IMMIGRANT ANCESTORS

---

*A List of 2,500 Immigrants
to America before 1750*

Edited by
FREDERICK ADAMS VIRKUS

Baltimore
GENEALOGICAL PUBLISHING CO., INC.
1986

Excerpted and reprinted from
The Compendium of American Genealogy, Volume VII
Chicago, 1942
Reprinted: Genealogical Publishing Co., Inc.
Baltimore, 1963, 1972, 1976, 1978, 1980, 1986
Copyright © 1942
Copyright © renewed 1970
Genealogical Publishing Co., Inc.
Baltimore, Maryland
All Rights Reserved
Library of Congress Catalogue Card Number 64-1935
International Standard Book Number 0-8063-0513-4
Made in the United States of America

PREFACE

The Compendium of American Genealogy is a series of seven volumes published by the now defunct Institute of American Genealogy. Its purpose was to record in permanent form the lineages of those whose ancestors were among the earliest settlers of America. Because many names of immigrant ancestors appeared frequently in the records, it was decided to avoid repetition by placing these in a special section at the end of each volume. We have reprinted this section from the seventh and last volume of the series as this seemed more complete than the listings that appeared in preceding volumes.

IMMIGRANT ANCESTORS

Following is a list of about 2,500 of the Immigrant Ancestors whose names appear so frequently in the published lineage records of this work that repetition of the identical data would be burdensome, and superfluous. Hence, where the following names appear in the lineage records, the cross-reference (qv) is employed to refer the reader to this particular section of this volume where all the authentic data available, pertaining to these names, may be found.

It should be understood, however, that this is not a list of all the Immigrant Ancestors mentioned in the lineage records in this work. The larger number of immigrant ancestors mentioned in this volume do not appear in the following list because their names have appeared only once, or only occasionally, and the data pertaining to them will be found in the lineage records.

ABBE (Abbey), John (1613-abt. 1690), from London, Eng., in the "Bonadventure," 1634 or 35; granted land at Salem, Mass., 1637/38; an early settler at Wenham, 1646; d at Salem; m Mary – (b Eng., abt. 1615-20-d Wenham, Sept. 9, 1672); m 2d, Nov. 25, 1674, Mrs. Mary Goldsmith (widow of Richard).

ABBOTT (Abbot), George, "of Andover" (b Bishop's Stortford, Co. Herts, Eng., 1615/16, bap. there, May 22, 1617-d Andover, Mass., Dec. 24, 1681/82; son of George [bap. May 28, 1587-living 1628], m Elizabeth–), came with Rev. Ezekiel Rogers in same ship with future wife, 1637; first settler at Andover, Mass., 1643; house he built still in possession of descendants; m at Roxbury, Mass., Dec. 12, 1646, Hannah Chandler (bap. Bishop's Stortford, May 22, 1630-d June 11, 1711), dau. of William Chandler (qv).

ABBOTT, George, "of Rowley" (prob. b in Eng.-d Rowley, Essex co., Mass., 1647); came from Eng., 1642; settled at Rowley, where his name heads the list of 54 inhabitants to whom house lots were registered in 1643; m in Eng.

ABBOTT (Abbitt), Robert (d Branford, Conn.. Sept. 31, 1658); came from Eng. and settled at Watertown, Mass., 1634; later at Wethersfield, Conn., 1636-40, at New Haven, 1642; mem. ct., 1642; granted land at Totoket (now Branford), removed there, 1645; m prob. as 2d wife, Mary – (who m 2d, 1659, John Robbins).

ABELL (Abel), Robert (b prob. in Eng.-d Rehoboth, Mass., June 20, 1663; s. of George Abell, who m Frances –, of Hemington, Leicestershire, Eng.); first record at Weymouth, Mass., where he desired to be made freeman, Oct. 19, 1630; later at Rehoboth; m Joanna –, who survived him (she m 2d, at Rehoboth, Mass., June 4, 1667, William Hyde of Norwich, Conn.).

ADAMS, George (d Oct. 10, 1696); first record of him is his marriage at Watertown, Mass., 1645; at Cambridge Farms (now Lexington), 1664; soldier in King Philip's War; m at Watertown, 1645, Frances –.

ADAMS, Henry, "of Braintree" (b Barton Saint David, Somersetshire, Eng., abt. 1583, where at least 4 generations of his ancestors had lived; d at Braintree, Mass., Oct. 6, 1646; son of John Adams of Barton St. David); came from Eng. 1638, and settled at Braintree, Mass., where he was granted 40 acres of land, Feb. 24, 1639/40; was maltster and yeoman; m in Eng., Oct. 19, 1609, Edith (1587-1673), dau. of Henry Squire (1563-abt 1640); she m 2d, 1651, John Fussell of Weymouth and Medfield.

ADAMS, Jeremy (b in Eng.-d Hartford, Conn., Aug. 11, 1683); came to N.E. with Rev. Thomas Hooker's co., 1632 and settled at Cambridge;

freeman, 1635, and possessed a town-lot; went with Hooker to Hartford, Conn., 1636, being an original propr. of that town; sent by Gen. Ct., 1638, with Capt. Mason and 4 others, to treat with the Indians; land grants of 30 acres, 1639, and 340 acres, 1661/62, at what later became Colchester; was constable and custom-master; kept the inn, at which the General Court held its meetings for many yrs.; m abt. 1637, Rebecca – (d 1678), widow of Samuel Greenhill, from Staplehurst, Kent, Eng.; m 2d, 1678, Rebecca (1638-1715), dau. of John Fletcher, and widow of Andrew Warner, Jr.; issue all by 1st marriage.

ADAMS, John (d 1633), came in the "Fortune," Nov. 9, 1621; settled at Plymouth, Mass.; m at Plymouth, after 1623, Ellen Newton, who came in the "Ann," 1623 (she m 2d, 1634, Kenelm Winslow, qv).

ADAMS, John, "of Cambridge" (b Kingweston, Eng., 1622-d Menotomy, now Arlington, Mass., 1706; son of Henry Adams, qv); came with his parents, 1638; was millwright at Cambridge; returned to Eng. to administer property, returning to N.E., 1651; m Ann–(d after 1714).

ADAMS, Robert (b Ottery St. Mary, Eng., Oct. 10, 1602-d Newbury, Mass., Oct. 12, 1682; son of Peter, of Ottery St. Mary, Devonshire); from Eng., 1635, and settled at Ipswich, Mass.; at Newbury, 1640-1680; tailor; m Eleanor Wilmott (d June 12, 1677); m 2d, Feb. 1678, Sarah Glover (d Oct. 24, 1697), widow of Henry Short.

ALDEN, John (ca. 1599-1687), 7th and last surviving signer of the Mayflower Compact; in Capt. Myles Standish's Duxbury Co., 1643; gov.'s asst., 1632-50, 86; dep. Gen. Ct., 1641, 42, 44, 49; mem. Council of War, 1646 et seq.; actg. dep. gov., 1664-77; m at Plymouth, Mass., before 1624, Priscilla (d after 1650), dau. William Mullins (qv).

ALDERMAN, William (d 1697), from Eng.; at Windsor, Conn., 1671; later at Simsbury; m 1679, Mary, dau. John Case, m Sarah, dau. of Hon. William Spencer (qv).

ALDRICH (Aldridge, Eldridge), George (d 1683), from Eng. to Dorchester, Mass., 1631; freeman, 1636; was at Braintree, 1644; one of the first settlers at Mendon, 1663; m 1629, Catherine Seald (1610-91).

ALEXANDER, Archibald (b Manor Cunninghame, Ire., Feb. 4, 1708-d Augusta [now Rockbridge] Co., Va., after 1773, eldest son of William Alexander of Co. Donegal, Ire., and descended from the house of Mac Alexander of Tarbet, Kintyre, Scotland); came from N. of Ire. with his bro. Robert, 1736, and settled at New Providence, Pa.; removed to Augusta (now Rockbridge) Co., Va., 1747; *m* in Ireland, Dec. 31, 1734, his cousin, Margaret (*d* July 1755). dau. of Joseph Parks of Donegal; *m* 2d, Augusta Co., Va., 1757, Margaret (or Jane) M'Clure of Augusta Co.

ALEXANDER, James (*b* Scotland, 1691 or 93-*d* 1756; second son of David, of the Ward of Muthill, Scotland, and a descendant of the 1st Earl of Stirling); was officer of engineers in the army of the Pretender, and was forced to flee from Scotland shortly after the uprising of 1715, coming to New Jersey, where he was made surveyor-general of East and West Jersey, 1716; was successively receiver-gen. of quit rents, advocate-gen., mem. King's Council, and attorney-gen.; *m* 1720/21, Mary (1693-1760), widow of David Provoost, and dau. of John Spratt, of Scotland.

ALGER, Thomas (prob. *b* Eng.-prob. *d* Bridgewater, Mass.), from Eng. abt. 1665, and settled at Taunton, Mass., where he was granted land; later at Bridgewater; *m* at Taunton, Nov. 14, 1665, Elizabeth, dau. of Samuel Packard (qv).

ALLEN, see also Alling, Allyn.

ALLEN, Edmund (also called Edward), from Scotland to N.E., 1636, settled at Ipswich, Mass., was at Suffield, Conn., before 1683, later at Northfield, Mass.; *m* Sarah Kimball (*d* June 12, 1696).

ALLEN, George (1568-1648), from Weymouth, Eng., in Rev. Joseph Hull's company; settled nr. Lynn, Mass., 1635; was at Weymouth, Mass.; in company with others obtained a grant, 1637, and founded Sandwich, Mass., settled there, 1638; 1st dep. Gen. Ct., 1640-44; constable 1639; freeman; the house erected by George Allen, 1646, was in good repair, 1860, but was taken down, 1880, situated at Sandwich, Mass., about a quarter of a mile from the Friends Meeting House on the main road to the cape; *m* 1st, in Eng.; *m* 2d, 1624, Katherine—(*b* 1605), she *m* 2d, John Collins, Sr., of Boston.

ALLEN, James (*d* Medfield, Mass., Sept. 27, 1673), prob. came from Colby, Norfolk, Eng., with his uncle Rev. John Allin (Savage says bro., the will says "cousin"), 1635; settled at Dedham, Mass., 1637; lands granted, 1638; one of the first 13 settlers of Medfield; *m* 1638, Anna Guild (1616-73).

ALLEN, Ralph (*d* 1698; apparently was son or bro. of George Allen, qv); Quaker, reported in vicinity of Boston, 1628; at Newport, R.I., 1638, Weymouth, Mass., 1639, Rehoboth, 1643; Sandwich, 1645; *m* 2d, 1645, Easter, or Esther, dau. of William Swift (qv).

ALLEN, Samuel (*b* Braintree, Co. Essex, Eng., ca. 1588-*d* Windsor, Conn., Apr. 1648), came to N.E., 1632; settled at Windsor, Conn., 1635; *m* Ann–.

ALLEN, Samuel (son of George, qv; *d* Braintree, Mass., 1665), came to N.E. and settled at Braintree, Mass., 1629; at New Towne (Cambridge), 1632, at Braintree, 1635, at Sandwich, 1637; freeman, May 6, 1635; *m* Ann—(*d* Sept. 29, 1641); *m* 2d, Margaret–, widow of Elder Edward Lamb.

ALLEN, Walter (1601-81), at Newbury, Mass., ca. 1640; moved to Charlestown, ca. 1652; bought 60 acres nr. the Concord boundary, Watertown Farms (later Weston), 1665, and 200 acres, 1669; to Charlestown, ca. 1673; *m* Rebecca–.

ALLEN, William (1602-79), from Manchester, Eng., with the Dorchester Company, 1623; settled at Cape Ann, 1623; removed to Salem, 1626, thence to Manchester, 1640; freeman, 1630; *m* 1629, Alice–(1603-32); *m* 2d, Elizabeth Bradley.

ALLEN, William (*d* 1686), from Eng.; settled at Salisbury, Mass., 1639; *m* Ann (*d* 1678), dau. Richard Goodale, from Eng. to Salisbury, Mass., 1638.

ALLERTON, Isaac (ca. 1586-1659), 5th signer of the Mayflower Compact; dep. gov. Plymouth Colony, 1621-24, asst., 1624, 31, 33; removed to New Amsterdam ca. 1639; one of the Eight Men of New Netherland, 1643; purchased a tract of land, and built a warehouse and residence, 1647, where Peck Slip now is; lived at New Haven, Conn.; *m* 1st, at Leyden, Holland, 1611, Mary Norris (*d* in 1621); *m* 2d, at Plymouth, Mass., bet. 1623-27, Fear (*d* 1634), dau. Elder William Brewster (qv); *m* 3d, before 1644, Joanna – (*d* 1682).

ALLING (now Allen), Roger (*d* New Haven, Conn., Sept. 27, 1674), settled at New Haven at beginning of settlement, 1639; a signer of the compact; deacon; treas. of colony, 1661 and later; *m* Mary (*d* Aug. 16, 1683), dau. of Thomas Nash (qv).

ALLIS, William (*b* prob. in Essex, Eng., bet. 1613 and 1616-*d* Hatfield, Conn., Sept. 6, 1678); came with Winthrop's fleet, 1630, settled at Braintree; had grant from Boston of 12 acres for 3 heads; freeman, 1640; removed to Hadley 1661; selectman, 1662; lt. of cavalry; dea.; *m* 1641, Mary – (*d* 1677), *m* 2d, June 25, 1678, Widow Mary Graves, née Brownson (her 1st husband was John Wyatt; she *m* 4th, 1682, Samuel Gaylord).

ALLYSON, John, see Alston.

ALLYN, Hon. Matthew (1604/05-1670/71; son of Richard, will proved 1652, *m* Margaret –): from Eng. to Charlestown, Mass., 1632; freeman, Cambridge, 1635; settled at Hartford, Conn., 1637, later at Windsor; rep. Mass. Gen. Ct., 1636; dep. from Windsor, Conn., 1648, 57; asst., 1658-67; commr. to United Colonies, 1660-64; *m* 1627, Margaret Wyatt, from Eng., of royal descent.

ALLYN, Robert (*b* Eng., 1608-*d* New Haven, Conn., 1683), bro. of William Allen of Manchester (qv); from Eng., 1637, and settled at Salem; admitted to ch., 1642; propr. Jeffries Creek (Manchester), 1648; freeman, 1649; removed to New London, Conn., 1651; and to Norwich, at its first settlement, 1659; constable 1669; returned to New London, where Allyn's Point perpetuates his memory; *m* Sarah–.

ALMY (Almey or Almond), William (*b* prob. at Dunton-Bassett or South Kilworth, Leicestershire, Eng., 1600-*d* Portsmouth, R.I., abt. Apr. 1677; only son of Christopher Almey of South Kilworth; executor of father's estate, 1624); came to N.E., 1631; went home and returned with wife and 2 children in 1635, and settled at Lynn (Saugus); one of the founders of Sandwich, 1637; sold his lands there and removed to Portsmouth, R.I., land grant, 1644; freeman, 1655, later juryman and commnr.; *m* at Lutterworth, Eng., abt. 1626, Audrey Barlowe (1603-living 1676).

ALSOP, Richard (1660-1718), from Eng. to Newtown, L.I., as youth; commissioned capt. Newtown troop of horse; inherited the estate of his uncle, Thomas Warnell; *m* 1686, Hannah (1666-1757), dau. of Capt. John Underhill (qv).

ALSTON, John (1610-87), of the Inner Temple and Parvenham, Eng., was granted tract embracing most of Fairfax Co., N.C.; *m* 1634, Lady Dorothy, dau. of Sir John Temple.

ALSTON (Allston), John (bap. Felmersham, Bedfordshire, Eng., Dec. 5, 1673-*d* Chowan Co., N.C., 1758; s. of John, qv); came to Carolina colony, prob. in 1710; settled on Bennett's creek, where Gatesville, N.C., now stands, 1711; landgrants to sons in 1713; juror, 1715, grand-juror, 1721-24; justice of the peace and associate justice, 1724-29; held military rank of capt., major and col. after 1725; was sheriff of Chowan Co., several terms; vestryman, St. Paul's parish; *m* abt. 1700, Mary (*b* ante 1687-*d* after 1758), dau. of John Clark, *m* Mary Palin, of Pasquotank, N.C.

ALVORD, Alexander (ca. 1620-87), from Eng., bet. 1636-40, settled at Windsor, Conn., 1645, at Northampton, Mass., 1661; *m* Oct. 29, 1646, Mary (*b* July 6, 1617-*d* before 1683), dau. Richard Vore (or Voar).

AMBLER, Richard (ca. 1611-1699; son of Richard [1587-1637]; g.son of Thomas, of Kiddington-in-Lindsay, nr. Yorkshire, Eng.); came to Watertown, Mass., ca. 1638; at Weymouth, 1640, Boston, 1643, Stamford, Conn., 1649; freeman, 1669; with his son, Abraham (Abram), and others bought from the Indians "the hopp-ground" (now called Bedford), Westchester Co., N.Y., 1699; a leader of the little company which founded the 1st church at Bedford, of which his son Abraham was minister, 1689 et seq.; *m* 1st, Sarah – (mother of all his children, all *b* Watertown); *m* 2d, Elizabeth – (*d* Mar. 27, 1685).

AMES, Thomas, see Eames.

AMES, William (*b* Bruton, Somersetshire, Eng., Oct. 6, 1605-*d* Braintree, Mass., Jan. 1, 1653/54), came from Eng. to Duxbury, Mass., as early as 1640; later at Braintree; freeman, 1647; *m* 1639/40, Hannah –.

AMMIDOWN (Amidon), Roger (*d* 1673), Huguenot refugee from Rochelle, France, to Eng., thence to Salem, Mass., ca. 1637, at Weymouth, 1640, Boston, 1643, Rehoboth, 1648; freeman, 1657; received land grants, 1658, 62, 65; *m* Sarah–(*d* 1668); *m* 2d, 1668, Joanna (1642-1711), dau. George Harwood, *m* Jane–.

AMORY, Jonathan (*b* Bristol, Eng., Mar. 14, 1654-*d* Charleston, S.C., 1699; son of Thomas Amory, *m* Ann Elliott); from Eng. via Jamaica. to S.C., Aug. 29, 1682; mcht.; apptd. by the crown as advocate gen. in S.C. admiralty courts, 1697; speaker of House of Commons, S.C., at time of his death from the "plague"; extensive landholder thru grant and purchase; also receiver for the public treasury, 1639; *m* abt. 1679, Rebecca (*d* abt. 1685), widow of David Houston, of Ireland; *m* 2d, Martha—.

ANDERSON, Richard (*b* 1585), from London in the "Merchant's Hope," to Va., 1635; was of Gloucester Co.

ANDERSON, Robert (ca. 1733-1825), from Ireland to Phila., Pa., 1755, thence before 1764, to Delaware; to Botetourt Co., Va., 1769; *m* 1764, Margaret Neely (1738-1810).

ANDREWS, Henry (*d* 1652), an original purchaser at Taunton, Mass., 1637; built first ch. there and in payment received "Calf Pasture," 1647; dep., 1639, 42, 43, 47, 49; *m* Mary–(ca. 1610-1655).

ANDREWS, William (prob. *b* in Hampsworth, Eng.-*d* East Haven, Conn., Mar. 4, 1675/76: Savage says *d* Jan. 3, 1664): carpenter came to Boston, in the "James" of London, 1635; freeman, 1635; removed to New Haven, Conn., where he signed the compact, 1639; built first meetinghouse there, 1644: lt. of arty. co., May 22, 1648; kept the inn under direction of Gen. Ct. for many yrs.: *m* in Eng., Mary– (*d* Jan. 3, 1663); *m* 2d, 1665, Anna (Tapp) Gibbard (*d* 1701), dau. of Edmund Tapp, of Milford, and widow of William Gibbard.

ANGELL, Thomas (*b* Eng. abt. 1618-*d* Providence, R.I., 1694); came in the "Lyon," Dec. 1630, arrived in Boston, Feb. 5, 1631, going soon after to Salem; winter of 1635 at Seekonk, and made the settlement at Providence before July 1636; signed the compact, Aug. 20, 1637; signed agreement for a form of govt. for colony, 1640; successively commr., juryman, constable; freeman 1655; *m* Alice Ashton (*d* 1695).

ANTHONY, John (*b* Hempstead, Eng., 1607-*d* Portsmouth, R.I., July 28, 1675; son of John Anthony, physician of London); came in the "Hercules," 1634; settled at Portsmouth, R.I.; freeman, 1641; corpl., 1644; received land grant at Wadding River, Nov. 14, 1644; apptd. to "keep a house of entertainer," May 25, 1655; commr., 1661; purchased house and 3 acres at Portsmouth, Dec. 3, 1663; sold this and other land, Nov. 7, 1666; dep. Gen. Ct., 1666-72; *m* Susanna Potter (*d* 1675).

APPLETON, Samuel (*b* Little Waldingfield, Suffolk, Eng., 1586-*d* Rowley, Mass., June 1670; son of Thomas, *m* Mary Isaack); gent., armiger; came from Eng. to Ipswich, Mass., with 2d wife and family, 1635; freeman, May 25, 1636; granted 460 acres of land on the Hamilton town line bet. Ipswich River and Mile Brook; dep. Gen. Ct., 1637; mem. grand jury, 1641: resided at Rowley, Mass.; *m* 1st, Preston, Eng., Jan. 24, 1616, Judith Evarard (*d* ca. 1630); *m* 2d, ca. 1633, Martha –.

ARMISTEAD, John (1635-98), Gloucester Co., Va.; was justice before 1675; high sheriff, 1675; burgess, 1685; lt. col. of horse, 1680; col. and county lt., 1685; mem. Council, 1688-98; *m* Judith Robinson.

ARMISTEAD, William (bap. 1610-ante 1660; son of Anthony, of Deighton Park, in the West Riding of Yorkshire, Eng., *m* Frances Thompson), came to Va., 1635; a patentee of Elizabeth City Co., 1636; *m* 1651, Anne –;

ARMOUR, James, from Ireland, settled at Unionville, Conn.; *m* 1751, Margaret Anderson.

ARMS, William (supposed to have been *b* on Isle of Jersey, 1654-*d* Deerfield, Mass., Aug. 25, 1731), came from either the Isle of Jersey or Guernsey, presumed to have assumed the name of Arms, as no one of that name is found on either of the islands; was a knitter of stockings; first known as soldier under Capt. William Turner at Hadley, Mass., Apr. 6, 1676; in Indian fight at Great Falls, May 17, 1676: at Hatfield, Mass., 1677; at Deerfield, abt. 1684; constable, 1699; tithing-man, 1700: at Sunderland, Mass., 1714-22; returned to Deerfield abt. 1722; *m* Nov. 21, 1677, Joanna (*b* abt. 1653-*d* Nov. 22, 1729), dau. of John Hawks, of Hadley, Mass.

ARNOLD, Thomas (bap. Eng., Apr. 18, 1599-*d* Smithfield, R.I., Sept., 1674; son of Thomas, of Cheselbourne, Dorsetshire, Eng.); came in

the "Plaine Joan," 1635, ship's record says "age 30 yrs."; settled at Watertown, Mass.; freeman, May 13, 1640; moved before 1661, to Providence, R.I.; sold rest of his Watertown holdings in 1661 and 1662; dep. Gen. Assembly, R.I., 1666, 67, 70-72; *m* in Eng., –; *m* 2d, 1640, Phebe (bap. 1612-*d* ca. 1688), dau. of George Parkhurst, Sr.

ARNOLD, William (*b* Eng., June 24, 1587-*d* 1676; son of Thomas, *m* Alice Cully of Cheselbourne, Eng., and half-bro. of Thomas, qv); brought his family to N.E., May 1, 1635, and was at Hingham for awhile; removed with Roger Williams to Pawtuxet, 1638, and was one of the 13 original proprs. of Providence Plantations; signed agreement for the first form of govt., 1640; commr. from Providence to Gen. Ct. of R.I., 1661; *m* Christian (*b* 1583), dau. of Thomas Peake.

ASPINWALL, Peter (*b* Eng. ca. 1612-*d* Brookline, Mass., 1687), came to Dorchester Ma. 1630; freeman, 1645; settled at Muddy River (Brookline), ante 1650; *m* ca. 1645, Alice Sharp; *m* 2d, Feb. 12, 1662, Remember (1638-1701), dau. of Peter Palfrey (qv).

ASTON, Lt. Col. Walter (1606/07-Apr. 6, 1656; son of Walter, of Longden, Stafford Co., Eng.; g.g.son of Sir Walter, knighted 1560); from Staffordshire, Eng., to Va., ca. 1628; burgess, Shirley Hundred, 1629-30, 31-32, 32-33, Charles City Co., 1642-43; justice of the peace; named lt. col. militia, Charles City Co., Sept. 17, 1655; patented 590 acres, July 26, 1638, on Kimage's Creek, of which land 200 acres, known as "Cawsey's Care," were purchased by a deed dated Feb. 7, 1634, from John Causey, as heir of Nathaniel Causey (the rest of this land was due Aston for the transportation into Va. of ten persons); patented an additional 250 acres, Charles City, Apr. 10, 1643; buried at Westover, on James River; permission to probate his will was granted in Charles City, January 25, 1657; *m* Miss Narbow (or Warbow); *m* 2d, Hannah Jordan (*d* post 1656).

ASTOR, John Jacob (*b* Waldorf, Duchy of Baden, July 17, 1763-*d* New York City, Mar. 29, 1848; son of Johann Jacob Astor, a bailiff of Waldorf); went to London, 1780, and engaged in manufacture of musical instruments as employee of bro. George's firm; came to Baltimore, Md., Mar. 1784, as agent of firm with consignment of goods; during voyage to America, his conversations with officers of the Hudson Bay Co. had interested him in the fur trade and having disposed of his goods he entered the employ of a fur dealer; established his own fur business and amassed a fortune of $250,000 in six years, which he invested mainly in N.Y. City real estate; continued in fur trade and real estate investments until he was reputed to be the richest man in America; *m* 1786, Sarah, dau. of Adam Todd, *m* Sarah Cox.

ATHERTON, Humphrey (*b* Lancashire, Eng., 1609-*d* Sept. 16, 1661; prob. son of Edmund Atherton, of Lancashire); came in the "James," 1635; settled at Dorchester, Mass., 1636; freeman, May 2, 1638; dep. Gen. Ct., 1638, et seq.; speaker of the house, 1653; mem. council of war for United Colonies, 1645; capt. Dorchester company, May 16, 1646; capt. of A. and H. A. Co., 1650, 1658; commr. of United Colonies, 1653; asst., 1645-1661; supt. of Indian affairs, 1658; maj. gen. of Mass. Colony, 1661; died from fall from his horse which stumbled over a cow lying in the road: *m* in England, Mary Wales (*d* 1672).

ATKINSON (Adkinson, Atkeson), John (*b* ca. 1640), from Boston, Mass., to Newbury Ca. 1663, *m* 1664, Sarah Myrick.

ATLEE (At Lee), William (*b* Fordhook House, Brentford, Eng., abt. 1700-*d* Phila., Apr. 27, 1744, son of Samuel Atlee of Brentford, Eng.); was first of the name to reach America; came 1734 as private sec. to Lord Howe, Gov. of Barbados; *m* June 1, 1734, Jane Alcock (*d* Lancaster, Pa., Jan. 18, 1777), dau. of an English clergyman and cousin of William Pitt, first Earl of Chatham (it is said she was maid of honor to the queen).

ATWATER, David (*b* Royton Manor in Lenham, Co. of Kent, Eng., bap. Oct. 8, 1615-*d* New Haven, Conn., Oct. 5, 1692; son of John, *m* Susan –); settled at New Haven, Conn., 1638, with bro. Joshua and sister Ann; signed plantation covenant, June 4, 1639; large landowner; freeman, 1665; *m* bet. 1643-1646, Demaris (*d* Apr. 1, 1691), dau. of Thomas Sayre (qv).

ATWOOD, Harman or Herman (*d* 1651; son of Dea. John, of St. Martin's Parish, Surrey, Eng., *m* Joan Coleson), to Boston, 1642; **mem.** A. and H.A. Co., 1644; freeman, 1645; dea. of Old North Ch.; *m* 1646, Ann (*d* 1661), dau. William Copp (qv); she *m* 2d, 1652, Thomas Saxton.

ATWOOD (Wood), John (bap. Dec. 24, 1614-*d* 1676; son of John, *m* Joan Coleson); came from Eng., 1635; propr. of Plymouth, Mass., 1635-36, where he owned land; constable; on grand jury; removed to Plympton; *m* Sarah (*d* 1701), dau. Richard Masterson, *m* Mary Goodale.

AUSTIN, Richard (*b* ca. 1598), from Eng. in the "Bevis," to Charlestown, Mass., 1638; tailor; brought wife and two children.

AVERILL (Averell), William (*b* Ash, nr. Farmingham, Kent, Eng., bet. 1611 and 1613-*d* 1653, will proved Mar. 29, 1653), settled at Ipswich, Mass., before Mar. 2, 1637, when he received his first grant of land from that town; *m* in Eng. ca. 1631 or 32, Abigail Hynton, or Hinton (*d* 1655).

AVERY, Christopher (*b* Eng. abt. 1590-*d* New London, Conn., buried Mar. 12, 1679; son of Christopher, of Newton Abbott, Co. Devon, Eng.); came in the "Arbella," 1630; settled at Gloucester, Mass.; weaver; selectman, 1646, 52, 54; took freeman's oath, Salem, June 29, 1652; sold land in Gloucester and removed to Boston, where he purchased home, Mar. 18, 1658; removed to New London, Conn.; freeman, Colony of Conn., Oct., 1669; *m* 1616, Margery Stevens (or Stephens), who did not come to America.

AVERY, Capt. James (1620-1700; son of Christopher, qv), of New London, Conn., 1650; acquired large tracts of land at Groton, Conn., and built the homestead "Hive of the Averys," 1656; selectman, 1660-80; commr., 1663-78; lt. Train Band, New London, 1665; ens., lt. and capt. in King Philip's War, cdr. of soldiers from Stonington, New London and Lyme thruout the war; asst. Gen. Ct., 1656-80; asst. judge Prerogative Ct.; *m* 1643, Joanna Greenslade (1622-bet. 1693-98); *m* 2d, Abigail (Ingraham) Chesebrough.

AVERY, William (1621-Mar. 18, 1686/87; son of Robert, of Wokingham, Berkshire, Eng.; g.son of Robert, of Pile, or Pyle, Somerset, Eng.), from Parish of Barkham, Berkshire, Eng.; settled at Dedham, Mass., ca. 1650; physician and surgeon; mem. A. and H. A. Co., 1654, sgt., 1655, lt., 1673; lt. in Dedham Co., Suffolk Regt., King Philip's War; settled at Boston, ca. 1679; propr. apothecary shop, and a book store; buried in King's Chapel Bury-ground, Tremont St., Boston; *m* ca. 1644, Margaret (*d* Sept. 28, 1678), dau. of William Allright, of Eng.; *m* 2d, 1679, Mary (Woodmansey) Tappin (ca. 1629-May 21, 1707), dau. of Robert Woodmansey, of Boston, and widow of John Tappin.

AXTELL, Daniel (*d* 1686), merchant in London; came to S.C., ca. 1680; received land grant for 3,000 acres, 1680; made landgrave, 1681; *m* Lady Rebecca Holland (*d* 1720), came to S.C., 1683, received grants of about 3,780 acres, 1696, 1704, 07, 11.

AYER (Eyer, Eyers, Ayres), John (*b* Eng., 1590 or 92-*d* Haverhill, Mass., Mar. 31, 1657; son of Thomas, *m* Elizabeth Rogers); came in the "James," 1635, settled at Newbury, Mass.; received land in the "first division," at Salisbury, 1640; removed to Ipswich, 1646, to Haverhill, 1647; *m* Hannah – (1598-July 13, 1686).

BABCOCK (Badcock), James (*b* in Eng., 1612-*d* Westerly R.I., June 12, 1679); came from Eng., bet. 1630 and 1640; settled at Portsmouth, R.I., by 1642; blacksmith; admitted inhabitant, Feb. 25, 1642; ordered by town, with Richard Morris, to repair all arms, 1643 and 1650; 10 acres were ordered "laide out" to him; freeman, July 10, 1648; mem. of com. for "tryall of the general officers"; assessor, 1650; mem. Gen. Ct. for Portsmouth, 1657, 8, 9; removed to Westerly, R.I., Mar. 1662; *m* 1st, Sarah – (*d* 1665, or later); *m* 2d, 1669 (?), Elizabeth – (she *m* 2d, Sept. 22, 1679, William Johnson.

BABSON, James (*d* on voyage to America, 1632), *m* Isabella–(*b* ca. 1579-*d* 1661), came with her infant son, James, 1632; admitted inhabitant at Salem, Mass., 1637; to Gloucester, Mass., ante 1644; midwife, and called "Mother Babson"; the son: James (*d* Dec. 21, 1683; *m* 1647, Eleanor Hill).

BACHE, Richard (*b* Settle, Yorkshire, Eng., Feb. 23 or Sept. 12, 1737-*d* July 29, 1811; son of William, *m* Mary Blyckenden); was settled at Phila. as a merchant, 1760; sec. of Province of Pa., 1775-76; register-general, 1775-76; was postmaster general under the crown, 1776-82; mem. Board of War, 1777; a protestant against the Stamp Act, and held with the Revolutionists; *m* Phila., Oct. 3 or 29, 1767, Sarah (*b* Sept. 11 or 99, 1743 or 44-*d* Oct. 5, 1808), only dau. of Benjamin Franklin, of Phila.

BACHILER, see Batchelder.

BACKUS, William (*d* 1664), from Eng. with his two sons, William and Stephen, in the "Rainbow," 1637, to Saybrook, Conn.; a founder of Norwich, 1659; *m* 2d, ca. 1660, Anne (Stenton) Bingham (*d* 1670), widow of Thomas Bingham.

BACON, Edmund (1641-1705; cousin of Nathaniel Bacon, called the "Rebel"), from Eng. to New Kent Co., Va., 1660; patented 443 acres on Pamunkey River, 1687; capt. Va. Militia, 1684-1700; high sheriff; vestryman; *m* Anne, dau. Capt. George Lyddall, from Eng., col. of Colonial troops, mil. and civil officer of the Colony, 1699.

BACON, Michael (bap. Winston, Co. Suffolk, Eng., Dec. 6, 1579-*d* Apr. 18, 1648; son of Michael, *m* Elizabeth Wylie; descended from Roger Bacon, who aided the barons against King John: the Bacon estates were confiscated by the Crown, but were restored in 1216); came from Eng. and signed the Dedham, Mass., agreement, 1633; returned to Eng.; apparently went to Ire., 1633, thence returned to Dedham, 1640, with wife, 3 sons and 3 daus.; made one of proprietors, 1640; signed church covenant of Dedham; granted land to town for a highway, 1644; *m* Eng., Sept. 20, 1607, Grace Blowerses; *m* 2d, Eng., Alice – (*d* Apr. 2, 1647/48).

BACON, Nathaniel (*d* Oct. 1673), perhaps came from Stretton, Co. Rutland, Eng.; settled at Barnstable, Mass., 1640; tanner and currier; proposed as freeman, 1645; constable, 1650; rep., 1652-1665; asst. of Plymouth Colony, 1667-1673; mem. council of war, 1658 and 1667; large landowner; *m* Dec. 4, 1642, Hannah (living 1691), dau. of Rev. John Mayo, of Barnstable.

BACON, Nathaniel (*b* ante 1630-*d* Jan. 27, 1705; son of Nathaniel, of Bramford, Eng.; g.s. of Thomas, *d* 1610), came abt. 1649; settled at Mettabesett (now Middletown), Conn., 1650; received large legacies from his "Unkell" Andrew Bacon, who had no children; *m* Anne (*d* July 6 1680), dau. of Thomas Miller of Stretton Parish; *m* 2d, Apr. 17, 1682, Elizabeth Pierpont.

BACOT, Pierre (*b* Tours, France, abt. 1670-*d* 1702; son of Pierre Bacot, *m* Jacqueline Menissier, and g.son of Pierre, *m* Jeanne Moreau); came from France, 1694, settled at Goose Creek, abt. 19 miles from Charleston, S.C.; planter (one account seems to show that Pierre, who was *b* 1638 and *d* near Charles-town, 1702, was the father of Pierre, the immigrant above; that he came from the vicinity of Tours, France, to Charles Town, Carolina, 1685, with wife Jacquine Menessier, who *d* 1709, and sons Daniel and Pierre; that in 1699 and 1700 grants of land were made to Pierre, Sr., in St. Andrew's Parish, lands which are now part of the well known Middleton Place, near Charleston, and that the sons Daniel and Pierre removed to Goose Creek); *m* Jacquine (*d* 1709), dau. of Abraham Mercier, *m* Jacquine Selipeaux.

BADGER, Giles or Gyles (*b* Eng.-*d* Newbury, Mass., July 10 or 17, 1647), settled at Newbury, by 1635; farmer; *m* 1st, abt. 1642, Elizabeth (bap. Jan. 16, 1622), dau. of Capt. Edmond Greenleaf (qv); she *m* 2d, Richard Brown, of Newbury.

BAILEY, John (1590-1651), from Eng. in the "Angel Gabriel," 1635; settled at Salisbury, Mass.; weaver; yeoman at Newbury, 1651; *m* —— (*d* in Eng.).

BAILEY (Baily, Bayly, Bailie), Richard (1619-1647), from Eng. in the "Bevis," to Lynn, Mass., 1638; later at Rowley; one of a company to set up the first cloth mill in America; selectman and overseer of the poor several yrs.; *m* Edna (Lambert) Holstead(?), perhaps sister of William Holstead.

BAIRD, John (*b* Scotland, abt. 1730-kld. at Grant's Fort, near Pittsburgh, Pa., Sept. 14, 1758), prob. came from Ayr, Scotland, before 1747; first settled in Chester Co., Pa., where he is on assessment list of 1747; is called the ancester of the Baird family of Washington Co., Pa.; served as an English officer, Braddock's army; served against Fort Duquesne, and shared in "Braddock's Defeat" of July 9, 1755; also said to have served in Gen. Forbes' expdn., 1758; supposed to have *d* in service; *m* Phila., abt. 1755, Catharine McLean or McClean (July 19, 1733-Nov. 28, 1802).

BAIRD (Beard), Thomas (1608-78), from Scotland with Gov. John Endicott, to Naumkeag (Salem), Mass., 1628.

BAKER, Alexander (*b* London, Eng., 1607 or 1611-*d* Boston, 1685), came in the "Elizabeth and Ann," 1635, with his wife Elizabeth, and daus. Elizabeth and Christiana; was a proprietor of Gloucester, before 1642; removed to Boston, where he was a rope and collar maker; admitted to Boston church with wife, Oct. 4, 1645, when his first 7 children were bap.; freeman, May 6, 1646; *m* abt. 1632, Elizabeth Farrar? (*b* abt. 1612).

BAKER, Edward (1600?-1687), from Eng. 1630; settled at Saugus (Lynn), Mass.; freeman, 1638; to Northampton, Mass., 1657; landowner; held several town offices; returned to Lynn; *m* Joan-, or Jane-(*d* 1693).

BAKER, Francis (*b* Great St. Albans, Hertfordshire, Eng., 1611-*d* Yarmouth, Mass., July 23, 1696), came in the "Planter," 1635; tailor; settled at Yarmouth; admitted inhabitant, June 1, 1641; became a cooper; settled near Follen's Pond, at the head of Bass River; surveyor of highways, 1648; freeman, 1657; was in Eastham, Mass., 1659; *m* June 21, 1641, Isabel (*d* Yarmouth, May 16, 1706), dau. of William Twining.

BAKER, Col. Henry (1640-42-1712), from Eng. to Isle of Wight Co., Va., ca. 1665; burgess, 1692-93; justice of Orphans' Court; styled maj. and col.; *m* Mary (1666-1734), dau. of Edward Bennett of London, mem. Va. company of colonizers.

BAKER (Backer), Thomas (*b* Eng., Sept. 29, 1618-*d* Easthampton, L.I., N.Y., Apr. 30, 1700), came to America, 1639; settled at Milford, Conn., and enrolled as a "free planter," Nov. 29, 1639, and as a mem. of the church; removed to Easthampton, L.I., 1650; received several allotments as a proprietor; chosen a "townsman," 1650-62; with John Hand apptd. "to go vnto keniticut for to bring vs vnder their government," Mar. 19, 1657/58; compact bet. Easthampton and Conn. Colony, May 3, 1658, by John Hand and Thomas Baker, and Thomas was elected by the Gen. Ct. of Conn., one of the magistrates to that ct., 1658-63; went to Huntington as agent of town to confer with agents of the other towns to consider their grievances against the English government, Sept. 24, 1681; foreman of grand jury, 1665; overseer, 1666; constable, 1667; apptd. justice of ct. of assizes in N.Y., Southampton and Southold, L.I., 1675-85; *m* June 20, 1643, Alice (*b* Eng., May 22, 1620-*d* Amagansett, L.I., Feb. 4, 1708/09), dau. of Ralph Dayton, of New Haven, Conn., and East Hampton, L.I.

BALCH, John (1579-1648), from Bridgewater, Somersetshire, Eng., in company with Capt. Robert Gorges, 1623, to Cape Ann; removed to Salem, Mass., 1626; granted land and built house at North Beverly which is still standing; freeman, 1630; held many town offices; *m* Margaret-(*d* 163-); *m* 2d, Agnes Patch (*d* 1657).

BALDWIN, Henry (*d* 1697/98), from Eng. ca. 1640; settled at Woburn, Mass.; freeman, 1652; selectman, 1681; deacon, 1686-97; *m* 1649, Phebe (bap. 1632-*d* 1716), dau. Ezekiel Richardson (qv).

BALDWIN, John (buried Milford, Conn., June 21, 1681), came from Eng., in the "Martin"; settled at Milford, Conn., 1639; joined church, Mar. 19, 1648; removed to Newark, N.J., about 1668, but returned to Milford; sgt. Conn. militia, 1658; *m* 1st, Mary—; *m* 2d, 1653, Mary Bruen (*d* Sept. 2, 1670).

BALDWIN, John (*b* Eng.-*d* Dec. 25, 1687), from Eng., abt. 1640; settled at Billerica, Mass., as early as 1655; farmer; had grant of land, 1657; petitioner for land in Chelmsford, 1653; freeman, 1670; mem. garrison No. 6 at James Patterson's, 1675; *m* May 15, 1655, Mary (bap. Nov. 17, 1638), dau. of Thomas Richardson (qv).

BALDWIN, Joseph (*b* Cholesbury, Buckinghamshire, Eng., 1609-*d* Hadley, Mass., Nov. 2,

1684; g.son of Richard, *m* 1552, Ellen Apoke); settled at Milford, Conn., 1639; free planter, Nov. 20, 1639; removed to Hadley, ca. 1663; freeman, 1666; *m* Hannah-(joined ch., 1644); *m* 2d, Isabel (Ward) Catlin Northam (*d* 1676), widow of both John Catlin and James Northam; *m* 3d, Elizabeth (Hitchcock) Warriner (*d* Apr. 25, 1696), widow of William Warriner.

BALDWIN, Nathaniel (*d* 1658; 2d son of Richard, of Cholesbury, Co. Bucks, Eng.), from Eng., 1638; cooper, Milford, Conn.; removed to Fairfield, 1641; *m* Abigail (*d* Mar. 22, 1648), prob. sis. of William Camp; *m* 2d, Joan-, widow of Richard Westcott (she *m* 3d, Thomas Skidmore).

BALDWIN, Richard (bap. 1622-*d* 1665; son of Sylvester, who *d* on voyage to America); from Eng. in the "Martin," to Milford, Conn., ca. 1636; frequently appeared as atty. in Gen. Ct. at New Haven; free planter, 1639; joined the church, 1641; town clerk, 1648; rep. Gen. Ct., 1660-65; *m* Elizabeth (*d* 1688), dau. John Alsop, of Eng., *m* Temperance Gilbert.

BALL, Edward (1642 or 44-living 1724; prob. son of Alling Ball, Wiltshire, Eng., to Conn., *m* twice), at Branford, Conn., Mass.; a founder and first settler at Newark, N.J., 1667; sheriff, Essex Co., N.J., 1693; apptd. with Daniel Dod, to run north boundary of Newark, 1678; *m* ca. 1664, Abigail (*b* 1650), dau. Thomas Blatchley, *m* Susanna Ball.

BALL, John (1580-1655), said to have come from Wiltshire, Eng., 1630; settled at Watertown, Mass.; removed to Concord, Mass., 1640; freeman, 1650; *m* Joanna King.

BALL, Col. William (*b* London, Eng., ca. 1615-*d* "Millenbeck," Lancaster Co., Va., Nov. 1680), with royalist forces in battles of Naseby and Marston Moor; fled to Va.; settled in St. Mary's Parish, Lancaster Co., where he built "Millenbeck"; merchant and planter; burgess, 1670-80; *m* London, Eng., July 2, 1638, Hannah (*d* 1695), dau. Thomas Atherold (*b* ca. 1590), of Burgh, Co. Stafford, Eng., *m* Mary Harvey.

BALLARD, Thomas (1630-Mar. 1689), from Eng., settled in James City Co., Va.; clk. of York Co., 1652-89; burgess, 1666, 1680-84; speaker, 1680; mem. Council, 1666, 75, 78, 79; vestryman, Williamsburg, 1674; styled maj.; *m* Anne (*d* 1678), dau. of William Thomas, *m* Anne-.

BALLARD (Ballord), William (bap. 1603-ca. 1639), from Bradwell, Co. Suffolk, Eng., in the "James," 1635, to Boston; to Saugus (now Lynn), Mass.; freeman, 1636; mem. Quarterly Ct., 1636; mem. A. and H. A. Co., 1638; *m* Mary-; *m* 2d, Elizabeth-(ca. 1609-post 1641).

BALLARD, William (*b* Eng., ca. 1617-*d* Andover, Mass., July 10, 1689), probably came in the "Mary and John," 1634; settled at Andover ca. 1644; farmer; in King Philip's War, 1675-76; lived at Salem; mem. A. and H. A. Co.; *m* Grace – (*d* Andover, Apr. 27, 1694).

BALLOU, Maturin (*b* Eng. bet. 1610-20-*d* 1661-63), was at Providence, R.I., ante 1645/46, when he subscribed to agreement for grant of 25 acres from the town; freeman at Warwick, 1658; *m* ca. 1646-49, Hannah (ca. 1627-ca. 1715), dau. of Robert Pike, of Providence.

BANCROFT, Thomas (*b* Eng., 1622-*d* Aug. 19, 1691), from Eng. to Dedham, Mass., ca. 1645; settled at Reading ca. 1652; styled lt.; *m* Jan. 31, 1647, Alice (*d* Jan. 29, 1648), dau. of Michael Bacon (qv); *m* 2d, Sept. 15, 1648, Elizabeth (Oct. 4, 1626-May 11, 1711), dau. of Michael Metcalf (qv).

BANGS, Edward (*b* Eng., 1591/92-*d* Eastham, Mass., 1678; accepted son of John, of Panfield, Co. Essex, Eng., *m* 1586/87, Jane Chavis), shipwright; came from Eng. in the "Anne," to Plymouth, Mass., 1623; received grant of 4 acres; freeman, 1633; mem. jury, 12 times; grand juror, 4 terms; mem. various town coms., 1633-44; assessor, 1634-36; removed to Eastham, 1644; capt. of the guard against Indians; dep. Gen. Ct., 1650, 52, 63; town treas., 1646-65; *m* prob. 2d, 1623/34, Lydia, dau. Robert Hicks; *m* 3d, ca. 1635-37, Rebecca (Hobart or Tracy?).

BANKS, John (*d* Jan. 22, 1684/85), at Windsor, Conn.; clk. for weights and measures, 1643; to Fairfield, ca. 1645; dep. many terms, 1651-80; commr., 1666; mem. Council of War, 1675, 76; mem. N.Y. Assembly conv., 1674; auditor colony accounts, 1680, 82; called sgt. and lt.; *m* Mary, or Marie (*d* ca. 1657), dau. of Charles Taintor;

m 2d, Jan. 18, 1658, Mary–(*d* 1693/94), widow of Thomas Sherwood (qv).

BANTA, Epke Jacobs, from nr. Harlingen, Friesland, Holland, in the "De Trouw," with wife and 5 sons, 1659; settled at Flushing, L.I.; bought grist mill, Jamaica, L.I., 1671; removed to Bergen (now Jersey City), N.J., ante 1675; mem. Ct. of Oyer and Terminer, 1679; removed to Hackensack, 1681; *m* in Holland, Sitska–(1624-ca. 16¹⁵).

BARBER (Barbour), George (*b* Eng. ca. 1615-*d* Apr. 13, 1685), came from Eng. ca. 1635; settled at Dedham, Mass., by 1640; mem. artillery company, 1646; freeman, 1647; original proprietor of Medfield, Mass., 1651; representative, 1668-69; was the chief military officer; *m* Nov. 24, 1642, Elizabeth Clark (1617-83), who came in the "Truelove," 1635.

BARBER, Dr. Luke (*d* 1671), from Eng. in the "Golden Fortune," 1654; settled in St. Mary's Co., Md.; received land grant of 1,000 acres for services rendered in Battle of the Severn; of "Wickham Hall"; dep.; lt. gov., Md.; mem. Gov.'s Council; dep. gov.; *m* in Eng., Elizabeth Younge.

BARBER (Barbour), Thomas (*b* perhaps Bedfordshire, Eng., ca. 1614-*d* Windsor, Conn., Sept. 11, 1662), sailed from London, Mar. 16, 1634/1635, in the "Christian," landed at Dorchester, Mass., but settled at Windsor, Conn., 1635; sgt. in Pequot War; granted abt. 600 acres of Massaco lands, 1641; freeman, 1645; *m* Oct. 7, 1640, Jane, or Joan–(*d* Windsor, Sept. 10, 1662).

BARCLAY, John (*b* Uri, Scotland, 1659-*d* Perth Amboy, N.J., bet. Apr. 22 and 29, 1731; son of Col. David Barclay, of Uri, Kincardineshire, Scotland, and Lady Katharine Gordon); settled in East N.J., 1684, where his bro. Robert the "Apologist for the Quakers" (living in England), was one of the 24 proprietors, and for whom he served as attorney-in-fact till he left the Quakers and followed George Keith into the Church of England, bet. 1697 and 1701; dep. surveyor, 1688; receiver general of colony, 1692; dep. sec. and register of Province, 1695; commr. ct. of small debts, 1696; register Ct. of Chancery, 1698; clerk of Provincial Ct., 1699; surrogate of East Division of Province, 1716; dep. N.J. Assembly from Amboy, 1704; *m* bet. 1699 and 1702, Katharine–(prob. buried Perth Amboy, N.J., Jan. 6, 1702/03).

BARCROFT, Ambrose (bap. Colne Parish, Lancashire, Eng., Apr. 12, 1681-drowned in Delaware River, Pa., Dec. 20, 1724; son of Thomas and Elizabeth [Leigh] Barcroft, of Foulridge and Noyna, Colne Parish, and descended from Gilbert de Berecroft, who was deprived of his manor by William the Conqueror, 1068, which was restored, 1094); Ambrose came from Eng., bet. 1716 and 1722, and settled in Solebury Tp., Bucks Co., Pa., before June 8, 1723; *m* Whalley Parish, Lancashire, June 23, 1702, Maria Walsham (*d* Foulridge Hall, Lancashire, 1705); *m* 2d, Elizabeth–.

BARKER, Samuel (buried in Old Swedes Churchyard, Wilmington, Del., 1720; prob. son of John and Mary Barker, of Aston Manor, Claverley Parish, Co. Salop, Eng., and desc. of Randulph de Calverhall, of Salop, 1200), Quaker, came from Eng., 1682; settled at "Barkers Bridge," in what is now New Castle Co., Del., on a tract of 200 acres which he purchased from William Penn.

BARNARD, John (*b* 1604-buried June 23 or 27, 1646); sailed from Ipswich, Eng., Apr. 10 or 30, 1634, in the "Elizabeth," settled at Watertown, Mass.; freeman, 1634/35, proprietor of Watertown, 1636/37; selectman, 1644; *m* Phebe–(*b* 1607-*d* Aug. 1, 1685).

BARNARD, Thomas (*b* Eng. ca. 1612-kld. by Indians, 1677), came from Eng. ca 1634, settled at Salisbury, Mass., 1640; received land in first division, 1640, and 1643; planter; removed to Amesbury, Mass., 1654; selectman; moderator; was a proprietor of Nantucket, July 1659; grand juror, Salisbury, 1665; *m* Eleanor, or Helen–(*d* Nov. 27, 1694); she *m* 2d, July 19, 1681, George Little (qv).

BARNES, Charles (son of William, of Grancourt, East Winch, Co. Norfolk, Eng.), came from Eng. to Mass.; settled at Easthampton, L.I., N.Y., and was 1st schoolmaster there, 1655-63; received land grant, 1657; returned to Eng.; *m* 1657-58, Mary, dau. John Hand (qv).

BARNES, Thomas (*b* Eng., 1636-*d* 1679; son

of Thomas, of Barking, Co. Essex, Eng.); sailed from London, abt. May 30, 1656, in the "Speedwell," settled at Marlborough, Mass., 1656; *m* Abigail, dau. of Thomas Goodnow, of Sudbury, Mass.

BARNES, Thomas (will proved, Mar. 6, 1689), from Eng. to Hartford, Conn.; original propr., 1639; removed to Farmington, Conn.; served in Pequot War; sgt. Farmington Train Band, 1651; *m* Mary––.

BARNEY, Jacob (*b* Bradenham, Bucks., Eng., abt. 1601-*d* Salem, Mass., Apr. 28, 1673), said to have come from Swansea, Wales, abt. 1630, perhaps in the "Lyon;" settled at Salem, by 1634; tailor; freeman, May 14, 1634; dep. to Gen. Ct. 1635, 38, 47, 53, 65; *m* Elizabeth–.

BARNWELL, "Tuscarora" John (*b* Co. Meath, Ire., 1671-*d* Beaufort, S.C., June 1723 or 24; descended from Barnwells of Crickston, Co. Meath, Ire.); came from Dublin, Ire., settled near Charleston, S.C., before 1700; styled col.; dep.-sec. of Colony, 1702; clerk of Council; served under Col. William Rhett against the French and Spaniards; comptroller of the Colony, 1707; mem. Commons House of Assembly, and Gov.'s Council of S.C.; dep. surveyor-general; col.-commander of first expedition against Tuscarora Indians, 1712; apptd. col. of forces of S.C., 1715; agent for Province in London during revolution of 1719; *m* 1704, Anne Berners, dau. of an English merchant of Charleston.

BARRELL, George (*d* Sept. 2 or 11, 1643; son of George, *m* Dorothy, of St. Michaels, S. Elmham, Co. Suffolk, Eng.); came from St. Michaels to Boston, 1638; cooper; admitted townsman. Nov. 19, 1638: "granted to have that acre of ground at Spectackoll Island which was passed over to him by Goodman Smith," June 29, 1640; admitted to church, Sept. 12, 1641; freeman, May 10, 1643; *m* Ann–.

BARRETT, James (*b* Eng., 1615-19-*d* Aug. 16, 1672), came from Eng., settled in Mass. Bay Colony, 1635; removed to Malden, Mass.; *m* Hannah, or Anna (*b* abt. 1615-*d* Aug. 16, 1672?), dau. of Stephen Fosdick (qv).

BARRINGER (Baringer, Beringer), John Paul (*b* Germany, June 4, 1721-*d* Cabarrus Co., N.C., Jan. 1, 1807); came to America, 1742-43; settled in Pa.; removed to Mecklenburg, N.C. (afterward Cabarrus), ca. 1743-46; built family home "Poplar Grove," Mt. Pleasant, N.C.; mem. Com. of Safety of Mecklenburg Co.; *m* 1750, Ann Elizabeth ("Ain lis") Iseman; *m* 2d, 1777, Catherine Blackwelder (1755-1847).

BARROWS (Barrow, Barrus), John (*b* Eng., 1609-will dated Plymouth Colony, Mass., Jan. 12, *d* Feb. 18, 1691/92); sailed from Yarmouth, Eng., May 10, 1637, prob. in the "Mary Ann;" settled at Salem, Mass., 1637, where he was a proprietor; cooper; fence surveyor, 1644; removed to Plymouth before 1665; *m* Ann–(*b* Eng. 1597); *m* 2d, Deborah–.

BARSTOW, William (*b* Eng., 1612-*d* Scituate, Mass., Jan. 1, 1668/69; son of Matthew, of Shelf, near Halifax, Yorkshire, Eng.); prob. came from Yorkshire, Eng., sailed Sept. 20, 1635, in the "Truelove"; settled at Dedham, Mass., 1635; removed to Scituate (in that part set off in 1727, and became Hanover, Mass.), before 1649, when he was made freeman; ship-builder; built first bridge over North River at Stoney Beach, 1657, where he also kept tavern; selectman; highway surveyor; mem. com. to perambulate the patent line, 1666; *m* May 8, 1638, Anna Hubbard (she *m* 2d, John Prince, qv).

BARTHOLOMEW, William (*b* Burford, Oxfordshire, Eng., 1602/03-*d* Charlestown, Mass., Jan. 18, 1680/81; son of William, *m* Friswide Metcalf); came in the "Griffin," Sept. 18, 1634, in company with Rev. Zachary Symmes, Mrs. Anne Hutchinson, and Rev. John Lathrop; freeman, Mar. 4, 1634/35; granted land at Ipswich, Apr. 25, 1635; rep. to Gen. Ct. at Boston, 1635-37, 41, 47, 50; mem. grand jury, Sept. 19, 1637; town clerk; county treasurer, 1654; mcht.; commr.; removed to Boston abt. 1660; county treasurer. 1666; *m* at Burford, England, Ann Lord (*d* Charlestown, Jan. 29, 1682/83).

BARTLETT, Richard (*b* Wiltshire, Eng., 1575-*d* Newbury, Mass., May 25, 1647; son of Edward Bartlett, of Co. Kent, Eng.); came in the "Mary and John," 1634, settled at Newbury, Mass.

BARTLETT, Robert (*b* Eng. 1603-06-will proved, Oct. 29, 1676), came from Eng., July 1623, in the "Anne," landed at Plymouth; one of first purchasers of land at Dartmouth, Mass.; served in Capt. Myles Standish's company, 1632; freeman, 1633; cooper; surveyor; m 1628, Mary (b ante 1612-d 1678 or 83), dau. of Richard Warren, Mayf. Pil. (qv).

BARTLETT, Robert (b 1603-slain by Indians, Mar. 14, 1676), came in the "Lyon," 1632; settled at Cambridge, Mass., 1632; original propr. Hartford, Conn., 1639/40; freeman, 1645; chimney viewer, 1650; removed to Northampton, Mass., ca. 1655; constable, 1655; townsman, 1657, 64; selectman, 1658, 63; juryman, 1659; m Anne–(d 1676).

BARTON, Thomas (b Co. Monaghan, Ire., 1730-d New York City, May 25, 1780), grad. U. of Dublin; came to America and settled at Phila., Pa., 1,51; tutor in the academy which afterwards became the U. of Pa.; returned to Eng., 1754, and was there ordained in the Established Church; returned to America, 1755, and settled at Lancaster, Pa.; rector of St. James' Episcopal Ch., Lancaster, 1759-77; Loyalist; because of political beliefs, removed to N.Y. City, Oct. 3, 1778; served as chaplain in Gen. Howe's army; m 1753, Esther Rittenhouse (b 1737-d 1774, buried in the "Coleman pew," St. James' Ch., Lancaster), sister of David Rittenhouse, the astronomer, and dau. of Matthias Rittenhouse; m 2d, Mrs. Lee Normandie, née Braid, of New York.

BARTOW, Rev. John (b Crediton, Co. Devon, Eng., 1670-72-d Westchester, N.Y., Feb. 9, 1726; son of Dr. Thomas, of Crediton, m Grace Snell; g.s. of Gen. Peter Bartow); grad. Christ's College, Cambridge, 1692; entered ministry and became curate of Pampisford, Co. Cambridge, 1694; sent to N.Y., by the Propagation Society of Eng., landed in New York, Sept. 29, 1702; the trustees of Westchester voted him land, 1704; founded St. Peter's Ch., Westchester; pastor there abt. 22 yrs.; m Freehold, N.J., Sept. 17, 1705, Helena (b 1681), dau. of John Reid, of Middrew Castle, Kirkliston, Scot., later of Freehold, N.J., m Margaret Miller.

BASCOM (Bascomb, Baskecomb), Thomas (d Northampton, Mass., May 9, 1682), came from Scotland, in the "Mary and John," landed at Nantucket, Mass., May 30, 1630; settled at Dorchester, 1634; removed to Windsor, Conn., 1639; later to Northampton, Mass., 1655; apptd. commr., May 1655 and 57; rep. Gen. Ct., 1658; constable, 1666, 68; freeman, 1670; took oath of allegiance, Feb. 8, 1678/79; m ante 1639, Avis, or Advice – (d Feb. 3, 1676).

BASS, Samuel (b Eng. bet. 1595-1600-d Sept. or Dec. 30, 1694, or Jan. 10, 1695), came from Eng., with Winthrop, 1630; settled at Roxbury, Mass., 1630; admitted freeman, May 14, 1634; removed to Braintree (now Quincy), Mass., 1640; 1st deacon of the church and served for 50 yrs.; dep. Mass. Gen. Ct., 1641-53, and afterward; m Ann, or Anna –, possibly Rawson (b ca. 1600).

BASSETT, John (d New Haven, Conn., Feb. 15-20, 1652/53), came from Eng., 1624, in the "Truelove"; removed from Boston to New Haven, Conn., 1642-43; mentioned in the New Haven Colonial records as "old man Bassett"; took the oath at New Haven, 1644; bought land at Stamford, 1651/52; m in Eng., Margery – (d Stamford, Conn., bet. June 1653 and May 1656).

BASSETT (Basset, Bassite), William (will proved June 5, 1667), came in the "Fortune," to Plymouth, Mass., Nov. 19, 1621; blacksmith and gunsmith; freeman, 1633; served in Pequot War; removed to Duxbury, abt. 1638; dep. Gen. Ct., 1640-43; mem. Capt. Standish's mil. co., 1643; constable, 1652; original propr. of Bridgewater, and early settler there, 1655; had large library; m ca. 1621, Elizabeth Neil (?); m 2d, post 1651, Mary (Tilden) Lapham, dau. of Nathaniel Tilden (qv), and widow of Thomas Lapham.

BATCHELDER (Bachiler), Rev. Stephen (b 1560/61-d Hackney, near London, Eng., 1660, aged nearly 100), a noted English divine of Hampshire: B.A., Oxford U., 1586; came in the "William and Francis" arriving at Boston, Thursday, June 5, 1632; went to Lynn, where his dau., Theodate, lived; ordered by the court at Boston "to forbeare exercising his giftes as a pastor or teacher," Oct. 3, 1632, which restriction was removed, Mar. 4, 1633; freeman, 1635; removed to Ipswich, Mass., 1636; to Winnicunnet, N.H., 1638, which was named Hampton at his request; removed to Casco, Me., 1647; returned to Eng.,

1654, where he d; m 1st wife in Eng., where she d; m 2d, Eng., Helen – (1583-1642 or 44); m 3d, 1648, Mary –.

BATES (Bate), Clement (bap. Jan. 22, 1595-d Sept. 17, 1671; son of James [d 1614], of Lydd, Eng., and bro. of James [qv]; descended from Thomas Bate [d 1445], of Lydd, All Hallows); came from Eng. with James in the "Elizabeth," 1635, settled at Hingham, Mass.; had land allotted him there; tailor; freeman, 1636; granted 5 acres, 1635; selectman, 1637; mem. of com. to divide remaining part of "Conyhasset," 1640, 43; one of 7 men apptd. to order the affairs of the town, 1647; surveyor at Hingham, 1655; m Ann, or Anna – (1595-1669).

BATES (Bate), James (bap. Dec. 2, 1582-d 1655/56; bro. of Clement, qv); from Eng. in the "Elizabeth," to Dorchester, Mass., 1635; husbandman; freeman, 1636; selectman, 1637-38, 42, 51; ruling elder; rep., 1641; m 1603, Alice Glover (b ca. 1583-d 1657), of Saltwood, Eng.

BATES, John (1598 or 1600-ca. 1666), from Eng. in the "Southampton," 1623; at Piercey's Hundred, 1624; later in Bruton Parish, Middletown, Va.; m Elizabeth–.

BATHURST, Lancelot (1646-1704-05; son of Sir Edward, Bart., of Co. Sussex, Eng.), from Eng. to Va., ante 1680; granted 1,200 acres in New Kent Co., 1683; examiner of records, 1689; high sheriff, Nex Kent Co., 1698; prominent lawyer; dep. atty. gen., Henrico Co., 1684; justice, 1699, 1702; m in Eng., Susanna–.

BATTLE, John (b Yorkshire, Eng.-d ca.1690), prob. from Ireland to Va., 1654; resided on west fork of Nansemond River, Va.; in Pasquotank Co., N.C., 1663; received large land grants from Sir William Berkeley; m Elizabeth–.

BAUDOUIN, Peter, see Bowdoin.

BAUMAN, see Bowman.

BAXTER (Baxstar), Gregory (d June 21, 1659), prob. from nr. Rowton, Eng., in Winthrop's fleet, 1630; settled at Roxbury, Mass., 1630; freeman, 1632; removed to Braintree, 1640; m Margaret Paddy (d Feb. 13, 1661/62), sis. of William Paddy, treas. Plymouth Colony, 1640-53.

BAXTER, Lt. Thomas (d June 22, 1713), from Scotland to Yarmouth, Mass.; m 1679/80, Temperance (d Mar. 12, 1745/46), dau. Capt. John Gorham (qv), and widow of Edward Sturgis.

BAYARD, Col. Nicholas (b Alphen, Holland, ca. 1644-d New York, N.Y., bet. 1707-11; bro. of Petrus [qv]; son of Samuel Bayard, m Ann Stuyvesant, who came from Holland in the "Princess," to New Amsterdam, 1647), came with his mother; clk. of Common Council, 1664; sec. to Gov. Peter Stuyvesant; surveyor; alderman; sec. of Colony, 1672; mayor of New York, 1685; mem. gov.'s council, 1685, 1687-89, 1691-98; col. of New York militia, 1685; m 1663/64, Judith Varleth, who was condemned as a witch at Hartford, Conn., 1662, but pardoned by Gov. Peter Stuyvesant; dau. of Casper Varleth.

BAYARD, Petrus (b Holland, 1635-d 1699; son of Samuel Bayard, m Ann Stuyvesant, sister of Gov. Peter); from Holland in the "Princess," to New Amsterdam, 1647; lived for a time in Del.; received land grant for Bombay, Hook Island, 1675; returned to New Amsterdam where he was large landowner; m 1674, Blandina (d 1702), dau. Dr. Hans Kierstede (qv).

BAYLESS (Baylis, Baylies, Bayliss, Bayles), John (1617-82), from Eng. to Bermuda, 1635; to America in the "Truelove"; settled at New Haven, Conn., 1654; at Southold, L.I., 1656; purchased from the Indians, 1664, with some associates, about 200,000 acres, where Newark, Paterson, and Passaic now stand; and same was deeded by John Bayles and associates to Philip Carteret, then gov. of N.J., 1665, both deeds are recorded at Trenton, N.J.; m Rebecca –.

BAYNTON, Peter (b Bedminster, Eng.-d 1710), resided in Pa. on Del. River, 1686; in New Castle Co., Del., 1689; justice, 1693; returned to Eng. for several yrs.; was a chirurgeon at Phila., 1710; m 1st, a dau. of Col. Paris, of Charleston; m 2d, Mary Budd; m 3d, – Wheeler.

BEACH, John (1623-77), came to New Haven, Conn., 1640 or 43; removed to Stratford, Conn.; purchased house and lot, 1660; freeman, 1669; town crier, 1671; King Philip's War; m Mary, dau. of Thomas Staples, of Fairfield.

BEACH, Richard (b ca. 1620), from Eng. to Watertown, Mass., 1635, thence to New Haven Colony, and signer of the Compact of 1639; removed to New London, 1667; m ca. 1640, Catherine

(Cook) Hull (*b* 1620), widow of Andrew Hull, of New Haven.

BEACH, Thomas (*d* 1662), from Eng. to Quinnipiack (New Haven), Conn., ca. 1638; took oath of allegiance, 1654; at Milford, 1658; *m* 1652, Sarah (1635-70), dau. of Richard Platt.

BEAL (Beale, Beall, Beals), John (1588-1688), from Eng. in the "Diligente," to Hingham, Mass., 1638; freeman, 1639; dep. Gen. Ct., 1649-59; *m* Nazareth Hobart (*d* 1658); *m* 2d, 1659, Mary, widow of Nicholas Jacob.

BEALE, Thomas (1626-ante 1700), from Eng., 1640; settled on York River, Va., 1645; mem. Royal Council, 1674; *m* Alice –.

BEALL, Alexander (1649-1744; son John, *m* Margaret Ramsay), from Scot., settled in Montgomery Co., Md.; owned "Friendship Enlarged," which extended from (now) Washington, D.C., to Burnt Mills, on Sligo Creek; *m* Elizabeth Dick.

BEALL (Beal, Beale), Col. Ninian (*b* Largo, Fifeshire, Scot., 1625-*d* 1717), as prisoner of Cromwell was exiled to Barbados, 1650; to Prince Georges Co., Md., ca. 1652; later planter in Calvert Co., Md.; lt., 1668, 76; dep. surveyor, Charles Co., 1684; chief mil. officer, Calvert Co., 1689; maj. Calvert Co. militia, 1689; high sheriff, 1692; col. of militia, 1694; mem. Gen. Assembly, 1697-1701; Md. Gen. Assembly passed "Act of Gratitude" for distinguished Indian services, 1699; ruling elder, and "Father of Presbyterianism in Md."; *m* Elizabeth Gordon (*d* in Scotland); *m* 2d, 1668-70, Ruth (1652-1707), dau. of Richard Moore, of St. Marys Co., Md., *m* Jane–.

BEARD, Thomas, see Baird.

BEARDSLEY (Beardslee, Berdsley, Bersley), William (1605-61), from Eng. in the "Planter," to Mass., 1635; extensive land owner; founder of Stratford, Conn., 1639; dep. Gen. Ct., 1645-51; *m* Mary–.

BEATTY, Charles (ca. 1712-1772; son of John Beatty, officer British Army, *m* Christiana Clinton, who came to America, *m* with her brother, Col. Charles Clinton, of N.Y.), came from Ireland, 1729, to Forks of Neshaminy, Pa., 1743; chaplain in French and Indian War; hon. A.M., Princeton, 1762, and trustee same, 1763-72; missionary to Indians, commr. to the Barbados to collect funds for Princeton Coll.: *m* Ann, dau. John Reading, pres. Provincial Council of N.J.

BEAUCHAMP, Edmund (ca. 1625-1691; son of Sir John, one of the stockholders who financed the Mayflower expdn.; g.son of Thomas Beauchamp, of Cosgrove, Co. Northampton); from Eng. ante 1665; settled in Somerset Co., Md.; clk. and keeper of records of Somerset Co., 1666, 1674-92; *m* 1666, or 68, Sarah (*d* 1734), dau. Ambrose Dixon, *m* Mary Peddington, of Va. and Md.

BEAUMONT, William (1607/08-1699), from Eng. in the "Elizabeth," 1635, settled at Saybrook, Conn.; *m* 1643, Lydia (1624-1686 or 88), dau. Nicholas Danforth (qv).

BECKWITH, Matthew (*b* ca. 1610-*d* 1680), from Eng. to Saybrook Point, Conn., 1636; later at Branford, at Hartford, 1645, and later at Lyme and New London; a founder of the Ch. at Lyme; *m* Elizabeth–; she *m* 2d, Samuel Buckland.

BEECHER, John (1623-59), from Eng. with his widowed mother, Hannah – (1600-58), arriving at Boston, Apr. 26, 1637; settled at Quinnipiack, Conn.

BEEKMAN, Wilhelmus (1623-1707; son of Hendrick), from Holland, in the "Princess," to New Amsterdam with Peter Stuyvesant, 1647; vice dir. of the colony on South River, 1658-64; lt. Burgher Corps of New Amsterdam, 1652-58, of New Orange, 1673-74; schout and commissary at Esopus, 1664; lt. militia, 1673; dep. mayor of N. Y., 1681-83; *m* 1649, Catalina (*d* 1700), dau. Hendrick de Boogh, of Albany.

BEERS, James (*d* 1694; son of James, of Gravesend, Co. Kent, Eng., and descended from Antony Bere, Gravesend, 1486); came to America with his uncle, Richard Beers (qv), 1635, thence to Watertown, Mass., thence Fairfield, Conn.; *m* Martha, dau. of John Barlow.

BEERS, Richard (*d* 1675), from Eng. to Watertown, Mass., 1635; capt. in King Philip's War, and killed at Northfield, Mass.

BEHETHLAND, Capt. Robert, Gent., from Eng. in the "Sarah Constant," to Jamestown, Va., 1607; accompanied Capt. John Smith on

expdns. to negotiate with Indians; *m* Mary Nicholson.

BELDEN (Bayldon, Belding), Richard (bap. Kippax, Co. York, Eng., 1591-*d* 1655; son of Sir Francis Baildon or Bayldon, Kt., *m* 2d, Margaret, dau. Richard Goodrick of Ripston), came to Wethersfield, Conn., 1635; apptd. town herder, 1646.

BELKNAP, Abraham (1589-1643), from Eng. with two brothers, Joseph and Thomas, 1637, settled at Lynn, Mass.

BELL, Francis (*d* 1690), from Eng., settled at Wethersfield, Conn.; an original settler of Stamford, 1641; rep. Gen. Ct., 1641; lt. militia, 1643; commr., 1664; gov.'s asst.; *m* Rebecca–(*d* 1684).

BELL, Thomas (1618-78), from Eng. to Jamestown, Va., 1635; *m* Mary, dau. Capt. John Neal.

BELLINGER, Capt. Sir Edmund (desc. Walter Bellinger, of Northumberland, who was granted coat-of-arms, 1475), from Westmoreland Co., Eng., 1674, settled on James Island, S.C.; landgrave, 1698; surveyor gen.; receiver of public moneys, 1700; *m* ca. 1680, Sarah Cartwright; issue: Edmund, 2d landgrave.

BELLOWS, John (ca. 1623-1683), from Eng. in the "Hopewell," before he was 12 yrs. old; settled at Concord, Mass., 1635; to Marlborough, 1660; *m* 1655, Mary (1637-1707), dau. John Wood, *m* Mary–.

BEMIS (Bemiss, Beamis), Joseph (1619-1684), from Eng. to Watertown, Mass., 1640; soldier King Philip's War; was often selectman; *m* Sarah –.

BENEDICT, Thomas (1617-90), from Eng. to Mass., 1638; at Southold, L.I.; mem. Colonial Assembly from Hempstead; finally at Norwalk, Conn., where was deacon, selectman, town clk. and dep. to Gen. Ct.; *m* Mary Bridgum, or Bridgham (*d* aet. 100).

BENJAMIN, John (1598-1645), from Eng. in the "Lion," to Boston, 1632, large landed propr. at Watertown, freeman, 1632; constable, 1633; *m* 1619, Abigail (1600-87), dau. Rev. William Eddy.

BENNETT (Bennet), James (*d* 1659), from Eng. to Concord, Mass., 1639; to Fairfield, Conn., 1644; *m* Hannah (*b* 1617), dau. Lt. Thomas Wheeler (*d* 1654), from Eng. ca. 1644, *m* 1613, Ann Halsey.

BENNETT (Bennet), Richard (*d* 1675), came to Va. ca. 1626, and settled in Nansemond Co.; burgess, 1629, 31; mem. Council, 1639-49, 1658, et seq.; removed to Md., 1649; apptd. by Parliament one of the three commrs. to reduce Va and Md., Dec. 1651; gov. of Va., 1652-55; went to Eng. 1655, as agent for the colony; maj. gen. militia, 1665; *m* Mary Ann Utie.

BENSON (Bensen), Dirck (*d* Albany, 1659), removed from Gröningen to Amsterdam, Holland; came with wife to New York, ca. 1648; granted land at Fort Orange (Albany), 1653, resided there the following year; as a carpenter, helped construct the new church at Albany, 1656, and loaned the deacons 100 guilders, 1658; *m* Catalina Berck (1625-post 1663); she *m* 2d, Harmen Thomase Hun.

BENT, John (1596-1672; son of Robert, 1566-1631), from Penton-Grafton, Co. Hants, Eng., in the "Confidence," 1638; settled at Sudbury, Mass.; freeman, 1640; received land grants, 1639, 1640, 1655; selectman, 1641; justice, 1648; one of three to lay out highway from Watertown (part now Weston), to Framingham, Mass.; in expdn. against Ninigret, 1654; a petitioner for Marlborough, 1656; *m* ca. 1644, Martha–(*d* 1679).

BENTON, Andrew (1620-83; son of Edward); from England to Watertown, Mass.; first settler of Milford, Conn., 1639; fence viewer, 1663-64; juror, 1664; freeman, 1665; collector of minister's fees, 1667; *m* 1649, Hannah (*d* 1670), dau. of George Stocking; *m* 2d Ann (*d* 1686), dau. of John Cole (the "bewitched man" for whom Nathaniel Greene and his wife were hanged, 1663).

BERGEN (van Bergen), Hans Hansen (1600-1653/54), native of Norway, came from Holland in the "Salt Mountain," to New Amsterdam, 1633; owned large plantation on Manhattan Island; *m* 1639, as her 1st husband, Sarah (1625-85), daughter Joris Jansen de Rapalje (qv).

BERNARD, Col. William (1598-1665), from Eng. in the "America," to Va., 1625, settled in Isle of Wight Co.; mem. Council, 1642-60; *m* Lucy (Higginson) Burwell, dau. of Capt. Robert Higginson, and widow of Lewis Burwell, of Carter's Creek, Gloucester Co.

BERNON, Gabriel (1644-1736; son of Andre, m Suzane –), a Huguenot, from Rochelle, France; imprisoned 2 yrs. because of religious faith; fled to Eng.; came to America, June 1688; founder of first three P.E. churches in R.I.; m 2d, 1714, Mary Harris.

BERRIEN, Cornelius Janse (d 1689), Huguenot; fled from France to Holland, thence came to New Amsterdam, 1669, settled at Flatbush, L.I.; removed to Newtown, L.I., 1685; was deacon and tax commr.; m Jannetje, dau. of Jan Stryker (qv).

BERRYMAN (Berriman, Bereman, Berreman), Thomas (will dated 1689), to S.I., 1686; administrator of the estate of Marrym Thomas, of Bergen, N.J., 1686; m Jane–(will dated 1701).

BETTS, Richard (1613-1713), from Eng. to Ipswich, Mass., 1648; removed to Newtown, L.I., 1656; capt., 1663; mem. Provincial Assembly of N.Y., 1665; high sheriff of Yorkshire, L.I., 1678-81.

BEVERLY, Maj. Robert (1630-86), from Eng., 1663, settled in Middlesex Co., Va.; large landholder; clk. Ho. of Burgesses; cdr. all Va. mil. forces, 1676; mem. Council; m 1666, Mary Carter (1637-78); m 2d, Katherine Hone.

BIBB, Benjamin (1640-1702), said to have come from Wales to Va.; received land grant, King William Co., ca. 1685; was deeded land in Hanover Co., Va.; m Mary–(d post 1702).

BICKNELL, Zachary (1590-1636), from Eng. with Rev. Joseph Hull, to Weymouth, Mass., 1635, of which he was a propr.; m at Weymouth, Eng., Agnes Lovell (d 1643).

BIDDLE, William (1630-1712), from Eng. to New Jersey, 1681, becoming one of the proprietors of West Jersey; was pres. bd. of trustees and Council Proprietary of West Jersey, Gov.'s Council, Gen. Assembly, and was justice; m 1665, Sarah Kemp (1634-1709).

BIGELOW (Baguley, Biglo, Biglow), John (1616/17-1703), from Eng., ca. 1630, settled at Watertown, Mass., 1642; soldier Pequot and King Philip's wars; m 1642, Mary (1628-91), dau. John Warren; m 2d, 1694, Sarah, dau. Joseph Bemis.

BILES (Byles), William (d 1710), an "Eminent Friend"; from Dorchester, Eng., in the "Eliza and Sarah," to Del., 1679; large landowner in Bucks Co., Pa.; mem. pre-provincial govt., Jan. 4, 1681, before arrival of William Penn; justice Uplands Ct.; signer of Penn's Great Charter; mem. first Council, Phila., Mar. 10, 1683, "William Penn presiding in person"; judge Ct. of Inquiry, 1700; the first known meeting of Friends in Pa. was held in his house, just below the Falls of Neshaminy, May 2, 1683; m 2d, Joan, or Jane Atkinson.

BILLINGS (Billing), William (ca. 1629-1713), from Eng. to Dorchester, Mass., ante 1649; settled at Stonington, Conn., 1658; m Feb. 12, 1657/58, Mary – (d 1718).

BILLINGTON, John (d 1630), 26th signer of the Mayflower Compact; m before 1605, Eleanor – (d 1643).

BINGHAM, Thomas (1642-1730), from Eng. to Saybrook, Conn., 1659, later a founder of Norwich, and at Windham, 1693; m 1666, Mary (1648-1726), dau. Jonathan Rudd, of New Haven, Conn.

BIRCHARD, Thomas (d 1684), came in the "Truelove," 1635; an original propr. of Hartford, 1636; rep., 1650-51; m Mary – (d 1655).

BISBEE, Thomas (1589-1674; son of John, m Dorothy Austin), from Eng., to Scituate, Mass., 1634; dea.; dep. Gen. Ct.; m 1619, Anne Baseden.

BISSELL, John (1591-1677), from Eng. to Plymouth, Mass., 1628, settled at Windsor, Conn., before 1640; established "Bissell's Ferry" across Connecticut River, under charter from King Charles, still operated by his descendants; dep. 1648; soldier King Philip's War; capt. of Windsor Troop, 1676; q.m. troop of horse, 1677; m Mary Drake (d 1641).

BIXBY, Joseph (bap. 1621-d Apr. 19, 1701; son of George, m Ann Cole), from Eng. to Ipswich, Mass., ca. 1640, where held public offices; m 1647, Sarah (Wyatt) Heard (1619-1704).

BLACK, John (1768-1849), Presbyn. minister, ed. U. Glasgow; came from Ireland to Phila., ca. 1797; prof. Western U. Pa.; m Elizabeth, dau. Andrew Watters, from Scotland, 1773, soldier in Am. Rev. (m Margaret, dau. Alexander Thomson, from Scotland to Pittsburgh, 1784).

BLACKSHAW, Randall (son of Capt. Ralph

[?], of Hollongee, Cheshire, who commanded a company under Charles I, and lost in the civil war most of the fortune and estates inherited from his father); came in the "Welcome" with William Penn, 1682; present when Penn signed the Shackawaxon treaty with the Delaware Indians; helped build the first Quaker meeting house in Pa., 1692; m Mary Burgess.

BLAINE, James (d 1792), from Ireland with his first wife, ca. 1745, settled in Toboyne Tp., Cumberland Co., Pa.; m Elizabeth–; m 2d, Elizabeth Carskaden.

BLAIR, John (1720-71), from Scotland to Cumberland Co., Pa., ca. 1740; of Fogg Manor, Chester Co., Pa.; v.p., trustee and first prof. of theology of Coll. of N.J. (Princeton), 1767-71; m 174–, Elizabeth, dau. of John Durburrow.

BLAISDELL, Ralph (d 1650), came in the "Angel Gabriel," to York, Me., 1635; settled at Salisbury, Mass.; m Elizabeth– (d 1667).

BLAKE, William (bap. Pitminster Parish, Co. Somerset, Eng., July 10, 1594-d Aug. 25, 1663; son of William, of Pitminster; g.son of John, of Over Stowey, Somerset), from Eng. to Dorchester, Mass., ca. 1636; freeman, 1638/39; selectman, 1645, 47, 51; town clk., 1656-64; founder of Agawam, Mass.; mem. A. and H.A. Co.; m at Pitminster, Sept. 27, 1617, Agnes (Thorne) Bond (bap. July 12, 1594-d July 22, 1678), dau. of Hugh Thorne.

BLAKEMAN, Rev. Adam, D.D. (1598-1665), ed. Christ Coll., Eng.; established 1st ch. at Stratford, Conn., and was one of the first settlers there, 1640.

BLAKESLEY (Blakeslee, Blakeslie), Samuel (d May 17, 1672), from Eng. with his brother Thomas, in the "Hopewell," ca. 1635; brought their blacksmithing equipment; settled first at Boston Neck; thence New Haven, Conn.; later Thomas went to Woodbury and settled, while Samuel remained at New Haven; m Dec. 3, 1650, Hannah, dau. of John Potter, of New Haven, m Elizabeth –.

BLANCHARD, Thomas (d 1654; desc. of Alain Blanchard, of Rouen, France, 1418, patriot executed by British after surrender at Rouen); came from Lorraine, France, to Eng.; from Eng. in the "Jonathan," to Charlestown, Mass., 1639; was at Braintree, 1646-50; Charlestown, 1651, et seq.; m 2d, 1637, Agnes (Bent) Barnes (d on voyage); m 3d, Mary –, of "Noodle's Island," Boston Harbor.

BLAND, Theodoric (1629-Apr. 23, 1671; son of John [1573-1632], an eminent merchant of London and a member of the Virginia Company); came to Va., 1654, and settled at "Westover," Charles City Co.; speaker House of Burgesses, 1659 and 61, and mem. Council, 1665-71; m Ann (d 1687), dau. of Richard Bennett (qv).

BLAUVELT, Garret Hendricks (1620-83), shoemaker, from Holland to Rensselaerwyck, N.Y., 1637; settled at New Amsterdam, 1646; m 1646, Marritie (ante 1625-ante 1679), dau. Lambert Huybertsen Moll, of Bushwick, L.I., m Tryntye Pieters.

BLEECKER, Jan Jansen (1641-1732), from Holland to N.Y. at 16 yrs. of age, and settled at Fort Orange (Albany), 1658; Indian commr.; mem. Assembly, 1698-1701; mayor of Albany, 1700-1701; capt. in Indian war, 1684; m 1667, Margaritta (1647-1733), dau. Rutger Jacobsen Van Schoenderwoert.

BLISS, Thomas (ca. 1580-1650), from Eng. to Braintree, Mass., 1635; settled at Hartford, Conn., 1639, where he was a propr.; m in Eng., ca. 1610, Margaret Lawrence (1594-1684), she removed to Springfield, Mass., after husband's death, where she received a land grant, 1651.

BLODGETT (Blogget), Thomas (1605-42), from Eng. in the "Increase," to Cambridge, Mass., 1635; freeman, 1636; m in Eng., Susanna –.

BLOODGOOD (Bloetgoet), Frans Jansen (1635-1676), from Holland to New Amsterdam, 1659; chief officer of Dutch militia, privy councillor to gov. at time of surrender of colony to British, 1675; magistrate, 1673; dep. to New Orange, 1674; m in Holland, Lysbeth Jans.

BLOOMER, Robert (b 1634), settled at Setauket, L.I., later at Rye and New Rochelle, N.Y.; m ca. 1670, Rachel–; m 2d, Sarah–.

BLOSSOM, Thomas (d 1633), from Eng., in 2d voyage of the "Mayflower," 1629 (a passenger in the "Speedwell" which returned to British port, 1620); settled at Plymouth; removed later to Barnstable; a deacon; m Ann–.

BLOTT, Robert (d 1665), came to Charlestown, Mass., 1634; freeman, Roxbury, Mass., 1635; m Susanna–(d 1660).

BLOUNT, Capt. James (ca. 1620-will proved July 17, 1686), from Eng.; in Isle of Wight Co., Va., 1655; moved to Chowan Precinct, Colony of Carolina, 1669; owned "Mulberry Hill"; mem. House of Commons, 1671; m 2d, 1665, Ann (Willis) Rascoe, of Ipswich, Mass. (she m 3d, Seth Sothell, m 4th, Col. John Lear, of Nansemond Co., Va.).

BOARDMAN (Boreman), Samuel (b Banbury, Eng., ca. 1615-d Wethersfield, Conn., Apr. 1675), arrived at Boston, 1638; settled at Ipswich, Mass.; at Wethersfield, Conn., 1641; first customs master, 1659; dep. Gen. Ct., 1657, and for 18 yrs.; gov.'s asst., 1676; m 1641, Mary (ca. 1623-Aug. 1684), dau. of John Betts.

BODDIE, William (ca. 1635-1717), from Eng. to Isle of Wight Co., Va., 1655; Quaker; received grant of 6,700 acres land from Gov. Berkeley for transporting 134 emigrants; m Anne –; m 2d, 1679(?), Elizabeth – (1650-99); m 3d, Mrs. Mary Edwards.

BOGARDUS, Dominie Everardus (b 1607-d Dec. 27, 1647), ed. U. of Leyden, Holland; apptd. chaplain to the sick at Elmina, Guiana (then Brazil), by Dutch West India Co., 1630-32; returned to Holland; ordained minister Dutch Ref. Church, 1632; came to New Amsterdam in the "Zontberg," 1633; pastor Dutch Ref. Ch. at New Amsterdam, 1638-47; resigned and started for Holland in the "Princess," which was shipwrecked off Wales; m 1638, as her 2d husband, Anneke (Webber) Jans (1605-63), widow of Roelof Jansen, and dau. of Wolfert Webber (b 1565), said to have been son of William, 9th prince of Orange and later King of Holland.

BOGART (Bogaert), Gysbert Cornelisen (d 1665), from Holland to New Amsterdam, 1661; resided at Rensselaerwyck; m Derkje–; m 2d, 1663, Mary, widow of John Jochams Kelder.

BOGERT (Bogaert), Jan Laurensz, commonly referred to as Jan (Lowesen) Louwe (born 1630-40), from Holland in the "Bonte Koe," to Bedford, L.I., 1663, settled at Bogert's Point, Harlem, 1672, at New York, 1707; magistrate 1675-76; m Cornelia Everts.

BOLLES, Joseph (1608-78), from Eng. to Winter Harbor, Me., ante 1640; removed to Wells, Me.; town clk., 1654-64; m Mary – (supposed to have been dau. of Morgan Howell, who bequeathed her all his property, will probated, 1679).

BOLLING, Robert (Dec. 26, 1646-July 17, 1709; son of John, m Mary–); came from Eng. at 14 yrs. of age, 1660, settled at Kipnax, Prince George Co., Va.; col., Prince George Co.; burgess; justice of Charles City Co. before 1698; high sheriff, 1699; surveyor, 1702; col. and county lt., 1705-09; m 1st, 1675, Jane (d 1678), dau. Lt. Thomas Rolfe (son of John, m Princess Pocahontas); m 2d, 1681, Anne, dau. Maj. John Stith, m Widow Jane Parsons.

BOLTWOOD, Robert (d 1684), from Eng. to Hartford, Conn., 1648, settled at Hadley, 1659; freeman, 1661; sgt. of militia; operated a corn mill, 1677; m Mary–(d 1687).

BOND, John (bap. 1624-d 1674/75), from Eng. ca. 1639; was at Newbury, Mass., 1642; removed to Rowley, 1660, thence to Haverhill; m 1649, Esther Blakely (or Hester Blakely).

BOND, Robert (1599-1677), came from Co. Kent, Eng., to Lynn, Mass., 1635; settled at Southampton, L.I., 1643; at Easthampton, 1648; a founder of Elizabethtown, N.J., 1665; rep., 1666; took oath of allegiance, 1665; m Hannah, dau. Richard Ogden; m 2d, Mary (Calkins) Roberts, dau. of Hugh Caldine, or Calkins, and widow of Hugh Roberts.

BOND, William (1625-95; son of Thomas; g.son of Jonas); from Eng. with his brothers, John and Thomas; settled at Watertown, Mass.; m Sarah, dau. of Nathaniel Biscoe.

BOOGHER, Nicholas (b 1690; desc. of Peter Bucher, granted coat of arms, 1450, for mil. service), from Germany in the "Friendship," to Pa., 1727; m Katherine–.

BOOKER, Edward (1590-1648), an English refugee in Holland; came to York Co., Va., 1648; mem. Council; m a sis. of Richard Glover.

BOONE, George (1666-July 27, 1744; son of George, of Bradnich, nr. Exeter, Eng., m Sarah Uppey); landed at Phila., Pa., Sept. 29, 1717;

settled in Berks Co., 1718; founded and named Exeter Tp.; mem. Gwynedd Monthly Meeting, later of Exeter Meeting; landowner; d Exeter, Pa.; m 1689, in Eng., Mary Milton (1669-Berks Co., Pa., Feb. 2, 1740), dau. of John Maugridge, of Eng., m Mary Milton; they were g.parents of Daniel Boone, the pioneer.

BOORAEM, see Van Boerum.

BOOTHE, Richard (1606/07-1688), from Eng., an original settler at Stratford, Conn., 1639; m 1640, Elizabeth Hawley (sister of Richard Hawley).

BORDEN, Richard (1595/96-1671), from Eng. with his wife and two sons to Portsmouth, R.I., 1635; surveyor; owned large tracts in R.I. and in Monmouth Co., East Jersey; freeman, Portsmouth, 1641; gov.'s asst., 1653, 54; commr., 1654-57; treas., 1654-55; dep. Gen. Ct., 1667, 70; resident of Gravesend, L.I., 1665; m 1625, Joan (1604-88), dau. Richard Fowle.

BOSTWICK (Bostock), Arthur (Dec. 22, 1603-post Dec. 10, 1680), from Tarporley, Cheshire Co., Eng., to Stratford, Conn., ca. 1640; m Jan. 8, 1627, Jane, dau. of Rev. Robert Whittel.

BOSWORTH, Edward, from Eng. in the "Elizabeth Dorcas," 1634; d as the ship was entering Boston harbor; his widow, Mary, and children settled at Hingham, where she d 1648.

BOURNE, Richard (d 1682), from Eng. to Lynn, Mass., 1637; one of the early settlers at Sandwich, Mass.; dep. General Court; mem. Council of War, 1675; m Martha Hallett; m 2d, Ruth (Sargent) Winslow.

BOURNE, Thomas (ca. 1581-d 1664), came to Plymouth, Mass., 1636; "the eldest of the Marshfield settlers"; dep. Gen. Ct.; on guard duty at his garrisoned home, 1643; m Elizabeth – (ca. 1590-1660).

BOUTON (Boughton), John, or Jean (1615-1704/05; son of Count Nicholas, Huguenot); from Gravesend, Eng., in the "Assurance," to Boston, Dec. 1635; settled at Hartford, later at Norwalk and Danbury, Conn., where he d; rep. Gen. Ct., 1671; m Joan Turney; m 2d, 1656, Abigail (1640-72), dau. of Matthew Marvin (qv); m 3d, ca. 1673, Mary – widow of Jonathan Stevenson.

BOUTWELL, James (ca. 1625-ca. 1651), from Eng., was at Salem, Mass., 1638, m Alice –.

BOWDITCH, William (1640-81), from Eng. to Salem, Mass., 1671; collector of the port; m Sarah–.

BOWDOIN (Baudoin), Pierre (d Boston, Mass., Sept. 1706), Huguenot physician from Rochelle, France, to Dublin, Ireland, 1685; to Casco, Me., 1686; received grant of 100 acres, Casco Bay, 1687; to Boston, 1690; m in France, Elizabeth– (1643-1720).

BOWEN, Griffith (d bet. 1671-76), from Wales to Boston, ca. 1638; freeman, 1639; later at Roxbury; returned to Eng., and was living at London, 1670; m Margaret, dau. Henry Fleming, of Wales.

BOWEN, Richard (1600-75), from Wales to Weymouth, Mass., 1640, with his wife and children, settled at Rehoboth, 1642; dep. Plymouth Gen. Ct., 1651; m Ann (or Anna)–; m 2d, Elizabeth – (d 1675).

BOWIE, John (1688-1759), from Scotland to Md., ca. 1705 or 06; settled nr. Nottingham, Prince George's Co., Md.; m 1707, Mary (d 1750), dau. of James Mullikin.

BOWIE, John (d 1789), from Scotland to Va. ca. 1742, settled on the Rappahannock; m 1745, Judith Catlett (d 1798).

BOWLES, John (d 1680), from Eng. in the "Hopewell," to Roxbury, Mass., 1636; admitted to the church, 1640; mem. A. and H. A. Co., 1645; m Elizabeth Heath.

BOWMAN (Bauman), Hans Dieterick (d Jan. 1761), from the Palatinate, Germany, in the "Adventurer," 1727; settled in Marlboro Tp., Phila. (now Northampton) Co., Pa.; erected a mill on Perkiomen Creek; removed to the Towamensing region in the Blue Mtns., 1754; m Eva Elizabeth– (she m 2d, Nicholas Kern, Jr.).

BOWMAN, Nathaniel (b Westwood Hill, nr. Leek, Eng., 1608-d Jan. 26, 1681/82; son of John [bap. 1578], m Anne, dau. Anthony Beresford), from Eng. in the Winthrop Fleet, 1630; settled at Watertown, Mass.; removed to Cambridge Farms, ca. 1650; m Anna–.

BOWNE, John (1626/27-1695; son of Thomas), from Eng. to Flushing, L.I., 1649; built the old

Bowne house there, 1661; *m* 1656, Hannah (ca. 1637-1677), dau. Lt. Robert Feake; *m* 2d, 1679/80, Hannah Bickerstaffe (*d* 1690); *m* 3d, 1693, Mary dau. James Cock.

BOWNE, John (ca. 1630-1684; son of William), of Salem, Mass.; at Gravesend, L.I., 1645: removed to Monmouth Co., N.J., 1665; one of 12 original patentees of Monmouth Co., 1665; patentee of Middletown, N.J., 1672; commd. as pres. of the ct., to hold a ct. at Middletown and Shrewsbury, N.J., 1677; judge, 1679; justice of the peace, 1679; maj. of militia, 1683; mem. of Assembly, and speaker, 1668, 75, 80, 81, 83; *m* Lydia (bap. 1646), dau. Rev. Obadiah Holmes (qv).

BOWNE (De La Bowne), William (*d* 1677), Huguenot, from Yorkshire to Salem, 1629, to Boston, 1631, to L.I., 1646; patentee of Gravesend and its magistrate 7 yrs.; associate in Monmouth Patent, 1665; mem. Assembly of Patentees and Deputies of N.J., 1669; *m* Anne –.

BOYDEN, Thomas (*b* 1613), from Eng. in the "Francis," 1634, settled at Scituate, Mass.; freeman, 1647; removed to Boston, 1650, and later at Medfield, Watertown and Groton; highway surveyor, 1659/60; *m* Frances– (*d* 1658); *m* 2d, 1658, Hannah (Phillips) Morse.

BRACE, Stephen (ca. 1644-1692), Eng. to Swansea, Mass., 1667; to Hartford, Conn., 1669; hatter; *m* ca. 1666, Elizabeth–(1644-1724).

BRACKETT, Anthony (killed by Indians, Sept. 28, 1691/92), from Eng., settled at Sandy Beach, nr. Portsmouth, N.H., 1623; received grants of over 200 acres; selectman, 1655, served several terms; later at Exeter; killed by Indians; *m* —(also killed by Indians, 1691/92).

BRACKETT, Richard (1611/12-1691), at Boston, Mass., 1632; removed to present site of Quincy, 1639; cdr. militia of Braintree; mem. A. and H. A. Co.; dep. Gen. Ct., 1655-80; *m* Alice–.

BRADBURY, Thomas (1610/11-1694/95; son of Wymond, of the Brick House, Wicken Bonant, *m* Elizabeth Whitgift), was at York, Me., 1634, later at Ipswich, Mass.; freeman, Salisbury, 1640; town clk.; school teacher; justice; dep. from Salisbury to Mass. Gen. Ct., 1651, 52, 56, 57, 60, 61, 66; capt. militia; recorder, Norfolk Co. 6 yrs.; asso. judge; *m* 1636, Mary (*d* 1700), dau. John Perkins (qv).

BRADFORD, William (bap. 1590-1657), 2d signer of the Mayflower Compact; gov. of the Colony 31 years; asst. 1634 et seq.; *m* 1st, at Leyden, Holland, 1613, Dorothy (1597-1620), dau. John May; *m* 2d, Plymouth, Mass., 1623, Alice (Carpenter) Southworth (1590-1670), widow of Edward Southworth.

BRADLEY, William (1619-91), soldier in Cromwell's army; came to New Haven with Theophilus Eaton, 1637; admitted freeman, 1644; started settlements at Wallingford and North Haven; on standing committee to manage affairs of Wallingford; rep. Gen. Ct. 6 terms; *m* 1650, Alice, dau. of Roger Pritchard.

BRADSTREET, Simon (1603-97; son of Simon, a non-conformist of Eng.); from Eng. with Gov. Winthrop, 1630; settled at Andover; first sec. of Colony of Mass. Bay, 1630-36, asst., 1630-78, commr. United Colonies, 1643, 1663-66, dep. gov., 1672-76, gov., 1676-86 and 1689; *m* 1628, Anne (*d* 1672), dau. Gov. Thomas Dudley; *m* 2d, Anna (Gardner) Downing.

BRAINERD (Brainard), Daniel (1641-1715), brought from Eng. to Hartford, Conn., at 8 yrs. of age, 1649; a propr. and settler of Haddam, Conn., ca. 1662; justice of the peace; deacon; freeman, 1669; commr., 1669; constable, surveyor, fenceviewer, assessor, collector; dep. Gen. Ct., 1692-1706; *m* ca. 1663 or 64, Hannah (1641-91), dau. of Gerard Spencer (qv); *m* 2d, 1693, Elizabeth (Wakeman) Arnold; *m* 3d, 1698, Hannah (Spencer?) Sexton, widow of George Sexton.

BRANCH, Christopher (1600 or 02-1681 or 82; son of Lionel); from Eng. to Va., 1619/20; land patent, 1634, of 100 acres, "Arrowhattocks," Henrico Co., Va.; permanent home was called "Kingsland," Chesterfield Co., Va.; patented 350 acres, 1636; burgess, 1629; justice, Henrico Co., 1650; tobacco inspector, 1639; *m* 1619, Mary, dau. of Francis Addie, of Darton, Yorkshire, Eng.

BRANCH, Peter (1596-1638), from Eng. in the "Castle," 1638, but *d* on shipboard; his will was the first recorded at Boston; *m* in Eng. 1623/24, Elizabeth Gillame (*d* 1632).

BRASHAER (Brasseuir), Benjamin or Benoist (*d* 1663), Huguenot from France to Va., ante 1640; removed to Md., 1658; settled in Calvert Co.; commr., 1661; granted citizenship by Cecil Calvert, Lord Baltimore, 1663; *m* Mary–(*d* 1663?).

BRATTLE, Capt. Thomas (ca. 1624-1683), mcht., Boston; capt. militia; a founder of Old South Ch.; selectman; *m* 1656 or 57, El'zabeth (1638-82), dau. of Capt. William Tyng, *m* Elizabeth Coytemore.

BRATTON, Capt. Robert (1712-85), from Ireland to Orange (now Augusta) Co., Va., 1733; capt. French and Indian War, 1756-58; mem. council of war for protection of Va. frontier, 1756; owner of 2,284 acres in Augusta Co., and other lands (uncle of Col. William Bratton, comd. at Battle of Huck's Depot, in Am. Rev., whose g.son was Brig. Gen. John Bratton, C.S.A.); *m* Ann (McFarland) Dunlap, desc. of chief of Clan MacFarlane, and widow of Capt. Alexander Dunlap (qv).

BRAYTON, Francis (1611-92), from Eng., settled at Portsmouth, R.I., 1642; freeman, 1655; commr., 1662, 63; mem. R.I. Gen. Assembly, 1669-71, 79, 84; mem. Grand Jury; *m* Mary– (*d* ca. 1692).

BRECKENRIDGE, Alexander (*d* 1744), a Scottish Covenanter, from Scotland via Ireland, 1728, to Phila., Pa., settled in Orange Co., ca. 1739; *m* Jane –.

BREED (Bread, Braid), Allen (1601-1690/91), a Quaker, from Eng., 1630, with Gov. Winthrop, settled at Lynn, Mass.; freeman, 1681; a grantee from the Indians of Southampton, L.I., but returned to Lynn, 1645; juryman, selectman; *m* 1622, Elizabeth Wheeler; *m* 2d, 1656, Elizabeth– (*d* 1695), widow of William Ballard and William Knight.

BRENT, Giles (*b* 1600), treas. Province of Md.; cdr. Kent Island; dep. gov. and lt. gen. 1643-44; lord of Ft. Kent Manor.

BRENTON, Gov. William (*b* Hammersmith Eng.-*d* Newport, R.I., 1674), *m* Martha Burton.

BRERETON, Thomas (1720-87, desc. Sir William Bereton, lord high marshal and chief justice of Ireland, under Henry VIII), came from Ireland in command of the privateer "Betty," 1761, settled at Baltimore; *m* 1781, Sarah, dau. Thomas John Marshall, Northampton Co., Va.

BREWER, Daniel (*d* 1646), from Eng. in the "Lion," to Boston, 1632; freeman, 1634; settled at Roxbury; *m* Joanna– (1602-88).

BREWER, John (*d* 1635; son of Thomas, of London, *m* Miss Drake): came from Eng.; owner of "Brewer's Neck," and "Stanley Hundred"; burgess for Warwick River, 1629-30; commr. and mem. of Council, 1632; *m* Mary–.

BREWSTER, Francis (lost in Capt. Lamberton's "Great Ship," 1646), merchant, New Haven, Conn., 1641; *m* Lucy–; their son, Rev. Nathaniel, was pastor at Setauket, L.I., 1664-95.

BREWSTER, William (1566/67-1644), 4th signer of the Mayflower Compact; a ruling elder of the church, 1620-44; dep. 1636; chaplain of military co.; *m* ante 1593, Mary– (*b* ca. 1569-*d* 1627).

BRIDGE, John (1576-1665), was admitted freeman at Cambridge, Mass., 1635; dep. Gen. Ct., 1637, 39, 41.

BRIDGMAN, James (*d* 1676), from Eng. before 1640, to Hartford, Conn., settled at Agawam (Springfield), Mass., 1645; a first settler of Northampton, 1654; *m* Sarah – (*d* 1668).

BRIGGS, Clement (1595-1650), from Eng. in the "Fortune," settled at Plymouth, Mass., 1621; *m* 1631, Joan Allen.

BRIGGS, John (1609-90), Quaker; was admitted inhabitant of Newport, R.I., 1638; later at Portsmouth and Kingston, R.I.; dep. Gen. Ct., 1664, et seq.; gov.'s asst., 1648; R.I. commr., 1654, et seq.; *m* Sarah Cornell, sis. of Thomas Cornell (qv).

BRIGGS, Richard, one of the grantors of the town of Taunton, Mass., 1672; *m* 1662, Rebekah Hoskin.

BRIGGS, William (ca. 1620-ca. 1687), tailor at Boston, Mass.; planter, ante 1642; removed to Lyme, Conn., ca. 1665/66; returned to Boston, post 1680/81; *m* ca. 1640, Mary–(ca. 1622-post 1695).

BRIGHAM, Thomas (1603-53), came from Eng. in the "Susan and Ellen," 1635; freeman at Cambridge, Mass., 1636; constable, 1639; juryman, 1639; selectman, 1640-42; *m* 1637, Mercy Hurd (1615-93).

BRIGHT (Brecht), Michael (1706-94; son of Johannes, *m* Ann Katharine Hoffman), came from Germany, 1726, settled at Germantown, Pa.; original settler and landed propr., Heidelberg. Pa.; *m* 1728, Margareta (1708-78), dau. of Jacob Simone, from France.

BRINCKERHOFF, Joris Dircksen (1609-61), from Province of Drenthe, Holland, 1638; resided on Staten Island, then later at Brooklyn, where he had land grant, 1646; magistrate, 1654-60; elder Brooklyn Ch., 1656, et seq.; *m* 1631, Susanna Dubbels (*d* ca. 1677).

BRINSMADE, John (1617-73), from Eng. 1637, settled at Charlestown, Mass., at Stratford, Conn., 1650, rep. Conn. Gen. Assembly; *m* Mary Carter.

BRINTON, William (1630-1700), from Eng. to Delaware Co., Pa., 1684; mem. and founder of Concord Meeting, Delaware Co., Pa.; *m* ca. 1659, Ann (1635-99), dau. of Edward Bagley.

BRISCOE, Dr. John (*b* ca. 1590-*d* St. Marys Co., Md.; son of Leonard, of Crofton Hall. Eng.); said to have accepted the invitation of Cecilius Calvert, 2d Lord Baltimore, and to have become one of the Gent. Adventurers who came to Md., 1634, in "The Ark" and "The Dove" expdn., to serve as the official doctor to the colony; *m* in Eng., Elizabeth Du Bois, of the Huguenot family of Count De Roussey, 1110, Marquis Du Bois, whose descs. fled to Eng. to escape religious persecution.

BROCKENBROUGH, Col. William (*d* 1701; desc. Lord Lt. Brockenbrough, of London Tower, Eng., 1413), from Eng. to Mass., thence to Northern Neck of Va.; settled at "Tappahannock," now Essex Co.; *m* Mary Dalton.

BRODHEAD, Capt. Daniel (*b* West Riding of Yorkshire, Eng.-*d* 1667), officer in army of Charles, II; from Eng. as capt. of grenadiers with Col. Richard Nicolls, 1664; c.-i.-c. English militia at Kingston, N.Y., 1665; *m* in Eng., 1660, Ann (*d* 1703), dau. Francis Tye.

BROKAW (Broucard), Bourgon (*b* 1645), Huguenot, fled from France to Holland, thence to New York, settled at Newtown, L.I., 1675; *m* Catherine Le Febre.

BRONSON (Brownson, Bronson), Richard (*d* post 1648), from Eng. with sons Richard and John (1600-80), to Cambridge, Mass., 1633, to Hartford, Conn., 1636; thence to Farmington, 1641.

BROOKE, John (*d* 1699), from Eng. in the "Britannia," 1699, landed in New Jersey, where he and his wife *d* shortly after; *m* Frances –.

BROOKE, Robert (*b* London, Eng., June 3, 1602-*d* July 20, 1663), of royal descent; B.A., Wadham Coll., Oxford, 1620, M.A., 1624; ordained, 1627; from Eng. in his own ship with his family and 28 servants, June 30, 1650; settled at De la Brooke Manor, on the Patuxent River, Charles Co., Md.; cdr., 1650; pres. Provincial Council, 1652; acting gov., 1652-53; *m* Feb. 25, 1627, Mary Baker (*d* 1634; dau. of Thomas Baker, of Battel, Co. Sussex, Eng. [desc. John Baker, granted arms by Edward III, 1327-77], *m* Mary Engham, desc. Allen Engham, of Parish of Woodchurch, Co. Kent, under King John, 1204-16); *m* 2d, May 11, 1635, Mary (*b* London-*d* Nov. 29, 1663), dau. of Roger Mainwaring, D.D., dean of Worcester, bishop of St. David's, 1636.

BROOKS (Brookes, Brooke), Thomas (ca. 1613-1667), from Eng. in the "Susan and Ellen," to Watertown, Mass., where he was assigned land, 1631; admitted freeman, 1636; removed to Concord. Mass., 1636, where he became a large landowner, 1638, dep. Gen. Ct., 1642-62; capt. 1643; *m* Grace – (*d* 1664).

BROUWER, Adam (*d* ca. 1698), from Cologne, Germany, 1642, to New Amsterdam; to Brooklyn, ca. 1647; occupied the old mill; mem. Brooklyn Dutch Ref. Ch., 1677; *m* 1645, Magdalena Jacobs (ca. 1624-post 1698), dau. Jacob Verdon.

BROWN (Browne), Chad (*d* ca. 1665), from Eng. in the "Martin," to Boston, 1638; signer of the Providence Plantations Compact; settled at Providence; pastor of Bapt. Ch., Providence, after Roger Williams, 1642; *m* Sept. 11, 1626, Elizabeth Sharparrowe.

BROWN, John (1584-1662), shipbuilder; came from Eng., 1633/34, to Plymouth Colony, 1634; became citizen, 1635; mem. Bd. Assts. 18 yrs.; an original purchaser of Taunton, 1637; served in militia, 1643; commr. United Colonies, 12 yrs.; mem. Council of War; patentee with Edward Winslow of Rehoboth, moved there, settled at Wanamoosit (now Swansea), 1645; *m* Dorothy– (1584-1674).

BROWN (Browne), John (1601-1636/37): from Hawkden, Eng., in the "Lion," to Boston, Mass., Sept., 1632; *m* Dorothy –.

BROWN, John (1631-97), from Eng. to Boston, 1632; removed to Falmouth, 1678, later at Watertown; *m* 1655, Esther, dau. Thomas Makepeace.

BROWN, Peter (1587-1633), 33d signer of the Mayflower Compact; freeman, 1633; *m* at Plymouth, 1624/25, Mrs. Martha Ford; *m* 2d, bet. 1627-31, Mary– (living Jan. 1633/34).

BROWN (Browne), Thomas (bap. at Ch. of St. Peter and St. Paul, Lavenham, Suffolk, Eng., Jan. 10, 1605-*d* 1688), from Eng. with his bro., Rev. Edmund Brown, 1637; a propr. of Sudbury, Mass.; freeman, 1639; trooper in Middlesex Co., 1675; *d* at Cambridge; *m* Bridget– (*d* 1681).

BROWNE (Brown), Abraham (1590-1650; son of Thomas, of "Swan Hall," Hawkedon, Suffolk Co., and desc. of John Browne [*b* ca. 1330], of the Borough of Stamford, Co. Lincoln, alderman of Stamford, 1376-77; John Browne [*d* 1442], whose munificence built All Saints' Ch., Stamford; William Browne [*d* 1489], of Stamford, alderman, sheriff of Rutland, founder of Browne's Hospital, Stamford; and Christopher Browne [*d* 1518], of Stamford and Tolethorpe Manor, Co. Rutland, sheriff of Rutland); came from "Swan Hall," in Winthrop's fleet, to Watertown, Mass., 1630; freeman, 1631; *m* Lydia – (*d* 1686).

BROWNE, Mrs. Christian (*d* 1641), from Eng. 1640, with her three sons, George, William and Henry, to Salisbury, Mass., with its first company of settlers and received grants of land there.

BROWNELL, Thomas (1608-64), from Eng., 1638; settled at Portsmouth, R.I.; freeman, 1655; commr., 1655, 61, 62, 63; *m* 1637, Ann (1606-65), dau. of Richard Bourne.

BROWNING, Nathaniel, from Eng., 1636; settled at Warwick, R.I., 1645; *m* Sarah, dau. of William Freeborn.

BROYLL, John (*d* 1733/34), from Germany to Culpeper Co., Va., 1717; *m* ante 1717, Ursley–.

BRUEN, Obadiah (bap. Dec. 25, 1606-1680/81; son of John, of Stapleford, Cheshire, Eng., desc. of Robert Le Bruen, of Bruen Stapleford, 1230, also desc. of Edward, I, of Eng.), to Gloucester, Mass., 1640; selectman, 1642; freeman, 1642; rep. 4 times; to New London, Conn., 1651; town clk. 15 yrs.; commr., 1660; grantee of royal charter of Conn., 1662; mem. com. which purchased site of Newark, N.J., 1666, and settled there, 1667; *m* 1632, Sarah– (1609-post 1681).

BRUSH, Thomas (*b* probably ca. 1610-ca. 1675), from Eng., was at Southold, L.I., before 1653, removed to Huntington, L.I., 1656; admitted freeman, 1664; *m* Rebecca, dau. John Conclyne.

BRYAN, Alexander (1602-79), from Eng. to Milford, Conn., 1639; gov.'s asst., 1668-79; *m* Ann– (*d* 1661); *m* 2d, widow of Samuel Fitch.

BRYAN, George (1730-91; son of Samuel, of Dublin, Ireland), came from Ireland to Phila., Pa., 1751; mem. Stamp Act Congress, 1765; a founder of the British Colony, Pictou, in Acadian N.S.; father of the Pa. Constn. of 1776, chief lawmaker of Pa. during Am. Rev.; author of the First General Emancipation of Negro Slaves in History, the Pa. Abolition Act of 1780; pres. Exec. Council; justice Supreme Ct. and High Ct. of Errors and Appeals of Pa.; *m* 1757, Elizabeth Smith.

BRYAN, William, Marquis of Thomond (1655-1742), from Ireland to Isle of Wight Co., Va., 1689; settled on Albemarle Sound, N.C., 1722; high sheriff, and justice of peace, Bertie Co.; mem. Assembly for Pasquotank Co.; *m* 1689, in Eng., Lady Alice (1656-1729), dau. of Lord Needham, Viscount of Killorey.

BRYAN, William Smith, "Prince William of Ireland" (son of Sir Francis of Co. Clare, Ire.; desc. of James Fitzmaurice Fitz-Gerald, 10th Earl of Desmond); attempted to gain throne of Ireland during Puritan Rebellion and was exiled to Va. by Cromwell, 1650; landed at Gloucester Beach with his family; settled in Gloucester Co.

BRYANT, Stephen, from Eng. to Plymouth, Mass., 1632; constable, 1633; m Abigail, dau. of John Shaw.

BUCKINGHAM, Thomas (d 1657), from Eng. to Boston, 1637; settled at Quinnipiack (New Haven), Conn.. 1638; dep. Gen. Ct., m Hannah –.

BUCKLAND, William (d 1683), from Eng. in the "Elizabeth and Dorcas," 1634; received grant at Hingham, Mass., 1635; removed to Rehoboth, Mass., ca. 1655; grand juror, 1656; constable, 1657; took oath of fidelity, 1658; donated funds for King Philip's War; m in Eng., Mary (ca. 1611-1687), dau. of Edward Bosworth (qv).

BUCKMINSTER, Thomas (d 1656), from Wales; received grant at Boston, 1640; freeman, 1646; lived at Muddy River (now Brookline); m in Eng., Johanna–(d 1676); she m 2d, 1661, Edward Garfield.

BUCKNER, John (ca. 1631-1701), came from Eng. to Gloucester Co., Va., ca. 1667, at which time he acquired a land patent there; vestryman Petsworth Parish, Gloucester, 1671; burgess, 1683; clk. of Gloucester Co.; was instrumental in bringing to Va. the first printing press; collector High Ct. of Admiralty, 1680; clk. of House of Burgesses; m 1661, Deborah Ferrers, of Eng.

BUDD, Lt. John (d 1678), from Eng. to Hampton, Mass., in the "Swallow," 1633; planter at New Haven, 1639; moved to Southold, L.I.; dep. Gen. Ct., New Haven, 1653; rep. town of Rye, Westchester Co., N.Y., 1666, 68; m Katharine Brown.

BUDD, Thomas (1646-1697/98; son of Rev. Thomas, rector of Martock, Co. Somerset, Quaker ca. 1657, m 1645, Johanna Knight); Quaker; came to East Jersey, 1668; propr.; went back to Eng. but returned in the "Kent," 1678, with his family and his bros., William, John and James; settled at Burlington, N.J.; mem. gov.'s council, 1681-83; mem. Assembly, 1682, 83, 85; receiver-gen., land commr., agt. for colony to Eng., 1684, etc.; author of "Good Order Established in Pa. and N.J. in America," 1683; also of a proposal to create vocational education in the public school and the appropriation of public lands for educational purposes; m 1667, Susannah (d 1707/08), dau. of William Robinson.

BUDD, William (1649-1722; son of Rev. Thomas [1615-70], of Somersetshire, Eng., matriculated at Merton College, Oxford, 1633, B.A., 1633, M.A., 1636; vicar of Montacute, 1639; became interested in the teachings of George Fox the Quaker; sequestered to the vicarage of Kingsbury, 1646; 4 of his 5 sons came to this country, 1668-84, settling in W. Jersey and Phila.); William settled in Province of West Jersey, 1684-85; mem. N.J. Assembly from Burlington Co., 1685; justice of the peace, 1703, 05, 06; judge of the Supreme Ct., 1705; commd. judge Superior Ct. Common Pleas, Burlington Co., 1705, 06, 14; m Ann Claypoole (1652-1722).

BUELL (Buel), William (1610-81), from Eng., 1630, settled at Dorchester, Mass., then to Windsor, Conn., 1635; landed propr. there; m 1640, Mary Post (d 1684).

BUFFUM, Robert (d 1669), from Eng. to Salem, Mass., 1634; mem. Train Band of Salem; m 1638, Widow Tamasine Thompson.

BUFORD, Richard (Beauford) (b 1617), from Eng. in the "Elizabeth," 1635, settled in Christ Ch. Parish, Lancaster Co., Va. (now Middlesex Co.); m 1635, a dau. of John Vaulx (or Vause).

BUIST, Rev. George (b 1770; son of Arthur, Laird of Pittuncarthy Abernathy, Co. Fife, Scotland), from Scotland to Charleston, S.C., 1793; m Mary Somers.

BULKELEY (Bulkeley, Buckley), Peter (1583-1659), grad. St. John's Coll., Cambridge, Eng., 1608; came in the "Susan and Ellen," to Cambridge, Mass., 1635, first settler and minister at Concord, and founder of the 12th church in the colony; his library formed the nucleus of Harvard Coll. library; m Jane (d 1626), dau. Thomas Allen; m 2d, 1634, Grace (d 1669), dau. Sir Richard Chetwode (or Chitwood).

BULL, Henry (1610-94), from Eng. to Roxbury, Mass., 1635; removed to Boston, 1637, to Portsmouth, R.I., 1638; corp. and sgt., 1638-39; gov.'s asst. 1674-75; gov. of R.I., 1685-86 and 1689-90.

BULL, Thomas (ca. 1606-1684), from Eng. to Boston, 1635; settled at Hartford, Conn., 1636; lt. Pequot War, 1637; capt. of Hartford company in defense of Saybrook, 1675; dep. Gen. Ct., 1648-49.

BULLITT, Joseph (ca. 1653-1692; son of Benjamin Bullett, a Huguenot, who left France after the revocation of the Edict of Nantes, 1685); was settled in Charles Co., Md., before 1676, m ca. 1685, Elizabeth, dau. Capt. Randolph Brandt.

BULLOCK, Richard (1622-67), from Eng., 1643/44, settled at Rehoboth, Mass.; freeman, 1646; town clk., 1659-67; excise collector; one of two men appointed to regulate trade with the Indians; m 1647, Elizabeth Ingraham (d 1659); m 2d, Elizabeth Billington.

BUMSTEAD, Thomas (1611-77), from Eng. to Roxbury, Mass., 1640; removed to Boston, 1642; mem. A. and H. A. Co.; m Susanna –.

BUNCE, Thomas (1612-83), of Scotch ancestry; a propr. of Hartford, Conn., 1636; soldier in Pequot War, 1637.

BUNKER, George (d 1658; son of William, a Huguenot, who went from France to Eng.); came from Eng., 1634; settled at Ipswich, Mass.; original settler at Topsfield, Mass.; m Jane Godfrey.

BUNNELL, William (b 1617), from Eng., 1638; an early settler at Wallingford, Conn., m 1640, Annie (d 1653/54), dau. of Benjamin Wilmot.

BUNYAN, James (son of William, and g.son of John, author of "Pilgrim's Progress"): of Kingston, Jamaica; was in New York, 1748; merchant; m Margaret Grant, of Kingston.

BURBANK, John (ca. 1600-1682), from Eng. to Boston, ante 1639, settled at Rowley, Mass., 1640; freeman, 1640, propr.; overseer, 1661-62; m Ann–; m 2d, 1643, Jemima–(d 1692/93).

BURCHARD, Thomas (1595-1657), from Eng. in the "Truelove," to Boston, 1635; removed to Saybrook, Conn., 1639, later to Hartford; dep. Gen. Ct.; m Mary Andrews (1597-1655).

BURDICK, Robert (1635-92), from Eng. to Newport, R.I., 1651; freeman, 1655; a founder of Westerly, R.I.; dep. Colonial Assembly; m 1655, Ruth (1640-91; first white child b at Agawam), dau. Samuel Hubbard.

BURGAMY, William (1739-1819), from France to Ga. and S.C.; soldier in Am. Rev.; captured by British at Augusta, 1780, but escaped; m 1759, Susan Hawkins (1742-1846).

BURGESS, Thomas (1603-85), from Eng. to Salem, Mass., ca. 1630; settled at Sandwich, 1637; was an original mem. of the church there, and dep. Gen. Ct., 1646, et seq.; m Dorothy –.

BURGESS, Col. William (1622-86), from Wales, settled in Anne Arundel Co., Md.; mem. Assembly and Council of Md.; col. of foot; justice High Provincial Ct.; cdr.-in-chief Provincial forces; m 1st, Elizabeth, dau. of Edward Robins.

BURLINGAME, Roger (ca. 1620-1718), from Eng., was at Stonington, Conn., 1654, settled finally at Meshanticut, R.I., ca. 1660; mem. Town Council; m ca. 1663, Mary (d 1718), dau. John Lippitt.

BURNHAM, John (1618-Nov. 1694), from Norwich, Co. Norfolk, Eng., in the "Angel Gabriel" to Mass., 1635; settled at Ipswich; deacon; soldier Pequot War, 1637; m Mary–.

BURNHAM, Thomas (1619-94; son of Robert, m Mary Andrews; came in the "Angel Gabriel," to Cape Cod, Mass., 1635; settled at Ipswich, Mass.; carpenter; surveyor, 1646; propr., 1647; freeman, 1653; corpl., 1662, ens. mil. co., 1675; lt., 1683; signer Ipswich petition, 1681-82; dep. Gen. Ct. from Ipswich, 1683, 84, 85; selectman; m 1645, Marie (1624/25-1715), dau. of Thomas Lawrence, St. Albans, Eng., m Joan Antrobus.

BURR, Jehu (1600-72), from Eng. with Gov. Winthrop, to Roxbury, Mass., 1630; freeman, 1631; a founder of Springfield, 1636; settled at Fairfield, Conn.; rep. Gen. Ct.; commr. United Colonies; m – Stedman.

BURR, Jonathan (1604-41), from Eng. to Dorchester, Mass., 1639; died of smallpox; m Frances – (1612-82).

BURR, Simon (1617-1691/92), from Eng., settled at Hingham, Mass., 1647; overseer, 1659; surveyor, 1660-62; freeman, 1664; juror for Co. Ct. of Suffolk, 1675; m 2d, 1648, Hester–(d 1692/93).

BURRAGE, John (1616-85), from England to Charlestown, Mass., ca. 1636; freeman, 1637; m 1654/55, Joanna Stowers.

BURRELL, John (bap. 1597-1649), from Eng. to Wethersfield, Conn., ca. 1637-39, later at Milford; m 1622, Hester Winchester.

BURROWS, Robert (d 1682), from Eng. in the "Arbella," 1630, with Gov. Winthrop; first ferryman across Thames River; early settler at Mystic, Conn., 1657; to Wethersfield, Conn., 1641; propr. Marblehead, Mass., 1649; at New London, Conn., 1650; m Mary–(1605-72), widow of Samuel Ireland.

BURSLEY, John (d 1660), from Eng. to Weymouth, Mass., 1629; freeman, 1630; removed to W. Barnstable, 1639; m Nov. 28, 1639, Joanna Hull, dau. of Rev. Joseph Hull (qv).

BURT, Henry (ca. 1590-1662), from Eng., 1638; settled at Roxbury, Mass.; a founder of Springfield; mem. com. to lay out lands, 1642; mem. first Bd. of Selectmen, 1644-54; contributed funds to purchase lands from Indians, 1644; mem. prudential com. to administer affairs of the town, 1646-47, 1650-54; clk. of writs, 1649-62; apptd. to conduct religious services on the Sabbath, 1656-57; m 1619, Eulalia Marche (1600-90).

BURT, James (1622-80), from Eng., 1635, settled at Taunton, Mass.; m Anna – (d 1665).

BURTON, Boniface (d 1730), from Eng. to Lynn, Mass., ca. 1632.

BURWELL, Maj. Lewis (1621-58), from Eng. ca. 1640; settled at Fairfield, on Carter's Creek, Gloucester Co., Va., ca. 1640; m Lucy, dau. of Capt. Robert Higginson.

BUSH, John (1613-70; son of Reynold, of Messing, Co. Essex, Eng.), from London, Eng., in the "Alexander," to Boston, 1635; settled at Wells (now Me.), Mass., ca. 1640-42; twice elected to try small causes; constable, 1653; preacher, 1662; was at Watertown; said to have d at Cape Porpoise, Me.; m Grace–(she m 2d, Richard Palmer).

BUSHNELL, Francis (1576-1646), from Eng. to New Haven Colony, 1638; settled at Guilford, Conn., 1639; m Rebecca Holmes (?).

BUTLER, Richard (d 1684), from Braintree, Co. Essex, Eng., to Cambridge, Mass., 1632; freeman, 1634; a founder of Hartford, Conn., 1636; juror, 1643, 44, 47, 48; dep. Gen. Ct., 1656-60, apptd. clerk thereof, 1658; grand juror, 1660-62; selectman, 1649, 54, 58; deacon; m 2d, Elizabeth Bigelow (d 1691).

BUTLER, Thomas (b 1720; 3d son of Edmund, 8th baron of Dunboyne); settled nr. Lancaster, Pa., 1748, where he purchased large tracts of land and founded the first Episcopal Church (St. John's) in that section; m Eleanor Parker (their 5 sons were officers Cont. Army).

BUTT (Butts), Robert (d 1676; son of Joshua, of Warrington Hall, Kent, Eng.), came from Eng., 1640, settled in Lower Norfolk Co., Va.; m Ann Riddlehurst.

BUTTERFIELD, Benjamin (d 1688), was at Charlestown, Mass., 1638, at Woburn, 1640; an original propr., at Chelmsford, 1654; m Anne – (d 1661); m 2d, Hannah Whittemore, widow.

BUTTOLPH, Thomas (1603-67), from Eng. in the "Abigail," to Boston, 1635; glover and leather dresser; freeman, 1641; constable, 1647; m Anne (Harding?), (ca. 1610-80).

BUTTON, Matthias (d 1672), from Eng. to Salem, Mass., 1628, with Gov. Endicott (qv); at Ipswich, Mass., 1641, d Haverhill, Mass.; m Lettice – (d 1662).

BYLES, William, see William Biles.

BYRD, William (1652-1704; son of John Byrd, of London, m Grace, dau. of Capt. Thomas Stegg [d 1651], speaker Va. House of Burgesses), came from Eng., 1674; settled nr. the Falls of the James River, Va.; established "Westover"; was burgess, councillor, auditor and receiver-general; m 1673, Mary (1652-99), dau. of Col. Warham St. Leger Horsmanden, from Eng., to Charles City Co., Va., was burgess and councillor.

CABANISS, Henri, a Huguenot, from France in the "Mary and Ann." 1687, to Nottaway Co., Va., m Marie–; m 2d, Magdalene–.

CABELL, William (1699 or 1700-1774), grad. London Coll. of Surgery and Medicine; surgeon in British Navy; settled in Henrico (now Nelson) Co., Va., 1724/25, established "Warminster," 1742, capt. militia, under sheriff, co. coroner, justice, burgess several yrs.; m 1726, Elizabeth (1705-56), dau. Samuel Burks, of Hanover Co., Va.; m 2d, 1762, Margaret Meredith.

CABOT, John (bap. Apr. 7, 1680-1742; son of Francis Cabot, of Trinity Parish, Isle of Jersey, m 1663, Susanne Gruchy), from Isle of Jersey to Salem, Mass., 1700, with bros. Francis and George; prominent importer and exporter;

large landowner; m 1702, Anne (1678-1767), dau. of Joseph Orne, g.dau. of Dea. John Orne, Salem, 1631.

CADWALADER, John (1677/78-1734), from N. Wales to Pa., 1697; freeman, 1705; settled at Merion, Pa.; mem. Common Council and Provincial Assembly; m 1699, Martha Jones (d 1747).

CADY, Nicholas (1615-ante 1712), from Co. Suffolk, Eng., bet. 1628-30; resided at Cambridge, Watertown, and Groton, Mass.; surveyor, constable, fence-viewer; mem. Capt. Mason's Train Band, Watertown; in King Philip's War; m 1646, Judith (b 1630), dau. William Knapp, of Groton.

CALEF (Caleff, Califf), Robert (ca. 1648-1719), from Eng., settled at Boston ante 1688, later at Roxbury; m ante 1671, Mary–(d 1720).

CALHOUN (Colhoon, Colquhoun), James (1694-ca. 1772), from Ireland with his wife, four sons and one daughter, to Pa., 1733, removed to Wythe Co., Va., to Abbeville Co., S.C., 1756, m Catherine Montgomery.

CALKINS (Calkin, Caulkin), Hugh (1600-90), from Wales to New London, Conn., 1638, arrived at Plymouth, Mass., 1640; mem. Conn. Assembly, 1672-83; dep. Mass. Gen. Ct., from Gloucester, New London and Norwich, Conn.; a founder of Gloucester, 1644; m Ann –.

CALVERT, Leonard (1606-47; son of George, first Lord Baltimore, and brother of Cecil, second Lord Baltimore), sent as first gov. of Md. by his brother, who had obtained a charter for the colony, 1632; arrived, 1634, with the "Ark of Avalon" and the "Dove"; gov. Palatine of Md., 1633-47; founded St. Mary's, the first capital, 1634; m Anne Brent.

CAMP, Nicholas (b 1597-d ca. 1653), from Eng. to Salem, Mass., 1630; a founder of Milford, Conn.; m 1st, Sarah Beard (d 1645).

CANBY, Thomas (1668-1742; son of Benjamin Canby, m Mary Baker), from Eng. in the "Vine," 1683, to Bucks Co., Pa.; mem. Pa. Assembly and justice several yrs.; m 1693, Sarah Jerves; m 2d, 1709, Mary Oliver (1677-1721), she came from Wales in the "Welcome," with William Penn, 1682.

CANDLER, Daniel (d 1765), from Ireland, 1735, settled in Bedford Co., Va., nr. present city of Lynchburg; m Anna –.

CANFIELD, Matthew (1604-73), from Eng. settled at New Haven, Conn., ante 1637; to Norwalk, 1652, to Newark, N.J., 1666-67; patentee of royal charter of Conn.; collector for Yale Coll., 1645; assessor, 1646-48; surrogate, 1658-60; mem. Conn. Gen. Ct., 1650-66; officer cav. troop of Conn., 1655-60; judge Fairfield Co., Conn., and Newark, N.J., 1654-73; m ante 1643, Sarah (1620-ca. 1673), dau. Hon. Richard Treat (qv).

CANFIELD, Thomas (d 1689), is supposed to have come from France via Eng. to America ca. 1634; with bros., Timothy and Matthew, settled at Milford, Conn., 1639; rep. Gen. Ct., 1674-76; sgt. Milford Train Band, 1669; m 1646, Phoebe Crane.

CAPEN, Bernard (1552-1638), from Eng., 1632; original grantee of Dorchester, Mass., propr., 1633; freeman, 1636; his was the first tombstone of the Mass. Bay Colony, and is now preserved by the N.E.H.G.S., Boston; m 1596, Joan (d 1653, aet. 75), dau. of Oliver Purchase.

CAPERS, William (d 1718), Eng. to S.C., ca. 1686; received grants in S.C., 1694; m Mary–(d 1720).

CAREW, John, see Cary.

CAREY, John, Quaker, from Eng., 1681; settled in William Penn's Colony, Bucks Co., Pa.; m Mary–.

CARHART, Thomas (1650-1695/96; son of Anthony, gent., of Co. Cornwall, Eng.); arrived at New York, 1683, as private sec. to Col. Thomas Dongan, gov. Province of N.Y.; removed to Staten Island; apptd. clerk of Richmond Co., 1691; m 1691, Mary (b 1668), dau. of Robert Lord, m Rebecca, dau. of Maj. William Phillips, of Saco, Me.

CARLETON, Edward (1605-51), came from Eng. to Rowley, Mass., 1638; freeman, 1642; rep. Gen. Ct., 1644, 47; returned to Eng., 1651; m Eleanor, dau. Sir Thomas Denton.

CARMAN, John, from Eng. with John Eliot (qv), arrived Mass. Bay, Nov. 3, 1631; mem. Mass. Gen. Ct., 1634; one of 12 grand jurors of Essex Co., Mass., July 27, 1636; a founder of Hempstead, L.I.; with Rev. Robert Fordham he purchased land from the natives; received patent, Nov. 16, 1644, from Gov. William Kieft, covering 120,000 acres of land from river to sea, with full powers, civil and political, to organize towns, build forts, establish courts of justice, and to use and exercise the Reformed religion which they professed; freeholder; m Florence Fordham.

CARPENTER, Alexander, of Wrentham, Eng.; removed to Leyden (?) because of being a Dissenter; thought to have stopped at Yarmouth for a time.

CARPENTER, William (1576-1659-70), from Eng. in the "Bevis," 1638, to Weymouth, Mass., but returned to Eng. in the same ship; left son Capt. William (1605-59), who also came in the "Bevis," with his wife Abigail (ca. 1606-1687), and family; he settled at Weymouth, later at Rehoboth, Mass.; freeman, 1640; will mentions Latin, Greek and Hebrew books.

CARPENTER, William (1605-85; son of Richard, of Amesbury, Wiltshire, Eng., who was bro. of William, qv), from Eng. to Boston; an original settler at Providence, R.I.; a founder of 1st Bapt. Ch. in America; m Elizabeth, dau. William Arnold.

CARR, Caleb (Dec. 9, 1616-Dec. 17, 1695; son of Benjamin, of London, a desc. of Sir William Carr, 10th Baron of Fennerhurst); came from England in the "Elizabeth Ann," 1635; settled at what later became Bristol, R.I.; removed to Newport; freeman, 1655; town commr., 1654-62, gen treas., 1661-62; justice Gen. Quarterly Session and of Inferior Ct. of Common Pleas; gov. of R.I., 1695; m 1653, Mercy Vaughn (1630-Sept. 21, 1675); m 2d, Sarah (Clarke) Pinner (1651-1706), dau. of Jeremiah Clarke (qv), and sis. of Gov. Walter Clarke.

CARR, George (1599-1682), from London, Eng., 1633, to Ipswich, Mass.; a founder of Salisbury, Mass., 1640; m 2d, Elizabeth (d 1691), dau. of Rev. Thomas Oliver (qv).

CARR, Col. Thomas (1655-post 1724), from Eng., settled at Topping Castle, Caroline Co., Va.; justice, 1702; high sheriff, 1708-09; obtained a patent for 546 acres in St. John's Parish, King William Co., Va., 1701, for transportation of 11 persons into the colony; m 1676, Mary Garland.

CARRINGTON, George (1711-89; son of Dr. Paul Carrington, from Eng. to the Barbados), came from Bermuda to Goochland Co., Va., abt. 1723; m 1732, Anne, dau. Col. William Mayo, who laid out the city of Richmond, Va.

CARROLL, Charles (1660-1720), from Ireland to Md., 1688, as atty. gen. of Md. for Lord Baltimore, m 1689, Martha Underwood (d 1690); m 2d, 1693, Mary (d 1742), dau. Henry Darnall.

CARTER, John (d 1669), from Eng. to Va., 1649, settled at "Corotoman," Lancaster Co., Va.; burgess from Nansemond, 1649, from Lancaster, 1654. 1657-60; mem. Council, 1657-58; col. comd. expdn. against Rappahannock Indians, 1654; m Jane Glyn; m 2d, Eleanor (Eltonhead) Brocas, dau. of Richard Eltonhead; m 3d, Anne, dau. Cleave Carter; m 4th, Sarah (d 1668), dau. Gabriel Ludlow; m 5th, Elizabeth Shirley.

CARTER, Nicholas (1629-81), from Eng. ante 1652; settled at Stamford, Conn.; a founder of Elizabethtown, N.J.. ca. 1665; m a relative of Robert Watson, of Windsor, Conn.

CARTER, Rev. Thomas (b 1610-d Sept. 5, 1684; son of James, of Hinderclay, Co. Suffolk, Eng.), grad. St. John's Coll., Cambridge, 1629; from Eng., prob. in the "Planter," 1635; to Dedham, Mass., 1636; to Watertown; freeman, 1637; first minister at Woburn, Mass., 1641; ordained 1642 (see portrait of his ordination, Vol. VI, p. 716); m 1638. Mary (1614-87), dau. George Parkhurst, of Watertown.

CARTER, Capt. Thomas (1630/31-1700), from London, Eng., to Nansemond Co., Va., 1650; later of "Barford," Lancaster Co., Va.; purchased a large plantation on the Rappahannock River; commr. Lancaster Co. Ct., 1663; dep., 1663-65; burgess, 1667; vestryman Christ Ch. and St. Mary's; capt. Lancaster militia, 1667; m 2d, 1670, Katherine (1652-1703), dau. of Edward Dale (qv).

CARTWRIGHT (Cartright), Edward (1640-1705), expert fisherman; constable at Isle of Shoals, N.H., 1671; removed to Nantucket, Mass., 1672/73; m 1st, —; m 2d, Elizabeth (1651-1729), dau. of John Trott, of Nantucket, m Mary, dau. of Stephen Batson, and g.dau. of Simon Trott, of Cape Porpoise, Me.

CARVER, John (d 1621), 1st signer of the Mayflower Compact; 1st gov. Plymouth Colony, 1620-21; m Katharine (d 1621), dau. of Alexander White, and widow of George Liggott.

CARVER, Robert (b prob. Eng., ca. 1594-buried 1680), nephew of John Carver (qv); of Marshfield, Mass.; granted land at Green's Harbor, 1638; mem. Train Band, 1643; one of twelve men who were willing to pay "for one to teach school," 1645; juryman; surveyor of highways; freeman, 1648; m Christian–(d 1658).

CARY (Carew), John (b Bristol, Somersetshire, Eng., 1610-d Oct. 31, 1681; son of Sir William, mayor of Bristol, Eng., 1611), ed. in France; from Eng. to Plymouth, Mass., 1634; propr. and settled at Duxbury, Mass., 1637; was at Braintree, 1652; constable, Bridgewater, 1656; town clk., 1657; selectman, 1667-79; m 1644, Elizabeth (d 1680), dau. Francis Godfrey, carpenter and bridge builder, Duxbury, m Elizabeth–.

CARY, Miles (b Bristol, Eng., 1620-d Warwick Co., Va., June 10, 1667; son of John, of Bristol, m Alice Hobson, and nephew of James Cary, of N.E.), settled in Warwick Co., Va., ca. 1645; royal naval officer for James River; col. and county lt., 1659-67; burgess, 1659-63; mem. Council, 1663-67; lived on an estate known as "Magpie Swamps," obtained from his father-in-law; owned two houses in Bristol. Eng.. 2,000 acres in Va., numerous slaves, a mill and a store; m ante 1646, Anne, dau. of Capt. Thomas Taylor, burgess of Warwick Co.

CASSEL, Johannes (1639-91), from Germany with his wife, Mary –, in the "Jefries," 1686; mem. committee of the first Council of Germantown.

CASTLE, Henry (1613-98), Eng. to Fairfield, Conn., 1635; thence to Woodbury, Conn.; m ca. 1666, Abigail (d 1725), dau. of Thomas Dickerson, m Mary– (she m 2d, Daniel Finch).

CATLETT, Col. John (b 1622-killed by Indians at Port Royal, Va., 1670), from Kent Co., Eng., to Va. ca. 1650; resided in Essex Co.: col. of militia; magistrate; justice of the peace; commr. to settle boundary line between Md. and Va.; accompanied John Lederer on his 3d exploration of the country west of the Blue Ridge; m 1654, Elizabeth, dau. Capt. William Underwood, and widow of Francis Slaughter.

CATLIN, John (d 1644), said to have gone from Eng. to Barbados, thence to Va.; at Wethersfield, Conn., ca. 1640; trader; juror at Hartford, 1644; m 1641-42, Isabella Ward (d 1676), sister of Lawrence Ward (she m 2d, James Northam, and 3d, Joseph Baldwin, qv).

CATLIN, Thomas (1600-90), from Eng., 1640, to Hartford, Conn.; chimney viewer, 1647, 48, 53; surveyor highways, 1655; townsman, 1659; constable, 1662-74; m 1646, Mary – (d ante 1675); m 2d, Widow Mary Elmer, or Elmore.

CECIL, John, from Eng., 1658, settled in St. Marys Co., Md.

CHACE (Chase), William (1595-1659), from Eng. with Gov. Winthrop to Roxbury, Mass., 1630; freeman, 1634; at Scituate, 1645, thence to Yarmouth; m in Eng., Mary – (d 1659).

CHAMBERLAIN, Edmund, from Eng. to Woburn, Mass., before 1647; removed to Chelmsford, 1655; freeman, 1665; m 1647, at Roxbury. Mary Turner (d 1669); m 2d, at Malden, 1670, Hannah Burden.

CHAMBERLAIN (Chamberlin), William (ca. 1620-1706), from Eng., settled at Woburn, 1648; removed to Billerica, 1654; m 2d, Rebecca Shelley (d in prison on charge of witchcraft, 1692).

CHAMBERLIN, Henry (1595-1674), from Hingham, Co. Norfolk, Eng., in the "Diligent," 1638; settled at Ipswich, Mass.; freeman, 1638/39; to Hingham; m Joan–, or Jane–.

CHAMPION, Henry (ca. 1610-11-Feb. 17, 1708), said to have been of Huguenot ancestry; at Saybrook, Conn., 1647; freeman at Lyme, 1670; m 1647. Sarah–; m 2d, 1697/98, Deborah Jones.

CHAMPLIN, Geoffrey (d before 1695), admitted inhabitant of R.I., 1638, freeman 1640, was at Portsmouth, Newport and Westerly.

CHANDLER, William (bap. Oct. 12, 1595-d 1641/42; son of Henry [ca. 1560-1618], and desc. of Thomas), from Bishop's Stortford, Co. Herts, Eng., to Roxbury, Mass., 1637; freeman, 1640; m 1st, Alice (Ales) Thurgood (d 1625); m 2d, 1625, Annie (or Agnes), dau. of Francis Bayford (she m 2d, 1643, John Dane, m 3d, 1660, Dea. John Parmenter).

CHANNING, John (1684-1731), from Eng. to Boston, ca. 1715; settled at Newport, R.I.; *m* Mary (Antram) Antrim.

CHAPIN, Samuel (Oct. 8, 1598-Nov. 11, 1675; son of John, of Paignton, Devonshire, Eng., *m* Philippa Easton); settled at Roxbury, Mass., 1635; freeman, 1641; removed to Agawam (Springfield), Mass., 1642; deacon; constable, 1645; selectman, 1644-51; commr., 1652; apptd. by Gen. Court of Colony of Mass. Bay to govern there; *m* Feb. 9, 1623/24, Cicely (bap. Feb. 21, 1601/02-Feb. 8, 1682/83), dau. of Henry Penney.

CHAPLINE, Isaac (*b* ca. 1584), ens. Royal Navy; from Eng. in the "Starr," as King's Council under Lord Delaware, 1610; settled in "Chaplaine's Choyce," south side of James River, 1622; *m* ca. 1606, Mary Calvert (*b* ca. 1586), to America, 1622, in the "James" with son John and 4 servants.

CHAPMAN, Edward (*d* ca. 1678), from Eng. to Boston, 1639; grantee of Ipswich, 1642, later at Rowley; *m* 1642, Mary (*d* 1658), dau. Mark Symonds; *m* 2d, Dorothy, dau. Richard Swann, and widow of Thomas Abbot, of Rowley, Mass.

CHAPMAN, Ralph (1615-71), from Eng., 1635; received land grant; bought ferry privilege at New Harbor Marshes, 1645; at Marshfield, Mass., ca. 1650; *m* 1642, Lydia Wills, Willis, or Wells.

CHAPMAN, Robert (1616-Oct. 13, 1687), from Eng. to Boston, 1635; removed to Saybrook, Conn.; served in Pequot and King Philip's wars; dep. Gen. Ct. 43 sessions; gov.'s asst., 1660-61, 1669, 1681-84; commr., 1664-80, 1685-87; grand juror several times; capt. Train Band, 1675; town clk.; *m* 1642, Ann (*d* 1685), dau. of Thomas Bliss (qv).

CHASE, Aquila (1618-Dec. 27, 1670), from Eng. in the "John and Francis," 1636, to Mass.; settled at Hampton, N.H., 1640, at Newbury, Mass., 1646; *m* Ann (1620-87), dau. of John Wheeler.

CHASE, William, see William Chace.

CHAUNCY, Charles (bap. 1592-1672), B.A. Trinity Coll., Cambridge U., 1613; from Eng. to Plymouth, Mass., 1637; pastor at Scituate, 1641-53; 2d pres. Harvard Coll., 1654-1671/72; *m* 1630, Catharine, dau. Robert Eyre, of Salisbury, Eng.

CHENEY, John (*d* 1666), from Eng. to Roxbury, Mass., ca. 1635; settled at Newbury, 1636; freeman, 1637; selectman; shoemaker; was drowned at Roxbury; *m* in Eng., Martha –.

CHENEY, William (1604-67), arrived at Boston, ca. 1635; resided at Roxbury, 1640; a founder of Roxbury Free School; assessor, 1648; selectman; *m* Margaret (Burdge or Mason), (*d* 1686).

CHESEBROUGH, William (1594-1667), from Eng. in the "Arbella," with Winthrop's fleet to Boston, Mass., 1630, founder and first white settler of Stonington, Conn.; dep. Colony of Mass. Bay and Gen. Assembly of Conn.; *m* Anne Stevenson.

CHESTER, Leonard (1609-48), from Eng. to Watertown, Mass., 1633; removed to Wethersfield, Conn., 1636; *m* Mary (Sharpe) Wade (or [Wade] Sharpe).

CHEVALIER, Peter (ca. Dec. 1, 1695-1769; son of Jean, Huguenot exile, from Normandy, after the revocation of the Edict of Nantes, 1685, to Flanders, later to Eng. where he, with wife and children, were naturalized, Apr. 1687, *m* Jeanne de Creguy); settled in America, 1715 or 20; *m* Mary Wood.

CHEW, John (1590-1655), from England in the "Charitie," to Jamestown, Va., 1622; was col., burgess from Hog Island and from York Co., and justice from York Co.; removed to Md. ca. 1653; *m* Sarah –.

CHEW, Col. Samuel (1634-77; son of John, qv); col. provincial forces of Md., 1675; mem. Council; burgess, chancellor; sec. Province of Md.; *m* 1658/59, Ann (*d* 1695), dau. of William Ayers, of Nansemond Co., Va.

CHICKERING, Francis (*d* 1658), from Eng., in 1637; freeman at Dedham, Mass., 1640; mem. A. and H. A. Co.; dep. Gen. Ct., 1644-53.

CHILDS (Child), Benjamin (*d* 1678), Aughton, Co. York, Eng., to Roxbury, Mass., ca. 1630; one of those who erected first church at Roxbury; *m* 1650, Mary (ca. 1635-1707), dau. Griffith Bowen (qv).

CHILDS (Child), William, from Eng. to Mass., ca. 1630; freeman, Watertown, Mass., 1634; large landowner; *m* probably in Eng.

CHILES, Lt. Col. Walter (*d* 1653), from Eng. in his own ship, 1637/38; settled in Charles City

Co., Va.; burgess, 1643-46, 49-52; speaker Va. House of Burgesses; mem. Council, 1651; *m* Elizabeth –.

CHILTON, James (*d* 1620), 24th signer of the Mayflower Compact; *m* Susanna – (*d* 1621).

CHILTON, John (1630-ca. 1708; son of John Chilton, of "Chilston Manor," Kent, Eng., *m* Catherine Heneage), to Va. with two bros., 1660; purchased a tract on Currioman Bay on the Potomac, named it "Currioman"; the town of Chiltons, once on his land, is named for him; *m* Jane–.

CHIPMAN, John (*b* ca. 1614), from Eng. in the "Friendship," to Boston, 1631; settled at Barnstable, Cape Cod, where he was ruling elder of the church, 1670; *m* 1646, Hope (1629-83), dau. of John Howland (qv).

CHITTENDEN, William (1593-1660/61), from Eng. to New Haven, Conn., 1639; removed to Guilford, and founder of the church there, 1639; trustee of land purchased from the Indians; lt. of Colonial forces; magistrate; rep. Gen. Ct.; *m* Joanna (*d* 1668), dau. Dr. Jacob Sheaffe.

CHOATE, John (1624-95), from Eng. to Ipswich, Mass., 1643; admitted freeman, 1667; *m* Anne–.

CHOUTEAU, Rene Auguste (*b* Bearn, France, 1723-*d* 1776), from France to New Orleans, La.; formed the firm of Maxtent, Laclede & Co., to develop the trade of Upper Louisiana; *m* 1748-49, Marie Therese Bourgeois (1733-1814), an orphan (parents were members of Court of Spain, eloped to America and *d*), reared by Ursuline Nuns at New Orleans; left her husband because of brutal treatment; with Pierre Laclede, settled at St. Louis, 1763; known now as the "Mother of St. Louis."

CHURCH, Richard (1608-68), carpenter, from Eng. in Winthrop's fleet, 1630; settled at Plymouth, 1633, at Charlestown, 1653, Hingham, 1657, Sandwich, 1664; freeman, 1632; soldier in Pequot War; *m* 1636/37, Elizabeth (*d* 1669/70), dau. Richard Warren, Mayf. Pil. (qv).

CHURCH, Richard (1610-67; son of Richard, of Braintree, Co. Essex, Eng.); settled at Hartford, Conn., probably ca. 1636, where his name appears on Founder's Monument; drew 12 acres in first land divided, 1639; freeman, 1658; one of sixty persons who founded South Hadley, Mass., 1650; *m* in Eng., 1627, Anne, dau. of Edward Marsh.

CHURCHILL, John (*d* Jan. 1, 1662/63), from Eng. to Plymouth, 1643; *m* Dec. 18, 1644, Hannah (1623 in Eng.-Dec. 22, 1690), dau. of William Pontus, at Plymouth, 1633; she *m* 2d, Giles Ricard. whom she survived.

CHURCHILL, Josiah (1615-86), from Eng., 1635; settled at Wethersfield, Conn., ca. 1641; soldier Pequot War, constable, town surveyor; *m* ca. 1638, Elizabeth (ca. 1616-1700), dau. Nathaniel Foote (qv).

CHURCHILL, William (1649-1710), from Eng., 1669, settled in "Bushy Park," Middlesex Co., Va., on the Rappahannock River; burgess, 1691-92; mem. Assembly, 1704; mem. Va. Council, 1705; warden and vestryman of Christ Ch., Middlesex Co.; *m* 1703, Elizabeth (Armistead) Wormley, dau. of Col. John Armistead (*d* ante 1703), mem. Va. Council, from 1688.

CILLEY, Robert, see Seeley.

CLAFLIN (MackClaflin, MackClaphlan, Macklathlan, MacClaflin), Robert (*d* 1690), from Scotland to Wenham, Mass., 1661; soldier in French and Indian War; *m* 1664, Joanna Warner.

CLAGGETT, Capt. Thomas (*b* 1635-40-will proved 1706; son of Col. Edward, *m* Margaret, dau. Sir Thomas Adams, Lord Mayor of London), officer British Navy; Eng. to Md., ca. 1670; large landowner; *m* Sarah Patterson, or Pattison.

CLAIBORNE (Clayborne), William (1587-1676), from Eng. to Va. with Governor Wyatt, 1621; sec. of state of Va., 1625, et seq.; mem Council, 1625-60; made treas. for life, 1642; dep. gov., 1653; comd. against Indians, 1629 and 1644; had one grant of 24,000 acres of land in King William Co., Va.; one of three commrs. apptd. to rule Va. under Cromwell; *m* Elizabeth Butler.

CLAPP (Clap), Roger (1609-92), from Eng. to Dorchester, Mass., 1630; lt. Dorchester mil. company, 1644; 2d sgt., A. and H. A. Co., 1646, lt. 1655; capt. at the Castle, 1665-86; dep. Gen. Ct., 1652-73; *m* 1633, Joanna (1617-95), dau. of Thomas Ford.

CLARK (Clarke), Christopher (1681-1754), Quaker, from Eng. via the Barbados, ca. 1710;

purchased or patented 50,000 acres of crown lands in Hanover, Albemarle and Louisa cos., Va.; capt. Hanover Co. militia, 1727; high sheriff, 1731; justice, Louisa Co., 1742; overseer of Friends Meeting nr. Sugar Loaf Mtns., 1749; law partner of Nicholas Meriwether; *m* ca. 1709, Penelope (*d* post 1754), dau. of Edward Johnson.

CLARK, Daniel (1623-1710), from Eng. ca. 1639, a first settler at Windsor, Conn., 1639; settled at Hartford, 1644; sec. Colony of Conn., 1658-66; asst., 1662, 64, 67; dep. 1657-61; magistrate, 1662-64; named asst. in charter of Charles II; *m* 1644, Mary, dau. Thomas Newberry (qv); *m* 2d, Mrs. Martha Pitkin Wolcott.

CLARK, John (1614-74), from Eng., 1632; admitted freeman, at Newton, Mass., 1632; an original settler at Hartford, Conn., 1636, soldier Pequot War; dep. for Hartford, 1641-44, for Saybrook, 1649-60, for Milford, 1666-68; *m* Mary, dau. John Coley (Cooley); *m* 2d, Mary, dau. of Joyce Ward, and widow of John Fletcher.

CLARK (Clarke) Nathaniel, from Eng. to Newbury, Mass., before 1663; freeman, 1668; *d* on board schooner "Six Friends," in expdn. against Quebec; *m* 1663, Elizabeth, dau. Henry Somerly.

CLARK, Richard (1613-16-1697), Eng. to Barbados, 1634/35; to Southampton, L.I., ca. 1650; at Southold, 1661, whale striker and boat carpenter at Southold, L.I., 1667; to Elizabeth, N.J., 1678; in Indian war, 1657; shipbuilder and planter; *m* Elizabeth–(*d* 1724).

CLARK (Clarke), Thomas (1599-1697), said to have been mate of the "Mayflower;" came from Eng. in the "Anne," 1623, to Plymouth, Mass.; at Harwich, 1670; rep. Gen. Ct., 1651-55; soldier in Pequot War; *m* 1634, Susanna Ring; *m* 2d, Alice Nicholas (widow), dau. Richard Hallett.

CLARKE, Charles (1721-85), from Eng., was settled in Cumberland (now Powhatan) Co., Va., 1745; *m* Marianne, dau. Abraham Salle.

CLARKE, Hugh (1613-93), from Eng. to Watertown, Mass., 1638; removed to Roxbury, 1657; freeman, 1660: mem. A. and H. A. Co.; *m* Elizabeth – (*d* 1692).

CLARKE, Jeremiah, or Jeremy (1605-52), from Eng. to R.I. ca. 1638; at Portsmouth, 1640; settled at Newport; 1st constable of Newport; was asst. pres., regent and actg. gov., and treas. of R.I. Colony, 1648; *m* Frances (Latham) Dungan (1611-77), dau. of Lewis Latham.

CLARKE, John (1609-76), from Eng. to Boston, 1637; driven from Mass. as a follower of Mrs. Hutchinson, 1638, and was a founder of Newport, R.I.; made treas. of Colony, 1649, and sent to Eng., 1651, to prevail on Council of State to revoke extra powers given to Coddington; dep. gov. R.I. and Providence Plantations, 1669, 70; again agt. in London; wrote book entitled "Ill News from New England"; twice married.

CLARKE (Clark), Joseph (1618/19-ca. 1694), from Eng., 1637; settled at Boston, 1638; removed to Newport, R.I., one of founders of Baptist Church there; gov.'s asst., dep. Gen. Assembly; finally settled at Westerly, R.I.; *m* 2d, Margaret – (*d* 1694).

CLARKE, Richard, 36th signer of the Mayflower Compact; *d* Plymouth, Mass., bet. Jan. 11 and Apr. 10, 1621.

CLARKE (Clark), William (1609-90), from Eng. in the "Mary and John," 1630, with Matthew Grant, to Nantasket, Mass.; at Dorchester, Mass., before 1635; selectman, 1641-50, 64; removed to Northampton, 1660; townsman, 1660; rep. Gen. Ct., 1663, and for 13 yrs.; lt., 1661, and in King Philip's War; juryman; co. judge 14 yrs.; commr.; mill owner; one of the incorporators of the First Ch. (Congl.) at Northampton; *m* ca. 1637, Sarah Strong (*d* 1675); *m* 2d, 1676, Sarah–, widow Thomas Cooper, of Springfield, Mass.

CLARKSON, Matthew (*b* in Eng., 1666-*d* New York, July 20, 1702); settled in New York, 1685; sec. of Province of New York, 1689-1702; clk. of Council; register and examiner of the Ct. of Chancery; clk. of Supreme Ct. of Judicature and register of the Prerogative Ct.; *m* 1692, Catharine, dau. of Gerrit Van Schaick, of Albany, N.Y.

CLAY (Claye) John (*b* ca. 1588; son of Sir John Clay, of Wales); called "The Grenadier"; from Eng. in the "Treasurer," 1613; in Powhatan Co., Va.; resided in Charles City Co., 1624;

settled finally nr. Jamestown, Va.; *m* Anne–, who came in the "Ann," 1623.

CLAYPOOLE, James (1634-87; desc. of Edward I; son of Sir John, *m* Marie Angell; g. son Sir Adam, *m* Dorothy Wingfield; g.g.son James, *m* Joan Hansen; g.g.g.son John, of King's Cliffe, *m* a dau. of Thomas Metcalf), from Eng. in the "Concord," 1683; had previously bought 5,000 acres from William Penn; settled a colony at Germantown, Pa.; treas. Free Soc. of Traders of Pa.; judge Provincial Ct.; mem. Gov.'s Council, and of the Assembly; *m* 1657/58, Helena Merces, of Bremen, Germany.

CLAYTON, John (1665-1737; son of Sir John); from Eng. to Va., 1705; was atty. gen., recorder, burgess, etc.; *m* Anne Page.

CLAYTON, William (son of Thomas); from Chichester, Eng., in the "Kent," to N.J., 1677, settled at Burlington; one of several commrs. from London sent out by proprs. of N.J. to purchase land from the Indians; moved to Pa. nr. Chester; mem. Provincial Council, presided at 1st meeting under govt. of William Penn; actg. gov. of Pa., 1684-85; mem. Gov.'s Council during drafting of Great Charter; he and Daniel Francis Pastorious were first two judges of Phila.; *m* Prudence –.

CLEEVE, George (ca. 1575-ca. 1667), from Eng.; first settler at Casco (now Portland), Me.; gov. Province of Lygonia, Me., 15 yrs.; *m* Joan –.

CLEMENT (Clemens, Clements, Clemence), Robert (bap. Dec. 14, 1595-*d* Sept. 29, 1658), from Eng., 1642, with three sons and two daughters, settled at Haverhill, Mass., where he was justice and asso. judge for Norfolk Co.; *m* 1st, ante 1615, Lydia – (*d* 1642); *m* 2d, ante 1657, Judith – (*d* 1669).

CLEMENTS, Geoffry (*d* 1609), Oxford, Eng.; shareholder in the London Virginia Co. which colonized Jamestown; *m* Elizabeth, dau. of Sir Cuthbert Fuller; as Widow Clements, came to Va. in the "George," 1611; settled at Jamestown (she *m* 2d, 1623/24, Capt. Ralph Hamor).

CLEVELAND, Moses (1624-1701/02), from Ipswich, Co. Suffolk, Eng., with his master, a joiner; settled at Woburn, 1641; freeman, 1643; served in King Philip's War; *m* 1648, Ann (ca. 1626-ante 1682), dau. Edward Winn.

CLINTON, Charles (1690-1773), from Ireland to Mass., 1729; settled at New Britain, N.Y., ca. 1732, *m* Elizabeth Denniston.

CLOPTON, William (*b* ca. 1655-*d* ante 1733), from Eng. to York Co., Va.; was clerk of vestry, St. Peter's Church, New Kent Co., 1697-1704, mem. vestry until 1728; constable, Hampton Parish; mem. Council; *m* 1679, Ann (Booth) Dennett (1647-1716), dau. of Robert Booth (*m* Frances–), and widow of Capt. Thomas Dennett, of York Co., Va.

COALE, William (*b* Bristol, Eng., 1592-*d* 1669), Quaker minister, from Eng., 1618, settled in Va., later in Anne Arundel Co., Md.; *m* Hester –; *m* 2d, Hannah – (*d* 1669); *m* 3d, Elizabeth, dau. Philip Thomas.

COATES, Thomas (1659-1719), from Eng. to Phila., Pa., 1683; *m* 1696, Beulah Jacques.

COBB, Henry (1596-1679), from Eng. to Plymouth, Mass., ca. 1629; at Scituate, 1633; a founder of Barnstable, 1639; a deacon; rep. Gen. Ct., 1645-51; *m* 1631, Patience Hurst (*d* 1648); *m* 2d, 1649, Sarah, dau. Samuel Hinckley.

COBURN, Edward, see Colburn.

COCKE (Cox), Richard (1600-65), from Eng. to Henrico Co., Va., ca. 1627; lt. col., Henrico Co., 1632; sheriff; burgess from Weyanoke, 1632, from Henrico Co., 1644-54; patented 3,000 acres on James River, Henrico Co., 1636; *m* 1st, an English lady; *m* 2d, ca. 1647, Mary, dau. of Walter Aston (qv).

CODD, Col. St. Leger (g.son of Sir Warham of royal descent); mem. Va. Company; came to Va., thence to Md.; *m* Anna, dau. of Richard Bennett, colonial gov. of Md., and widow of Governor Bland.

CODDINGTON, William (1601-78), from Eng. with Winthrop's fleet, 1630; returned to Eng. but came again to Boston, 1633; removed to Newport, R.I., 1636; asst. Mass. Bay Colony, 1630-37; treas., 1634-36; dep. from Boston, 1636-37; chief exec. of Aquidneck, 1638, of Newport, 1639-40; gov. of Portsmouth and Newport, 1640-47; gov.'s asst., 1647; pres. of four united towns, 1648-49; commr., 1656-63; dep., 1666; gov.'s asst., 1666-67; dep. gov., 1673-74; gov., 1674-76, 78; *m* Anne Brinley.

CODMAN, Robert (*d* 1678), from England to Charlestown, Mass., 1630.

CODRINGTON, Simon, mem. Va. Company, 1615; said to have been the "First individual Englishman to own in his own right a foot of land in America"; his grant from the Va. Co., according to memorandum now preserved in the British museum, was for 100 acres of land, and bore the date Mar. 6, 1615; *m* Agnes, dau. of Richard Seacole, of Didmarton.

COE, Robert (1595-ca. 1687), from Eng. in the "Francis," 1634; freeman, Watertown, Mass., 1634; founder of Wethersfield, Conn., 1636; a purchaser of Stamford, 1640; asst. judge, 1643; dep. Gen. Ct., 1643; one of those who formed the 1st English settlement at Hempstead, L.I., 1644; a founder of Newtown, L.I., 1652; one of the 1st settlers at Jamaica, L.I., 1656; magistrate, and rep. of the town in Gen. Conv. at Hartford, 1664; *m* Anna – (1591-1674).

COFFIN, Tristram (1605 or 09-1681; son of Peter Coffin, *d* 1628; g.s. Nicholas Coffin, *d* 1613), came from Eng., 1642; at Salisbury, and Haverhill, Mass., 1642, removed to Newbury, ca. 1648; returned to Salisbury, 1654/55; a founder of Nantucket, 1660, where he was chief magistrate, 1671, commissioner, 1655; *m* ca. 1630, Dionis Stevens (*d* after 1682).

COGGESHALL, John (ca. 1581-1647), from Eng. with his wife and three children, to Roxbury, Mass., 1632; freeman, 1632, removed to Boston, 1634, where he was selectman and dep. Gen. Ct.; settled at Providence Plantations, 1637; pres. Colony and Providence Plantations, 1647; gov.'s asst., 1640-44; moderator, 1647; *m* Mary – (1604-84).

COGSWELL (Coggeswell), John (1592-1669; son of Edward, *m* Alice –); from Westbury Leigh, Eng., in the "Angel Gabriel," to Ipswich, Mass., 1635; *m* 1615, Elizabeth (*d* 1676), dau. of Rev. William Thompson, first minister at Braintree. *m* Phyllis –.

COIT (Coyte), John (*d* 1659), shipwright, from Wales to Mass. ca. 1634; granted land at Salem, Mass., 1638; removed to Gloucester, 1644, to New London, Conn., 1650; selectman, 1648; *m* Mary Jenners (1596-1676).

COLBURN (Coburn, Colburne), Edward (1618-1712), from Eng. in the "Defense" to Boston, 1635; settled at Insw'ch; moved to Dracut; soldier mil. co. of Chelmsford, during King Philip's War; *m* Hannah–.

COLDEN, Cadwallader (1687-1776; son of Rev. Alexander, of Berwickshire, Scotland), grad. U. Edinburgh, 1705; came to Phila., Pa., where he practiced medicine until 1718, when he removed to N.Y. City; lt. gov. and acting gov.; *m* Nov. 11, 1715, Alice Christy, of Scotland.

COLE, James (*b* 1600), from Eng. to Saco, Me., 1632; settled at "Coles Hill," Plymouth, Mass., 1633; in Pequot War; surveyor of highways; *m* 1624, Mavy, dau. Mathieu De L'Obel, physician to William of Orange and James I; g.dau. Jean De L'Obel, French lawyer.

COLEMAN, Henry (*b* 1594), from Eng.; in Elizabeth City Co., Va., 1632; secured grant for 1,000 acres; *m* Catherine–.

COLEMAN, Thomas (1598-1674), from Eng., 1630; an original propr. of Hadley; *m* 2d, Mrs. Frances Wells (*d* 1674).

COLES, John (1705-Oct. 16, 1747), from Ire. to Va. when a very young man; reputed to have built first house where Richmond now stands; *m* Mary Ann, dau. of Isaac Winston, of Va. (their dau. Sarah, *m* 2d, Colonel John Henry and was mother of Patrick Henry; their dau. Lucy, *m* 2d, William, younger brother to John Coles, whose dau. Mary, *m* John Payne and was mother of Dolly Payne [Todd] Madison who *m* James Madison; their son John, Jr., was g.father of Sarah Angelica Singleton, who *m* Abram, son of Martin Van Buren).

COLES, Robert (1598-before 1655), from Eng. to Roxbury, Mass., to Ipswich; removed to Ipswich, 1633; a founder of Providence, R.I.; dep. Gen. Ct.; *m* Mary Hawkhurst.

COLEY (Cooley), Samuel (*d* 1684), from Eng. to Mass. Bay Colony, 1631; an original settler at Milford, Conn., 1639; joined church, 1640; *m* Ann, dau. of James Prudden.

COLGATE, Robert (1758-1826), from Eng. to Harford Co., Md., 1795; settled in Delaware Co., N.Y.; *m* Mary Bowles.

COLLETT, Jeremiah (*d* 1706), of Devizes,

Wiltshire, Eng.; prob. arrived in Chester Co., Pa., ca. 1682, as he was listed a juror June 13, 1682; sheriff, 1684, 85; justice cts. of Quarter Session and Common Pleas, 1693; *m* 1681, Jane May–.

COLLIER, William (1620-82), from London, Eng., 1670; settled in York Co., Va.; later to New Kent Co., where he was lt. col., 1675; *m* 1655, Sallie– (1636-80).

COLLINS, Edward (1603-89), from Eng., settled at Cambridge, Mass., 1638; freeman, 1640; dep. Gen. Ct., 1654-70; mem. A. and H. A. Co.; deacon: *m* in Eng., Martha –.

COLLINS, Henry (1606-87), from Eng. in the "Abigail," with his family and servants to Lynn, Mass., 1635; mem. Salem Ct.; selectman, etc.; *m* Ann – (*b* 1605).

COLLINS, John (1616-70), from London, Eng., ca. 1636; settled at Boston and Braintree, Mass.; freeman, 1646; mem. A. and H. A. Co., 1644; had land grant, Braintree; *m* ante 16440, Susannah–.

COLT (Coult), John (*d* 1730), from Eng. to Dorchester, Mass., 1625; removed to Hartford, Conn., 1638, thence to Windsor, *m* Mary Fitch.

COLTON, George (*d* 1699), from Eng. to Springfield, Mass., 1644; later at Longmeadow; q.m. Hampshire Co. troop, 1663; served in King Philip's War; dep. Gen. Ct., 1669, 71, 77; *m* 1644, Deborah Gardner (*d* 1689).

COMBES (Combs, Coombs, Combe, Coomes), Richard, from Eng. before 1690, settled at Hempstead, N.Y.; *m* Elizabeth –.

COMSTOCK, William (1595-bet. 1680-83), from Eng. to Wethersfield, Conn., 1637, later at New London; soldier in Pequot War; *m* 1625, Elizabeth – (1608-post 1665).

CONANT, Roger (bap. 1592-1679), from Eng. in the "Ann," to Plymouth, Mass., 1623, with his wife and son Caleb; removed to Nantasket (Hull), to Gloucester, 1625, to Salem, where he built the first house, 1626: freeman, 1630: gov. Colony of Cape Ann, 1625-26, Salem, 1627-29; rep. Gen. Ct., of Mass., 1634; *m* 1618, Sarah Horton.

CONDIT (Cunditt), John (*d* 1713), from Eng. or Wales with his son Peter, 1678; settled at Newark, N.J.; weaver; purchased land, 1689, 91; *m* 2d?, post 1678, Deborah–(living 1713).

CONKLIN (Conkling, Conklyne), Ananias (ca. 1600-1684), from Eng. to Salem, Mass., ca. 1635-37; freeman, 1642; removed to Southhold, L.I., 1652; to Huntington, L.I., 1653; established first window-glass works in America; *m* 1631, Mary Launders; *m* 2d. Susan—.

CONNABELL (Conable), John (1649/50-1724), "citizen and joyner," from London, 1674, settled at Boston; freeman, 1690; tithingman; served King Philip's War, for which his son Samuel received grant of land at Fall Town, 1736; *m* 1st, in Eng., ca. 1672. ——— (*d* Boston, ca. 1687); *m* 2d, 1688/89, Sarah (1666-67-ante 1700), dau. Peter Clayes of Wells, Me.. *m* Hannah Littlefield; g. dau. John Clayes of Watertown.

CONOVER, Wolfert Gerretse, see Couwenhoven.

CONVERSE (Conyers, Convers), Edward (1590-1663: son of Christopher, *m* Mary Halford); from Eng. to Mass., 1630, with Gov. Winthrop; settled at Salem; granted land at Charlestown, 1631: a founder of Woburn; granted first ferry to Boston, 1631; selectman at Salem, 1635-40; deacon; dep. Gen. Ct., 1660; *m* Jane Clark (*d* ante 1617); *m* 2d, in Eng., 1617. Sarah – (*d* Jan. 14, 1662).

CONWAY, Edwin (1610-1675), from Co. Worcester, Eng., ca. 1640; granted land in Va., 1644; settled in Lancaster Co., *m* 1640. Martha, dau. of Richard Eltonhead, *m* Ann, dau. of Edward Sutton.

COOK (Cooke), Ellis (ca. 1618-79), went from Lynn, Mass., abt. 1644, and settled at Southampton, L.I., ca. 1644; *m* Martha (1630-after 1690), dau. John Cooper (*b* 1594), from Eng. in the "Honewell," 1635.

COOK, Henry (ca. 1600-1691), propr. Salem, Mass., 1638; *m* 1639, Judith Birdsall (*d* 1689).

COOK, Josiah (ca. 1610-1673), from Eng., was at Plymouth, Mass., 1633/34; constable, 1646; dep., 1647; grand juror, 1656; *m* 1635, Elizabeth (Ring) Deane.

COOK (Cooke), Walter (*d* 1694/95), from Eng. ante 1643, settled at Weymouth, Mass.; freeman, 1653; a founder of Mendon, Mass., 1659; propr. and selectman; *m* Experience –; *m* 2d, Catherine –.

COOKE (Cook), Aaron (bap. Bridport, Co. Dorset, Eng., Mar. 20, 1613/14-*d* Northampton, Mass., Sept. 5, 1690; son of Aaron Cooke, of Thorncombe, and Bridport, Co. Dorset, Eng., *m* Elizabeth Chard, she *m* 2d, 1616, Thomas Ford), came with his mother and stepfather, Thomas Ford, in the "Mary and John," 1630; resided at Dorchester, Mass., Windsor, Conn., Northampton, Mass., Westfield, Mass.; freeman, 1635; juror many yrs.; town warner, 1656; pvt., lt., capt., and maj. mil. co.; capt. Troop of Horse, 1657/58; granted land at Northampton, Mass., 1659/60; settled there, 1661; tithingman; selectman several terms; commr., 1663; dep. Gen. Ct. many yrs.; wolf hunter; kept an ordinary, 1668-72; cdr. garrison at Westfield, 1675; returned to Northampton, 1678; *m* ca. 1637, ――(*d* post 1645); *m* 2d, ca. 1649, Joan (*d* 1676), dau. of Nicholas Denslow; *m* 3d, 1676, Elizabeth (*d* 1687), dau. of John Nash, of New Haven, Conn.; *m* 4th, 1688, Rebecca (Foote) Smith, dau. of Nathaniel Foote and widow of Philip Smith.

COOKE, Francis (*b* 1577-*d* 1663), 17th signer of the Mayflower Compact; *m* at Leyden, Holland, 1603, Hester Mahieu, a Walloon and Huguenot (*d* bet. 1666-75), came in the "Anne," 1623.

COOKE (Cook), Thomas (*b* Earls Coign, Essex, Eng., 1603-will proved 1677), from Eng. to Boston ca. 1630 or 36, to Taunton, Mass., 1637; mem. Plymouth Colony militia, 1643; to Portsmouth, R.I., 1643; dep. 1664; road commr. for colony; *m* Mary—.

COOLEY, (Coley), Benjamin (*b* ca. 1617-*d* Aug. 17, 1684), from Eng. to Mass., settled at Longmeadow; selectman, 1646; ensign Hampshire regt.; *m* 1642, Sarah-(*d* 1684).

COOLEY, Samuel, see Coley.

COOLIDGE, John (bap. 1604-*d* 1691; son of William Cooledge, *m* Margaret Mayse); the Colonist; came from Cottenham, Cambridgeshire, Eng., 1630, settled at Watertown, Mass.; the frame for his house was brought from Eng. and the house was standing until after 1800; freeman, 1636; selectman, 1638-42, 1664-66, 1668-69, 77, 80, 82; dep. Gen. Ct. of Mass. Bay, 1658; *m* ca. 1627, Mary – (1604-91).

COOPER, Thomas (1617-75), from Eng. to Boston in the "Christian," 1635; at Windsor, Conn., 1641; to Springfield, Mass., 1643; freeman, 1649; selectman, 19 yrs.; dep. Gen. Ct., 1668; ens. Springfield Co., 1657; lt., killed by Indians; *m* Sarah-.

COOPER, William (1649-1709), Quaker, from Snapt, Yorkshire, Eng., to Bucks Co., Pa., 1699; at his house was held the first Quaker meeting in Bucks Co. 1700; *m* ca. 1672, Thomasin -.

COPE, Oliver (ca. 1647-97), from Eng., with William Penn on his 2d voyage, and settled at "Backington," on Naaman's Creek, New Castle Co., Pa., now in Del., 1683; *m* Rebecca – (*d* 1728).

COPP, William (bap. Nov. 9, 1589-*d* 1670; son of Thomas [1539-1628], elder of Bewsall, Warwickshire, Eng., *m* 2d, 1576, Isabel Gunne), from Eng. bet. 1635-40; admitted mem. First Ch. at Boston, 1640; cordwainer; *m* 1614, Anne Rogers; *m* 2d, 1634, Goodeth, or Judith Itchenor (*d* 1670).

CORBIN (Corbyn), Clement (1626-Aug. 1, 1696, aet. 70), from Eng. to Roxbury, Mass., 1638; settled at Muddy River before 1655; at Woodstock, Conn., 1687; *m* Dorcas Bookmaster, or Buckminster (1629-1722).

CORBIN, Henry (1629-Jan. 8, 1676; son of Thomas Corbin, Esq., of "Hall End," Polesworth, Co. Warwick, Eng.), of London; draper; came to Md. in the "Charity," 1654; settled in Lancaster Co., Va.; established "Buckingham Lodge," on South side of Rappahannock River, also owned "Pickatone" in Westmoreland and "Corbin Hall," in Middlesex; justice of Lancaster Co., 1657; vestryman, Christ Ch., Middlesex; burgess Lancaster Co., 1658-60; mem. Council, 1663; justice Middlesex, 1673; *m* ca. 1655, Alice (*d* ca. 1684), widow of Rowland Burnham, and dau. of Richard Eltonhead, of "Eltonhead," Lancaster Co., Va.

CORLISS, George (1617-86; son of Thomas), from Eng., settled at Newbury, Mass., ca. 1639; moved to Haverhill, built a loghouse in "West Parish," 1647, the farm was later known as "Poplar Lawn"; *m* 1645, Joanna Davis (their dau. Mary [1646-1722], *m* 1663, William Neff [*d* 1689, aet. 47], captured, 1697, with Mrs. Hannah [Emerson] Dustin, by a party of 12 Indians and carried off toward Can., they, Mrs. Dustin, Mrs. Neff, and Samuel Leonardson, a youth captured

previously, rose in the night, Mar. 30, and killed 10 out of the 12 Indians, with the scalps they returned to Haverhill and later went to Boston; they were rewarded by the Gen. Ct. of Mass. with money and grants of land; two monuments were erected to their memory, one in Haverhill and the other, a duplicate, on Dustin's Island, see Vols. II and IV).

CORNELIUS, Aaron (*d* ca. 1696), from Vlessengen, Holland, as capt. of the "Canary Bird," 1645, to "Nieu Nedderlands," settled at Flushing, L.I.; with 99 others obtained a patent from Gov. William Kieft for all the land now comprising the town of Flushing, 1645; *m* Patience-.

CORNELL (Cornil), Thomas (ca. 1595-ca. 1655/56), from Eng. with the 2d Winthrop expdn. to Boston, 1636; removed to Portsmouth, R.I., 1654, and was freeman there; settled at Flushing, L.I., 1643; ensign Portsmouth militia, and served under Gov. Kieft against Indians; *m* Rebecca Briggs (1600-73).

CORNING, Samuel (*d* 1694), from Eng., was at Salem, Mass., 1638; later at Beverly, Mass., where he founded a church, 1667; *m* Elizabeth –.

CORWIN, Matthias (bet. 1590-1600-*d* 1658), from Eng., 1634, to Ipswich, Mass.; an original settler at New Haven, Conn., and Southold, L.I.; *m* Margaret (Morton?).

COTTON, John (1585-1652), grad. Cambridge U., 1606; from Eng. in the "Griffin," to Boston, 1633; teacher of first Ch. in Boston; freeman, 1634; author of nearly 50 books; *m* 2d, in Eng., Sarah (Hankredge) Story.

COTTON, Thomas (1657-1730), of Peviston, Yorkshire, Eng., *m* London, Eng., 1689, Bridget (*b* 1673), dau. Dr. Leonard Hoar (3d pres. Harvard, *m* Bridget Lisle).

COULT, John, see Colt.

COURSEN, Peter (ca. 1577-1648), a Huguenot refugee to New Amsterdam, N.Y., progenitor of the Corson-Coursen family in America.

COURTS (Courte), Sir John (*d* 1697), from Eng. to Md., 1637/38, settled in St. George's Hundred, Charles (now Montgomery) Co.; burgess; mem. Md. Assembly; mem. Gov.'s Council; *m* 1654, Margaret-.

COUWENHOVEN (Van Couwenhoven, or Conover), Wolfert Gerretse (*b* ca. 1588-*d* 1661), from Holland, 1630; as overseer of farms for the Patroon Van Rensselaer; freeholder in Midwout, 1637, 41; commr. from the colony to Holland, 1653; schepen of New Amsterdam, 1654; great burgher, 1657; *m* Neeltje -.

COVELL, Nathaniel (*d* 1687), from Chelmsford, Eng., 1653, settled at Marshfield, Mass.; was a bound servant of Gov. Edward Winslow and by him transferred to Peregrine White; he and his father-in-law settled the town of Chatham; *m* Sarah Nickerson (*d* 1702).

COWLES (Cole), John (1598-1675), from Wales to Mass., 1635; settled at Hartford, Conn., 1636, at Farmington, 1640; constable, 1647; at Hartford, 1656-64; surveyor, 1659; at Hadley, Mass., 1664; dep. Gen. Ct., 1653-54; *m* Hannah-(*d* 1684).

COX, Richard (1600-65), see Richard Cocke.

COX, Thomas (*d* 1681), from Eng., was at Marshpath Kills, at head of Newtown Creek, L.I., 1665; a patentee of Monmouth tract, East Jersey; settled at Middletown, N.J., 1665; founder Bapt. Ch., Middletown; overseer, deputy, town agent; with three others, was chosen to make prudential laws for the newly formed settlement of Middletown, 1668; received 240 acres, 1675, 269 acres, 1676; juryman; dep. to meet gov. and council at Woodbridge, 1676; *m* 1665, Elizabeth Blashford.

CRABB (Crabbe), Richard (1594-1680), from Suffolk, Eng., in the "Puritan," 1634, to Boston, 1634; at Wethersfield, Conn., 1639; with Robert Coe founded Stamford, Conn.; later to Jamaica, L.I.; dep. Gen. Ct. from Wethersfield, 1639-41; *m* –Coe; *m* 2d, Alse–, widow of Peter Wright.

CRANE, Henry (1621-1709), from Eng. to Dorchester, Mass., 1654; *m* Tabitha Kinsley; *m* 2d, 1655, Elizabeth, dau. of Stephen Kinsley, of Milton, Mass.

CRANE, Henry (1635-1711), settled at Wethersfield, Conn., 1655; at Guilford, 1664, later at Killingworth; one of the first settlers of what is now Clinton, Conn.; gov.'s asst. and dep. Gen. Ct.; *m* Concurrence Meigs.

CRANE, Jasper (1590-1680), from Eng. to Mass. about 1635, an original propr. of New Haven, Conn., 1639; a first settler of Newark,

N.J., 1666; magistrate; rep. Gen. Ct., 1653-58; gov.'s asst., 1662-67; dep. Provincial Assembly of East Jersey, 1667-73; *m* Alice –.

CRANSTON, John (1626-80), arrived in Newport ante 1644; capt. and maj. of militia; capt. of all forces of the Colony in King Philip's War; atty. gen.; gov. 1678; licensed and recorded Doctor of Physic and Chirurgery; *m* 1658, Mary (1611-1711), dau. of Jeremy Clarke (qv).

CRAWFORD, John (1600-76), a cadet of the Kilbirnie Crawfords; from Ayrshire, Scot., to Jamestown, Va., 1643, settled in James City Co.; killed during Bacon's Rebellion.

CRESAP, Thomas (1702-88), from Yorkshire, Eng. to Md., 1715; col. Cont. Army, founder of "Sons of Liberty," first patriotic society in U.S.; surveyor; noted Indian fighter; burgess; col. of the Provincials, 1730-70; *m* 1726, Hannah Johnson; *m* 2d, Mrs. Milburn (*d* Old Town, Md., 1788).

CROASDALE, Thomas (*d* 1684), from Eng. in the "Welcome," 1682; settled in Bucks Co., Pa.; *m* 1664, Agnes Hathernthwaite (*d* 1686).

CROCKER, William (1612-92), from Eng. to Scituate, Mass., ca. 1634; removed to Barnstable, 1639; rep. Gen. Ct., 1670, 71, 74; *m* Alice–(*d* 1684).

CROCKETT, Thomas (1606-79), from Scot., in the "Pied Cow"; owner of Piscataqua Plantation, 1633; living at Kittery Point, 1640; given 187 acres in Crockett's Neck, 1643, by Thomas Gorges; he was Braveboat Harbor ferryman, 1648; took Oath of Submission at York, 1652, and received 48 acres; returned to Kittery; constable, 1657; had the Piscataqua Ferry, 1659; *m* Ann–(living 1701, aet. 84).

CROSBY, Richard (ca. 1646-1718; desc. Sir John Crosby [*d* London, 1475], built Crosby Hall), purchased 1,000 acres in Pa. from William Penn, 1681; came to America, 1682, and located at Middletown, Chester Co., Pa.; to Ridley, 1684, where he erected a house and mill, since known as Crosby's Mill place; tax collector; Episcopalian; *m* 1670, Ellinor Done.

CROSBY, Thomas (ca. 1575-1661), from Eng. to Cambridge, Mass., 1640, settled at Rowley, 1641; *m* 1600, Jane (bap. 1581-1662), dau. William Sotheron.

CROSMAN, Robert (*d* 1692), from Eng. before 1642, settled Dedham, Mass.; mem. A. and H. A. Co.; *m* 1652, Sarah Kingsbury, of Dedham, Mass.; *m* 2d, 1687, Martha Eaton, of Bristol, Mass.

CROSS, Robert (1612-93), from Eng. in the "Mary and John," 1635, settled at Ipswich, Mass., 1639; soldier in Pequot War; *m* – (*d* 1677).

CROW, John (1606-85; son of John), came in the "Lion"; a first settler of Hartford, Conn.; moved to Hadley, Mass., but later returned to Hartford; *m* Elizabeth, dau. of Elder Goodwin, who also came in the "Lion."

CROWNINSHIELD (von Kronsheldt), Johannes Caspar Richter (bap. 1644-*d* 1711), came to Lynn, Mass., ca. 1670; *m* 1694, Elizabeth (*b* 1679), dau. of Jacob Allen.

CULVER, Edward (1600-85), a Puritan, from Eng., 1635, a founder of Dedham, Mass., 1636, later at New London, Conn.; served in Pequot, Narragansett and King Philip's wars; *m* 1638, Anne, dau. of John Ellis.

CUMMINGS (Cummins), Isaac (1600-77), from Scotland to Topsfield, Mass., ca. 1630; removed to Watertown, Mass., 1635; propr. at Ipswich, Mass., 1639.

CUNNINGHAM, Andrew (1654-1735), from Scotland to Boston, ca. 1680; glazier; mem. Scots Charitable Soc., 1684; *m* at Boston, 1685, Sarah, dau. William Gibson.

CURRIER, Richard (*b* Eng. or Scot., 1616/17-*d* 1686/87), planter and millwright, Salisbury and Amesbury, Mass.; an original settler of Salisbury; *m* 1st, Ann–(*d* 1667).

CURRY, Robert (1741-80), from Ireland, 1771, with his wife and son, James; officer Am. Rev.; killed by Indians, Northumberland Co., Pa.; Presbyn.; *m* at Belfast, 1770, Jane McWilliams.

CURTIS (Cuttris), Henry (*d* 1678), from Eng. to Watertown, Mass., 1635; an original propr. of Watertown, 1636, of Sudbury, 1639; *m* 1640, Mary, dau. of Nicholas Guy.

CURTIS, John (1577-1640), from Eng. in the "Lion," to Boston, 1632, thence to Roxbury, Mass.; *m* 1610, Elizabeth Hutchins (*d* 1658).

CURTIS, William (1592-1672), from Eng. in the "Lyon" to Roxbury, Mass., 1632; freeman, 1633; settled at Stratford, Conn.; *m* Sarah Eliot (1600-73), sister of Apostle John Eliot.

CURTIS (Curtiss), William (*b* ca. 1611-*d* Dec. 21, 1701), from Eng. to Roxbury, Mass., 1632, settled at Stratford, Conn., 1649; capt. Stratford Train Band, also Fairfield forces; mem. Com. of Safety, 1673; dep. Gen. Ct.; *m* Mary Morris; *m* 2d, Sarah Marvin, widow of William Goodrich.

CUSHING, Matthew (1588-1660), from Eng. in the "Diligent," to Hingham, Mass., 1638; *m* in Eng., 1613, Nazareth (1586-1681), dau. Henry Pitcher.

CUSHMAN, Robert (1580-1625), a leader and financial agt. at Leyden of the Mayflower Pilgrims, was a passenger in the "Speedwell," which was compelled to return to Eng., but came in the "Fortune," 1621, but returned to Eng. one month later; *m* 1606, Sarah Rider; *m* 2d, at Leyden, 1617, Mary Singleton, who came to Plymouth with her family after 1625.

CUTLER, James (1606-94), from Eng. to Watertown, Mass., 1634; removed to Cambridge; at Lexington, 1651; soldier King Philip's War; *m* Anna – (*d* 1644); *m* 2d, 1645, Mary, widow of Thomas King; *m* 3d, Phebe, dau. John Page.

CUTLER, John (1600-38), from Sprauston (Norwich), Eng.; a founder of Hingham, Mass., 1635, and settled there permanently, 1637; *m* 1625, Mary – (*d* 1681).

CUTLER, Richard (1621-93), from Eng. with his mother, Elizabeth; was freeman at Cambridge, 1641; mem. A. and H. A. Co.; officer Cambridge militia.

CUTTER, Mrs. Elizabeth (1575-1663), from Eng., settled at Cambridge, Mass., 1640; *m* in Eng., Samuel Cutter (*d* in Eng.).

CUTTING, Leonard (1724-94), from Eng. to New York, 1750; pastor at New Brunswick, N.J., Hempstead and Oyster Bay, L.I.; prof. King's Coll.; *m* a dau. of John Pintard, alderman of New York.

CUTTING, Richard (1623-1695/96), from Eng. in the "Elizabeth," 1634, to Watertown, Mass.; selectman; freeman, 1690; *m* Sarah–(1625-85).

CUTTS, Robert (*d* 1674), with bros. John and Richard, came to N.E.; shipmaster; resided for a time at Barbados; returned to Kittery, Me.; *m* 2d, Mary Hoel, of Barbados (she *m* 2d, post 1675, Capt. Francis Champernowne).

DABNEY (D'Aubigne, De Bany, De Bony), Cornelius or Corneille (*b* ca. 1640-*d* ante 1701; son of Theodore); Huguenot; had land grants in New Kent Co., Va., 1664, 66, 68; settled at Manakin Town, Va.; prob. *m* ca. 1668, Susanne – (*d* 1724); among their children was: Cornelius (*d* 1764), fled from France after revocation of Edict of Nantes, 1685, to Eng. or Wales; came to Va. bet. 1715-20, and settled in Hanover Co.; *m* in Eng., – (*d* in America); *m* 2d, 1721, Sarah Jennings.

DADE, Maj. Francis (*b* Eng., 1621-*d* at sea, 1663; son of William [1579-1659], of Tannington, Co. Suffolk, Eng., *m* 1st, Mary Wingfield, *d* 1624/25), came to Va. under assumed name of John Smith, 1651; after the Restoration visited Eng., but *d* while on voyage back to Va.; *m* ca. 1650, Behethland (ca. 1635-will 1720), dau. Maj. Thomas Bernard, *m* Mary, dau. Robert Behethland (she *m* 2d, 1664, Maj. Andrew Gilson).

DAGGETT (Dogget, Doggett, Dogett), Thomas (1607-Aug. 18, 1692), from Eng. in the "Mary Anne," of Yarmouth, Eng., to Salem (or Concord), Mass., May 1637; resided at Weymouth for a time; settled in Marshfield, Mass., 1652; farmer, selectman, juryman, constable, surveyor; *m* 1st, – (*d* June 23, 1642 at Concord, Mass.); *m* 2d, 1643, at Weymouth, Elizabeth (Humphrey) Fry (*b* Eng.-*d* Weymouth, Mass., 1652; widow of William Fry; dau. of Jonas Humphrey, of Dorchester, Mass., *m* Frances –); *m* 3d, at Marshfield, Aug. 17, 1654, Joane Chillingsworth (*b* prob. Eng.-*d* Marshfield, Sept. 4 1684; widow of Thomas Chillingsworth).

DAINGERFIELD, William (desc. Sir Philip, of Co. Worcester, Eng.); English gentleman, came to Essex Co., Va., before 1660; established "Greenfield"; *m* Frances –;

DALE, Maj. Edward (*d* Feb. 2, 1695), from Eng. to Lancaster Co., Va., among the royalists who sought refuge in Va., after the death of Charles I, 1649/50; justice; 1st clk. Westmoreland Co., Va., 1653; clk. Lancaster Co., Va., 1665-74; maj. of militia; high sheriff, 1670-80; burgess, 1677, 82-83; *m* Lady Diana (*b* Prestwould, ca. 1625), dau. of Sir Henry Skipwith (*b* 1589), knight and baronet of Prestwould, Leicestershire, Eng., *m* Amy Kempe.

DAME (Dam), John (ca. 1610-1693/94), from Eng., 1633, settled at Dover, N.H.; dea. First Parish Ch., 1675; received valuable land grants; held many town positions; *m* Elizabeth, dau. Lt. William Pomfret, town clk.

DAMON, John (*b* 1620-*d* Apr. 8, 1708), from Eng., to Dedham, Mass., 1640; freeman, 1645; an original founder of Reading, Mass.; *m* ca. 1645, Abigail (*d* 1713), dau. Richard Sherman, of Boston.

DANA, Richard (*d* 1690), early settler on south side of the Charles River, Cambridge, Mass.; constable, 1661; grand juror, tithingman, surveyor of highways, 1665; bought land at Shawshine; signer petition adhering to govt.; *m* ca. 1648, Ann Bullard (*d* 1711).

DANFORTH, Nicholas (*b* ca. 1585-*d* Apr. 1638), from Framlingham, Eng., 1634; to Cambridge, Mass., 1635; selectman, 1635-37; rep. Gen. Ct., 1636-37; mem. com. to build bridge, 1635; *m* Elizabeth Symmes (*d* in Eng., 1629).

DANFORTH (Danford), William (ca. 1640-post 1720), from Eng. or Ire., 1677; settled at Ipswich, Mass.; *m* 2d, ca. 1680, Sarah Thurloe.

DANIEL, Capt. William (will probated 1698), first of record in Middlesex Co., Va., when he received a patent for 115 acres; served on jury, 1674, 77, 79; constable, 1676; vestryman, Christ Ch. Parish, 1684-96; ch. warden, Great Ch., 1685-87; justice, 1684; capt. Middlesex Co. militia; *m* Jocebed— (*d* bet.1694-98)

DANIELS, Robert (*d* 1665), from Eng., settled at Watertown, Mass., ca. 1636; an original patentee of Sudbury, Mass.; *m* 1st, Elizabeth (*d* 1643), dau. Samuel Morse, *m* Elizabeth Jasper.

DARCY, Edward, see Dorsey.

DARLING, Denice (*d* 1717, aet. 77), settled at Braintree, Mass., 1640; propr. and settler, Mendon, Mass., 1677-78; *m* 1662, Hannah, dau. of John Francis, *m* Rose–.

DARNALL, Col. Henry (*d* 1711; son of Philip), came to Province of Md., 1672; held estate "The Woodyard"; was collector port of St. Mary's; col. of horse; dep. gov. of Md.; *m* Elinor, dau. of Richard Hatton, and widow of Thomas Brooke.

DASHIELL, James (1634-97), Eng. to Northumberland Co., Va., 1653; to Somerset, Md., 1663; surveyor of highways; burgess; *m* 1659, Ann Cannon (1639-ca. 1697).

DAVENPORT, John (1597-1670), grad. Magdalen Coll.; as a non-conformist fled to Holland, 1633, thence to Boston, in the "Hector," 1637; a founder of New Haven, Conn., 1638; pastor First Ch., Boston, 1668-70; *m* Elizabeth Wolley (1603-76).

DAVENPORT, Thomas (*b* ca. 1589/90-*d* Nov. 9, 1685; said to have been related to Rev. John Davenport of New Haven, Conn., both bore the same coat armor and are thought to have been g.sons of Henry Davenport, of Coventry, Eng., *m* Winifred, dau. of Richard Barnabit), from Eng. to Dorchester, Mass., 1638; admitted to Dorchester Ch., 1640; freeman, 1642; constable, 1670; *m* Mary Forth (bap. 1589/90-*d* Oct. 4, 1691).

DAVIS, Capt. Christopher, "Kit" (1616-ca. 1680), from Eng. to Mass. Bay Colony, ca. 1636; settled at Fort Orange, N.Y., 1640; removed to Ulster Co., N.Y., ca. 1652; in Esopus Indian wars; *m* Cornelia (*d* 1657), dau. Andries de Vos; *m* 2d, Maria Martensen.

DAVIS (Davies), David, from Wales to Newcastle, Del., 1760, brought by his father, who purchased 30,000 acres from William Penn; one of the founders of the Welsh Tract, Pa.

DAVIS, Dolor (1593-1673), master builder, from Kent, Eng., to Cambridge, Mass., 1634; settled at Duxbury, 1635, Barnstable, 1643, and again in 1666; Concord, 1655-66; petitioner for the grant of the Town of Groton, 1656; one of the twenty of the Plymouth Colony who had lands granted to them at Concord, Mass., 1658; sec. to 1st colonial gov. of Mass. Bay Colony; *m* Margery Willard (sister of Lt. Simon Willard, of Kent, Eng.); *m* 2d, 1671, Mrs. Joanna Bursley.

DAVIS, Samuel, Presbyn. minister, came under auspices of Soc. for Propagation of the Gospel in Foreign Parts, 1692, settled at Lewes, Sussex Co., Del.; *m* Mary Simpson.

DAVIS, William (1617-83), from Eng. ca. 1635, was at Roxbury, Mass.; freeman, 1673; *m* Elizabeth – (*d* 1658); *m* 2d, Alice Thorp (*d* 1667); *m* 3d, Jane – (*d* 1714).

DAWES, William (1620-69; son of William, who came to America, 1628, but later returned to Eng.); bricklayer; came in the "Planter," to Braintree, Mass., 1635; freeman, 1646; settled at Boston, 1652; *m* Susanna, dau. of John Mills.

DAY, Anthony (1617-1707), from Eng. in the "Paule," 1635; an original settler at Leominster, Mass.; later at Salem and Ipswich.

DAY, Robert (1604-48), from Eng. in the "Elizabeth," 1634, to Cambridge, Mass.; freeman, 1635; an original settler of Hartford, Conn., 1636; *m* in Eng., Mary –; *m* 2d, Editha, sister of Dea. Edward Stebbins.

DAYTON, Ralph (1588 or 98-1658), from Ashford, Co. Kent, Eng., to Boston, ca. 1636; at New Haven, Conn., 1639; constable; signer of Covenant, 1639; cordwainer; settled at Southampton, L.I., 1648, later at Easthampton; *m* 1616/17, Alice (Goldhatch) Tritten.

DEANE (Dean), Walter (ca. 1615-1693; son of William), from Eng. to Boston, 1637; settled at Dorchester, Mass.; later at Taunton; freeman; dep. Plymouth Ct., 1640; selectman many terms; mem. mil. co., 1639-43; a founder and stockholder in first permanent and successful iron works in America, Taunton, 1652; active during King Philip's War; deacon; *m* in Eng., Eleanor, dau. William Cogan.

DEARBORN, Godfrey (1599-Feb. 4, 1686), from Eng., 1638; with his son Henry, settled at Exeter, N.H., 1639; selectman, 1648; removed to Hampton, N.H., ca. 1650; j.p. and town clk.; large landowner; *m* —(*d* bet. 1650-62); *m* 2d, 1662, Dorothy–, widow of Philemon Dalton.

DE COURCY, Col. Henry (1620-95), from Eng. with Leonard Calvert, to Md., 1634; sec. of Md., 1660-61; chief justice of provincial cts.; col. comdg. forts of Cecil and Kent cos., 1670, 76, 81; burgess, Talbot Co., Md., 1694-95; mem. Gov.'s Council, 1660, 70, 76, 84; *m* Elizabeth (Smith) Carpenter.

DeFOREST (DeFrees), Jesse (ca. 1575-1624), Walloon leader of the Huguenots, from France, recruited the first band of colonists for New Amsterdam; led another expdn. to South America, 1623; *m* 1601, Marie du Cloux.

de GRAFFENRIED, Christopher (*b* Switzerland-*d* Oct. 27, 1742; son of Landgrave, Baron Christopher V, who visited America, founded New Bern, S.C., *m* Regina Tscharner); "brought over a colony of Swiss Palatines to North Carolina in 1709"; after marriage "moved first to Phila., to Maryland, and lastly to Va.," settled permanently in Prince Edward Co., Va., maintaining a town house in Williamsburg; *d* on his plantation on the James River; *m* Feb. 22, 1714, at Charleston, S.C., Barbara (Needham) Tempest (1688-June 26, 1744), dau. of Sir Arthur Needham of Wymondsley, Hertfordshire, Eng.

DeKAY, Willem (1606-68; son of Guillaume de Kay, director in Dutch West India Co.); came from Holland to New Amsterdam before Gov. Kieft; was fiscal or treas. of the colony, 1641.

DELAFIELD (de la ffelde), John (1748-1824?), from Eng. in the "Vigilant." to New York, 1783; was founder and pres. Mutual Ins. Co., and of United Ins. Co., large landowner; established "Sunswyck" on the East River opposite Blackwell's Island; was created count of the Holy Roman Empire; *m* 1784, Ann (1766-1839), dau. of Joseph Hallett.

DELAMATER, Claude LeMaistre (1611-83), fled from France to Flanders, thence to Amsterdam, 1652; came to New Amsterdam, 1652; settled at Flatbush; magistrate, Harlem, 1666-73; dea., 1675; *m* 2d, 1652, Hester (*d* 1710), dau. of Pierre DuBois.

De la MONTAGNE, Dr. Johannes, Huguenot physician, from Holland to New Amsterdam, 1637; *m* Rachel Monjour.

DELANO (de la Noye, de Lannoye), Philippe (bap. Leyden, Holland, Dec. 7, 1603-*d* Bridgewater, Mass., 1661); from Holland in the "Fortune," to Duxbury, Mass., 1621; soldier Pequot War; *m* Dec. 19, 1634, Hester Dewsbury; *m* 2d, 1657, at Duxbury, Mary (Pontus) Glass (*b* Leyden, ca. 1625-*d* Feb. 2, 1690), dau. of William Pontus and widow of James Glass.

DEMAREST (des Marest) David (1620-93; son of Jean des Marest [*b* 1596]; desc. of Baudouin, Seigneur des Marest, and also from his son, Baudouin des Marest, "who made over to the Abbey of Mount St. Andre in 1190 several heritages situated in the Seigniory des Marest"),

Huguenot, fled from France to the Province of Zeeland, Netherlands, 1640, later to Mannheim, Germany; came with his wife and four children in the "Bonte Koe" to New Amsterdam, 1663; del. from S.I., to the Gen. Assembly of New Netherlands, 1664; a founder of New Haarlem (now Harlem), and purchased land there, 1665; overseer, 1667-68, 1671-72; schepen, 1673; magistrate, 1673, 75; bought several thousand acres from the Tappan Indians, 1677; founded the French Ch. at Kinderkameek; m 1643, Marie (1623-80), dau. Francois Sohier, m Marguerite de Herville.

DEMING, John (ca. 1615-ca. 1705), from Eng. to Wethersfield, Conn., 1635; rep. Gen. Ct. 50 sessions; one of the patentees named in the Royal Charter of Conn., 1662; m 1637, Honour, dau. Richard Treat (qv).

DENISE (Nyssen, DeNyse), Theunis (d 1661), from Binneck, Utrecht, Holland, to New Amsterdam, N.Y., 1638; to Flatbush, L.I., 1655; magistrate at Brooklyn, 1658-61; m 1640, Phabea (Faelix) Seals, widow of John Seals, from Co. Devon, Eng. (she m 2d, 1663, Jan Cornelisze Buys).

DENISON (Denyson), William (1586-1653/54; son of John Denyson [d 1582], of Bishops Stortford, Eng., m Agnes —); came in the "Lyon," 1631, bringing his three sons, Daniel, Edward and George, and their tutor, Rev. John Eliot (qv); settled at Roxbury, Mass.; freeman, 1632; dep. Gen. Ct., 1635; mem. Roxbury militia, 1636; m in Eng., Nov. 7, 1602, Margaret (Chandler) Monck (b Eng., 1586-d Roxbury, Feb. 23, 1645), who came in 1632.

DENNIS, John (1612-79), from Eng. in "Ye Merchants Hope," to Va., 1635, settled in Northumberland Co., ca. 1651.

DENSLOW, Nicholas (1577-1666), from Eng. in the "Mary and John," 1630, settled at Dorchester, Mass.; to Windsor, Conn., ca. 1636; in Pequot fight, Mystic, Conn., 1637; m 2d, Elizabeth Dolling (1585-1669).

DENT, Thomas (1628-76), from Eng. to St. Marys Co., Md., 1650; was high sheriff and justice county ct.; m Rebecca, dau. of Rev. William Wilkinson.

DENTON, Richard (1586-1662/63), grad. Cambridge U., 1623; from Eng. with Gov. Winthrop in the "Arbella," to Boston, 1630; was at Watertown, Mass., 1634, at Wethersfield, Conn., 1635, at Stamford, 1641-44, later at Hempstead, L.I.; founded Congl. church at Stamford and said to have been the founder of Presbyterianism in America.

DE PEYSTER, Johannes (1620-85), a Huguenot, from Holland to New Amsterdam, 1645; cadet of Burgher Corps at New Amsterdam; burgomaster, dep. mayor of New Amsterdam and New York, and commissioner; m Cornelia Lubberts.

DE PRE, Josias, see Du Pre.

DE PUY (Du Puy), Nicholas (d 1691), from Paris to Holland, thence to America in the "Good Ship Pemberton Church," 1652 or 62; settled at New Amsterdam; m Catherine Renard (or De Vos or De Vaux?).

DERBY, Roger (b 1643), from Eng. to Boston, 1671; removed to Ipswich; settled at Salem, Mass., 1681; was a chandler; m in 1668, Lucretia Hillman (d 1689); m 2d, Elizabeth (Hasket) Dynn, dau. Stephen Hasket, and widow of William Dynn.

DEVEREUX, John (ca. 1615-ca. 1695), from Eng. to Salem, Mass., bet. 1630-36; at Marblehead, 1637; freeman, 1683; owned the Devereux Farm, celebrated in Longfellow's poem, "Driftwood"; m Ann – (d 1708, aet. 88).

DEWEY, Thomas (d 1648), from Eng. to Boston, 1631; settled at Dorchester; freeman, 1634; settled at Windsor, Conn., 1635; cornet of the troop; m 1638/39, Frances –, widow of Joseph Clark.

De WITT, Tjerck Claessen (1620-1700; son of Claes, of Groothalt, Zunderlandt), from Holland to New Amsterdam, N.Y., ca. 1653; to Albany, 1657; settled at Kingston, 1661; magistrate, 1661, 62; sgt. Ulster Co. militia; m 1656, Barbara Andrieszen Van Amsteram (d 1714).

DE WOLF, Balthasar (1620-96), was at Hartford, Conn., 1656, settled at Lyme, Conn., 1668; mem. militia; m Alice –.

DEXTER, Gregory (1610-1700), from Eng., 1644, settled at Providence, later at Warwick, R.I.;

clergyman; commr., 1651-54; pres. of the colony, 1653-54; dep. Gen. Ct., 1654-55; m Abigail Fullerton.

DEXTER, Thomas (d 1677), from Eng., was at Sudbury, Mass., ca. 1638; admitted freeman, 1640; was the first white settler at Marlborough, Mass., ca. 1657; soldier King Philip's War; m Mary—.

DEYO, Christian (1620-86), Huguenot, from France to the Palatinate, thence to Kingston, N.Y., 1676; one of 12 New Paltz patentees; called the "Grandpere of New Paltz"; m 1643, Jean Verbeau.

DICKERMAN, Thomas (d 1657), Eng. to Dorchester, Mass., 1635; tailor; also owned land at Boston Neck, 1652, 56; m Ellen– (she m 2d, John Bullard, removed to Medfield, Mass., ante July 14, 1663).

DICKINSON, Nathaniel (1600-76), from Eng. to Watertown, Mass., 1634; removed to Wethersfield, Conn., ca. 1636; town clk., 1645; to Hadley, Mass., 1659; served in Hampshire Guard; a founder of Hopkins Acad.; deacon; dep. Gen. Ct., 1642; rep. 1646-56; m in Eng., 1630, Anna–, widow of William Gull.

DIGGES (Diggs), Col. Edward (1620-21-1675; son of Sir Dudley [b 1583], Master of Rolls, m Mary Kemp); came from Eng. ca. 1650, settled at Belfield, Warwick Co., Va.; mem. Council; auditor gen.; gov. of the Colony, 1656; was zealous in fostering silk mfg. and in order to furnish the colonists with proper teachers he imported two Armenians skilled in this industry; provincial agent to Eng.; m Elizabeth Page (d ca. 1691).

DIKE, Capt. Anthony (d 1638), from Eng. in the "Anne," 1623, served in Pequot War; m Tabitha–.

DIMMOCK (Dimmick, Dymoke), Elder Thomas (d 1658 or 59), from Eng., settled at Dorchester, Mass., 1635, at Hingham, 1638, Scituate, 1639, Barnstable, 1640; m Ann (d 1683), dau. of Wm. Hammond, and g.dau. of Elder William Penn (father of William Penn, of Pa.).

DINGLEY, John (1608-58), from Eng. to Lynn, Mass., 1637; removed to Sandwich, 1637, to Marshfield, 1644; m Sarah –.

DIXON (Dixson), William (ca. 1662-1708; son of Henry, m Rose–), from Ire. to New Castle Co., Del., 1688; Quaker; m ca. 1690, Ann, dau. William Gregg, from Ire.

DOANE, John (1591-1686), from Eng. to Plymouth, Mass., 1630; removed to Eastham, 1644; gov.'s asst., 1632, 33, 39; mem. Plymouth mil. company, 1643; dep. Gen. Ct., 1639-42 and 1649, et seq.; m Ann –.

DODGE, Richard (ca. 1602-1672), from Eng., 1629, and settled at Salem, Mass.; donated large sum to Harvard Coll., 1653; a founder of Beverly, Mass., 1667; m Edith – (1603-78).

DODGE, William (1605-90), from Eng. in the "Lyon's Whelp," 1629, to Salem, Mass.; freeman, 1637; a founder of church at Beverly.

DOGGETT, Thomas, see Thomas Daggett.

DOLE, Richard (1622-1705), from Eng. to Parker River, old Newberry, Mass., 1639; dep. 1673; m in 1647, Hannah Rolfe (d 1678); m 2d, 1679, Hannah, widow of Capt. Samuel Brocklebank.

DOOLITTLE, Abraham (1619/20-1690), from Eng., was at Boston, 1640; removed to New Haven, Conn., 1644, to Wallingford, Conn., 1670; dep. Gen. Ct. from New Haven and Wallingford; mem. Vigilance Com. in King Philip's War; m Joane Allen (1625-61); m 2d, 1663, Abigail Moss.

DORR, Edward (1647/48-1733/34), from Eng. to Rowley, Mass., 1674; selectman; m 1st, 1679, Elizabeth (1656-1719), dau. Thomas Hawley.

DORSEY (Darcy), Edward (d 1659), from Eng. to Va., ca. 1642; acquired land nr. the Severn river in Anne Arundel Co., Md., 1650; drowned off the Isle of Kent in Chesapeake Bay, 1760; "Hockely-in-the-Hole" was patented to his sons, 1664; m Anne–.

DOTY, Edward (d 1655), 40th signer of the Mayflower Compact; in the "First Encounter," 1620; m 2d, at Plymouth, Mass., 1635, Faith (d 1675), dau. Tristram Clark.

DOUGHTY, Rev. Francis, from Eng.; preacher at Taunton, Dorchester, 1639; received grant at Maspeth (now Newtown), L.I.; first Puritan minister at New York City, and first to preach in English language there; m Bridget–.

DOUGLAS, William (1610-82), came with his wife and two children to Gloucester, Mass., 1640; freeman at Boston, 1640; settled at New London, Conn., 1659, rep. Gen. Ct.; m Ann (d 1685), dau. of Thomas Mattle.

DOW, Henry (b Ormsby, Eng., 1608-d 1659; son of Henry), from Eng. to Watertown, Mass., ca. 1638; to Hampton, 1649; dep. Gen. Ct., 1655-56; m 1630, Jane Nudd; m 2d, 1643, Margaret Cole, of Dedham (she m 2d, Richard Kimball).

DOWD (Doude, Dowde, Dowdy), Henry (d in 1668), from Eng. to Guilford, Conn., 1639; m Elizabeth – (d 1683).

DOWS (Dowse), Lawrence (1613-92), from Eng. to Charlestown, Mass., 1640; m 1st, Martha – (d in 1644); m 2d, Margery (ca. 1625-1714), dau. of Robert Rand, Eng. to Charlestown, m Alice Sharp.

DRAKE, Capt. Francis (ca. 1625-Sept. 24, 1687; desc. of John Drake, Devonshire, Eng.), and wife Mary-(d July 29, 1688), from Co. Meath, Ire., settled at Portsmouth, N.H., ca. 1650; to Piscataway Tp., Middlesex Co., N.J., 1668; surveyor and ens., Portsmouth; selectman, constable. j.p., co. judge, and militia capt., July 15, 1675-May 30, 1687, Piscataway.

DRAKE, John (1600-59; son of William); from Devon Co., Eng., to Boston, 1630; settled at Windsor, Conn., ca. 1639; m Elizabeth Rogers (d 1681).

DRAKE, Thomas (1628-92), came to Weymouth, Mass., 1653/54; served in King Philip's War; m ante 1659, Jane, dau. Thomas Holbrook; m 2d, 1681, Millicent (Ford) Carver, dau. of William Ford.

DRAPER, James (1618-94; son of Thomas Draper); a Puritan, came from Eng. bet. 1647-50, settled at Roxbury, Mass.; m 1646, Miriam (1625-97), dau. of Gideon Stansfield, m Grace Eastwood.

DRAYTON, Thomas, from Eng. to the Barbados, thence to Cape Fear River, N.C., 1671; settled at Drayton Hall, on Ashley River, nr. Charleston, S.C., ca. 1680.

DRINKER, Philip (1596-1647), from Eng. in the "Abigail," to Charlestown, Mass., 1635: freeman, 1637; kept the first ferry over the Mistick River, 1640; m Elizabeth – (b 1603).

DRURY, Hugh (1616-July 6, 1689), from Eng. to Boston, Mass.; lt. colonial wars; m ca. 1645, at Sudbury, Mass., Lydia (b Barkhamstead, Co. Herts., Eng., 1627/28-d Boston, Apr. 5, 1675), dau. of Edmund Rice (qv).

DU BOIS, Louis (1626-95; son of Christien, Huguenot, of Lille, France); came in the "St. Jean Baptiste," to New Amsterdam, 1661; a patentee of New Paltz, N.Y., 1664; mem. first Ct. of Sessions; led expdn. against Indians, 1663; m at Mannheim, Germany, 1655, Catherine, dau. of Matthew Blanshan, or Blanchan, at Hurley, 1670.

DU BOSE (Du Boce), Isaac (1665-1743), a Huguenot, from France to Jamestown, on south side the Santee River, nr. Charleston, S.C., ca. 1689, after the revocation of the Edict of Nantes: m Susanne Couillandeau.

DUDLEY, Edward (d ante Feb. 6, 1655; son of Robert, of Bristol, m Miss Green); from Eng. to Va., 1637; settled in York Co.; removed to Lancaster (part now Middlesex) Co.; m Elizabeth (d 1691), dau. of Hester Pritchard, of Bristol.

DUDLEY, Francis (1640-living 1702), settled at Concord, Mass.; m 1665, Sarah (1640-1713), dau. of George Wheeler, of Concord.

DUDLEY, Thomas (bap. Yardley, Hastings, Northants, Eng., Oct. 12, 1576-buried Roxbury, Mass., July 31, 1653), came in the "Arbella"; dep. gov. Colony of Mass. Bay 13 yrs., gov.'s asst. 7 yrs., and gov., 1634, 40, 45, 50; commr. United Colonies, 1643, 47, 49; lt. col., Suffolk Co., Mass., 1636; commr. of mil. affairs, 1636; founder of Harvard Coll., 1637; name on new charter of Harvard Coll., 1650; pres. of the Confederacy, 1643, 47, 49; m in Eng., Apr. 25, 1603, Dorothy Yorke (b Eng., 1582-buried Roxbury, Dec. 27, 1643); m 2d, 1644, Catherine, dau. of Dr. John Dighton, and widow of Samuel Haigborn or Hayburn (she m 3d, Rev. John Allen, of Dedham, Mass.).

DUER, William (1747-99; son of John, one of his majesty's council for Antigua, m Frances, dau. Gen. Frederick Frye, of Brit. Army),

served with Lord Clive in India, came to New York, ca. 1768; del. Cont. Congress. asst. sec. of the treas.; m Lady Catharine, dau. Maj. Gen. William Alexander, Earl of Stirling (m Sarah, dau. Philip Livingston, 2d lord of the manor).

DUNBAR, Robert (1630-93), from Dunbar, Scot., 1655; settled at Hingham, Mass.; bought land from Richard Dwelle, 1671-72; freeman; took oath, Apr. 21, 1679; m Rose-(d 1700).

DUNHAM, Hon. and Dea. John (1588/89-1668), in Plymouth Colony ante 1631; was elected dep. Gen. Ct., Plymouth. 1639-64: mem. Council of War; dea. of ch. at Plymouth under Elder Brewster; was a widower with 3 children when m at Leyden, Holland, Pilgrim Colony, 1622, to Abigail, dau. of Thomas Bailliou, m Anne–, probably Huguenot refugees as the name occurs frequently in publications of the Huguenot Soc. of London, and is identified with Baliol, Scotch King, and with Bella Aqua, of ancient Eng. Abigail Baillou, still resident at Leyden, witness at marriage of a sister, June 1624.

DUNLAP, Capt. Alexander (1716-44), from Ireland to Augusta (now Rockridge) Co., Va., and also came to Augusta Co., Va., Capt. James and William Dunlap (these three leaving many distinguished descendants), and to Knoxville, Tenn., came Hugh Dunlap (Knoxville's first mcht., and among whose sons were Gen. Richard Gilliam Dunlap, Sec. of War of the Republic of Texas, and William Claiborne Dunlap, M.C., Tenn.), all four immigrants being related; was capt. of horse, 1743; first settler in the Pastures region of the Valley of Va.; grantee by orders of council of lands (unpatented) on Greenbrier river. (now) W.Va.; m Ann McFarland (b Scotland), said to have been desc. of a chief of Clan MacFarlane (she m 2d. Capt. Robert Bratton).

DUNNING, Theophilus (b prob. Devonshire, Eng.), from Eng. ante 1642; granted land at Salem, Mass.; to Newtown, L.I.; called "the fisherman"; m ante Mar. 13, 1642.

DUNSTER, Rev. Henry (bap. 1609-d 1659/60), grad. Magdalen Coll., Cambridge, Eng., B.A., 1630, M.A., 1634; came to Boston, 1640; first pres., Harvard Coll., 1640-54, and for several yrs. its sole teacher; settled at Scituate, 1654; m 1641, Elizabeth (ca. 1627-1690), probably dau. of Hugh Atkinson, of Eng.

DU PONT de Nemours, Pierre Samuel (1739-1817), ex-pres. Constituent Assembly and of the Conseil des Anciens. of France: sec. Provisional French Govt., 1814, statesman and author, arrived at Newport, R.I., with his sons, Jan. 1, 1800; m Nicole-Charlotte-Marie-Louise Le Dee de Rencourt (or Roccourt), (1743-74).

DU PRE (Deupree, DePre, Dupree), Josias, Huguenot from France, 1686, settled nr. Charleston, S.C.; granted 750 acres on eastern branch of Cooper River, 1703; m Martha–.

DU PUY, Barthelemy (1653-1743). captain of Household Guards, of Louis XIV: in battles in Flanders: escaped to Germany, 1685, at revocation of Edict of Nantes: to England, 1699, to Virginia 1700: m Countesse Susanne La Villian.

DUPUY Nicholas, see De Puy.

DURAND, John (1667-1727), Huguenot, from France to New York, 1694: settled at Milford, Conn., 1696; surgeon in expdn. to Can., 1709; m ca. 1698, Elizabeth, dau. of Richard Bryan.

DURANT, George (b Eng., Oct. 1, 1632), in Mar. 1661, Kilcocamen, great Indian chief of Yeopims deeded to him for a "valuable consideration" a tract of land bearing the name of Wecocomeke (a peninsula now called Durant's Neck), this is the earliest recorded deed in history of N.C.; with Samuel Pricklove, established 1st permanent settlement in N.C. at Durant's Neck, 1661; atty. gen., Grand Council, Albemarle Co., 1679; resided at Durant's Neck, 1691; an acknowledged leader in public affairs; with Culpeper led the Culpeper rebellion against unjust restriction of trade; m Jan. 4, 1658, Ann Marwood, of Northumberland Co., Va.

DURYEA (Durje), Joost (d 1727), a Huguenot, from France to New York, ca. 1675; m Magdalena Le Fehre.

DUSTIN, Thomas (1652-1729; son of Thomas [d 1662], of Richmond Island, nr. Dover, N.H., 1632, later at Haverhill, Mass., m Elizabeth, dau. John Wheeler), settled at Haverhill, Mass.; m Hannah (1657-post 1709), dau. of Michael Emerson (qv); see Vols. II and IV, for portraits of monument erected to her memory.

DUTTON, John, from Eng. with Gov. Winthrop, 1630; settled at Reading, Mass.; *m* Mary Neeld.

du TRIEUX, Philip, see Truax.

DUVAL (Duvall, Du Val), Mareen (*d* 1694), a Huguenot refugee, settled in Anne Arundel Co., Md., on land patented to him by Lord Baltimore in 1650, and surveyed for him under name of Laval, 1659; served against Nanticoke Indians, 1678; commr. for laying out towns, 1683; *m* 2d, Susanna—; *m* 3d, Mary Stanton (she *m* 2d, Col. Henry Ridgely I, and 3d, Rev. Jacob Henderson).

DWELLE (Dwelley), Richard (ca. 1630-1692; son John), from Eng.; an incorporator of Lancaster, Mass., 1653; to Hingham, thence to Scituate; in King Philip's War; *m* 2d, 1690, Elisabeth Simmons (*d* 1708).

DWIGHT, John (*d* 1660), from Eng. to Watertown, Mass., 1634, settled at Dedham, 1635, and founded the Church of Christ; was one of the five trustees of the first free school in America supported by a town tax, 1644; freeman, 1638; selectman 16 yrs.; *m* Hannah–(*d* 1656); *m* 2d, 1658, Elizabeth (*d* 1660), widow of William Ripley.

DYER (Dyar, Dyre), William (*d* 1667), from Eng. to Boston, 1635; disarmed as a supporter of Wheelwright, 1637, disfranchised and driven from the colony, 1638; one of 18 original proprs. of R.I.; sec. Providence Plantations, 1639; col. of R.I., 1640-42; gen. recorder, 1647-48; commr. at Newport to act against the Dutch, 1648; commr. to the Assembly from Providence, 1655, from Warwick, 1661, from Newport, 1662; *m* Mary – (executed, 1660, on Boston commons, for preaching Quakerism).

EAMES, Anthony (1595/96-1686), from Eng., was a propr. of Charlestown, Mass., 1634; removed to Hingham, 1636, to Marshfield, 1650; dep. Gen. Ct., 1637-38, 43; capt., Hingham mil. company, 1644-45.

EAMES (Ames), Thomas (1618-80), from Eng. ca. 1634; settled at Dedham, 1640, finally on Mount Wayte, Framingham, Mass.; *m* Margaret –; *m* 2d, Mary, dau. of John Blamford, and widow of Jonathan Paddlefoot; she and five children killed by Indians and four other children captured in King Philip's War, of whom Samuel escaped.

EARLE, Sir John (1614-60; son of Sir Richard, of Dorset Co., Eng.), from Eng., ca. 1649-52, with his wife and three children, and for paying the passage of 34 persons received land grants aggregating 1700 acres located on Earle's Creek and Yeocomico River, now Westmoreland Co., Va., which, exclusive of other patents subsequently granted by the lords proprietors of the Northern Neck, descended in a single male representative for 100 yrs.; *m* Mary Symons (1619-59).

EARLE (Earl), Ralph (*b* Aug. 25, 1605-*d* 1678; son of Raulphe, *m* Margaret Browne), came to Boston, 1634; at Newport, R.I., 1638; at Portsmouth, R.I., 1649, later a townsman of Dartmouth, Mass.; was one of the petitioners for a charter, 1638; capt. of troops, 1667; *m* in Eng., June 29, 1631, Joan (bap. 1609), dau. of Richard Savage.

EASTMAN, Roger (bap. Charleton, Eng., Apr. 4, 1610-*d* Salisbury, Mass., Dec. 16, 1694; son of Nicholas, of Charleton, *m* Barbara –); came in the "Confidence," 1638, settled at Salisbury; *m* 1639, Sarah (Smith?), (1621-97).

EASTON, Nicholas (1593-1675), *b* Wales; came to N.E. with his two sons, Peter and John, 1634; was at Ipswich, Mass., 1634; removed to Newbury, 1635; built the first house at Hampton, 1638; settled in R.I., 1639, and built the first house at Newport, 1639; pres. of R.I., 1650-51 and 1654; dep. gov., 1670-71; gov. under royal charter, 1672-1674.

EATON, Francis (*d* 1633), 23rd signer of the Mayflower Compact; *m* 1st, Sarah – (*d* 1621); *m* 2d, probably Governor Carver's maid servant; *m* 3d, at Plymouth, Mass., 1624 or 25, Christian Penn (*d* ca. 1684), she *m* 2d, Francis Billington.

EATON, John (1595-1668), Eng. to Mass., ante 1639; at Salisbury and Haverhill; cooper; propr., 1639, 1646-48; grand juror, 1646; one of five "prudential men" to manage town affairs, Salisbury; *m* in Eng., 1618, Anne–(*d* 1660).

EATON, John (1611-58), from Eng. in the "Elizabeth and Ann," 1635; freeman at Water-

town, Mass., 1636; surveyor of boundaries; built bridge across St. Charles River; removed to Dedham, 1637; *m* 1630, Abigail Darmont.

EATON, Theophilus (1590-1657; son of Rev. Richard, vicar of Great Budworth, Cheshire, Eng.); with Rev. John Davenport to Boston, 1637; a founder of Quinnipiack (New Haven), Conn.; gov., 1639-57; *m* 2d, in Eng., 1619, Ann, widow of David Yale and dau. George Lloyd, bishop of Chester.

EATON, Col. William (1680-1749), from Leicester, Eng., to nr. Petersburg, Va.; settled in Edgecombe Co., N.C., ca. 1739; high sheriff, mem. N.C. Colonial Assembly; *m* Mary Rives.

EDDY, Samuel (1608-87; son of Rev. William Eddy, ca. 1550-1616, vicar of St. Dunstan's, Cranbrook, Eng., *m* Mary Fosten), came from Eng. in the "Handmaid," with his brother, John, to Plymouth Colony, 1630; settled finally at Swansea, Mass.; *m* Elizabeth - (1601-89).

EDES, John (Mar. 31, 1651-1693; son of John, of Essex Co., Eng.; g.son John [*d* Apr. 12, 1658], A.B., St. John's Coll., Cambridge, 1610, M. A., 1614, rector, 41 yrs.; g.g.son Henry of Bocking, Co. Essex, Eng.); came from Lawford, Co. Essex, Eng., to Charlestown, Mass., 1655; King Philip's War; *d* Middlesex, Mass.; *m* 1674, Mary, dau. of Peter Tufts (qv).

EDSALL, Samuel (1630-1706), from Eng. in the "Triall," to Boston, 1648; settled at New Amsterdam, 1655-68; founder of Bergen, N.J.; mem. Council, Province of East Jersey, 1668, and Province of N.Y., 1689-91; Indian interpreter, New Castle on the Delaware, 1675-76; *m* 3d, Ruth, dau. of Richard Woodhull (1620-90), of Setauket, L.I., from Eng. ante 1648, *m* Debora –.

EDSON, Samuel (bap. Fillongley, Warwickshire, Eng., Sept. 5, 1613-*d* July 19, 1692; son of Thomas, *m* Elizabeth Copson); came to Salem, Mass., ca. 1639; removed to Bridgewater, 1650; *m* in Eng., 1638, Susanna Orcutt (1618-Feb. 20, 1699, aet. 81):

EDWARDS, Dr. John (son of Thomas, g. son of Richard, of Co. Lancaster, Eng.), from Wales, to Va., 1620 or 23, settled in Northumberland Co., and later in Lancaster Co.; *m* Elizabeth–.

EDWARDS, William (1620-85; son of Rev. Richard Edwards, *m* Ann, prob. dau. of Henry Munter), from Eng. with his mother and stepfather, –Cole, to Hartford, Conn., 1639; freeman, 1658; chimney-viewer, 1668; mem. Troop of Horse, 1658; *m* 1645, Agnes–, widow of William Spencer.

EELLS (Ells, Eels, Eales), John (1575-1653), from Eng. to Dorchester, Mass., 1629; freeman, 1634; removed to Hingham, and in 1645 to Newbury; called the "beehive maker."

EGGLESTON, Begat (1590-1674), from Eng. in the "Mary and John," to Dorchester, Mass.; removed to Windsor, Conn., 1635; an original member of Warehams Church (second Congl. church organized).

ELDERKIN, John (*b* 1616-*d* 1687), from Eng., 1637; built first merchant vessel ever owned in New England; went to Lynn, Dedham, Reading, Providence, New London, building churches, mills and other buildings; finally settling in Norwich, Conn., where he died; *m* Elizabeth (Drake) Gaylord.

ELIOT (Eliot, Elliott), Andrew (1627-1704), from Eng. to Beverly, Mass., 1650; dep. Gen. Ct.; served in expdn. against Canada; *m* Grace Woodier.

ELIOT, Rev. John (1604-90, son of Bennett, *m* Letteye Aggar); grad. Jesus Coll., Cambridge U., 1622; came from Eng. in the "Lyon," to Boston, 1631; teacher of the church at Roxbury, 1632; known as the "Apostle to the Indians"; *m* 1632, Hanna Munford (or Mountford).

ELIOT, Philip (1602-57; brother of Rev. John), from Eng., was admitted freeman at Roxbury, Mass., 1636; mem. A. and H. A. Co.; col., Mass. militia; dep. Gen. Ct., 1654-57; commr. for Roxbury.

ELLERY, William (1643-96), from Eng., settled at Gloucester, Mass.; *m* Hannah Vinson.

ELLICOTT, Andrew (*d* 1766), from Eng., 1730/31 to Bucks Co., Pa., inventor, clock and astronomical instrument maker; *m* Mary Fox.

ELLIS, David, from Wales in the "Mary Margaret"; listed in muster of gov.'s men at Pashehaighs, Jamestown, 1624; *m* Margaret–, who came in the "Margaret and John".

ELLIS, Richard (bap. 1600-1694), from Eng. in the "Lion," to Boston, 1632; an original propr. of Dedham, 1636; ensign and lt.; dep., 1692-93; *m* Elizabeth French.

ELLSWORTH, Josiah (1629-89), from Eng., 1645, settled at Windsor, Conn.; *m* 1654, Elizabeth, dau. Thomas Holcomb.

ELLYSON, Hon. Robert, M.D. (*b* in Eng.), established in Md. ante 1643; sheriff, St. Mary's Co., 1643; removed to James City Co., Va.; burgess from that co., 1656, 1659-61, 63; magistrate; militia officer.

ELTINGE, Jan (1632-1729; son of Roelof), from Holland to New Amsterdam was settled on L.I., 1663; apptd. judge Court of Sessions of Ulster Co., N.Y., 1675; *m* 1677, Jacomyntje, dau. of Cornelis Barentse Slecht, who was at Esopus, N.Y., 1655.

ELY, Nathaniel (1605-75), from Tenterden, Co. Kent, Eng., in the "Elizabeth," to Cambridge, Mass., 1634; freeman, 1635; a founder of Hartford, Conn., 1636; constable, 1639; selectman; settled at Norwich, Conn., 1650; constable, 1654; rep. Gen. Ct., 1657; to Springfield, Mass., 1659; selectman, 1661, et seq.; *m* Martha–(*d* 1688).

ELY, Richard (1610-84), from Eng. to Boston, ca. 1660; a merchant; settled at Lyme, Conn.; *m* Joane Phipps (*d* 1660); *m* 2d, 1664, Elizabeth, widow of John Cullick, and sister of Col. George Fenwick.

EMERSON, Michael (1627-1715), from Eng. to Haverhill, Mass., 1656; *m* 1657, Hannah, dau. of John Webster, *m* Mary Shatswell.

EMERSON, Thomas (1584-1653), collector at Bishop's Stortford, Eng., 1636; came in the "Elizabeth Ann," and settled at Ipswich Mass., 1638; *m* 1611, Elizabeth Brewster.

EMERY (Emmerie, Emory), Anthony (1600-90), from Eng. in the "James," to Boston, 1635; removed to Newbury, Mass., thence to Dover, N.H., 1644, to Kittery, Me., 1648; freeman, 1652; selectman, 1652-59; constable, 1661; resident of Portsmouth, 1662; dep. Gen. Ct., 1672; rep. Gen. Assembly, 1680; *m* Frances –.

EMERY, John (1598-1683; son of John, *m* Agnes –); came in the "James," 1635; settled at Newbury, Mass.; freeman, 1641; selectman, 1661; surveyor of highways, 1668, 80; presented by grand jury for entertaining Quakers, the deposition alleging that "two mennequakers wr entertained very kindlie to bed and table & John Emmerie shok ym by ye hand and bid ym welcome"; *m* in Eng., Mary – (*d* 1649); *m* 2d, 1650, Mary (Shatswell) Webster.

EMLEY, William (*b* in Eng., 1648-1704), arrived in the "Kent," 1677; one of commrs. to buy West Jersey land from Indians; returned to America with family in the "Shield," 1678, and settled nr. present site of Trenton; mem. West Jersey Gen. Assembly; justice; land commr.; mem. Council; surveyor; boundary commr., boundary between N.Y. and N.J., 1687; *m* Ruth (Stacy?).

EMMONS (Emons), Thomas (*d* 1664), from Eng. to Newport, R.I., ca. 1638; freeman at Boston, 1652; *m* Martha –.

ENDICOTT, John (1589-1665), from Eng. in the "Abigail," to Salem, Mass., 1628; one of the 6 original purchasers of Mass. Bay from the Plymouth Council; named in the Royal Charter as one of the eighteen, and was named by his associates at head of 1st settlement at Salem; col. 3d Regt. Mass. Militia in first expdn. against the Pequot Indians, 1636; gen. in command of Block Island expdn., 1636; maj. gen., 1645-49; dep. gov., 1641, and gov. most of time, 1644-65; pres. United Colonies, 1658; *m* in Eng., Ann Gower: *m* 2d, 1630, Elizabeth Gibson.

ENNALLS, Bartholomew (1643-88), to Dorchester Co., Md.; burgess, 1678-82; received land patent from Lord Baltimore; *m* ca. 1660, Mary (Warren) Heywood; *m* 2d, Elinor Hill.

EPPES, Lt. Col. Francis (*d* 1655), said to have been of an armorial family; from Eng. to Prince George Co., Va., 1625; patented 1,700 acres in Charles City Co., 1635; rece'ved head rights for transportation of himself, 3 sons and 30 servants; settled on lands at junction of James and Appomattox rivers still held by family; commr., 1632; burgess, 4 terms; justice for Charles City Co., Va., 1639-45; capt. and lt. col Va. troops; mem. Royal Council, 1652; *m* in Eng.

ERSKINE, Christopher (1701-75; desc. John Erskine, Earl of Mar, of Scotland), came from Londonderry, Ire., to Abingdon (Bridgewater), Mass., 1725; *m* 1729, Susannah (1713-87), dau. of Cain Robinson.

ERSKINE, Sgt. John (*d* 1677), was with Sir Robert Carr during the attack on the Dutch on the Delaware, 1664; granted a house and lot adjoining Sir Robert Carr's; also granted land nr. New Castle; *m* Jane, or Jeane–(*d* post 1682).

ERWIN (Irwin), Nathaniel (1713-94), from North Ireland to Phila., Pa., 1740; moved to Bucks Co., Pa., finally settled in York Co., S.C.; *m* Mary—; *m* 2d, Leah Julian.

ESTABROOK, Rev. Joseph (1640-1711), from Eng., ca. 1660; grad. Harvard, 1664; minister at Concord; freeman, 1665; *m* 1668, Mary, dau. Capt. Hugh Mason (qv).

ESTES, Matthew (1645-1723; son of Robert, *m* Dorothy–), came from Eng. ante 1676; settled at Dover, N.H.; master mar'ner, and master of sloop, "Unity" of Boston; Quaker; *m* 1676, Philadelphia (Jenkins) Hayes (1645-1721), dau. Reginald Jenk:ns. *m* Ann–, of Lynn, Mass.

ESTEY, Jeffrey (1587-1657; son of Christopher, *m* Ann Arnold; g.son of Jeffrey Estey), came from Eng.; settled at Salem, Mass.; granted 20 acres, 1636; removed to Huntington, L.I., 1651; *m* 1606, Margaret Pote, Pitt, Pott, or Pett.

EUSTIS, William (*d* 1694); whose name first appeared on the tax list of Romey Marsh (now Chelsea), Mass., 1674; was at Charlestown, later at Malden, and at Boston; *m* Sarah – (1639-1713).

EVANS, Thomas (1651-1738; son of Evan ap Evan of Wales, and desc. Conan Tyndaethy, king of Wales, who died 818); came to Gwynedd, Delaware Co., Pa., 1698; *m* Ann –.

EVARTS, John (1601-69), from Eng., settled at Concord, Mass.; freeman, 1638; removed to Guilford, Conn., 1650; landed propr.; *m* 2d, 1663, Elizabeth–(*d* 1683), widow of John Parmelee.

EVERETT, Richard (*d* 1682), with his first wife, from Essex Co., Eng., to Cambridge, Mass., ca. 1634-35; with William Pynchon in settlement among the Indians on the Conn. River, 1636; settled at Dedham; freeman, 1646; constable and selectman; *m* 1st, Mary – (issue: six children); *m* 2d, 1643, Mary Winch (issue: five children).

EWEN, Col. Richard (*b* Eng.-*d* post 1674), to Md., 1649, probably Anne Arundel Co.; one of Cromwell's commrs.; mem. Severn's Provincial Council; speaker lower house; justice Anne Arundel Co.; sheriff; asst. cdr., regt.; *m* Sophia –.

EWING, Nathaniel (1692-Sept. 6, 1748; son of William, fled from Scot. to Ire., 1685), from Coleraine, Ire., to Cecil Co., Md.; *m* 1721, his 1st cousin, Rachel Porter.

EWING, Robert (*d* 1787), from Ireland with his brother Charles, to Bedford Co., Va., bet. 1735-47; clk. co. ct. many yrs.; elder Presbyn. ch.; in Lord Dunmore's war; *m* Mary (*b* 1730), dau. of Caleb Baker, *m* Catherine Hodwill.

EWING, Thomas (1695-1748), from Londonderry, Ireland, emigrated to Long Island, 1718; settled at Greenwich, West Jersey; *m* Mary Maskell.

FAIRBANKS (Fairbank), Jonathan (ca. 1595-1668), from Eng. with 4 sons in the "Speedwell," to Boston, 1633; settled at Dedham, 1636, and built there the house, still standing, said to be the oldest dwelling in America; *m* 1617, Grace Smith (*d* 1673).

FAIRCHILD, Thomas (ca. 1610-1670), from Eng., a founder of Stratford, Conn., 1639, and was first magistrate of the town; dep. Gen. Ct. of Conn., 1646, served 11 sessions; apptd. by the Gen. Ct. to press men for the Narragansett expdn.; *m* Emma, dau. of Robert Seabrook; *m* 2d, 1662, Catharine Craig, a widow.

FAIRFAX, William (1691-1757), from Eng. to the Bahamas, 1718, came to Salem, Mass., 1725; was Va. agt. for his cousin, 6th Lord Fairfax, 1733, established "Belvoir," Fairfax Co., Va., 1735; was burgess and pres. Colonial Council; *m* 1723, Sarah, dau. Thomas Walker; *m* 2d, ca. 1731, Deborah (1708-44), dau. Francis Clarke.

FANNING, Edmund (ca. 1620-1683; son Francis, sheriff, 1632, mayor of Limerick, 1644, transported to Connaught by Cromwellians, 1653-54), sentenced to Connaught, 1653-54; escaped with his wife to America and settled at New London, Conn., 1653; removed to Fishers Island, 1655; served in King Philip's War; *m* ca. 1649, Ellen–.

FARLEY, George (1615-93; son of Thomas, of Somersetshire, Eng., *m* Jane Hungerford), clothier, from Eng. in the "Lion," 1639; lived at Woburn, Mass., until 1653; moved to Billerica, where he built a commodious house which was used as a garrison in King Philip's War; Baptist; *m* 1641/42, Beatrice Snow; *m* 2d, 1653, Christian Births (*d* 1702).

FARNSWORTH, Matthias (1612-89; son of Joseph, *d* 1660); of Lynn, later of Groton, Mass.; *m* 2d, Mary (*d* 1717), dau. of George Farr, *m* Elizabeth Stower.

FARNUM, Ralph (1603-93), from Eng. in the "James," 1635, settled at Ipswich, Mass.; *m* Alice–.

FARWELL, Henry (1605-70), from Eng., 1636; one of original settlers of Concord, Mass., 1639; freeman, 1639; removed to Chelmsford: *m* 1629, Olive, dau. of Richard Welbie, *m* Frances Bulkley.

FAUNTLEROY, Col. Moore (1610-63; 2d son of John [bap. 1588], of Crondall, Hampshire, Eng., *m* 1609, Phoebe Wilkinson: and g.g.son of Tristram Fauntleroy [*d* 1538], of Michels Mersh, Hampshire, *m* Joan, dau. John Holt, of Crondall, and widow of Thomas Villiers, of Leicestershire, Eng.); came to Va., 1641; patented land, Upper Norfolk Co., called "Royes-Rest," 1643; removed to Northern Neck, Va.; purchased land from Rappahannock Indians, 1651; settled finally at "Crondall," Naylor's Hole, Lancaster (now Richmond) Co., Va.; *m* 2d, 1648, Mary Hill (dau. Capt. Thomas of Warwick Co., later of York Co., Va., *m* Mary, dau. Hon. Abraham Piersey, *m* Elizabeth Draper, of Weyanoke, on James River, Va.).

FAY, John (1648-90), Huguenot, refugee from France to England, thence in the "Speedwell," to Mass., 1656; lived at Watertown, later at Sudbury, and at Marlboro, 1675; *m* 1668, Mary (*d* ca. 1677), dau. of Thomas Brigham (qv); *m* 2d, 1678, Susanna, widow of Joseph Morse and dau. William Shattuck.

FEAKE, Robert (1610-63), from Eng. in Winthrop's fleet, 1630, settled at Watertown, Mass.; freeman, 1631; lt., colonial forces, 1632-36; dep. Gen. Ct., Colony of Mass. Bay, 1635-36; *m* Elizabeth (Fones) Winthrop, dau. of Thomas Fones, *m* Ann, dau. Adam Winthrop, *m* 2d, Ann Brown.

FEARING, John (*d* 1665), from Eng. in the "Diligent," to Hingham, Mass., 1638; selectman, 1648; constable, 1650; freeman, 1652; a deacon; *m* Margaret—.

FELLOWES (Felloe, Fellows), William (1611-77), from Eng. in the "Planter," to Ipswich, Mass., 1635; shoemaker; *m* a sister of John Ayres.

FELTON, Nathaniel (bap. 1615-1705; son of John, of Great Yarmouth, Norfolk, Eng., *m* 1612, Ellen Thrower), came from Eng. to nr. Felton Hill. Salem, 1633; at Salem Corners, 1653; constable, 1657; juryman, 1655; grand juror, 1676, 79, 83; apptd. ens., 1679; lt., 1681; *m* Mary (bap. 1627-1701), dau. Rev. Samuel Skelton, 1st minister at Salem, mem. Gov.'s Council, *m* 1619, Susanna Travis.

FENN, Benjamin (1612-72), from Eng. in the "Mary and John," to New Haven, Conn., ca. 1630; to Dorchester, Mass., 1631; settled at Milford, Conn., 1638; was gov.'s asst.; magistrate of colony and col. militia; *m* Sarah (1621-63), dau. Sylvester Baldwin.

FENNER, Arthur (1622-1703), was at Providence, R.I., 1650, or before; commr. for United Colonies, 1653, et seq.; gov.'s asst., 1657-90; dep. Gen. Ct., 1664-1700; cdr. Providence forces in King Philip's War; *m* Mehitable (*d* 1684), dau. of Richard Waterman.

FENTON, Robert, from Wales; first notice of him at Woburn, Mass., 1688; tax payer at Woburn, 1688-91, at Windham (now Mansfield), Conn., 1693-94; propr., 1703; *m* Dorothy–.

FERNALD, Reginald, or Renald (ca. 1595-1656), surgeon, from Eng. to Kittery, Me., 1626-30; settled at Portsmouth, N.H., 1631; was surgeon of a company of colonists sent by Mason and Gorges; was town clerk; clk. of ct., 1640; recorder, 1654; etc.; his lands included "Lady Claim" or "Doctor's" Island (since 1806 U.S. Navy Yard); *m* Johanna Warburton.

FERREE, Mme. Mary (Maria Warenbur) Warrenbuer (1650-1716; widow of Daniel [*d* in exile ante 1708], desc. Jean [Fuehre] LaVerree, a French Protestant, of Picardy who removed to Flanders at the revocation of the Edict of Nantes); went from Lindau in Bavaria, German Palatinate, to Eng., obtained letters patent for citizenship under the privy seal of Queen Anne, Aug. 30, 1708; visited William Penn in person and he covenanted with her for a grant of land in Pa.; arrived New York, Dec. 31, 1708, with 6 children, as a mem. of a party of French and Palatine refugees headed by Rev. Joshua Kocherthal from Lindau; went from Esopus, on the Hudson River, as a founder of Huguenot colony in the Pequea Valley, Lancaster Co., Pa.

FERRIS, Jeffrey (1610-56), from Eng., ca. 1634; admitted freeman at Boston, 1635; an original settler at Greenwich, 1642; *m* Susannah—; *m* 2d, Judy Barnes.

FERRY (Fere), Charles (1637-99; son of John of Eng., and desc. Duke of Lorraine, 1205), from Eng. ca. 1660/61; took oath of allegiance at Springfield, Mass., 1678; selectman, 1695; tithingman, fence viewer; *m* 1661, Sarah (1644-1740), dau. John Harmon.

FIELD, John (*d* 1686), from Eng. to Providence, R.I., 1637; commr. to Gen. Assembly; deputy; was at Bridgewater, Mass., 1655.

FIELD (Feild), Robert (1605-1673?), from Eng., was living at Newport, R.I., 1638, returned to Eng. ca. 1641, but came again, 1644; was patentee of Bayside, L.I.; landed propr. Newtown, L.I.; *m* Ruth Fairbank; *m* 2d, 1630, Elizabeth Taylor; *m* 3d, Charity—.

FIELD, Robert (1613-75), from Eng. in the "James," 1635; arrived at Boston; went to Providence, R.I., 1638; returned to Boston, 1650; *m* 1650, Mary (ca. 1630-living 1677), dau. Christopher Stanley, from London, 1635.

FIELD, Zechariah (1596-1666), from Eng., 1629; later at Dorchester, Mass., thence to Hartford, 1636, Northampton, 1659, to Hatfield, 1662: soldier Pequot War; *m* 1641, Mary-(*d* ca. 1670).

FILMER, Maj. Henry (*d* post 1673), from Eng. to Va. ante 1642, settled first at James City and later in Warwick Co.; burgess, James City Co., 1642-43; justice of Warwick, 1647; had land grants as early as 1637; officer British Army of Occupation; *m* Elizabeth –.

FINLEY, Michael (*b* 1683-*d* bet. 1747-50; son of Robert, *m* Margaret Lauder); from Ireland to Phila., Pa., 1734; settled on Neshaminy Creek, Bucks Co., Pa.; later in N.J.; removed to Sadsbury Tp., Chester Co., Pa.; *m* 1712, Ann, dau. of Samuel O'Neill, of Ireland.

FISH, John (bap. 1621-1686), from Eng., 1637; at Stratford, Conn., 1654, New London, 1655; settled at Stonington, Conn.; received land grant at Voluntown for services in King Philip's War; sch. master, Stonington, 1680; surveyor; Mary Ireland.

FISH, Jonathan (1610-63) from Eng. with his brothers, Nathaniel and John, to Lynn, Mass., ca. 1635; removed to Sandwich, Cape Cod, 1637, to Newtown, L.I., ca. 1659; *m* Mary –.

FISH, Thomas (*d* 1647), from Eng. to Portsmouth, R.I., 1643; *m* Mary–(*d* 1699).

FISHER, Anthony (bap. 1591-1671; son of Anthony Fisher, *d* 1640, *m* Mary Fiske); came from Eng. in the "Rose," to Boston, 1637, and settled at Dedham same yr.; dep. Gen. Ct.; mem. A. and Hon. Arty. Co.; freeman, 1645; selectman, 1644-66; rep., 1649; *m* Mary—.

FISHER, Daniel (1619-83), from Eng. to Boston, 1637, settled at Dedham same yr.; freeman, 1640; selectman, 1650-81; capt. co. of Foot, 1640; mem. A. and H. A. Co., 1640; dep. Gen. Ct., speaker 3 times; gov.'s asst., 1682; *m* 1641, Abigail (*d* 1683), dau. of Thomas Marriott, *m* Susanna –.

FISHER, John, from Eng. in the "Welcome," with William Penn, 1682; settled at Phila., Pa.; bought 900 acres nr. Cape Henlopen, Del., 1685; *m* Margaret Hindle.

FISHER, Joshua (1585-1674; brother of Anthony Fisher, qv; son of Anthony, *d* 1640, of "Wignotte," Suffolk, Eng., *m* Mary Fiske); came from Eng., 1640; *m* Elizabeth –.

FISKE, John (ca. 1601-77); A.B., Cambridge U., 1625; from Eng. to Cambridge, Mass., 1637, removed same yr. to Salem; freeman, 1637; teacher; ordained at Wenham, Mass., 1644, later at Chelmsford; *m* in Eng. Ann Gipps (*d* 1672); *m* 2d, 1673, Elizabeth, widow of Edmund Henchman.

FISKE, Nathan (ca. 1615-1676; said to have been son of Nathaniel, of Weybred, Co. Suffolk, Eng., *m* Dorothy Symonds), at Watertown,

Mass., 1642; freeman, 1643; selectman, 1673; m Susanna–.

FISKE, William (1613-54; desc. Symond Fiske, lord of the manor of Stradbaugh), came from Eng. with his brother, Rev. John, and two sisters, to Salem, Mass., 1637, freeman, 1642; settled at Wenham, Mass., 1640, where he was first town clerk, 1643-60; rep. Gen. Ct., 1646, 49, 50, 52; m 1643, Bridget Muskett, of Pelham, Eng.

FITCH, James (1622-1702), from Eng. to Hartford, Conn., 1638; admitted to the ministry at Saybrook, Conn., 1646; removed to Norwich, 1660, to Lebanon, Conn., 1696; chaplain King Philip's War; m 1648, Abigail (d 1659), dau. Rev. Henry Whitfield; m 2d, 1664, Priscilla (b 1641), dau. Maj. John Mason.

FITCH, Thomas (1612-1704), from Eng., 1637; settled at Norwalk, Conn., ca. 1651; freeman, 1657; dep. Gen. Ct., 1654-57; one of the wealthiest men in the colony; commr. for Norwalk, 1670-1674; clk. of Train Band, 1656; m 1632, Anna Stacie (Stacey); m 2d, Ruth Clark.

FITHIAN, William (will dated 1678), from Wales; first appeared at Boston; thence to Lynn and New Haven, Conn., finally settled at East Hampton, L.I., 1639; m Margaret–.

FITZHUGH, William (1651-1701; son of Hon. Henry, of Bedford Co., Eng.); from Eng., 1670, settled at Bedford, on the Rappahannock, Stafford Co., Va.; lt. col. Westmoreland Co., Va., 1683; burgess, 1678-87; col. Stafford Co., 1690; m May 1, 1674, Sarah Tucker (d 1701).

FITZRANDOLPH, see Randolph.

FLAGG (Flegg), Thomas (1616-98), from Eng. in the "Rose," to Boston, 1637; a propr. of Watertown, 1641; in Train Band until 1681; m Mary –.

FLETCHER, Robert (1592-1677), from England, 1630; a founder of Concord, Mass.; a founder of Chelmsford, later at Middletown, Conn.

FLINT, Thomas (1603-63), from Eng. to Boston, 1635; settled at Concord, freeman, 1637; magistrate; rep. Gen. Ct., 1638-41; gov.'s asst., 1642-51, 1653; m Ann –.

FLOOD, John (b ante 1600-d 1661), from Eng. to Va., in the "Swann," 1610; living at "Jordan's Journey," 1624; rep. Gen. Assembly, 1630, 32, 42, 45; Charles City, 1638; capt.: Indian interpreter, for this was allowed 4,000 lbs. of tobacco yearly; lt. col. Surry Co.; mem. legislature, 1652-55; m ante 1624, Widow Margaret Finch, who came in the "Supply," 1620, in which William Tracy brought the immigrants to Berkley Hundred.

FLOURNOY, Jacob (b Jan. 5, 1663; son of Jacques [b 1608], desc. of Laurant Flournoy, fled from Champagne, France, to Geneva, Switzerland, after the massacre of Protestants at Vassay, 1562, m Gabrielle Mellin, of Lyons), from Holland in the "Peter Anthony," 1700; settled nr. Williamsburg, Va.; had plantation at Manakintown, Va., 1704; m 2d. —(d Va.); m 3d, 1701, Madeline (Prodhom) Verreuil, widow of Moise Verreuil, of Rouen.

FLOYD, Richard (ca. 1620-ca. 1700), from Brecknockshire, Wales, 1650; first appears in 1656 as a resident of Setauket, L.I.; judge Suffolk Co.; col. militia; owner of considerable land by purchase and grant; one of 55 original proprs. of Brookhaven, L.I.; m Susannah–(d 1706, aet. 80).

FOLGER, John (1590-1660), from Diss. Co. Norfolk, Eng., 1635; settled at Watertown, Mass.; elder; m Meribeh (d ante 1664), dau. John Gibbs, of Eng.

FOLSOM (Foulsom, Foulsham), John (1615-81), from Eng. in the "Diligent," to Hingham, Mass., 1638; settled at Exeter, N.H., 1655; constable; m 1636, Mary, dau. Edward Gilman.

FOOTE, Nathaniel (1593-1644; son of Robert Foote, of Shalford, m Joane, dau. John Brooke), from Eng. to Watertown, Mass., 1630; freeman, 1634; settled at Wethersfield, Conn., 1636; rep. Gen. Ct., 1641-44; m in Eng., ca. 1615, Elizabeth Deming (ca. 1595-1653), sister of John Deming, one of the first settlers of Wethersfield, Conn. (she m 2d, ca. 1646, Thomas Welles, gov. of Conn.).

FORD, Matthew (b 1661), from Eng., settled at Bradford, Mass.; m 1684, Lydia Griffin (b 1664).

FORD, Thomas (ca. 1587-1676), of Powerstock and Bridport, Co. Dorset, Eng.; came in the

"Mary and John," 1630; settled at Dorchester, Mass.; freeman, 1631; mem. town governing com., 1633; removed to Windsor, Conn., 1637; propr.; dep. Gen. Ct., 1637-40; grand juror, 1643; to Northampton, Mass., ca. 1660 (Judge Henry N. Blake says: "Six Presidents of the United States were descended from Thomas Ford."); m at Powerstock, Co. Dorset, Eng., 1610, Joan Waye (d 1615); m 2d, Bridport, Co. Dorset, Eng., 1616, Elizabeth (Charde) Cooke (d 1643), mother of Maj. Aaron Cooke (qv); m 3d, at Windsor, Conn., 1644, Ann–, widow of Thomas Scott.

FORD, William (1604-76), from Eng. in the "Fortune," to Plymouth, Mass., 1621; was a miller at Duxbury, Mass.; later removed to Marshfield, Mass.; m Anna – (d 1684).

FOSDICK, Stephen (1583-1664), from Eng. to Charlestown, Mass., 1636; freeman, 1638; m 2d, in Eng., Sarah Wetherell.

FOSTER, Christopher (b 1603), from Eng. in the "Abigail," 1635; settled at Lynn, Mass.; a founder and constable; removed to Southampton, 1651; m Frances Stevens (b 1607).

FOSTER, John (b 1626-will proved 1688), from Eng. ca. 1649, settled at Salem, Mass.; m 1649, Martha (b ca. 1630), dau. Ralph Tompkins, m Katharine Aborn.

FOSTER, Reginald (ca. 1595-1681), from Eng. with wife Judith and seven children; settled at Ipswich, Mass., 1638; m 1st Judith-(d 1664); m 2d, 1665, Sarah, widow of John Martin.

FOULKE, Edward (1651-1741; son of Foulke Thomas Lloyd; desc. Edward I, of Eng.), scholar and writer; from Merionethshire, Wales, in the "Robert and Elizabeth," to Phila., Pa., 1698, with 9 children; owned 700 acre estate; a founder of Gwynedd, Pa.; m Eleanor (Hughes), dau. of Hugh Cadwalader Rhys, m Gwenn–.

FOWKE, Gerard (d 1669), gentleman of the bed chamber of Charles I, col. in Royalist Army; came to Va., 1650; merchant and wealthy planter; burgess from Westmoreland Co., Va., 1663; removed to Md.; m 2d, 1661, Anne Chandler.

FOWLER, Capt. Richard (son of Richard, of Northumberland, Eng., m Isabel Mather), of British Army; killed at Battle of Harlem Heights; m Sarah, dau. of Thomas Hunt, of Hunt's Point, N.Y.

FOWLER (Fowle, Fowlar), William (d 1661), from Eng. with Rev. John Davenport, to Boston, 1637; settled at New Haven, Conn., 1638, where he was 1st magistrate, asst., and dep. Gen. Ct.; at Milford, 1661; m Sarah–.

FOX, Thomas (ca. 1620-1658), from Eng. ca. 1640; freeman at Concord. Mass.; m Rebecca – (d 1647); m 2d, 1647, Hannah Brooks (d ca. 1690).

FRANCIS, Richard (1606-87), from Eng. to Dorchester, Mass., 1636, thence to Cambridge; a bricklayer; freeman, 1640; m 1638, Alce or Alice Wilcockes (Wilcox).

FRANCIS, Robert (1629-1712), from Eng., settled at Wethersfield, Conn., 1645; fence viewer; surveyor of highways, 1675; m Joane–(1629-1705).

FREEBORN, William (1594-1670), came to Boston in the "Mary and Francis"; a signer of the Providence Compact, 1636; freeman, 1655; commr., 1657; m Mary –.

FREEMAN, Edmund (b Pulborough, Co. Sussex, Eng., July 25, 1590-d Sandwich, Mass., Nov. 1, 1682), from Pulborough, Co. Sussex, Eng. in the "Abigail," 1635, with wife and four children; settled at Saugus, Mass., where he presented the colony with 20 corslets (armor); moved to Duxbury, 1637, where he was admitted freeman, 1637; was leader of the ten to settle Sandwich, Mass., 1639, and received the largest land grant; dep. Plymouth Colony, 1641; asst. to Gov. Bradford, 1640-47; mem. Council of War, 1642; presiding officer of a court of three "to hear and determine controversies and cawses," and later selected judge; m Elizabeth— (d 1675/1676).

FREEMAN, Henry (1672-1763; son of Joseph, b 1639, m 1666, Elizabeth Gosse), came from Eng. to Phila., and settled at Woodbridge, N.J.; judge Ct. Common Pleas; m in 1695, Elizabeth Bonne, or Bonue.

FREEMAN, Samuel, from Eng., in Winthrop's fleet, to Watertown, Mass., 1630; took oath of allegiance, 1639, and soon after returned to Eng., leaving family in Mass., and d soon after; m Mary –.

FRENCH, Edward (1598-1674), from Eng., with his wife and children, 1636; a founder of Ipswich, Mass., where he was a large landowner; removed to Salisbury, 1640; selectman; *m* Ann (*d* 1683), dau. of Bennett Swayne.

FRENCH, John (1612-92), from Eng. to Dorchester, Mass., 1630; removed to Braintree, 1640, the homestead, acquired 1640, or soon after, is still in the family; *m* Grace – (*d* 1681); *m* 2d, Elinor, dau. Rev. William Thompson, widow of William Veazey.

FRENCH, Thomas (1608-80), from Eng. to Boston, 1631; freeman, 1632; removed to Ipswich, in 1639; *m* Alice –.

FRENCH, William (1603-81), from Eng. in the "Defence," to Cambridge, Mass., 1635; an original propr. of Billerica, Mass., 1652; officer King Philip's War; rep. Gen. Ct.; mem. A. and H. A. Co.; *m* in Eng., Elizabeth Godfrey (1605-68); *m* 2d, 1669, Mary, widow of John Stearns and dau. Thomas Lothrop, of Barnstable.

FRICK, Conrad (*b* 1688, in Switzerland-1761; desc. Heinrich Frick, Zurich, Switzerland; of Celtic-Burgundian ancestry, traced to 1113); came from Rotterdam, in the "Pennsylvania," 1732, to Phila., Pa.; settled at Germantown, Pa.; naturalized 1749; *m* Barbara Enten.

FROST, Edmund (ca. 1610-1672; son of John), came from Eng. in the "Great Hope," to Cambridge, Mass., 1635; freeman, 1636; ruling elder of the Shepard Ch.; *m* Thomasine–; *m* 2d, Mary–; *m* 3d, widow of Robert Daniels.

FROST, Nicholas (1585-1663), from Eng. to Kittery, Me., 1634, where he had a garrison house; *m* 1610, Bertha Cadwalla.

FROTHINGHAM, William (ca. 1600-1651), from Eng. with Gov. Winthrop, 1630, to Mass.; one of original proprs. of Charlestown; took oath of allegiance, 1632; a deacon; *m* Ann–(1607-74).

FRY, Col. Joshua (*d* 1754), prof. William and Mary Coll., Williamsburg, Va., 1728-32; living in Goochland Co. when Albemarle Co. was cut off from Goochland, 1744; commr. Albemarle Co.; justice of the peace; co. lt., Albemarle Co.; presided at the first ct. of the co., 1744; apptd. col. of Va. regt., 1754, by Gov. Dinwiddie, while on way to Ft. Duquesne (now Pittsburgh, Pa.), he fell from his horse at Millis Creek, now Cumberland, Md., where he died; at his death, Lt. Col. George Washington then about 21, succeeded to the command; *m* Mary (Micou) Hill.

FRYE, John (1601-will proved Dec. 3, 1693), came from Basingstoke, Hampshire, Eng., in the "Bevis," 1638; settled at Newbury, Mass., later at Andover; *m* in Eng., Ann–(*d* 1680).

FULLER, Edward (bap. 1575-1621), 21st signer of the Mayflower Compact; *m* Ann – (*d* 1621).

FULLER, John (1611-Feb. 7, 1697/98), came to N.E., ca. 1635; settled at Cambridge Village (now Newton), Mass., ca. 1644; *m* Elizabeth–(*d* 1700).

FULLER, John (1619/20-June 4, 1666). from Eng. in the "Abigail," with his bro., William, 1635; settled at Ipswich, Mass.; removed to Salisbury, but returned to Ipswich, ca. 1648; surveyor, 1663; commr., 1664; *m* Elizabeth, dau. of Roger Fuller; *m* 2d, Elizabeth, dau. of Thomas Emerson (qv).

FULLER, Robert (*d* 1706), from Eng. in the "Bevis," 1638; settled at Salem, Mass.; purchased or held land rights and was propr., Rehoboth, 1645; freeman, 1658; *m* Sarah (*d* 1676), dau. Richard Bowen, from Eng. to Weymouth, Mass., 1640, at Rehoboth, 1643, *m* Elizabeth–.

FULLER, Samuel (*d* 1633), 8th signer of the Mayflower Compact; dea. of the church at Leyden and Plymouth; the first physician among the Pilgrims; asst., 1632; *m* 1st, Alice Glascock (*d* before 1613); *m* 2d, at Leyden, Holland, 1613, Agnes (*d* before 1617), dau. Alexander Carpenter; *m* 3d, at Leyden, 1617, Bridget Lee (*d* 1664).

FULLER, Lt. Thomas (*d* Sept. 28, 1690), from Eng.; at Dedham, Mass., 1642; surveyor, 1650/51; selectman, 1663; rep. Gen. Ct., 1673, 79, 86; commr., 1690; keeper of town's ammunition; *m* Nov. 22, 1643, Hannah Flower (*d* ante 1703).

FULLER, Thomas, of Woburn (1611-June 1698), from Eng.; at Woburn, Mass., 1640; blacksmith; sgt., 1656, lt., 1685; selectman, 1663, 64, 85; removed to Salem, Mass. ca. 1664; *m* 1643, Elizabeth, dau. of John Tidd, of Woburn; *m* 2d, 1684, Sarah (Nutt) Wyman (*d* 1688), dau. of John Nutt; *m* 3d, Harriet (Palmer) Wilson.

GAILLARD, Joachim (*b* 1625), from France upon the revocation of the Edict of Nantes, 1685; was in S.C. by Oct. 10, 1687, when he re-

---

ceived 600 acres in James Town precinct; settled on the Santee River, Craven Co.; *m* 1664, Ester Paparel.

GAINES, Thomas (son of Sir John, 1559-1606), came from Co. Brecon, Wales, ante 1650; settled in Va.

GALE, Edmond (*d* 1642), from Eng. to Newtown, Mass., ca. 1630.

GALLATIN, Albert (1761-1849), grad. U. of Geneva, 1779; came from Switzerland to Boston, 1780; served in Am. Rev.; purchased land in Fayette Co., Va., 1785, which later was included in boundary of Pa.; mem. Constl. Conv. of Pa., 1789, Ho. of Rep., 1790-92; elected to U.S. Senate, but was not seated; mem. 4th, 5th and 6th Congresses, 1795-1801; Sec. of the Treas., 1802-14, in Cabinets of Presidents Jefferson and Madison; minister to France, 1815-23, to Great Britain, 1826-27; *m* Hannah, dau. Commodore James Nicholson, U.S.N.

GALLUP (Gallop), John (1590-1650), from Eng. in the "Mary and John," arriving at Nantascot (changed to Hull, 1646), 1630; admitted freeman at Boston, 1634; *m* Crestabel –, who followed him to America with four children in the "Griffin," 1633.

GANO (Gerneaux), Francis (1620-1723), Huguenot; from the Island of Guernsey, France; was at New Rochelle, N.Y., 1661.

GARDINER (Gardner), George (1600-77; son of Rev. Michael Gardiner, rector of Holy Cross Ch., Greenford Magna); from Eng. in the "Fellowship," 1637; at Aquidneck, R.I., 1638; freeman, 1639; constable, 1642; commr., 1644; *m* 1630, Sara Slaughter; *m* 2d, ca. 1640, Herodias, or Horod (Long) Hicks; *m* 3d, Lydia Ballou.

GARDINER, Lion (ca. 1599-1663), officer English army, came from Holland in the "Bachilor" of only 35 tons, to Boston, 1635; settled at Saybrook, Conn.; built and commanded the fort at Saybrook during Pequot War; later at Easthampton, L.I.; 1st lord of the manor of Gardiner's Island, 1640; *m* in Holland, Mary Wilemson Deurcant.

GARDINER, Joseph (1601-79; son of Sir Thomas, Kt.), from Eng. to Newport, R.I., bet. 1635-40.

GARDNER, Thomas (1592-1674 or 77), from Eng. in the "Charity," to Cape Ann, Mass., as head of the Dorchester Co., 1624; removed to Salem, 1626; freeman, 1637; rep. Gen. Ct., 1637; capt. Train Band; *m* Margaret Tryer (or Fryer).

GARFIELD, Edward (*d* 1672, aet. 97), from Eng., ca. 1630; settled at Watertown, Mass.; had son Edward (1605-June 14, 1672), freeman, 1635, selectman, 1635, 55, 62; propr., *m* Rebecca- (*d* 1654, aet. 55), *m* 2d, 1661, Johannah Buckminster (will proved 1676), widow of Thomas Buckminster.

GARLAND, Peter, from Eng. to Charlestown, Mass., 1634; mariner; *m* Elizabeth–(1599-1687).

GARLAND, Peter, of the Sussex branch of the family in Eng.; came to Va., 1650; settled in York Co.

GARY, Charles, from Va. to S.C., name 1st appears in land grants in Newberry Co., 1767; planter; soldier Am. Rev.; *m* Elizabeth –.

GASSAWAY, Col. Nicholas (ca. 1619-1961/92; son of Thomas, of St.Margaret's Parish, Westminster, Eng., *m* 1631, Ann Callendgwood, or Collingwood); to Anne Arundel Co., Md., 1650; in mil. service, 1669, capt. 1678, maj. 1681, col. 1690; asst. cdr. of rangers, 1691; gentleman justice, 1679, et seq.; justice of the Quorum, 1685, of Superior Ct., 1691; mem. commn. to establish the ports of entry, 1683; mem. Grand Com. apptd. to govern Md., 1690; *m* Ann, dau. of Capt. Thomas Besson.

GATES, George (ca. 1634-1724), a Puritan, from Eng. to Hartford, Conn., ca. 1651; an original propr. of Haddam, 1661; rep. Gen. Ct., 1668-73; capt. colonial forces; *m* Sarah, dau. Nicholas Olmsted.

GATES, Stephen (*d* 1662; son of Thomas), from Norwich, Co. Norfolk, Eng., in the "Diligent," 1638; settled at Hingham, Mass.; a founder of Lancaster, 1654; *m* Anne Hill (*d* 1682/83; she *m* 2d, 1663, Richard Woodward, qv).

GAY, John (*d* 1688), from Eng. in the "Mary and John," to Watertown, Mass., 1630; freeman, 1635; a founder of Dedham, 1636; selectman; *m*

Joanna– (d 1691·), called "Widow Joanna Bald-wicke."

GAYLE (Gale), George (1670-1712; son of John, and desc. of James Gale, seated at Thirntoft, Yorkshire, Eng., 1523), came from Eng.; settled at Somerset, Md., 1690; m ca. 1700, Mildred (Warner) Washington (d 1701), g. mother of Gen. George Washington; m 2d, Elizabeth (d ca. 1736), dau. Levin Denwood, g. dau. Levyne Denwood, early settler on Eastern Shore of Va., 1633, justice and commr. of Northampton, Va., 1654.

GAYLORD, Dea. William (1585-1673), from Eng. in the "Mary and John," with his brother John, to Dorchester, Mass., 1630; freeman, 1630; signed first land grants at Dorchester, his own grant being dated 1633; selectman; rep. Gen. Ct.; removed to Windsor, Conn., which town he represented in the Gen. Assembly nearly 40 sessions; m Sara – (d 1657).

GEER (Geare, Gears, Gere), Thomas (1623-1722; 6th from Walter Geere, b 1450, of Heavitree, Exeter), from Eng. to Boston, 1635; settled at Enfield, Conn., ca. 1682; m Deborah Davis.

GEORGE, John (1604-78), from Eng., 1632; settled in Charles City Co., Va.; burgess, 1647-48, 52; mem. Council; maj., lt. col. and col. in command of Isle of Wight forces against the Indians; cdr. Elizabeth City Co. forces; m ante 1632, Jane–.

GERE (Geer, Gear), George (ca. 1621-1726, aet. 105; son of Jonathan, of Hewitree, Co. Devon, Eng.), from Eng. to Boston, 1635; settled at New London, Conn., 1651; soldier Pequot War; later at Preston, Conn.; m Feb. 17, 1658/59, Sarah (1642-post 1723), dau. of Robert Allyn (qv).

GERRISH, William (ca. 1617-1687), settled at Newbury, Mass., 1639; removed to Boston, 1678; capt., Newbury mil. company and cdr. of garrison there; capt. in King Philip's War; dep. Gen. Ct., 1650, et seq.; m 1645, Joan (d 1677), dau. of Percival Lowell (qv), and widow of John Oliver.

GEST, Henry (b 1658; desc. John Geste or Ghest, of Handsworth, nr. Birmingham, Eng.), from Eng. in the "Delaware," to Chester, Pa., 1686; m Mary –.

GIBSON, John (1601-94), early settler at Cambridge, Mass., 1635; Cambridge records show he owned many acres of land; planted linden trees; mentioned in Longfellow's "The Open Window"; m Rebecca–(d 1661); m 2d, 1662, Joanna– widow of Henry Prentice, of Cambridge.

GIFFORD, William (d Apr. 16, 1687), Quaker; from Eng. ante 1647; believed to have first emigrated to a southern port and afterward went north; before Stamford, Conn., Ct., ca. 1647, sentenced to be whipped, banished; earliest record at Sandwich, Mass., 1650; a propr. Monmouth, N.J., resided there, 1665-70; m 2d, July 16, 1683, Mary Miles (d Feb. 10, 1734).

GILBERT, Jonathan (1618-82; son of Thomas, qv), came from Eng. to Boston, 1635; was at Hartford, Conn., 1640, later at New Haven; innkeeper; was marshal Gen. Assembly; collector of customs; dep. Gen. Ct.; commr. United Colonies; m 1646, Mary (d 1650), dau. of Elder John White (or Whight); m 2d, 1650, Mary (d 1700), dau. of Hugh Welles and sister of Thomas Welles, of Hadley.

GILBERT, Dep. Gov. Matthew (1599-1679-80), from Eng. to Colony of Mass. Bay, ca. 1628; settled at New Haven, Conn.; one of 7 founders of the civil court, New Haven, 1639; one of 7 founders of First Ch. of Christ, New Haven, 1639; later dea.; judge of N.H. Colony, 1639-43, and of N.H. as part of Conn. Colony, 1665-71; dep. gov., N.H. Colony, 1661-63; provisional asst., Conn. Colony, 1664, and asst. (senator) Conn. Colony Gen. Ct., 1677; owned 600 acres; m Jane Baker (d 1706).

GILBERT, Thomas (1582-1659), from Eng. to Braintree, Mass.; granted land, 1639/40; removed to Windsor, Conn., ca. 1644; to Wethersfield, post 1654; m ca. 1615, Lydia–(d prob. 1654/55).

GILBERT, Thomas (d 1662; son of Thomas, qv), from Eng., 1635; received land grants at Springfield, Mass., 1655; selectman, 1660; m 1655, Catherine (Chapin) Bliss (d 1712), dau. Dea. Samuel Chapin (qv).

GILDERSLEEVE, Richard (1601-80), from Eng., 1635; propr. Wethersfield and Glastonbury, Conn., 1636, New Haven Colony, 1639, Stamford, Conn., 1641, Hempstead, L.I., 1644,

Newtown, L.I., 1652-59; dep. New Haven Ct.; magistrate; colonial commr. for Conn., 1664; constable of Hempstead under the Dukes laws, and surveyor; m Joanna Appleton (b 1601).

GILES, Edward (d 1650), from Wiltshire, Eng., to Salem, Mass., ca. 1633; freeman, 1634; m 1636, Bridget Very, a widow (will proved 1680).

GILLETTE (Gillet, Gillett), Jonathan (d 1677), from Eng. in the "Mary and John," with his wife and three children and his brother, Nathan, to Dorchester, Mass., 1630; freeman at Dorchester, 1635; removed to Windsor, Conn., 1636; constable, 1656; m 1634, Mary (1607-85), dau. of Rawkey or Rockey Dolbere, m Mary Mitchell.

GILMAN, Edward (1587-1681), from Eng. in the "Diligent," with his wife, five children and three servants, to Hingham, Mass., 1638; freeman same yr.; removed to Rehoboth, 1643; thence to Ipswich; settled at Exeter, N.H., 1652; m 1614, Mary Clark.

GILPIN, Joseph (1664-1741; son of Thomas Gilpin, col. in Cromwell's army and later became a Quaker; desc. Richard de Gaylpyn, 1206), from Eng. to Chester Co., Pa., 1696; m 1691/92. Hannah Glover.

GIST, Christopher (1655-91), from Eng. ante 1679; settled on the south side of the Patapsco River, Baltimore Co., Md.; mem. Grand Jury, 1682; justice, 1689; m ante 1679, Edith Cromwell (1660-94), sis. of William, John and Richard Cromwell, of Md. (she m 2d, Joseph Williams, and 3d, John Beecher).

GLIDDEN, Charles (ca. 1632-post 1707), from Eng. to Portsmouth, N.H., ca. 1660; took oath of fidelity at Exeter, 1677; granted land at Newmarket, N.H., 1697; m 1658, Eunice Shore (1640-1707).

GLOVER, Henry (1603-50; son of Thomas, m Margaret Deane), from Eng., 1640, to Medfield, Mass.; settled at Dedham, on grants given by King; m Abigail–.

GLOVER, John (1600-54; son of Thomas, of Rainhill Parish, Prescot, Co. Lancaster, Eng., m Margery Deane), mem. London Company, 1628; capt. of A. and H. A. Co. of London; from Eng. in the "Mary and John," 1630, to Nantasket; an incorporator of Dorchester, 1631; set up the first tannery in the colony; selectman, 1636-50; rep. Gen. Ct., 1636-52; asst., 1652-54; to Boston, 1650; mem. com. that examined and censured a work written by Col. William Pynchon; called "The Worshipful Mr. Glover"; m ca. 1625, Anna–.

GODDARD (Godard), William (1627-91; son of Gen. Edward, of Norfolkshire), from Eng. to Watertown, Mass., 1665; schoolmaster; soldier King Philip's War; m Elizabeth (d 1697), dau. Benjamin Miles.

GODFREY, Richard (1631-91), settled at Taunton, Mass., 1652; m Jane, dau. of John Turner.

GOFORTH, Aaron (d 1736), Quaker; from Eng. to Phila., Pa., 1711; m 2d, Tabitha Bethell (d 1721/22).

GOLD, Nathan, see Gould.

GOLDSBOROUGH, Nicholas (1639-70), from Malcolm Regis, nr. Weymouth, Dorsetshire, Eng., to Barbados, thence to America, 1670, settled at Kent Island, Md.; m ca. 1659, Margaret, dau. Abram Howes, of Eng.

GOLDTHWAITE, Thomas (1610-83), a cooper; from Yorkshire, Eng., 1630, settled at Salem, Mass.; m 1636, Elizabeth–; m 2d, 1671, Rachel, dau. of Lawrence Leach (qv).

GOODALE, Robert (1604-83), from Eng. in the "Elizabeth," 1634; was at Salem. Mass., 1634; propr., 1636; m Katherine– (b 1606).

GOODHUE, William (1612/13-1699), from Eng. aet. 24, settled at Ipswich, Mass.; deacon; moderator; selectman; rep. in Colonial Assembly; m 1634, Marjory Watson (d 1668); m 2d, Mary Webb, a widow; m 3d, Bethial–, widow of Joseph Grafton; m 4th, Remember Fisk.

GOODLOE, George (1639-1710), from Eng., ca. 1666; settled in Middlesex Co., Va.; mem. co. militia, 1687; landowner; m Mary–.

GOODRICH (Goodridge), William (1605-1647/48), from Eng. ca. 1635, settled at Watertown, Mass., 1636; m 1631, Margaret Butterfield (d 1682/83).

GOODRICH, William (d 1676; son of William, m Margery –); from Eng. ca. 1636; was at Wethersfield, Conn., 1643; ensign; dep. Gen. Ct., 1660-66; m 1648, Sarah (1631-1702), dau. of Matthew Marvin (qv).

GOODWIN, Christopher (prob. a son of Daniel, *m* Dorothy Barker), from Eng., 1647, settled at Charlestown, Mass.; *m* Mary–(*d* 1683).

GOODWIN, Ozias (1596-1683), from Eng. in the "Lion," to Newtown, Mass., 1632; one of first settlers of Hartford, Conn., 1636; *m* in Eng., Mary Woodward.

GOODYEAR, Stephen (1600-58), from Eng. to New Haven Colony, 1638; dep. gov., 1643-58; commr. for United Colonies, 1643, 46; lost at sea on return to Eng.; *m* Margaret –, widow of Capt. George Lamberton.

GOOKIN, Daniel (1612-87), from Eng., to Va., thence to Boston, Mass., 1644; resided at Roxbury and Cambridge; capt., 1648; maj. gen. Mass. forces, 1681; dep. Gen. Ct., 1649-51; speaker, 1651; gov.'s asst., 1652-86; commr. to the Indians, 1656; *m* 1639, Mary Dalling.

GORDON, James (ca. 1714-1768), from Ireland, with his brother, John, to Merry Pt., Lancaster Co., Va., before 1738; *m* Mary, dau. Col. Nathaniel Harrison.

GORDON, John (*d* 1780), from Ireland with his brother James, ca. 1738, settled in Lancaster Co., Va., later in Middlesex and Richmond counties; tobacco merchant; justice; *m* 1756, Lucy, dau. Col. Armistead Churchill.

GORE, John (*d* 1657 Roxbury), probably from Waltham Abbey, Essex, Eng., with wife, to Boston, 1635, settling in Roxbury as a freeman; *m* Rhoda Gardner.

GORHAM (Gorum), John (1621-1675/76; son of Ralph, who came from Eng., 1635, but returned to Eng.), was landowner at Yarmouth; resided at Barnstable and Plymouth, Mass.; capt. 2d Barnstable company in Great Swamp Fight, King Philip's War, 1675; *m* 1643, Desire (*d* 1683), dau. of John Howland (qv).

GORTON, Samuel (1592-1677), from Eng. to Boston, 1636; removed to Plymouth, Mass.; to R.I., 1638; settled at Warwick, R.I., 1641; dep. Gen. Ct., 1651, et seq.; commr. to Narraganset Indians; was a zealous religionist and co-worker with Roger Williams; sponsored adoption of "Emancipation of Slavery," 1651; *m* in Eng., Lady Mary Maplet.

GOULD, John, from Eng., 1664; landowner, Southampton, L.I., 1686; was at Elizabeth, N.J., 1690; *m* Sarah Axtell.

GOULD (Gold), Nathan (*d* 1694), from Eng. ca. 1643; settled at Milford, Conn., 1647, Fairfield, 1650; asst., 1657, 62, 94; mem. Gov.'s Council; rep. in 1st Colonial Congress in N.Y., 1690; mem. Com. of Defense against the Dutch, 1662; maj. of dragoons, 1675; *m* Martha–, widow of Edmund Harvey.

GOULD, Zaccheus (1589-1668; 6th from Thomas Gould of Boringdon, Co. Bucks, Eng.); early settler of Topsfield, Mass.; *m* Phebe Deacon.

GRAHAM, John (1694-1774), from Scotland to Boston, 1718; settled at Exeter, N.H.; chaplain Crown Point expdn.; *m* Abigail Chauncy.

GRANGER, Launcelot (1624-89), from Eng. to Ipswich, Mass., 1648; to Newbury, thence to Suffield, Conn., 1674; soldier in King Philip's War; *m* 1654, Joanna (1634-1701), dau. Robert Adams (qv).

GRANT, Matthew (1601-81), from Eng. in the "Mary and John," to Dorchester, Mass., 1630; freeman, 1631; a founder of Windsor, Conn., 1636; where he was town clerk and surveyor many yrs.; *m* 1625, Priscilla Grey (1601-44); *m* 2d, 1645, Susanna (1602-1665/66), dau. William Rockwell.

GRANT, Peter (*d* bet. 1709-12), Eng. to Nantasket, Mass.; charter mem. "Scots Charitable Soc. of Boston," 1657; to York Co., Me., and purchased land at Kittery, 1659; had grant of 120 acres nr. York Pond, 1674; *m* ca. 1664, Joan–, widow of his bro., James.

GRAY, Robert (1634-1718), from Eng., 1658, settled at Andover, Mass., 1659; *m* 1669, Hannah Holt.

GREELEY (Greele, Grele), Andrew (ca. 1617-1697), from Eng., ca. 1638; an original propr. of Salisbury, Mass.; at Haverhill, 1669; *m* Mary, dau. Joseph Moyse.

GREEN, James (ca. 1610-1687), from Eng. ca. 1634; freeman at Charlestown, Mass., 1647; *m* ca. 1638, Elizabeth (*d* 1687), dau. of Robert Newman, of Co. Kent, Eng.

GREEN (Greene), John (*b* 1606), from Enfield, Eng., 1635/36, settled at Quidnessett, R.I.; *m* 1642, Mrs. Joan Beggarly.

GREEN (Greene), Capt. Robert (1695-1748), from "Green's Norton," Northamptonshire, Eng., to Va. with his uncle, Sir William Duff, whose heir he became; settled in King Co., 1712; with uncle and Joist Hite held patent for 120,000 acres; settled finally in Culpeper Co.; burgess, 1736; capt. Orange Co. militia; vestryman St. Mark's Parish, 1731; *m* Eleanor Dunn.

GREEN (Greene), Thomas (1600-67), from Eng. to Lynn, Mass., 1635; later at Ipswich, Mass., and Malden, 1638; *m* Elizabeth (*d* 1658); *m* 2d, 1659, Frances –, widow of Richard Cook.

GREENBERRY, Col. Nicholas (ca. 1627-1697, aet. 70), came to Md. in the "Constant Friendship," 1674; settled at Greenberry's Point, Anne Arundel Co., Md.; mem. Council of Sir Lionel Copley; acting gov. Province of Md., 1693; chancellor and keeper of the great seal, 1692-94; *m* Anne – (1648-98).

GREENE, "Surgeon John" (1597-1658), from Eng. in the "James," to Boston, 1635; a founder with Roger Williams of Providence Plantations where he lived until 1643; with twelve other men purchased Narragansett from the Indians; a founder of Warwick, 1643; magistrate, dep., commr., etc.; *m* in Eng., 1619, Joanna Tattershall; *m* 2d, Alice Daniels; *m* 3d, Philippa – (*d* 1687, aet. 87).

GREENLEAF, Edmond (1573-1671), from Eng., 1635; capt. Indian wars; overseer of "collection of arms"; settled at Newbury, Mass., 1639; removed to Boston, 1650; *m* Sarah Dole (*d* 1663).

GREENOUGH, William (1641-93), from Eng. to Boston, and established a ship yard there; freeman, 1673; ensign A. and H. A. Co.; capt. King Philip's War; *m* Ruth, dau. Thomas Swift, of Dorchester; *m* 2d, Elizabeth (*d* 1688), dau. Elder Edward Rainsford; *m* 3d, 1688, Sarah Shobe, of Chelmsford.

GREGG, James (1678-1735), from Scotland to Ireland, 1690; came to Londonderry, N.H., 1718, a founder of that town; cdr. of company during war with eastern Indians, 1719; mem. N.H Assembly; *m* Janet Cargill (?).

GREGORY, Henry (*b* ca. 1570-*d* ante 1655) from Eng. to Boston, 1633; later at Springfield a founder of Stratford, Conn.

GRESHAM, Edward (son of Sir Thomas Gresham, Kt., seated at Tetsey, *m* Mary, dau of John Lennard, or Leonard); to Va. ca. 1650, located in New Kent Co.; ancestor of the Va Greshams; purchased abt. 500 acres of land which had been patented by Robert Joanes, 1658, which patent was renewed by patent direct to Edward Gresham, issued by Sir William Berkeley, Mar. 18, 1662; received grant from Gov. Berkeley of 111 acres in New Kent adjoining above grant, June 10, 1675; was granted 640 acres in New Kent, same locality, 1690.

GRIDLEY, Thomas (1620-ca. 1655), from Co. Essex, Eng., to Boston; to Hartford, Conn., 1636; at Windsor, 1637, 39, again at Hartford, 1637; served in Pequot War; original propr. of Northampton, Mass., 1653; *m* 1644, Mary D. Seymour (ca. 1622-1689).

GRIFFEN, Edward (1602-living at Flushing, L.I., 1698), sailed in the "Abraham," from London, Oct. 24, 1635, and settled on Palmer's Island, Va. (now Md.); thence to New Amsterdam, 1640; overseer of Flushing, 1680; *m* Mary– (living in 1698).

GRIFFIN, Jasper (1648-1718), from Wales to Southold, L.I., ca. 1675; maj. provincial militia: *m* Hannah –.

GRIFFIN, Matthew, from Eng., was at Saybrook, Conn., 1645; fortified same; served in King Philip's War; *m* at Charlestown, Mass., Aug. 29, 1654, Hannah (*b* 1636?-*d* Dec. 2, 1674), dau. of Robert Cutler, landed 1637, *m* Rebecca –.

GRIMBALL, Paul (*d* ante 1696), from Eng., 1682, with a communication from the Lords Proprs. containing among other things a commn. to grant 3,000 acres to "Mr. Paul Grimball, merchant, bound for Ashley River to settle there"; mem. Council: sec. of the Province, 1683; receiver gen. and escheator of the Province, 1688, and surveyor gen.; built his home on Edisto Island, where he lived until his death; *m* Mary Stoney (*d* bet. 1711-20).

GRINNELL, Matthew (*b* 1602; desc. Pierre Grinnell, 1480, Duchy of Bourgogne, France), a Huguenot refugee from France ca. 1630; freeman at Newport, R.I., 1638; removed to Portsmouth, 1655; m Rose –.

GRISWOLD, Edward (1607-91), from Eng., 1639; a founder of Windsor, Conn.; later settled at Killingworth; was dep. Gen. Ct., justice, deacon; built "Old Fort," at Springfield; rep. Gen. Assembly, 1658-61; m 1630, Margaret (d 1670), dau. of John Diamond; m 2d, 1672, Sarah Bevius, widow, of New London, Conn.

GRISWOLD, Matthew (1620-1698/99), from Eng. to Windsor, Conn., 1639; removed to Saybrook, 1644; a settler of Lyme; magistrate, dep., etc.; m 1646, Anne, dau. Henry Wolcott.

GRISWOLD, Michael (1597-1678; son of George. Kenilworth, Co. Warwick, Eng.), from Eng. to Wethersfield, Conn.; freeman, 1659; m Anne–.

GROVER, James, Sr. (d 1686), presumed to have gone from N.E. to Gravesend, L.I., 1648; set up the standard of Eng. at Gravesend, which was under Dutch rule, Mar. 9, 1655; sent to Oliver Cromwell, with letters, 1655, returning with a letter from Cromwell to the English inhabitants of L.I., 1657; grantee of Monmouth (N.J.) patent, 1663; lt. of 1st co. of militia in N.J., Dec. 1, 1663; mem. court at Portland Point, July 16, 1670; justice at Shrewsbury and Middletown, 1676; burgess for Middletown in first Assembly, 1668; dep. to treat with admirals and commanders of fleet of the States-General, 1673; m Rebecca –.

GRUBB, John (1652-1708; son of John, royalist), from Eng. to Burlington, West Jersey, 1677; settled at Grubbs Landing (now New Castle Co., Del.), Pa., 1682, later at Marcus Hook, Pa.; j.p.; mem. Council of Del. and twice mem. Pa. Assembly; m Frances (Vane?).

GRYMES, Rev. Charles (b 1612-d ca. 1661), had a parish in York Co., Va., 1644; large landowner in Northern Neck of Va.

GUILD (Guile), John (1612-72), one of the founders of Dedham, Mass., 1636; freeman, 1640; soldier King Philip's War; m 1645, Elizabeth Crooke (d 1669).

GULICK (Gullick), Joachim (will dated 1711), from Holland to Gravesend, L.I., 1653; patentee, 1670; overseer, 1680; ensign, 1689; settled at Six Mile Run, N.J., 1717; m ca. 1676, Jacomyntie, or Magdalena, dau. Teunis Van Pelt, from Holland in the "Rosetree," 1663.

GUNN, Dr. Jasper (1606-71), from the Highlands of Scotland in the "Defense," 1635; settled at Roxbury, Conn.; removed to Milford, Conn.; at Hartford, Conn., 1648; deacon, schoolmaster, atty. at Milford.

GUSTINE (Augustine Jean), John (1647-1719; son of Edmond Jean de le Tacq, dau. of Jean Le Rossignol); came from Isle of Jersey, 1675; at Falmouth (now Portland), Me.; sgt. King Philip's War; received grant of land from Thomas Danforth, gov. of Me., belonging to Mass. Bay Colony; m 1677, Elizabeth (b 1657), dau. John Browne (qv).

HACKETT, Capt. William (1635-1713), from Eng., commanded the "Endeavor," from Salisbury, Mass., on voyage to New York, 1671, the first time any ship had been a commercial carrier between the two ports; m 1666, Sarah, dau. of Thomas Barnard.

HAINES, see also Haynes.

HAINES, Richard (d 1682), from Eng., 1682, d on the voyage; his wife, Margaret, settled on Rancocus Creek, nr. Lumberton, Burlington Co., N.J.

HAIRSTON, Peter (1700?-1760?), officer in the army of Charles Edward Stuart, the Pretender; after the disastrous battle of Drummassie Moore (Culloden), where his son Peter was lost, he, then a widower, fled to Va., 1747, with 5 children, a man of means, he purchased large estates in Bedford, and nearby counties, Va.; his sons served in the House of Burgesses and as officers in colonial wars; two g.sons and one g.son-in-law were officers in Am. Rev.; wife was a dau. of an Irish gentleman, name now unknown.

HALE, Robert (d 1659), Puritan; from Eng. to Boston, 1630; joined the first church at Charlestown, 1632; mem. A. and H. A. Co.; surveyor; m Jane Cutter.

HALE, Samuel (1610-93), from Eng., was at Hartford, Conn., 1640, removed to Wethersfield; one of first proprs. of Norwalk, 1654; finally at what is now Glastonbury; served in Pequot

War, 1637; rep. Gen. Ct., for Norwalk, 1657 and later; m Mary Welles.

HALE, Thomas (1604-82), from Eng. to Newbury, Mass., 1634; freeman, 1638; removed to Haverhill, 1649; selectman there; later again at Newbury; resident of Salem, 1659; sgt. of militia; m in Eng., Thomasin Dowsett; m 2d, Margaret, dau. Sir Henry Tamorin.

HALL, John (1584-1673), from Eng., 1633, to Boston; settled at Cambridge; removed to Roxbury, 1634-39, to Hartford, 1640, Middletown, Conn., 1650; m Esther–.

HALL, John (1606-76), from Eng. to Boston, 1633, thence to Hartford, Conn.; at New Haven, 1639; a founder of Wallingford; soldier in Pequot War; dep. Gen. Ct., Conn., 1653-61; m Jane Wallen.

HALL, John (d 1696), from Eng. to Charlestown, Mass., 1630; m Bethia–.

HALL, Samuel (1648-1725), of New Haven, Conn.; King Philip's War; dep. Gen. Ct., 1698-1700; capt. Train Band, 1704; m Hannah Walker (1646-1728).

HALLETT, William (1616-1706?), from Dorsetshire, Eng., to Greenwich, Conn., ante 1647, thence to Hellgate, L.I., N.Y.; home and plantation at Hallett's Cove destroyed by Indians, 1655; to Flushing; sheriff, 1656; fined and imprisoned by Gov. Stuyvesant for religious tolerance; del. to Gen. Ct. of Conn.; commr. for Flushing; returned to Hellgate, L.I.; m—; m 2d, ca. 1647, Elizabeth (Fones) Feake (d 1673), dau. of Thomas Fones, and divorced wife of Robert Feake.

HALLOCK, Peter (b ca. 1590), "The Pilgrim"; from Eng. with Rev. Young and others, 1640; settled at Southold, L.I.; original purchaser of "Oyster Pond," now Orient; went back to Eng. but returned to America and settled at Mattituck, L.I.; m 1st, —(d in Eng.); m 2d, Widow Howell.

HALLOWELL, John (b 1647), a Quaker, from Eng. to Darby, Pa., 1682; removed to Abington, Pa.; m Mary, dau. Thomas Sharpe.

HALSEY, Thomas (1592-1678; son of Robert Halsey, d 1618, m Dorothy Downes), from Eng., settled at Lynn, Mass., 1637, where he owned 100 acres of land; a founder of Southampton, L.I., 1640; marshal, 1646; dep. Hartford Gen. Ct., 1664; adj. Train Band, 1650; m before 1627, Phoebe – (killed by two Pequot Indians, 1649); m 2d, 1660, Ann –, widow of Edward Johnes.

HAMLIN, Giles (1622-89), a sea captain for 50 yrs., came from Eng. to Middletown, Conn., 1654; was commr. for the United Colonies, 1666; dep. Gen. Ct., 1666-68, 1670-84; asst., 1685, 87, 89; m 1655, Hester, dau. John Crow, of Hartford.

HAMLIN (Hamblen), James (1606-1690), Huguenot from Eng. to Barnstable, Mass., ca. 1639; m 1628, Anne –.

HAMMOND, John (1643-1707), from Isle of Wight, to Annapolis, Md., 1685; burgess, 1692; judge High Ct. of Admiralty; col. forces of Anne Arundel Co., 1699; maj. gen. of Western Shore, 1707; m Mary Howard.

HAMMOND, Thomas (1603-75; son of William Hamonde, supervisor Manor of Melford, 1587; g. son of John Hamonde of Lavenham, will proved 1551), from Melford, Eng., ante 1636, settled at Hingham, Mass.; received land grant, 1636; mem. grand jury, 1637; freeman, 1636/37; to Cambridge Village (now Newton), ca. 1650; m 1623, Elizabeth (b ante 1604), dau. Robert Cason, of Eng., who m Prudence, dau. Robert Hammond, of Great Whelnetham, Eng.

HAMPTON, William (1586-1652), from London, Eng., to Va. in the "Bona Nova," 1621; settled first nr. old Point Comfort; planter; established "Hampfield," Gloucester Co., Va., 1652; m Joan – (b 1596), who came with their three children in the "Abigail," to Va., 1621.

HAND, John (1611-63), from Eng. ca. 1636; settled first at Lynn, Mass.; moved to Southampton, L.I., 1644; one of nine founders of East Hampton, 1648; magistrate, 1657-60; m Alice Stanborough, sister of Josiah Stanborough.

HANFORD (Handford), Rev. Thomas (1621-93; son of Eylin [Hatherly] Hanford [b 1588], as widow came from Fremington, Co. Devon, Eng., in the "Planter," 1635, and settled at Scituate, Mass.), from Eng. to Scituate, Mass.; freeman, 1650; ordained at Norwalk, Conn., 1652; m 1652, Hannah Newberry, of Windsor, Conn.; m 2d, 1661, Mary (Miles) Ince, dau. Hon. Richard Miles, and widow of Jonathan Ince.

HANSON, John (1630-will dated Dec. 12, 1713), with his 3 bros. was sent by Gustavus Adolphus, of Sweden, under Lt. Col. Johann Printz, to found a colony in America; landed at Fort Christiana, Delaware River (New Sweden), Feb. 15, 1643; to Kent Co., Md., 1653; later to St. Marys Co., Md.; to Charles Co., ca. 1656; *m* Mary, dau. Thomas Hussey.

HANSON, Thomas (*d* 1666), from Eng., was at Dover, N.H., before 1643.

HAPGOOD, Shadrach (1642-75), from Eng. in the "Speedwell," to Sudbury, Mass., 1656; killed in King Philip's War; *m* 1664, Elizabeth, dau. Nathaniel Treadway.

HARDENBERGH (Van Hardenbergh), Jan (*d* ca. 1659), from Holland to New Amsterdam ca. 1640, where he was a large land holder.

HARDING, Abraham (1605-55), from Eng. to Plymouth Colony, 1623; was at Dedham, 1638; settled at Braintree, 1642; *m* Elizabeth Harding.

HARDING, Richard (ca. 1585-ca. 1657), one of 3 bros. who came from Northampton, Eng., 1623; settled at Braintree at Weymouth; freeman, 1640; *m* 2d, 1630, Elizabeth Adams.

HARDY, George (1633-93), from Eng. to Isle of Wight Co., Va., ca. 1660; burgess, 1642-52; *m* Mary Jackson.

HARDY, John (1613-70), from Eng. to Va.; owner of the famous Hardy Mill; said to have been burgess, 1641-52; granted 1,150 acres in Isle of Wight Co., 1666; Olive Council (*d* post 1670).

HARLOW, Sgt. William (1624-91), from Eng. to Plymouth, Mass.; built house, 1677, from remnants of Pilgrim's fort, which is still standing, lt. gov. of Plymouth under Gov. Winslow; rep. Gen. Ct., 1673-75; selectman, 1666-91; *m* 1649, Rebecca, dau. Robert Bartlett (qv); *m* 2d, Mary, dau. of John Faunce, came in the "Anne," 1623, *m* Patience, dau. of George Morton (qv); *m* 3d, 1665, Mary Shelley.

HARMON, John (1617-1660/61; son of Francis); from Eng. to Boston, ca. 1636; resided at Roxbury; a settler at Springfield, Mass., 1644; constable; road supervisor; *m* 1640, Elizabeth – (*d* 1699), she *m* 2d, Anthony Dorchester.

HARRINGTON, Robert (1616-1707), from Eng. in the "Elizabeth," to Watertown, Mass., 1642-44; owned property at Watertown, Mass., 1642-44; freeman, 1663; selectman, 1697, 1681-83, 85, 1691-1700; *m* 1649, Susanna George (1632-94).

HARRIS, Capt. Thomas (1573 or 76-1658), from Wales, in the "Prosperous," 1611, settled in (now) Henrico Co., Va.; 2d in command in Indian wars; burgess, 1623-24, 1639-47; *m* Adria (*b* 1601), dau. Lt. Col. Thomas Osborne, came in the "Marmaduke," to Va. with Harris, first in command in Indian wars, 1621, burgess from Henrico Co., 1629-30, 1631-33.

HARRIS, Thomas (1600-86), from Eng. to Charlestown, Mass., 1630; signer of Providence Plantations Compact, 1637; served as dep. Gen. Assembly, gov.'s asst. and commr.; patentee in charter of King Charles, II, to R.I., 1663; *m* Elizabeth–(1576-1669).

HARRIS, Walter (*d* 1654), to Boston, 1632; freeman, 1641; at New London, 1652; *m* Mary Fry (*d* 1655).

HARRISON, Benjamin (ca. 1600-1648/49), from Eng. to Surry Co., Va., 1631; clk. of Council of Va., 1636-40; burgess, 1642.

HARRISON, Burr (1636-1706; son of Cuthbert), from Eng. to Va. ante 1670; sent by the House of Burgesses on a dangerous mission to the Piscataway Indians; *m* Sarah Frances Burdette.

HARRISON, Richard (*d* 1654; son of Thomas, an uncle of Gen. Thomas Harrison, the regicide; g.son of Richard, twice mayor of Newcastle-under-Lyme), came from West Kirby, Cheshire, Eng., 1640, settled at New Haven. Conn.; later removed to Branford; *m* Sarah Yorke.

HART, Edward, an Englishman, was one of the 18 incorporators of Flushing, L.I. 1645: as clk. of the town, 1657, he wrote a remonstrance against the persecutions of the Quakers and sent it to Gov. Stuyvesant, for which he was punished by the governor.

HART, Isaac (1628-99), from Eng. to Lynn, Mass., ca. 1637; to Reading, 1647; later at Lynnfield: *m* Elizabeth Hutchinson.

HART, John (1651-1714; son of Christopher and Mary–), came from Eng. to Byberry, Phila. Co., Pa., 1682; mem. 1st Pa. Assembly,

1683; signer 1st charter of govt. granted colonists by William Penn; *m* 1683, Susannah (*d* 1725), dau. John Rush (qv).

HART, Samuel (*b* 1622), from London, Eng., settled at Lynn, Mass., 1640; *m* 1653, Mary Needham (*d* 1671).

HART, Stephen (1605-1682/83; son of Stephen); from Eng. to Cambridge, Mass., 1632; freeman, 1634; settled at Hartford, Conn., 1635; one of original proprs. of Hartford; soldier Pequot War; rep. Gen. Ct., 1647-55; commr. for Farmington, 1653; a deacon; *m* 2d, Margaret–, widow of Arthur Smith.

HARTSHORNE, Richard (1641-1722; son of Hugh); came from Eng., 1669, as commr. from the Proprietors of E. Jersey; settled at Shrewsbury, N.J.; speaker of Assembly, 1687-1708; mem. Council; judge Ct. of Common Rights at Perth Amboy, 1698-99; *m* 1670, Margaret, dau. of Robert Carr, from Scotland, granted Connecticut Island, R.I.

HARVEY, John (1639-1702), from Eng., settled at Harvey's Neck, Perquimans Co., N.C.; was pres. of Council and actg. gov. of N.C.; *m* Mary –.

HASBROUCK (Hasbroucq), Abraham (*d* 1717), his family removed to the Palatinate previous to the revocation of Edict of Nantes, migrated to America, 1675; patentee of New Paltz, N.Y., 1677; *m* 1676, Maria Deyo (1653-1741), a fellow passenger in the same ship.

HASKELL, Roger (1613-67), from Eng. with his brothers William and Mark, to Salem (now Beverly), Mass., 1632; *m* a dau. of John Stone; *m* 2d, Elizabeth, dau. John Hardy.

HASTINGS, Thomas (1605-85), from Eng. in the "Elizabeth," to Watertown, Mass., 1634; selectman 5 yrs.; town clk. 3 yrs.; rep. Gen. Ct., 1673; *m* Susanna – (*d* 1650); *m* 2d, 1651, Margaret (1604-67), dau. William Cheney, of Roxbury, Mass.

HATCH, Thomas (ca. 1596-ante June 14, 1646; son of William Hatch), came from Wye, Co. Kent, Eng., ca. 1638; settled at Scituate, Mass.; freeman, 1638/39; *m* ca. 1622, Lydia–(she *m* 2d, ca. 1654, John Spring).

HATCH, Thomas (1603-61), from Eng. to Mass., 1634; freeman, 1634; received grant of 2 acres at Dorchester, 1634; to Yarmouth, 1638/39, to Barnstable, 1641; on mil. roll, 1643; took oath of fidelity, 1657; *m* ca. 1624-26, Grace–(living 1661).

HATCH, William (1598-1667), settled at Scituate, Mass., 1635; *m* Jane–.

HATHAWAY, Arthur, from Eng. to Dartmouth, Mass., 1630; said to have been at Marshfield, 1643, Plymouth, 1656; *m* and had Arthur (1635-1711), juror, selectman and magistrate, Dartmouth, 1671; *m* 1652, Sarah (1635-1713), dau. of John Cooke, and g.dau. of Francis Cooke, Mayf. Pil. (qv).

HATHORNE, William (1607-81), from Eng. in Winthrop's fleet, 1630, to Dorchester, Mass.; removed to Salem, 1636; dep. Gen. Ct., 1635, et seq.; first speaker House of Deputies, 1644, 45, et seq.; commr. United Colonies, 1650, 54, 73; maj., Salem mil. company; gov.'s asst., 1662-79; in charge mil. affairs of Marblehead, 1666; judge, 1667-78; *m* Ann – (*d* post 1681).

HAUGHWOUT (van Hagewout), Pieter Janse (ca. 1623-1661/62; prob. son of Johan Hagewolt, capt. troop of horse, at Drenthe, Holland, 1640), shoemaker, from Drenthe, Holland, to New Amsterdam in the "'Bonte Koe,'" 1660; settled at Flatbush (Brooklyn), N.Y., 1661; *m* ca. 1644, Femmetje Hermans; had sons: 1–Leffert Pieterse (ca. 1650-1704), Kings Co., N.Y., used surname Lefferts, *m* Abigail Auckse Van Nuyse; 2–Pieter Pieterse (ca. 1659-1715/16), settled in Richmond Co., S.I., used surname Haughwout, *m* 1683, Dirckje Egberts.

HAVEN, Richard (1616-1703), from Eng. to Lynn, Mass., 1640-45; sgt. King Philip's War; freeman, 1691; *m* Susanna (*b* ca. 1624-*d* 1682), dau. Thomas Newhall (qv).

HAWLEY, Joseph (1603-90), from Eng., 1629 or 30; was first town recorder of Stratford, Conn.; dep. Gen. Ct., 1665-87; *m* 1646, Katharine Birdsey (*d* 1692).

HAY, John (son of a Scottish soldier), came from the Rhenish Palatinate, ca. 1750, and settled in York Co., Pa.

HAYDEN (Heydon, Heaydon), John (*d* 1682), from Eng. in the "Mary and John," to Boston,

1630; propr. Dorchester, 1632; freeman, 1634; settled at Braintree; m Susanna –.

HAYDEN, William (1600-69), from Eng., with his brother John, in the "Mary and John," to Dorchester, Mass., 1630; a founder of Windsor, Conn., 1640; removed to Kennilworth (now Clinton), 1660; m 2d, Margaret Wilcoxson.

HAYES, George (1655-1725), from Scotland, 1680, settled at Windsor, Conn., 1682; removed to Simsbury; m Sarah – (d 1683); m 2d, 1683, Abigail Dibble (1666-post 1725).

HAYHURST, Cuthbert (ca. 1633-1683), Quaker minister, from Eng. to Pa., 1682, accompanied William Penn on his first voyage in the "Welcome"; purchased 500 acres on the Neshaminy Creek, Bucks Co., Pa.; the house still standing (1925), occupied by the Phila. Camp Fire Girls; m 1666, Mary (d 1686), dau. of Edward Rudd.

HAYNES, see also Haines.

HAYNES, John (1594-1654), from Eng., 1633; gov. Colony of Mass. Bay, 1635; a founder of Hartford, 1636, and gov. Colony of Conn., 1639, and alternate yrs. until his death; pres. 1st Gen. Ct., 1637; commr. United Colonies, 1650; col. of regt. raised against the Indians, 1636; m 2d. Mabel (b 1614), dau. Richard Harlakenden.

HAYNES, Walter (1583-1664/65), from Wilts., Eng., 1638; dep. from Sudbury, Mass., to Gen. Ct., 1641, 42, 43, 44, 46, 48, 51; m bet. 1612-16, Elizabeth – (d 1659).

HAYWARD (Haward, Howard) William (1614-59), from Eng., 1635; propr. Charlestown, Mass. 1637; removed to Braintree; dep. Gen. Ct., 1641; m Margery (d 1676), dau. of Thomas Thayer (bap. 1596-1665), from Eng. to Braintree, Mass., ante 1636, m 1618, Majorie (d 1672/73), dau. Abiel Wheeler (d 1614), m 1588, Jane Sheperd (d 1629)

HAZARD, Thomas (1610-80), ship-carpenter, surveyor and planter; probably originally from Nottinghamshire, Eng., but came immediately from Lyme Regis, Dorset, on the Channel, to Boston, Mass., 1635, with wife Martha and son Robert, where he was admitted freeman, 1636; thence to Portsmouth, R.I., where he was admitted freeman, 1638, as of Aquidneck; was a signer of the Compact for the settlement of Newport, R.I., 1639; admitted freeman and was apptd. with three others to lay out the town of Newport, 1639; apptd. mem. Gen. Ct. of Elections, 1640; was one of the founders of Newtown, L.I., 1652, where he was a magistrate under the Dutch, 1652-55; mem. Gov.'s Council, 1654; returned to Portsmouth, R.I., 1655, but again appears at Newtown, 1656 and 1665; m Martha – (d post 1669); m 2d, 1675, Martha (d 1691), widow of Thomas Sheriff, of Plymouth, Mass., and Portsmouth, R.I., she m 3d, Lewis Hues, of Portsmouth.

HAZELTINE, John (1620-90), from Eng., 1637, settled at Salem, Mass.; an original settler at Rowley, 1640; freeman, 1637-40; selectman, 1668; served in King Philip's War; m Jane Auter (d 1698).

HAZEN, Edward (d 1683), Rowley, Mass.; m Hannah, dau. Thomas Grant.

HEALD, John (d 1662), from Berwick on Tweed, Co. Northumberland, Eng., to Cambridge, Mass.; settled at Concord, Mass., as early as 1635; freeman, 1641; had 4 lots of land containing 68 acres, 1655; m Dorothy Andross.

HEALE, Nicholas (d 1657), from Eng., ca. 1650; planter, 1654; settled in York Co., Va., later in Lancaster Co.; justice, York Co., Va.

HEALY (Hele, Healey), William (1613-83), from Eng. ca. 1638; mem. of ch. at Lynn. Mass., 1640; at Roxbury, 1643, at Cambridge, 1653; prison-keeper, 1672-82; m 1643, Grace Ives (d 1649); m 2d, Mary Rogers; m 3d, 1653, Grace (1634-60), dau. Nicholas Buttrice; m 4th, 1661, Phoebe (d 1662), dau. of Bartholomew Greene (d 1638), of Cambridge; m 5th, 1677, Sarah (Cutting) Brown, dau. John Cutting, widow of James Brown.

HEBARD (Hibbard, Hibbert, Heberd), Robert (1612-84), from Eng., to Salem, Mass., ca. 1636; m Joanne–, dau. John Fairfield, m Isabel–.

HELM, Thomas (1731-1816), whose family had settled in Va.; was lt. 3d Va. Regt. in Am. Rev., 1776/77; removed to the Falls of Ohio, in Ky., 1779, established "Helm Place," Hardin Co.; m ca. 1760, Jean Pope (desc. Nathaniel Pope, from Eng. to Md., ca. 1635, mem. Md. Assembly, later settled in Westmoreland Co., Va.).

HEMENWAY (Hemmenway), Ralph, was a resident of Roxbury, Mass., 1633; was devoted to the interests of Apostle John Eliot; m 1634, Elizabeth Hewes (d 1686, aet. 82).

HEMPSTEAD, Robert (ca. 1600-1655), from Eng. to New London, Conn., 1643, where he was one of the first nine settlers; m 1646, Joanna Wyllie (d 1660).

HENDERSON, Thomas, from Dumfries, Scot. to Jamestown, Va., 1607; later to Blue Springs, Va., and Albemarle Co., Va.

HENRY, Rev. Robert (1720-67; a cousin of Patrick Henry, the statesman), from Scotland, 1740; A.B., Princeton, 1751; Presbyn. minister in Charlotte Co., Va.; m Jean (Johnson) Caldwell.

HENRY, Robert, from Scotland, 1722, settled in Chester Co., Pa.; m Mary Ann –.

HENSHAW, Joshua (1642-1719; son of William, of "Wavertree Hall," nr. Liverpool, Eng. [killed 1644, at the storming of Liverpool by Prince Rupert], m Katherine, dau. Evan Houghton), sent to America, 1652; settled at Dorchester, Mass.; d in London; m 1670, Mary Elizabeth (bap. 1654-1728), dau. William Sumner, m Elizabeth Clement; and g.dau. William Sumner (qv).

HERNDON, William (1649-1722), from Eng., patented large tracts of land in St. Stephen's Parish, New Kent Co., Va., Feb. 1673/74; m 1677, Catherine (1654-1727), dau. of Gov. Edward Digges, of Va.

HERR, Hans (1639-1725), from Switzerland to Lampeter, Lancaster Co., Pa., 1709; m 1660, Elizabeth (1644-1730), dau. John Kendig.

HERRESHOFF, Charles Frederick, scientist, linguist and musician; came from Germany and settled at Providence, R.I.; m Sarah, dau. John Brown, banker, Revolutionary patriot; mem. Congress: a founder Brown U.; desc. Chad Brown and Richard Warren (both qv).

HERRICK (Heyricke), Henry (1600-71; 5th son of Sir William [1557-1653], of Beau Manor, Co. Leicester, Eng., m 1596, Lady Joan, dau. Richard May, of London), came from Eng.; settled on "Cape Ann Syde," 1629; freeman, 1630; removed to Wenham, finally to Beverly, was a founder of the first church there; m Editha (b 1614), dau. Hugh Laskin.

HERSEY (Hersie, Harsie, Hearsey), William (1596-1658), from Eng., 1635; an original settler at Hingham, Mass.; freeman, 1638; mem. A. and H. A. Co.; m Elizabeth Croade.

HEWITT, John (1777-1857), from Eng. to Rockland Co., N.Y., 1796; m Ann Garnee (desc. Isaac Garnier, a Huguenot, from Isle de France to N.Y., 1692).

HEYDT, Hans Jost, see Hite, Joist.

HEYWARD, Daniel, from Eng. to Charleston, S.C., ca. 1672.

HICKOX, William (bap. Dec. 10, 1609-post 1645; son of Thomas, of Stratford-on-Avon, Eng., m Elizabeth Sturley), an original settler at Farmington; m Elizabeth–(d 1655; she m 2d, William Adams).

HICKS, Robert (d 1647), from Eng. in the "Fortune," to Plymouth, Mass., 1621; m 1596, Margaret Morgan (d 1607); m 2d, 1610, Margaret Winslow, who came in the "Ann," 1622.

HIGBEE, Edward (d 1699), Eng. to Mass., ca. 1630; landholder New London, Conn., 1647; bought farm at Hartford from an Indian Sachem, 1664; freeman, 1667; later at Huntington, Jamaica and Cold Spring Harbor, L.I.; m Jedidah, dau. Thomas Skidmore.

HIGGINS, Richard (b 1603), came from England to Plymouth, Mass., 1632; freeman, 1636; mem. Council of War, 1653; dep., 1647; selectman; a founder of Eastham, Mass., 1644; a planter in Piscataway, N.J., 1669; m 1634, Lydia Chandler; m 2d. 1651, Mary Yates.

HIGGINSON, Francis (1587/88-1630), A.B., Cambridge, 1609; elected at London mem. council of Colony of Mass. Bay, 1629, and came in the "Talbot," with wife and eight children (one of whom d on the passage) to Salem, Mass., 1629; was minister at Leicester, Eng.; ordained at Salem, 1629, and minister of the first church in the Colony; m Anne– (d 1640).

HIGLEY, Capt. John (July 22, 1649-1714), from Frimley, Surrey, Eng., settled at Windsor, Conn., 1664; m 1671, Hannah, dau. of John Drake; m 2d, 1696, Sarah Strong Bissell (Mar. 14, 1666-May 27, 1739).

HILDRETH, Richard (1605-Feb. 23, 1693), from Eng. to Cambridge. Mass.; freeman, 1643; one of five townsmen, 1645; apptd. collector of fines for Cambridge, 1646; fence viewer, 1649, 1653/54, 1664, 67; surveyor of highways, 1650, 52, 1661/62, 1666/67; to Chelmsford, Mass., 1656; selectman, 1656; called sgt., 1657; grand juror, 1657, 64; commr., 1661, 64; *m* Sarah–(*d* 1644); *m* 2d, ca. 1645, Elizabeth–(1625-93).

HILL, Clement (*d* 1708), from Eng. with the third Lord Baltimore, 1662/63, settled in Md.; high sheriff St. Mary's Co., 1674-76; mem. Lower House of Md. Assembly, 1677-85; mem. Council, privy councilor, vice regent, probate judge, etc.; *m* Elizabeth (Hatton) Gardiner, widow of Luke Gardiner, of St. Mary's Co., Md.

HILL, Peter (*d* 1667), from Eng. in the "Huntress," 1632/33, settled on Saco River, present site of Biddeford, Me.; mem. Assembly of Lygonia, 1648, and asst. of same.

HILL, Ralph (*d* 1663), from Eng. before 1638, to Plymouth, Mass.; selectman at Woburn, 1649; freeman, 1647; an original grantee of Billerica, Mass., 1653; *m* 1638, Margaret Toothaker (1607-83).

HILL, Robert, to Va., 1642, settled in Isle of Wight Co.; *m* ante 1642, Mary –.

HILL, William (*d* 1649), from Eng. in the "William and Francis," 1632, settled at Dorchester, Mass.; freeman, 1633; at Windsor, Conn., 1635, where he had land grants; dep. from Windsor, 1639-44; to Fairfield, 1644; dep., 1647-49; *m* 1619, Sarah, dau. Ignatius Jourdain.

HILLHOUSE, James (ca. 1687-1740, son of John), from Ireland, 1721; was 1st pastor of the first church at Montville, Conn.; *m* Mary, dau. Daniel Fitch; *m* 2d, Mary Sherwood.

HILLS, Joseph (1602-88), from Eng. in the "Susan and Ellen," 1638, to Charlestown, Mass.; an early settler at Mystic Side (later Malden), Mass., where he purchased a house and land; 1644; mem. Charlestown ch., 1647; freeman, 1647; dep. and speaker of the House, 1647; compiled first code of laws in N.E., 1647-48; capt. Malden mil. co.; *m* 1624, Rose Clarke; *m* 2d?, 1651, Hannah (Smith) Mallows.

HILLS, William (1608-83; son of Thomas, *m* Jane Scarborrow), from Upminster, Co. Essex, Eng., 1632; to Hartford, Conn., 1634; capt. militia; *m* 1632-35, Phyllis (1611-48), dau. Richard Lyman (qv).

HILLYER, John (*d* 1655), from Eng. to Windsor, Conn., a founder, 1639; *m* Ann –.

HILTON, Edward (*d* 1671), from Eng., 1623; a founder of Dover, N.H.; apptd. 1st magistrate, 1641; rep. Gen. Ct., 1652.

HINCKLEY, Samuel (1595-1662), from Eng. in the "Hercules," to Scituate, Mass., 1635; removed to Barnstable, 1639; *m* in Eng., 1617, Sarah Soule (*d* 1656); *m* 2d, Bridget Bodfish.

HINE, Thomas (*d* ca. 1696), settled at Milford, Conn.; granted 3 acres, 1646; name appears on the Milford Memorial Bridge as the founder of the town; *m* Elizabeth–(*d* post 1669).

HINMAN, Sgt. Edward (*d* 1681), from Eng. ante 1650; lived at Stamford, Conn., settled finally at Stratford; served in Indian campaign, 1644; *m* 1651, Hannah (*d* 1677), dau. of Francis Stiles.

HINSDALE, Robert (ca. 1617-1675), from Eng. to Dedham, Mass., ca. 1632; a founder of the church there; with three sons was slain by Indians at Deerfield, Mass., Sept. 18, 1675; *m* Ann Woodward (*d* 1666).

HITCHCOCK, Luke (*d* Nov. 1659), from Eng. ca. 1635, an original settler at New Haven, Conn., 1638; freeman, 1644; later at Wethersfield, Conn.; selectman and dep.; capt. early colonial wars; *m* Elizabeth Gibbons.

HITCHCOCK, Matthew, or Matthias (1614-69), from Eng. in the "Susan and Ellen," to Boston and Watertown, Mass., 1635; removed to New Haven; *m* Elizabeth –.

HITE (Hans Jost Heydt), Joist (*d* 1760-61), from Germany, in his own ship, the "Swift," bringing with him 16 families, to Kingston, N. Y., 1710, thence to Germantown, Pa., 1716; was the first white settler in Shenandoah Valley, Va., 1731; obtained grants for 140,000 acres and settled over 100 families there; justice first court of Orange Co.; *m* 1st, Anna Maria, dau. Louis DuBois, a Huguenot.

HOAG, John (1642/43-1728; son of Richard, *m* ante 1637, Joan –), Quaker; from Eng. or Wales with his father's family, 1650, to Boston; the family returned to Eng., he alone remaining; settled at Newbury, Mass.; a judge Salem witchcraft trials and dissented from the other

judges by opposing the persecution; *m* 1669, dau. of John Emery (qv).

HOARE (Hoar), Charles (*d* in Eng., will probated Dec. 21, 1638; son of Charles, of Gloucester, Eng., *m* Margery–), alderman, Gloucester, Eng., 1632-38; sheriff, 1634; *m* 1607?, Joanna Hinksman, or Henchman (*d* 1661), she came to America with 5 children, settled at Braintree, Mass.; buried in Old Quincy burying ground.

HOBART (Hobard, Hubbard), Edmund (1570-1646), from Eng. to Charlestown, Mass., 1633; freeman, 1634; constable; one of the first settlers at Hingham, 1635; dep. Gen. Ct., 1639, 40, 42; *m* 1600, Margaret Dewey.

HODGDON (Hodsdon), Nicholas, from Eng., 1634, settled at Hingham, Mass.; granted a house and lot, 1635-36; freeman, 1636-37; received land grants at Kittery, Me., 1656, 69, 73; *m* ca. 1639, Esther Wines (*d* 1647).

HODGE, Andrew (1711-89), from Ireland, with his brothers William and Hugh, settled at Phila., Pa., 1731; *m* Jane McCulloch.

HODGES, William (*d* 1654), from Eng. to Salem, Mass., before 1643, settled at Taunton; *m* Mary Andrews.

HOFFMAN, Martinus Hermanzen (*b* 1640; son of Herman, a native of Revel on the Gulf of Finland), from Holland to Esopus (Kingston), New Netherland, 1657; removed to New Amsterdam, later to Kingston, Ulster Co.; *m* 1663 Lysbeth Hemans; *m* 2d, Emmerentje Claesen de Witt.

HOGE, William (1660-1750), from Scotland ca. 1682, settled at Perth Amboy, N.J.; founder of Washington Co., Pa.; settled finally at Opequon, Va.; *m* Barbara Hume (1670-1745).

HOLCOMB (Holcombe), Thomas (*b* Pembrokeshire, Wales, or Devonshire, Eng., 1601-*d* 1657; prob. son of Gilbert Holcomb, *m* Ann–), came in the "Mary and John," 1630; settled at Dorchester, Mass., 1634; at Windsor, Conn., 1636; freeman; rep. Gen. Ct., Hartford; *m* Elizabeth Ferguson (*d* 1679), said to have been a fellow passenger on the "Mary and John."

HOLDEN, Justinian (ca. 1611-1691), from Lindsey, Co. Suffolk, Eng., in the "Francis," to Watertown, Mass., 1634; served in King Philip's War; landed propr.; constable, 1652; freeman, 1657; surveyor, 1672; *m* 1641, Elizabeth–(*d* 1672/73); *m* 2d, 1673, Mary (*b* ca. 1647), dau. John Rutter, of Sudbury, Mass., *m* Elizabeth–.

HOLDEN, Randall (1612-92), from Eng., was settled at Portsmouth, R.I., 1638; removed to Warwick; marshal and corp. at Portsmouth, 1638; gov.'s asst., 1647, et seq.; capt., 1664; dep. Gen. Ct. 1666-86; *m* 1648, Frances (1630-97), dau. of William Dungan, *m* Frances, dau. Lewis Latham.

HOLDEN, Richard (ca. 1609-1695/96; bro. of Justinian, qv), from Lindsey, Co. Suffolk, Eng., in the "Francis," to Watertown, Mass., 1634; an original propr. of Groton, Mass.; of Watertown, Cambridge and Woburn; *m* 1640/41, Martha (1620-81), dau. of Stephen Fosdick (qv).

HOLLADAY, John (*d* 1743), from Eng. to Spotsylvania Co., Va., 1702; *m* Elizabeth Brocas.

HOLLINGSWORTH, Valentine (1632-ca. 1711; son of Henry, of Ireland), a Quaker; came to Pa., 1682; settled on Shelpat Creek, Brandywine Hundred, New Castle Co. (now Del.), Pa.; mem. first Provincial Assembly of Pa., 1682-1683, et seq.; justice; signer of the Great Charter; *m* 1655, Ann Ree (1628-1671); *m* 2d, 1672, Ann (*d* 1697), dau. Thomas Calvert, of Ireland.

HOLLIS, John, from Eng. to Weymouth, Mass., 1642; removed to Wethersfield, Conn., 1644; *m* Elizabeth Priest.

HOLLISTER, John (ca. 1612-1665), from Eng., 1641, settled at Wethersfield, Conn., 1642; large landowner on east side Conn. River; freeman, 1643; collector, 1660; rep. Gen. Ct., Mass. and Conn.; lt. colonial forces; *m* Joanna (*d* 1694), dau. Richard Treat.

HOLMES, John (*d* 1667), from Eng. to Plymouth, Mass., 1632; 1st messenger Gen. Ct., 1638; *m* Sarah –.

HOLMES, John (*b* 1644), from Eng. to Dorchester, Mass.; an original propr. Woodstock Conn., 1686.

HOLMES, Rev. Obadiah (1607-82), from Preston, Lancashire Co., Eng.; ed. at Oxford U.; living at Salem, Mass., 1639; Newport, R.I., 1652-82; commr. from Newport to the Gen. Ct. of R.I.,

1655, 56, 58; one of the 12 original patentees of Monmouth Co., N.J., 1655, to whom Gov. Richard Nicholls granted nearly the whole of the present county; mem. of special Governor's Council, 1676; lt. in Plymouth militia; pastor Bapt. Ch., Newport, R.I., 1652-84; m in Eng., 1630, Catherine Hyde (1608-84).

HOLMES, Thomas (d 1690/91), received land at York, Me., 1671; at Dover, 1675; bought land at Berwick, 1676; his garrison house was burned by Indians, 1676; m Joanna, dau. William Freathy, of York, Me.

HOLT, Nicholas (1602-85), from Eng. in the "James," to Newbury, Mass., 1635; a woodturner; freeman, 1637; removed to Andover, Mass., 1644; m 1st, Elizabeth – (d 1656); m 2d, 1658, Hannah – (d 1665), dau. Humphrey Bradstreet, and widow of Daniel Rolfe; m 3d, 1666, – Preston, widow.

HOLTON, Joseph (1621-1705), from Eng., wheelwright; m Sarah (Ingersoll) Haynes, dau of Richard Ingersoll (qv).

HOLTON, William (1611-Aug. 12, 1691), from Eng. in the "Francis," 1634; one of first settlers of Hartford, Conn., and at Northampton, Mass., 1654, where he was justice and the first deacon; rep. Gen. Ct., 1664, 67, 69, 71; introduced the first motion known in American history for the suppression of intemperance; m Mary – (d Nov. 16, 1691)

HOLYOKE, Hon. Elizur (son of Edward), m 1640, Mary, dau. of Col. William Pynchon.

HOOKER, Thomas (1586-1647), A.B., Cambridge, 1608; fled from Eng. to Holland, 1630, thence in the "Griffin" to Boston, 1633; freeman, 1634; elected pastor of the 8th Ch., Newton, Mass., and moved with his congregation and family to Hartford, Conn., 1636, of which he was the founder; m at Amersham, Buckinghamshire, Eng., Apr. 3, 1621, Susannah, dau. of Richard Harkes, alias Garbrand, m Anne–.

HOOPER, Capt. Henry (d 1676), from Eng., settled in Calvert Co., Md., 1651, in Dorchester Co., 1667; m Sarah–.

HOOPES, Joshua (d 1724; son of John, Yorkshire, Eng., m Isabel–), cornet in Parliamentary army; came in the "Providence," with his wife and children, Daniel, Margaret, and Christian, arrived on Delaware River, Sept. 10, 1683; settled at Wakefield, Bucks Co., Pa.; mem. Falls Monthly Meeting of Friends; mem. Assembly, 1688-92, 1695-97, 1700, 01, 03, 1705-07, 08, 09, 11; a signer of the "Proprietary's Charter," which pledged allegiance to Queen Anne and denounced the Pope and doctrines of the Catholic Ch., 1701; m 1st, Isobel–(d 1691).

HOPKINS, Gerrard (or Jared), (d ante 1693/94), from Eng., was settled in Anne Arundel Co., Md., about the middle of the 17th Century; m Thomasin –.

HOPKINS, John (ca. 1613-1654), prob. from Coventry, Eng., to New Town (Cambridge), Mass., ca. 1630; received land grants, 1634, 35; freeman, 1635; a founder of Hartford, Conn., 1636; selectman, 1640; juror, 1643; charter mem. First Ch.; m ca. 1636, Jane (d 1679), dau. of John Strong (she m 2d, Nathaniel Ward, and 3d, Gregory Wolterton).

HOPKINS, Stephen (1583-1644), came in the Mayflower, 1620; as commissioner with Gov. Winslow, made treaty of peace with Massasoit, 1621; mem. expdn. which crushed Neponset's conspiracy, 1623; asst., 1633-36; mem. Council of War for the Colony, 1642-44; in Pequot War, 1637; m Constance Dudley; m 2d, 1617, or earlier, Elizabeth Fisher (d bet. 1640-44).

HOPKINS, Thomas (1616-84), Eng. to Boston, ca. 1633; settled in R.I., 1638; commr. at Providence; mem. Town Council; dep. Gen. Assembly, 1665; m Elizabeth–.

HOPKINSON, Thomas (1709-51), from Eng. to Phila., Pa., 1731; judge of vice admiralty, mem. Provincial Council, etc.; m Mary Johnson.

HOPPIN (Hopin), Stephen (1624-78), from Eng., was at Dorchester, Mass., 1653; also lived at Roxbury; m Hannah, dau. Thomas Makepeace.

HORD, John (1664-will proved 1749), from Eng.; in Christ Ch. Parish, Middlesex Co., Va., 1708, St. Ann's Parish, Essex Co., 1720; settled at "Shady Grove," Essex Co.; grand juror, 1721-24; surveyor of highways, 1731; m Jane–.

HORTON, Barnabas (1600-80; son of Joseph), from Eng. in the "Swallow," to Hampton,

Mass., 1635; to New Haven, 1640; to Southold, Suffolk Co., L.I., 1640; m 1629, Mary–.

HORTON, Thomas (d 1641; son of Joseph); came from Eng., in the "Mary and John," 1633; settled at Springfield, Mass., 1638; witnessed an Indian deed; m Mary Eddy.

HOSFORD (Horsford), William (d ante 1671), from Eng. in the "Elizabeth Bonaventure," 1633; received land grant, Dorchester, Mass., 1633; freeman, 1634; early settler at Windsor, Conn., 1637; ruling elder First Ch., 1637; commr.; removed to Springfield, Mass., preached there, Oct. 1652 to Oct. 1654; returned to Eng., 1654; and in 1656 gave land at Windsor, Conn., to his 3 children; m –(d 1641); m 2d, Jane–, widow of Henry Fowkes; she went to Eng., 1655, and was at Tiverton, Co. Devon, Eng., 1671.

HOSMER, James (bap. Dec. 1605-d Feb. 7, 1685; son of Stephen, of Hawkhurst, Co. Kent, Eng., m 1601/02, Dorothy Selden), came from London, 1635, with his wife Ann, 2 daus., and 2 maid servants; landed at Cambridge, Mass.; freeman, 1637; moved to Concord, Mass.; overseer of highways; m Ann–; m 2d, Mary–(d 1641); m 3d, Alice–(d 1664/65).

HOSMER, Thomas (bap. Jan. 2, 1602/03-d 1687; son of Stephen, m 1601/02, Dorothy Selden), from Eng., 1632; to Boston, Mass.; at Cambridge, Mass., 1633; selectman; freeman, 1635; to Hartford, Conn., ca. 1636; m Frances–(1602-75).

HOTCHKISS, Samuel (d 1663), from Eng. in the "Hector," with the Davenport colony; one of founders of New Haven, Conn., 1638; m 1642, Elizabeth Cleaverly (d 1681).

HOUGH, Richard (d 1705), from Co. Chester, Eng., in the "Endeavor," to Phila., Pa.; settled in Bucks Co., where he owned 2,500 acres; provincial councillor, 1693, 1700; mem. Assembly; justice of the peace Bucks Co. Ct.; drowned in Delaware River; m 1683, Margery (d 1719-20), dau. of John Clows, Quaker, from Eng. in the "Endeavor," mem. Pa. Assembly, 1683-84, m Margery –.

HOUGHTON (Hoghton), John (1624-84; son of John, II, who came in the "Abigail," 1635, but returned to Eng.), from Eng. in the "Abigail," to Mass., 1635; at Concord, and at Lancaster, 1652; m Beatrix –.

HOUGHTON, Ralph (1623-1705), from Eng., ca. 1636; settled at Lancaster, Mass., 1652; clk. of writs, 1656-82; rep. Gen. Ct., 1673-89; was constable, collector and town treas.; removed to Milton, Mass.; m Jane Stowe (1626-1700/01).

HOUSTOUN, Sir Patrick (1688-1762; son of Patrick): came to America with Gen. Oglethorpe, 1731, to found colony of Ga.; settled at Fredrica, St. Simons Island, Ga., 1732; was pres. of His Majesty's Council, Province of Ga.; m Priscilla Dunbar, who came from Eng. in same ship with him (with her brother Capt. Dunbar); their son John was twice colonial governor.

HOVEY, Daniel (1618-92; son of Richard, of Waltham Abbey, Co. Essex, Eng.), from Eng.; early settler at Ipswich, Mass., 1635; selectman, 1659; surveyor of highways, 1641-49, 50; constable, 1658; juror Ipswich Ct., 1649; joined Colony to Quabog (Brookfield), 1668; settled at Hadley before massacre at Quabog, 1675; returned to Ipswich, 1678; m ca. 1641, Abigail (d bet. 1676-83), dau. Capt. Robert and Elizabeth Andrews.

HOWARD, John (1620-1700), from Eng., 1638, settled at Roxbury, Mass.; one of 54 original proprs. of land at Bridgewater; surveyor; ens. in King Philip's War; dep. and rep. Gen. Cts.; commd. lt., 1689; innkeeper and carpenter, Bridgewater; m ca. 1651, Martha, dau. of Capt. Thomas Hayward (d 1691), came in the "Hercules," 1635, m Susanna –.

HOWARD, Joshua (ca. 1665-1738), from Eng. to Baltimore, Md., 1686; m Joanna O'Carroll (d 1763).

HOWARD, Matthew (1609-ante 1659), came to Va., ca. 1620, where he lived in Lower Norfolk Co.; to Anne Arundel Co., Md., 1649; large landowner; m ca. 1625, Ann–.

HOWARD, Samuel (b 1613), from Eng., 1635; m ca. 1645, Sarah, dau. Nicholas Stowers, from Eng. 1629, m Amy–.

HOWE (How), Abraham (d 1695), settled at Watertown, Mass.; a propr. of Marlborough, Mass., 1660; served in King Philip's War; m 1657, Hannah (1639-1717), dau. William Ward (qv).

HOWE, Edward (1575-1639), from Barkhampstead, Co. Herts, Eng., 1635; settled at Lynn, Mass., Sept. 19, 1635; rep. Gen. Ct.; *m* Elizabeth – (1585-1672).

HOWE, James (1605-1702), from Eng. to Roxbury, Mass., ca. 1637; freeman; settled at Ipswich before 1648; *m* Elizabeth (*d* 1693), dau. of John Dane.

HOWE (How), John (*d* 1687), from Eng., was at Sudbury, Mass., 1639; freeman, 1640; selectman, 1643; first white settler at Marlborough, Mass., ca. 1657, where he commanded a garrison house in King Philip's War; innkeeper; *m* Mary— (*d* ca. 1687).

HOWELL, Edward (1584-1655), from Eng. to Boston, 1639; had land grant of 500 acres at Lynn, Mass., before 1639; founder of Southampton, L.I., 1640; gov.'s asst. Conn. Colony, 1647-53; magistrate; mem. Legislature; *m* Frances – (*d* 1630); *m* 2d, Eleanor –.

HOWELL, William (1645?-1710), of Castle Bigot, provincial councillor, Wales (son of Morgan Howell, *m* Margaret Edwards, *m* 2d, Mary Thomas, widow, dau. of John and Joan Husband); came from Wales to Phila., among the earliest founders of Pa.; a surveyor and man of education he became one of the first magistrates, and the founder of Haverford Town, Pa.; 5 surviving children.

HOWES, Thomas (ca. 1595-1665), from Eng. to Salem, Mass., 1637; to Old Yarmouth, 1639; original grantee, and settled at Dennis (part now New Boston); constable, 1644; mem. Council of War, 1658; dep. Gen. Ct.; apptd. to receive "oil of the country," 1652; *m* Mary Burr.

HOWLAND, Henry (*d* 1671), from Eng., 1621-23; early settler of Duxbury, Mass., where he was constable; grantee of Bridgewater, 1645; *m* Mary (*d* 1674), dau. Henry Newland.

HOWLAND, John (ca. 1593-1673), 13th signer of the Mayflower Compact; asst., 1633-35; dep. Gen. Ct., 1641-69; in the "First Encounter," 1620; in command of Kennebec Trading Post, 1634; *m* at Plymouth, Mass., before 1624, Elizabeth (ca. 1607-1687), dau. John Tilley (qv).

HOYT, John (1610-87), from Eng., 1639; an original settler of Salisbury, Mass., 1640; killed by the Indians; *m* 1635, Frances – (*d* 1642); *m* 2d Frances –.

HOYT (Haight, Hoyte), Simon (*b* Somerset, Eng., Jan. 20, 1590-*d* Sept. 1, 1657), arrived in the "Abigail," Sept. 6, 1628; appeared at Charlestown, Mass., 1629; first settler of Dorchester, 1630; freeman, 1631; at Scituate, 1633-36, where he and his wife joined ch.; removed to Windsor, Conn., 1639, to Fairfield, 1645, at Stamford, 1658, where he died; *m* Deborah Stowers (1593-1625); *m* 2d. Susanna Smith (*d* 1674).

HUBBARD, George (1594-1685), from Eng. to Concord, Mass., 1633, was at Hartford, Conn., 1636, later was Indian agt. at Middletown; dep. Gen. Ct.; *m* 1640, Elizabeth Watts (*d* 1702).

HUBBARD, William (1594-1670), grad. Cambridge U. ca. 1620; came in the "Defense," to Ipswich, Mass., 1635; freeman, 1638; rep. Gen. Ct., 1638 and several yrs. following; settled at Boston, 1662; *m* probably 2d, Judith (*b* 1601), dau. of John Knapp, *m* Martha Blosse.

HUBBELL, Richard (1627-99, son Richard, of Worcestershire, Eng., *m* Sarah, dau. Francis Wakeman); from Eng. to Poquonnock, Conn., bet. 1633-39; settled at New Haven, 1647; sgt. of militia, Fairfield, Conn., 1677-99; dep. Gen. Ct., 1678; *m* 1650, Elizabeth (*d* 1664), dau. of John Meigs, Sr., *m* Thomasine Fry; *m* 2d, ca 1669, Elizabeth, dau. of Samuel Gaylor; *m* 3d, 1688, Abigail (Prudden) Walker, dau. of Rev. Peter Prudden (qv).

HUDSON, Daniel (1617-97), from Eng., 1639; settled at Watertown, Mass., 1640; later at Lancaster, Mass.; brickmaker and bricklayer; built first little red school house, Cambridge, Mass.; *m* Joanna—(1620-97), both killed by Indians.

HUGER, Daniel (1651-1711), Huguenot; from France, 1685; settled on the Santee River, S.C.; *m* Margaret Perdriau.

HUGHES (Hugh), John (1652-1736; son of Hugh Cadwalader Rhys by his wife Gwenn, dau. of Ellis Williams, Gentleman, of royal descent; descent that of the Hughes of Gwerclas, Wales; desc. Humphrey de Bohun X, Earl of Hereford, Essex and Northampton), came from Wales to Philadelphia in "Robert and Elizabeth," 1698; estate 500 acres at Gwynedd.

HULBERT (Hurlbut, Hurlburt), Thomas (ca. 1610-1675), from Eng., probably with Lion Gardiner in the "Bachilor," to Boston, 1635; was at Saybrook, Conn., 1637, later at Wethersfield; granted 160 acres for services under Lion Gardiner in Pequot War; dep. Gen. Ct. and constable, 1644; *m* Sarah –.

HULBURD (Hulbert), William (1611-94), from Eng. to Dorchester, Mass., 1630; freeman, 1632; at Windsor, Conn., 1636, at Hartford, later Northampton, Mass., 1655; *m* 2d, Ann –, widow of Samuel Allen, of Windsor, Conn.

HULL, George (1590-1659), from Eng.; was at Plymouth, Mass., 1629; resided at Boston and Dorchester, Mass., Windsor, Killingworth and Fairfield, Conn.; dep. Gen. Ct. of Conn., 1637; *m* 1614, Thamzen Michell.

HULL, Joseph (1594-1665; son of Thomas, *m* Joane Peson); B.A., St. Mary's Hall, Oxford U., 1614; from Eng. with a company of 106 persons, to Boston, 1635; founder of Barnstable, Mass.; later at Yarmouth and at York, Me.; clergyman; dep. Gen. Ct., 1638, 39; *m* Joanne –; *m* 2d, Agnes –.

HULL, Richard (*d* 1662), from Eng. to Dorchester, Mass., ca. 1632; freeman, 1634; at New Haven, Conn., abt. 1640; master of the watch, 1649.

HUME, George (1698-1760; son of Sir George, 9th Baron Wedderburn, Scotland, and desc. King Robert Bruce, King Malcolm II, and Edward, the Elder); from Scotland; surveyor for William and Mary Coll., 1727-29, and for Augusta, Spotsylvania, Orange and Culpeper cos.; laid out city of Fredericksburg, Va.; officer Colonial wars; *m* 1728, Elizabeth Procter (*b* 1700), of Va.

HUMPHREY (Humphreys), Michael (ca. 1620-post 1697), from Eng. to Windsor, Conn., 1642; freeman, 1657; settled at Simsbury, 1669; dep. Gen. Ct., 1670; *m* 1647, Priscilla (*b* 1626), dau. Matthew Grant (qv).

HUNGERFORD, Thomas (1602-63), from Eng. to Hartford, Conn., 1638; to New London, 1650.

HUNT, Peter (1610-92), one of the first settlers at Rehoboth, Mass.; lt., Rehoboth Train Band, 1654-82, and capt., 1682-92; mem Council of War, 1658, 85; dep. Gen. Ct., 15 yrs.; served in King Philip's War.

HUNT, Ralph (*d* 1677), Eng. to New York, 1652; lt. militia, 1665; surveyor of Indian lands, 1663-64; mem. Provincial Assembly, 1673; magistrate; a patentee of Newtown, N.Y.; *m* Elizabeth, or Ann, dau. Edward Jessup.

HUNT, William (1605-67; son of Robert, of Halifax, Yorkshire, Eng.); from Eng. to Concord, Mass.; freeman, 1641; *m* 1630, Elizabeth Best (*d* 1661).

HUNTINGTON, Simon (1583-1633), Puritan, from Eng., 1633, *d* at sea of smallpox; his wife, Margaret Barrett (dau. Christopher Barret, mayor of Norwich, Eng.), and three children arrived at Boston, 1633, settled at Roxbury, Mass.; she *m* 2d, 1635, Thomas Stoughton (qv).

HURD, John (*d* 1681), one of the earliest settlers at Windsor, Conn.; settled at Stratford, 1639, dep. Gen. Ct., 1657-58.

HURLBUT, Thomas (*b* Scotland-*d* 1689), to Saybrook, Conn., 1635; served in Pequot War; clk. Train Band, 1649; dep. Gen. Ct., 1644; blacksmith, Wethersfield, 1662; received grant for mil. services, 1671; *m* Elizabeth—(living 1689).

HUSSEY (Huzzey), Capt. Christopher (1598-1686), from Eng. in the "William and Francis," to Boston, Mass., 1632; lived first in Lynn; propr. of Hampton, N.H., 1637; mem. Mass. Gen. Ct., 1658-60, 72; one of the purchasers of Nantucket Island from Indians, 1659; mem. Royal Council of N.H., 1679-85; capt. of militia; *m* Theodate, dau. of Rev. Stephen Bachiler (qv).

HUTCHINS, John (1604-85), from Eng. to Newbury, Mass.; settled at Haverhill, 1640; soldier King Philip's War; *m* Frances–.

HUTCHINSON, William (1586-1642), from Eng. to Boston, Mass., 1634; freeman, 1635; removed to R.I., 1638; rep. Gen. Ct. of Mass., 1635-38; gov. of Portsmouth, R.I., 1639-40; *m* ca. 1612, Ann Marbury (ca. 1590-1643), distinguished religious teacher; was banished and with her husband and fifteen children went to the Narragansett country where they purchased Aquidnick Island from the Indians and founded the town of Portsmouth, R.I.; after her husband's death, went into the Dutch country west of New Haven, where she and most of her family were murdered by the Indians.

HYDE, Jonathan (1626-1711), from Eng., 1639; was at Newtown, Mass., 1647; settled at Cambridge, 1648; served in King Philip's War; *m* 1650, Mary (1633-72), dau. William French.

HYDE, William (ca. 1597-1681), from Eng. with Rev. Thomas Hooker, to Newton, Mass., 1633; removed to Hartford, Conn., 1636; an original propr. of Norwich, 1660.

HYNSON, Thomas (*b* 1621), from Eng. to Kent Co., Md., ca. 1650, he and Joseph Wickes were awarded a grant of 800 acres called "Wickcliffe," at the Eastern Neck, nr. the mouth of Chester River; commr. of Kent Island, 1654; high sheriff; burgess, 1659; *m* Grace –.

IDE, Nicholas (1620-1690), from Eng. with his widowed mother, 1636; settled at Rehoboth; freeman, 1648; surveyor of highways, 1662, 69, 74; *m* Martha (*d* 1676), dau. Thomas and Dorothy (Wheatlie) Bliss.

INGALLS, Edmund (*b* Skirbeck, Lincolnshire, Eng., ca. 1598-will proved Sept. 16, 1648; son of Robert; grandson of Henry), to Salem, Mass., 1628; at Lynn, Mass., 1629; *m* Ann–.

INGERSOLL, John (1615-84), from Eng. with his bro., Richard (qv); went from Salem, Mass., to Hartford, Conn., 1651; to Westfield, Mass., 1666; *m* 1651, Dorothy (*d* 1656), dau. Thomas Lord (qv); *m* 2d, 1657, Abigail (*d* 1666/67), dau. Thomas Bascom; *m* 3d, 1668, Mary Hunt (*d* 1690), sister of Jonathan Hunt and g.dau. of Gov. John Webster, of Conn.

INGERSOLL, Richard (*d* 1644), from Eng. to Salem, Mass., accompanied by bro., John (qv), 1628; granted 82 acres on the Cape Ann side, 1638, later granted 30 acres of meadow land; *m* 1611, Agnes, or Ann, Langley (*d* 1677), she *m* 2d, John Knight (qv).

INGHAM, Jonas (*d* 1755), from Eng. to New England, ca. 1705, removed to Trenton, N.J., thence to Bucks Co., Pa.; *m* Elizabeth – (*d* 1748).

INMAN, Abednego (1752-1831), from Eng., ca. 1765-67, settled at Limestone, Va., then at Danridge, Tenn.; maj. Am. Rev.; *m* 1778, Mary Ritchie (1757-1836).

INSLEE (Ilsley), William (1608-81), from Newbury, Wiltshire, Eng., in the "Confidence," to Newbury, Mass., 1638; *m* Barbara–(*b* ca. 1618).

IRISH, John (*d* 1677; son of Jonathan Irish, *m* Elizabeth Kirby), from Parish Clisdon, Somerset, Eng., to Plymouth, Mass., 1637; settled at Duxbury, Mass.; served in Pequot War; granted land at Little Compton, R.I.; *m* Elizabeth, probably Risley (*d* 1687).

IRVING, William (1731-1807), from Shapinsha, one of the Orkney Islands, came to New York, 1763; *m* Sarah Sanders (among their sons was Washington Irving, distinguished author).

ISHAM, Henry (1627-76; son of William; desc. of Thomas Isham [*b* 1456], Lord of Pytchley, Northamptonshire, Eng.), came directly from Eng. to Va., 1654; settled at Bermuda Hundred on the James River; merchant; *m* 1659, Katherine (Banks) Royall (will dated Oct. 10, 1686), of Canterbury, Eng., widow of Joseph Royall (qv).

ISHAM (Isum), John (*d* 1713), was at Newburyport, Mass., 1667; settled at Barnstable, Mass., 1670; *m* 1677, Jane (1664-1719), dau. Robert Parker, of Barnstable.

IVES, William (1607-48), from Eng. in the "Truelove," to Boston, 1635; an original settler at Quinnipiack (New Haven), Conn., 1638; signed the civil compact, 1639; soldier at New Haven in Indian alarms of 1642, 46; *m* 1641, Hannah – (who *m* 2d, William Bassett).

IZARD, Ralph (*d* 1710), from Eng. to Charleston, Carolina, 1682; settled in St. James' Parish, S.C.; mem. Council, 1700; justice; pres. Indian Commn.; *m* Mary –, widow of Arthur Middleton; *m* 2d, Dorothy –, widow of Christopher Smith.

JACKSON, Edward (1602-81), from Eng. to Newtown, Mass., 1643; freeman 1645; purchased farm of 500 acres from Gov. Bradstreet; selectman; dep. Gen. Ct. 18 sessions; aid of Apostle Eliot in evangelization of the Indians; gave 400 acres of land to Harvard Coll.; *m* Frances – (*d* 1648); *m* 2d, 1649, Elizabeth, dau. John Newgate, and widow of John Oliver.

JACOB (Jacobs), Nicholas (*d* 1657), from Eng. with his wife and two children to Watertown, Mass.; removed to Hingham, 1635; freeman, 1636; dep. Gen. Ct., 1648-49; selectman; *m* Mary – (*d* 1681).

JANNEY, Thomas (1633-Feb. 12, 1696), from Styall, Pownall Fee, Parish of Wilmslow, Macclesfield Hundred, Co. Chester, Eng., in the "Endeavor," to Bucks Co., Pa., July 29, 1683; minister Soc. of Friends; provincial councillor, mem. William Penn's Council, 1684, 85, 86, 91; justice of the peace for Bucks Co.; *m* Sept. 24, 1660, in Eng., Margery Heath.

JAY, Augustus (*b* France, Mar. 3, 1665-*d* New York, Mar. 10, 1751; son of Pierre Jay), Huguenot, from France, upon the revocation of the Edict of Nantes, 1685, settled at New York; *m* 1697, Anna (*b* 1670), dau. of Balthazar Bayard, *m* Maria Loockermans.

JAYNE, William (1618-1714), of New Haven, Conn.; removed to Brookhaven, L.I., 1676; trustee, Town of Brookhaven, 1701; moved to Setuaket, L.I., 1708; *m* 1675, Annie (Jennings) Biggs, dau. of John Jennings (1617-86).

JEFFERSON, John (1590-1660), from Eng. in the "Bona Nova," 1619; settled at "Osborne," Chesterfield Co., Va.; mem. First Va. House of Dels., 1619; burgess from Flower de Hundred.

JENKINS, John (1609-ca. 1690), from London, Eng., in the "Defense," to Plymouth, 1635; soldier Pequot War, 1637; soldier Narragansett Expdn., 1645; moved to Barnstable, 1652.

JENKINS, Thomas (1642-ca. 1729), from Wales to Md., ca. 1670; settled in Charles Co.; *m* 1669, Ann Spaulding.

JENKS (Jenckes), Joseph (1602-Mar. 1683), from Eng., 1643, settled at Lynn, Mass.; established the iron works at Lynn; was the first patentee in America, 1646; cut the dies for the "Pine Tree Shilling," 1652; built the first fire engine, 1654; inventor of the grass scythe; *m* 1st, –(*d* in Eng.); *m* 2d, Elizabeth–(*d* 1679).

JENNINGS, Charles (*d* 1705), from Eng.; clerk of Elizabeth City Co., Va.; *m* Mary– (1651-1710).

JENNINGS, Edmund (1659-1727), of "Ripon Hall," York Co., Va.; was atty. gen., sec. of state, pres. of the Council and acting gov.; *m* Frances, dau. of Henry Corbin (qv).

JENNINGS, Joshua (ca. 1620-1674/75), from Eng. to Hartford, Conn., ca. 1645; at Fairfield, 1650; *m* 1647, Mary Williams, of Hartford (she *m* 2d, 1680, George Slawson).

JEWELL, Thomas (*b* 1598-will dated, 1654), from Eng. to Mt. Wollaston, Mass., 1639; lived at Braintree; *m* Grisell –.

JEWETT, Joseph (bap. 1609-1660/61), Puritan, from Eng. in the "John," 1638; admitted freeman at Rowley, Mass., 1639; dep. Gen. Ct., 1651-54 and 1660; *m* 1634, Mary Mallinson (*d* 1652); *m* 2d, 1653, Ann (*d* 1660/61), widow of Bozoar Allen.

JEWETT, Maximilian (bap. 1607-*d* 1684; son of Edward [1580-1614], of Bradford, West Riding, Yorkshire, Eng., clothier, *m* Mary Taylor); from Eng. in the "John," to Boston, 1638; a founder of Rowley, 1639; deacon 50 yrs.; dep. Gen. Ct., 1641-76; *m* 1st, Ann – (*d* 1667).

JOHNSON, Edward (bap. 1598-1672), from Eng., 1630; freeman at Charlestown, Mass., 1630; was at Merrimac, 1632; a founder of Woburn, 1642; a founder of the A. and H. A. Co., 1637; lt., Middlesex Co. troop, 1643, capt., 1644; surveyor gen of the mil. stores of the colony, 1659; dep. Gen Ct., 1643-47, 1649-70, and speaker, 1655, historical author; *m* Susan Munnter (1598-1689).

JOHNSON, Elihu, of Conn., soldier in French and Indian War and Am. Rev.; *m* 1762, Sarah (Webb) Converse (*b* 1741), widow of Joshua Converse, and desc. Christopher Webb, from Eng. before 1645, and Henry Adams.

JOHNSON, John (1630-85), from Eng., to Rowley, Mass.; soldier King Philip's War; *m* 1655, Hannah, dau. Anthony Crosby.

JOHNSON, Col. Richard (*d* 1699), from Bilsby, Lincolnshire, Eng., to King and Queen Co., Va.; justice, New Kent, 1689; capt. of horse; mem. Council, 1696.

JOHNSON, Thomas (*d* 1714), from Eng. to Md., ca. 1660; settled in Calvert Co., ca. 1690, where he was Indian trader; *m* Mary, dau. Roger Baker, of Liverpool, Eng.

JONES, Capt. Lewis (*d* 1684), from Wales and Eng., 1635, settled at Weston, Roxbury or Belmont, Mass., ca. 1640; *m* Anne (*d* 1680), dau. of Deacon Simon Stone (qv).

JONES, Matthew (*b* 1640), Wales to Isle of Wight, Va., 1682, thence to Mulberry Island, Warwick Co.; *m* Elizabeth (Albridgton) Ridley, dau. Francis Albridgton.

JONES, Capt. Roger (1642-1701), came to Va. with Lord Culpeper, 1680, but returned to London, 1684/85; *m* Dorothy (*b* 1642), dau. of John Walker; *m* 2d, Priscilla Haddock.

JONES, Thomas (1598-1671), from Eng. in the 2d voyage of the "Mayflower," 1629; settled at Gloucester, Mass.; freeman, 1653; *m* Mary (*d* 1681), dau. of Richard North, *m* Ursula–.

JONES, Thomas (1665-1713), from Ireland to R.I., 1692; became ranger gen. of L.I., and maj. of Queens Co. regt.; *m* Freelove, dau. Capt. Thomas Townsend.

JORDAN, Arthur (1629-98), from Eng., settled in Surry Co., Va.; *m* 1654, Elizabeth, dau. of Richard Bavin.

JORDAN, Robert (1612-79), from Eng., ca. 1641; clergyman; preacher at Richmond Island, nr. Scarborough, Me., later at Falmouth, Me., and Portsmouth, N.H.; mem. Council of George Cleves, of Lygonia, 1648; apptd. one of four to govern Province of Me., 1665; *m* Sarah, dau. of John Winter.

JORDAN (Jourdan), Samuel (*d* 1623), came from France in the "Sea Venture," which was wrecked off Bermuda Coast; settled at "Jordan's Journey," on James River, 1610; mem. first legislative assembly in America at Jamestown, 1619; *m* Cicely—, came in the "Swan," 1611.

JOSLYN, Thomas (ca. 1591-1660/61) from Eng. in the "Increase" to Sudbury, then Hingham, Mass., 1635; propr.; then Watertown, then removed to Lancaster; *m* ca. 1615, Rebecca Marlowe.

JOY, Thomas (1611-78), from Eng. in the "Constance," 1635, was an architect and builder at Boston; supported Dr. Robert Child's petition for extension of the right of suffrage, 1646; settled at Hingham, 1647; mem. A. and H. A. Co., 1658; freeman Mass. Bay Colony, 1665; built Boston Town House, 1657; *m* 1637, Joan Gallup.

JUDD, Thomas (ca. 1608-1688), settled at Cambridge, Mass.; at Hartford, Conn., 1636; one of earliest proprs. of Farmington, Conn. 1644; settled at Northampton, Mass., 1679; dep. Gen. Ct. several yrs.

JUDSON, William (*d* 1662), from Eng. to Concord, Mass., 1634; one of first settlers at Stratford, Conn., 1639; moved to New Haven; *m* Grace—(*d* 1659).

KEASBEY, Edward, from Eng., ca. 1694; joined John Fenwick's colony of Quakers; founder of Salem, N.J., 1675; mem. Gen. Assembly; del. Provincial Congress; *m* 1701, dau. of Andrew Thompson, and widow of Isaac Smart.

KEELER, Ralph (1613-72), from Eng., settled at Hartford, Conn., ca. 1637; a first settler at Norwalk, Conn., 1650; *m* 1653, Sarah Whelpley.

KEEN (Kyn), Jöran (*ca.* 1620-1693), from Sweden in the "Fama," with Johan Printz, gov. of New Sweden, to Christiana, New Sweden (now Wilmington, Del.), 1643, and founded Upland. New Sweden (now Chester, Pa.).

KEENE (Keen), John (1578?-1649), from Eng. in the "Confidence," 1638; settled at Hingham, Mass.; mariner and inn-holder; *m* Martha– (1578-1638), *d* on board the "Confidence".

KEITH, James, of Mass. (*b* Keith, Scot., 1643/ 44-*d* 1719), entered Marischal Coll., Aberdeen, Scot., 1657; to Boston, Mass., 1664; ordained, Feb. 1664; settled at Bridgewater, Mass.; *m* 1st, 1668. Susanna (1640-1705), dau. Dea. Samuel Edson (qv).

KEITH, James, of Va. (*b* Peterhead, Aberdeenshire, Scot., Nov. 6. 1696-*d* Hamilton Parish. Va., 1758; son of Robert), ed. Marischal Coll., Aberdeen, Scot.; wounded in Battle of Sheriff Muir; attainted for attempts to return the Stuarts, 1719, and fled to Va., 1720; settled in Fauquier Co.; later rector St. John's. Henrico Co., 1730-33; of Hamilton Parish, 1733, et seq.; *m* 1733. Mary Isham Randolph (*b* 1718), dau. of Thomas, *m* 1712. Judith Fleming; and g.dau. of William Randolph (qv).

KELLOGG, Daniel (bap. 1630-1688/89; son of Martin, of Great Leighs. Eng., *m* Prudence Bird), prob. came with his bro. Joseph (qv), from Eng. to Norwalk, Conn., ante 1651; selectman, 1670; rep. 8 terms; *m* ante 1661, —; *m* 2d, 1665, Bridget (ca.1642-1689), dau. John Bouton, *m* Alice Pratt.

KELLOGG, Joseph (1626-1707), from Eng. to Farmington, Conn., 1651; freeman, 1654; a founder of Hadley. Mass., where the house he built

is still standing; commanded Hadley men, in the Falls fight; selectman; *m* 1650, Joanna– (*d* 1666); *m* 2d, 1667, Abigail (1646-1717), dau. Stephen Terry, of Windsor, Conn.

KELSEY, William (ca.1600-ca.1680; son of George), came from Eng. as mem. of the Braintree Company, 1632; had a grant at Cambridge, Mass.; freeman, 1635; to Hartford, Conn., 1636; to Killingworth, Conn., 1663; dep. Gen. Ct., 1671; *m* Bethia–(ca.1605-ca.1636).

KEMPTON, Ephraim (ca.1584-1645), came in the "Anne," 1623, to Plymouth, Mass.

KENDALL, Francis (1612-1708), from Eng. to Charlestown, Mass., 1640; one of the first settlers at Woburn, 1644; freeman, 1647; selectman 18 yrs.; *m* 1644, Mary (1630-1705), dau. of Sgt. John Tidd.

KENNON, Richard (*d* 1696), from Eng.; in Bermuda Hundred, Henrico Co., Va., 1670; mcht.; magistrate, 1678; burgess, 1685; owned "Rochedale"; bought "Conjurer's Neck," Chesterfield Co., 1677; *m* Elizabeth, dau. of William Worsham, of Va.

KENRICK (Kendrick), John (1605-86), from Bristol, Eng., with Rev. Richard Mather (qv), in the "James"; was at Boston, 1639; took freeman's oath, 1640; purchased 250 acres in Cambridge Village (now Newton), 1658, where he settled; *m* Ann Smith (*d* Nov. 15, 1656); *m* 2d, Judith–(*d* Aug. 23, 1687).

KENT, Daniel (1765-1844), from Ireland to Phila., Pa., 1785; settled in Chester Co., Pa.; *m* Esther Hawley (g.dau. of Benjamin Hawley, from London to Phila., 1723, settled at Goshen, Pa.).

KENT, Thomas (*d* 1656), from Eng., ca. 1640, an original propr. of Gloucester, Mass.

KETCHAM, Edward (*d* June, 1655), from Cambridge. Eng.; settled at Ipswich, Mass., 1635; to Southhold, L.I., and later to Stratford, Conn.; *m* at Cambridge, Eng., Aug. 22, 1619, Mary Hall; *m* 2d, Sarah–(who *m* 2d, Henry Whitney).

KEY, Moses (ca.1675-1748), from Scot., 1700; resided in Chester and Delaware cos., Pa.; Quaker; mem. Pa. Assembly from Delaware Co., 1723-24; *m* 1701, Elizabeth (*d* 1756), dau. John Yearsley, settled in Thomberg Tp., Delaware Co., Pa., *m* Elizabeth–.

KEY, Philip (1696-1764), from Eng., ca. 1720, settled in St. Marys Co., Md.; mem. Lower House of Md. Assembly several sessions; high sheriff, 1744-45; mem. Council, 1763-64; *m* Susanna, dau. John Gardiner (desc. Richard Gardiner, of St. Marys Co., Md.); *m* 2d, Theodosia (Lawrence) Trumphries.

KEYES, Solomon (*d* 1702), at Newbury, Mass., ante 1653; later at Chelmsford; *m* 1653, Frances (*d* 1708). dau. Thomas and Jane Grant.

KEYSER, Dirck (1635-1714; silk merchant, son of Dirck Gerrits Keyser by his wife Cornelia, dau. of Tobias Govertz Van Den Wyngaert, a writer and a Mennonite preacher); came from Bavaria to Pa., 1685; built the first stone house in Germantown, still standing; *m* Elizabeth, dau. of Peter ter Himpel; *m* 2d, Johanna Harpers Snoeck.

KIDDER, James (1626-76), from Eng. to Cambridge, Mass., 1649; later settled at Billerica; his dwelling used as a garrison house in King Philip's War, in which he was killed; *m* ca. 1649/50. Anna, dau. Elder Francis Moore.

KIERSTEDE, Dr. Hans (ca.1612-1666), from Maegdenburg, 1638, with Gov. Kieft, in the service of the West India Co.; first physician and surgeon to settle in New York; *m* 1642, as her 1st husband, Sarah Roelofse (*b* ca.1625, bap. 1634-*d* 1693), eldest dau. of the celebrated Anneke Jans.

KILBOURN (Kilborne), Thomas (1578-1639), from Wood Dighton. Cambridge, in the "Increase," 1635; settled at Wethersfield, Conn.; *m* 1604, Frances Moody (1584-1650).

KIMBALL, Richard (ca. 1595-1675), of Rattlesden, Suffolk; came in the "Elizabeth," 1634; settled at Watertown, Mass.; freeman, 1635; removed to Ipswich, ca. 1637; selectman, 1645; surveyor of fences, 1653; *m* ca. 1615, Ursula, dau. of Henry Scott, *m* Martha Whatlock, of Rattlesden, the latter coming to Mass. with her son after her husband's death; *m* 2d, 1661, Margaret – (*d* 1675), widow of Henry Dow.

KING, John (1629-1703; son of John, sec. for Ireland under reign of Queen Elizabeth, son of

Lord Edward, first archbishop of Ireland after the Reformation), was at Northampton, Mass., 1645, later at Hartford, Conn.; lt. and capt. Northampton forces; dep. Gen. Ct.; *m* Sarah, dau. William Holton; *m* 2d, Sarah, dau. William Whiting, and widow of Jacob Mygatt.

KING, John (*d* 1744), from Eng. to Boston, ca. 1710, later at Watertown, Mass., and Scarboro, Me.; *m* 1714, Sarah Allen; *m* 2d, 1718, Mary, dau. Benjamin Stowell.

KINGSBURY, Joseph (*d* 1676), from Eng. to Dedham, Mass., bet. 1628-30; freeman, 1641; *m* Millicent Ames.

KINGSLEY (Kinsley), John (*d* Jan. 6, 1678/79; desc. of Randulphus de Kyngesleigh, of Chester, 1120), from Hampshire, Eng., to Taunton, Mass., bet. 1630-34; to Dorchester, Mass., 1635; an organizer of the First Ch. of Dorchester, 1636; later to Rehoboth, settled in that part now in E. Providence, R.I.

KINNE (Kinney, Kene), Sir Thomas, knighted in Eng., 1618, for signal service rendered to govt.; fled to Holland to escape religious persecution; came to America, 1625.

KINSEY, John (*d* 1677), from Eng. in the "Kent" to Burlington, N.J., 1677; one of the commrs. for settlement of West Jersey; his son David (*d* 1687), came in the "Lyon" with a certificate of removal from the Bristol (Eng.) Quaker Meeting, dated 1682, to Phila.; owned 300 acres at Radnor, and a town lot, now a part of Independence Square, Phila.; *m* ca.1680, Maudlin–.

KIP (Kype), Hendrik Hendriksen (1600-1680), from Holland to New Amsterdam, bet. 1636-42; one of "The Nine Men," 1647, 49, 50; asst. to the director or gov.; mem. Council; schepen, 1656; great burgher, 1657; *m* 1624, Tryntie Lubberts; *m* 2d, ca. 1627, Tryntje Droogle; *m* 3d, Margaret de Marneil.

KIRBY, Richard (*d* 1686-88), at Lynn, Mass., 1636; removed to Cape Cod, 1637, to Sandwich, to Dartmouth, 1660; freeman, took oath of fidelity, 1684; *m* prob. Jane–.

KIRKBRIDGE (Kirkbride), Joseph (*d* Jan. 1, 1737), to Newcastle, Pa., with William Penn, 1682; *d* Phila.; *m* Phoebe Blackshaw.

KIRKHAM, Thomas (*d* ca. 1677), from Eng. ca. 1646; settled at Wethersfield, Conn., ca. 1648; taxgatherer, 1648-49.

KITCHELL, Robert (*b* Kent, Eng., 1604-*d* 1672), from Eng. with brothers-in-law, Henry Whitfield and William Chittenden, 1639; name stands first on Plantation Covenant, made on board "Confidence"; treas. of Conn.; dep.; a founder of Guilford and New Haven, Conn., and Newark, N.J., 1666; *m* 1632, Margaret, dau. of Rev. Edmund Sheaffe.

KNAPP, Nicholas (*d* 1670; son of Roger), came with Winthrop's fleet, 1630; settled at Watertown, Mass.; propr., 1636/37; removed to Wethersfield, Conn., thence to Stamford, 1649; *m* 1630, Elinor–(*d* 1658); *m* 2d, 1659, Unity–, widow of Peter Brown.

KNIGHT, John (1587-1670), from Eng. in the "James," to Ipswich, Mass., 1635; settled at Newbury, Mass.; innkeeper, selectman, constable; *m* in Eng., Elizabeth Vincent (*d* 1645); *m* 2d, Ann Langley (*d* 1677), widow of Richard Ingersoll (qv).

KNOWLES, John (*d* 1705), from Eng. to Cambridge, Mass., ca. 1650, later at North Hampton, N.H.; *m* 1660, Jemima Knapp.

KNOWLES, Richard (*d* 1670-75; prob. a son of Rev. John Knowles, who came to N.E., 1639), settled at Plymouth, Mass.; removed to Eastham, Mass.; shipmaster; surveyor, 1670; *m* 1637, Ruth (*d* 1687), dau. George Bower, *m* Barbara–.

KNOWLTON, Capt. William (1584-1632-34), *d* on voyage from Eng., and is said to have been buried in what is now Shelburn, N.S.; was part owner of vessel in which he sailed for America; *m* Ann Elizabeth Smith, as widow, settled at Ipswich, Mass., with her children.

KYN, Jöran, see Keen.

LADD, Daniel (*d* 1693), from Eng., in the "Mary and John," to Mass., 1634; was at Salisbury, ca. 1639; *m* Ann – (*d* 1694).

LAKE, Henry, from Eng. bet. 1645-49, to Salem, Mass.; removed to Dorchester.

LAMAR, Thomas (*d* 1714), Huguenot, from Wieres, France; settled in Va., ca.1660; in Prince Georges Co., Md., 1663; naturalized in Md.; settled at "The Fishing Place," Calvert

Co., Md., 1676; acquired large landed interests ante 1696; *m* Mary–; *m* 2d, Ann Pottinger (living 1714).

LAMB, Thomas (*d* 1646), Eng. to Roxbury, Mass., 1630; freeman, 1631; *m* 2d, 1640, Dorothy Harbittle.

LANE, Job (1620-97), from Eng., was at Rehoboth, Mass., 1644; freeman at Malden, 1656; resided at Bedford, Mass.; served in his own garrison house in King Philip's War; dep. Gen. Ct. from Bedford, 1678-79, from Malden, 1685, 93; *m* 2d, 1660, Anna Raynor (ca. 1632-1704).

LANGHORNE (Lacharn), John (11th gen. from Richard Lacharn of Pembrokeshire, Wales, *m* Joan, dau. of Sir Peter Russell, Kt.); came from Wales, ca. 1672; mem. Va. House of Burgesses, 1675; patented a large tract on James River in Warwick Co., Va., 1681; established "Gambell" in Warwick Co.

LANIER, John (ca. 1655-*d* 1719), from Eng., settled in Prince George Co., Va., as early as 1676; received land grant in Westover Parish, 1683, for importing 30 families into the colony of Va.; *m* Sarah –.

LANSING, Gerrit Frederickse (*d* 1679?), from Hasselt, nr. Zwoll, Providence of Overyssel, Holland, to New Amsterdam, ante 1650; purchased land at Albany; *m* Elizabeth Hendricks (she *m* 2d, Wouter Albertsen Van den Uythoff).

LARRABEE, Stephen, settled at Malden, Mass.; served in Narragansett War; to North Yarmouth but was forced to leave during King Philip's War; his children each received 10 acres of land for his services.

LATHROP (Laythrop, Lathropp, Lothrop), John (1584-1653), M.A., Queen's Coll., Cambridge, Eng., 1606; was pastor First Independent, or Congl. Ch. at London; came to Scituate, Mass., 1634, where he was first minister; removed to Barnstable, Mass., 1639, and was first minister there; *m* 1st, 1611, Harriet, dau. Rev. John Howse.

LAURENS, Andre (*d* post 1715-16; son of Jean), Huguenot; from La Rochelle, France to Eng. with his widowed mother, 1682, soon afterward to Ireland, thence to New Rochelle, N.Y., 1695, and settled at Charleston, S.C., 1715 or 16; *m* in Eng., Feb. 22, 1688, Marie Lucas (*d* 1715).

LAWRENCE, Benjamin (*d* 1685), from Accomac Co., Va., to Somerset Co., Md., thence to Anne Arundel Co., Md.; *m* Ann Ascomb; *m* 2d, 1676, Elizabeth (Talbott) Preston (ca. 1656-ante 1719), dau. of Richard Talbott, *m* Elizabeth, dau. of Richard Ewen.

LAWRENCE, John (bap. at Wissett, Eng., Oct. 8, 1609-*d* July 11, 1667; son of Henry, *m* Mary –): settled at Watertown, Mass., 1635; freeman, 1637; settled at Groton, 1662, where he was an original land proprietor of a 20-acre tract; mem. first Bd. of Selectmen; *m* Elizabeth – (*d* Aug. 29, 1663); *m* 2d, at Charlestown, Susanna (*d* July 8, 1668), dau. William Batchelder.

LAWRENCE, John (1618-99; *e.* son of Thomas [1588-1625], chief burgher of St. Albans, Co. Herts., Eng., *m* 1609, Joan Antrobus, who *m* 2d, Thomas Tuttle, of Ireland, and came in the "Planter" 1635, with her children, John, William [qv], and Marie Lawrence, and her three Tuttle children); he was an incorporator of Hempstead, L.I., 1644, and of Flushing, 1645; removed to Amsterdam, 1658; alderman; twice mayor of N.Y. City; councillor; deposed by Gov. Bellomont, restored and made a justice Supreme Ct. of N.Y.; *m* Susanna –.

LAWRENCE, Maj. Thomas (1625-1703), from Eng. to Flushing, L.I.; bought patent for Hell Gate Neck from Governor Dungan, 1686; maj. Queens Co. forces; *m* Mary –.

LAWRENCE, William (1623-80), from Eng. in the "Planter," 1635, with his brother John; lived at Ipswich, Mass.; was one of the first patentees of Flushing, L.I., 1645; mem. Queens Co. militia, 1665-80; cdr. Flushing company at surrender of New York to the Dutch, 1673; *m* 2d, Elizabeth Smith.

LAWRENCE, William (bap. June 13, 1630), from Eng. to L.I., ca.1660; to N.J., 1666; mem. Middletown Ct., 1670; mem. Gen. Ct., 1669; burgess, Elizabeth Town, 1671; overseer; *m* 2d, 1693, Elizabeth Scudder (*b* 1648), widow of Jan Albertus.

LAWSON, Hugh (1705-72; son of John Roger Lawson, *m* Mary McConnell; desc. of Cedric, crowned 519 A.D., and from Edward I, King of

England), came from Ire. in the "George and Anne," settled in Pa., 1727; justice 1st Co. Ct. of Lunenberg Co., Va., 1746; purchased land Rowan Co., N.C., 1757; *m* 1729, Mary, dau. Charles Moore, of Lancaster Co., Pa.

LAY, Robert (1617-89), of Lynn 1638; removed to Saybrook 1647; *m* 1647, Sarah Fenner (1616-76), widow of John Scully.

LEA (Lygh), John (1661-1726), Quaker, from Eng. in the "Canterbury," with William Penn on his second voyage, 1699, to Upland, nr. Chester, Pa., settled at Concord, Chester Co., Pa.; *m* in Eng., 1698, Hannah (Hopton) Webb (1665-1735).

LEACH, Lawrence (1580-1662), came to N.E. in the "Abigail," 1628; freeman, Salem, 1630; a founder of the First Ch. of Christ there, 1637; one of the "seven men" to manage the affairs of Salem, 1638-42; an early propr.; received land grant for 100 acres; farmer, millwright, and had an iron foundry; *m* Elizabeth-(*d* ca.1674).

LEARNED, William (1590-1646), from Eng., in the Winthrop Fleet, 1630; recorded at Charlestown, Mass., 1632; freeman, 1634; settled at Woburn, ca.1640; selectman, 1644; *m* Goditha –, or Judith–.

LEAVITT, John (1608-91), from Eng. in the "Diligent," to Dorchester, Mass., 1634; later at Hingham; freeman, 1636; dep. Gen. Ct., 1658-64; tailor; deacon; *m* (?) Mary Lovitt; *m* 2d, 1646, Sarah, dau. of Edward Gilman.

LE COMPTE, Sir Anthony (1618-73), Huguenot, of Picardy, France; fled to Eng. at time of religious persecutions and served in the army 11 yrs.; to America, 1655; settled in Calvert Co., Md.; granted patent for 800 acres on Horne Bay, 1659; justice, Dorchester Co., to 1671; *m* 1661, Esther Dottando (or Doatloan or Dotlando), of Dieppe, Normandy.

LE CONTE, Guillaume (1659-1710/11), a Huguenot, from France to Holland before the revocation of the Edict of Nantes, 1685; came to New York, 1698; *m* Marguerite DeValleau.

LEE (Leigh), John (1600-71), from Eng. to Mass., ca. 1635; settled at Ipswich; *m* Anne Hungerford.

LEE, Richard (*b* 1619-*d* 1684), called "The Cavalier"; came to Virginia in 1641; served as secretary of state under Governor Sir John Harvy; was the King's counsellor; became a large landowner in both York and Westmoreland counties; also served as Colonial secretary of Virginia under Sir William Berkeley; was member of Council and a justice; *m* Anne—.

LEE, Thomas (1710-69), *b* Barbados, came to Charleston, S.C.; *m* 1732, Mary Giles (*d* 1751).

LEETE, William (1613-83), clk. of Bishop's Ct., Cambridge, Eng.; Whitfield's company, one of the signers Plantation Covenant, shipboard, June 1, arriving at New Haven, July 10, 1639; one of the founders and first clk. Guilford, Conn.; propr. Leete's Island, Conn.; asst. of colony, dep. gov. and gov. New Haven Colony; asst. and dep. gov. Conn. Colony, succeeding Winthrop as gov. of Conn., 1676, dying in office, 1683; pres. of Congress of Commissioners, United Colonies of N.E.; protector of Goffe and Whalley, judges of Charles I; *m* Anne, dau. Rev. John Payne.

LEFFERTS, Leffert Pieterse, see Haughwout, Pieter J.

LEFFINGWELL, Thomas (1622-1714), from Eng. to Saybrook, Conn., 1637; a founder of Norwich and its first settler; dep. Gen. Assembly, 1661-1710; lt. King Philip's War; *m* Mary White.

LEGARE, Solomon (1662-1760); Huguenot, who with his mother Janette, fled from France to America after the revocation of the Edict of Nantes, and settled at Charleston, S.C., 1686.

LEGGETT (Legat), Gabriel (1635-1700), from Eng. to the Barbados, thence to New Amsterdam, ca. 1640; West Farms (now part of greater New York), 1661; became patentee of a large estate on Hunt's Point, also called Leggett's Point; *m* 1676, Elizabeth, widow of John Richardson, an original patentee of West Farms, 1664.

LEIDY (Ludwig, Lydig, Leydig), Carl (1678-1765), from Alsace-Lorraine, settled in Phila. Co., Pa., 1727; *m* Catherine –.

LELAND (Layland), Hopestill (1580-1655), from Eng. as early as 1624, settled at Weymouth; *d* at Sherborn, Mass.; son Henry (1625-80), at Dorchester, 1653; later at Sherborn; *m* Margaret Badcock.

LEONARD, James (1621-91), from Eng. to Md. after 1628; thence to N.E., and was at Providence, R.I., 1645; with his brother Henry, built the first iron foundry in Plymouth Co., at Taunton, Mass., 1652; defended his garrison house in King Philip's War; *m* Mary Martin; *m* 2d Margaret –.

LEONARD, Solomon (ca.1610-1675), from Monmouthshire, Eng., to Holland, thence to Bridgewater, Mass.; freeman, Plymouth, 1633; early settler at Duxbury; granted land, 1638/39; *m* Mary–.

LESTER, Andrew (*d* 1669), from Wales to Gloucester, Mass., 1641; freeman; to New London, Conn., 1651; constable, collector, 1668; *m* Barbara–(*d* 1653/54); *m* 2d, 1654/55, Joanna–, widow of Robert Hempstead; *m* 3d, 1661, Hannah (Brooks) Fox, dau. of Henry Brooks, and widow of Thomas Fox.

LEVERETT, John (1616-78; son of Thomas, who came from Eng. to Boston, 1633, and was ruling elder); freeman, 1640; mem. A. and H. A. Co., 1639, sgt., 1642, lt., 1652; agt. of Colony of Mass. Bay in Eng.; maj. gen. Mass. forces, 1663-73; rep. Gen. Ct., 1663, 64, 65, and speaker, 1663, 64; gov.'s asst., 1665-71; gov., 1673-78; *m* Hannah (ca. 1621-1646), dau. of Ralph Hudson (*b* 1593), *m* Marie (*b* 1592), dau. of John Twing, *m* Helen –; *m* 2d, ? Sara Sedgwick (1629-1704).

LEVERICH, Rev. William (1605-77), A.B., Emanuel Coll., 1625; from Eng., 1633, settled at Boston; removed to Sandwich, 1640, to Oyster Bay, L.I., 1653, to Newtown, 1669.

LEVERING, (John) Wigard (1648 or 49-1744/45; son of Rosier, *m* Elizabeth Van de Walle); came from Germany to Germantown, Phila., 1685; a first settler in Roxborough Tp., Pa., 1691, where he bought 500 acres and there died; *m* 1674, Magdalena Böker (ca. 1640-1717).

LEWIS, George (*d* 1662), from East Greenwich, Co. Kent, Eng., to Plymouth, Mass.; 1630; one of first makers of cloth at Scituate, 1634; a founder of Barnstable, 1639, where he died; *m* Sarah Jenkins; *m* 2d, Mary Fuller.

LEWIS, Henry (1671-1731), *b* in Wales, came to Pa.; mem. Pa. Assembly, 1700, 08, 09, 15, 18; *m* 1692, Mary Taylor.

LEWIS, "Pioneer" John (*b* Donegal Co., Ireland, 1678-*d* Feb. 1, 1762; son of Andrew, and g.son of William, Huguenot, from France to Wales after the revocation of the Edict of Nantes, 1685, thence to North of Ireland, where he *m* Mary McCollough, or McCleland); John fled from Ireland to Portugal, thence to Pa., ca. 1731; was the first white settler in now Augusta Co., Va., 1732, where he built "Ft. Lewis"; col. militia; justice; high sheriff; had 5 sons in Am. Rev.; *m* 1715/16, Margaret (1693-1775), dau. of the Laird of Loch Lynn, in Scotland.

LEWIS, Robert (*d* 1644), came in the "Blessing," to Salem, Mass., 1635; settled at Newbury, Mass.; *m* Elizabeth—.

LEWIS, Robert (*d* ca. 1656), from Eng. to Va., bought land Poropotank Creek, Gloucester Co., Va.; of record in York Co., 1644-46; traditionally a gen. of Va. militia; *m* Mary-(she *m* 2d, ca. 1656, Capt. Robert Langley).

LEWIS, William (1594-1683), from Eng. in the "Lion," to Boston, 1632; freeman, 1632; an original settler of Hartford, Conn., 1636; at Hadley, 1659; rep. Gen. Ct., 1662, for Northampton, 1664; settled at Farmington, ca. 1675; *m* Felix Collins (*d* 1671).

LEWIS, William (1610-71), from Eng., 1630, was a propr. in Cambridge, Mass. Bay Colony, 1630; returned to Eng. and *m* Amy Wells; was at Roxbury, 1639, where he was land owner and freeman, 1642; an original settler of Lancaster, Mass., 1653, where he died.

LIBBY (Libbey), John (ca. 1602-1682), from Eng. bet. 1630-35; granted land at Scarborough, Me., before 1640; first selectman, 1669; served in Indian wars; *m* Agnes –.

LIGON (Lygon), Lt. Col. Thomas (will made 1675; son of Thomas, of Elstone, Parish of Orcheson, St. George, Wiltshire, Eng., *m* Frances Dennis), at Calloudon, Warwickshire, Eng., 1630; to Va. as agt. for Sir William Berkeley, 1642; settled in Henrico Co.; burgess, 1655-56; j.p., surveyor; *m* a dau. of Dennis Pratt (*d* in Eng.); *m* 2d, ca. 1650, Mary (1625-1703/04), dau. of Capt. Thomas Harris (qv).

LILLIE, George (1638-91), from Eng., 1658, settled at Reading, Mass.; *m* 1st, 1659, Hannah Smith (*d* 1666); *m* 2d, 1667, Jane–.

LILLINGTON, Alexander (1643-97), dep. gov., 1693-95, pres. Council and asso. justice Supreme Ct. of N.C.; judge Precinct Ct., 1690-1695; *m* 2d, 1675, Elizabeth Cooper.

LINCOLN, Samuel (1619-May 26, 1690), from Eng. to Salem, Mass., 1637; settled at Hingham; *m* Martha–(*d* 1693).

LINDLY, Francis (*d* 1704), bro. of John from Eng. to Conn.; came to Branford, Conn.; herdsman; early settler at Newark, N.J.; sexton, 1672; *m* 1655, Susanna Culpepper (*d* ante 1704).

LINES, Ralph (*d* 1689), from Eng., 1639, settled at what is now New Haven, Conn.; he gave food and assistance to the 3 judges, Goff, Whaley and Dixon, who fled from Eng. for safety; *m* Alis–.

LINTHICUM, Thomas (1640-1701), Wales to Md. Colony, 1658; settled in Anne Arundel Co., Md.; landed propr.; Quaker; *m* Jane–.

LIPPINCOTT, Richard (*d* 1683), from Eng. to Dorchester, Mass., ca. 1639; freeman, 1640; removed to Boston, 1644; disagreed with church and was cast out from the community, 1651; returned to Eng.; again came to America and lived in R.I.; removed to N.J. and was a patentee of Shrewsbury, 1669; dep. Gen. Assembly of East Jersey, 1669-77; overseer; *m* Abigail – (*d* 1697).

LIPPITT (Lippett), John (*d* 1669), from Eng. to R.I., 1638, and became a landholder and commr. to form government under a charter, Colony of R.I. and Providence Plantations, 1647; landholder at Warwick, 1648.

LITCHFIELD, Laurence (1620-49), from Kent, Eng., to Scituate, Mass., 1639; mem. A. and H. A. Co.; served in colonial wars; *m* 1640, Judith Denniss (1620-85).

LITTELL (Little), Benjamin, from London, Eng. to Newbury, Mass., 1630.

LITTLE, George (*d* bet. 1693-94), from Eng. to Newbury, Mass., ca. 1640; *m* 1st, Alice Poor (1618-80); came from Eng. in the "Bevis," 1638; *m* 2d, July 19, 1681, Eleanor, or Helen –, widow of Thomas Barnard (qv).

LITTLE, Thomas (*d* 1671/72), from Eng., was at Plymouth, Mass., 1630; purchased 1000 acres at Marshfield, 1650; *d* at Scituate; mem. Plymouth mil. company; *m* 1633, Anne, dau. Richard Warren (qv).

LITTLETON, Col. Nathaniel, in Va., 1622; gov. of Accomac, 1652; burgess; *m* Anne, dau. of Henry Southey; *m* Elizabeth –.

LIVERMORE, John (1606-84; son of Peter), from Eng. in the "Francis," 1634, freeman, 1635; at Wethersfield, Conn., to 1640; at New Haven to 1647; corpl. New Haven company, 1647; settled at Watertown, Mass.; *m* Grace (1615-90), dau. Edmund Sherman (qv).

LIVINGSTON, Robert (1654-1728; desc. William, 4th Lord Livingston, of Callendar), from Scotland to Charlestown, Mass., 1673; settled at Albany, N.Y., 1674; large landholder, patented from Gov. Dungan, 1686, and confirmed by royal charter, 1715, erecting the manor and lordship of Livingston; mem. Council Province of N.Y., 1698-1701; mem. Assembly, 1709-11; *m* 1679, Alida (Schuyler) Van Rensselaer, dau. Philip Pieterse Schuyler, and widow of Rev. Nicholas Van Rensselaer.

LLOYD, Col. Edward (1605-95), from Wales to Va., ca. 1636; justice of Norfolk Co., 1645; burgess, 1644-45; removed to Md., 1649, settled on Greenbury Point, nr. Annapolis, Md.; mem. Md. Privy Council, 1656; cdr. Anne Arundel Co., 1650; signed treaty with Susquehanna Indians, 1652; burgess, 1658; mem. Provincial Ct., 1656; was Cromwell's commr. of Parliament; resided in London, 1688-95; *m* 1st, ca. 1646, Alice Crouch.

LLOYD, John, from Wales, settled at Camptown, N.J.; *m* 1765, Rebecca Ball (cousin of Mary Ball, mother of George Washington).

LLOYD, Thomas (1640-94), from Wales in the "Fortune," with William Penn, in 1682, to Pa.; mem. and pres. of the Council, and dep. gov. Province of Pa., during William Penn's ab-

sence; chief magistrate, 1684-93; first master of rolls and keeper of the great seal; *m* 1665, Mary (*d* 1680). dau. of Roger Jones, of Wales.

LOBDELL (Lobden), Nicholas, from Hastings, Kent, Eng.; at Hingham, Mass., 1635; received land grants; *m* twice.

LOBDELL, Simon (*d* 1717; desc. Count Nicholas Lobdell), from Eng. ca. 1645; settled at Milford, Conn., 1646; *m* Persis, dau. of Thomas Pierce. *m* Elizabeth –, of Charlestown, Mass.

LOCKE, Capt. John (1627-killed by Indians, 1696), from Yorkshire, Eng., to Dover, N.H., ca. 1644; later to Ft. Point (Newcastle); finally at Rye, N.H.; *m* ca.1652, Elizabeth, dau. of William Berry.

LOCKWOOD, Robert (*d* 1658), from Eng. in the "Arbella," 1630, with Winthrop's fleet to Salem, Mass.; propr. of Watertown, Mass., 1636; freeman, 1636; settled at Fairfield, Conn.; sgt. of Fairfield regt.; *m* Susannah (*d* 1660), dau. Capt. Richard Norman; she *m* 2d, Jeffrey Ferris.

LOGAN, Col. George, from Aberdeen, Scot., 1690; settled at Oyster Point (now Charleston), S.C.; master Provincial House, 1716; col. of regt. in expdn. against the Spaniards at St. Augustine, Fla.; *m* 1st, and by whom issue; *m* 2d, Martha–, widow of Gov. Robert Daniell.

LOGAN, James (1674-1751), came with William Penn, 1699, as his secretary, established "Stenton," in Phila. Co., Pa.; eminent educationalist; sec. of the province and clk. of the Council, 1701; commr. of property; justice Ct. Common Pleas, 1715-23, presiding judge, 1723; mayor of Phila., 1723; chief justice Supreme Ct., 1731-39; pres. Provincial Council and actg. gov., 1736-38; *m* 2d, Amy Child.

LOMBARD, Thomas (*b* ca. 1610-1662), from Eng. in the "Mary and John," 1630, settled at Dorchester, Mass., later at Scituate and Barnstable where he died; *m* Joyce –.

LONG (Longe), Robert (*b* Eng. 1590-*d* Charlestown, Mass., Jan. 9, 1663), came in the "Defense," to Boston, 1635, with 2d wife, 10 children and one servant; purchased the "Great House," Charlestown, 1636, for an inn; freeman, 1636; selectman; mem. A. and H. A. Co.; *m* Oct. 8, 1614, Sarah (1595-1631), dau. of John Taylor, of Eng.; *m* 2d, Elizabeth – (*b* 1605).

LONGLEY, William (1614-80; son of John, of Firsby, Lincolnshire, Eng.), settled at Lynn, Mass., as early as 1638; later at Groton; selectman; town clk., 1665-67; *m* Joanna Goffe (1618-98).

LONGSTRETH, Bartholomew (1679-1749), from Eng. to Edgehill, nr. Phila., Pa., 1699; *m* Ann Dawson.

LOOMIS, Joseph (1590-1658; son of John, *m* Agnes –); came to Boston in the "Susan and Ellen," 1638; woollendraper; settled on "The Island," at Windsor, Conn., 1639; dep. Gen. Ct., 1643-44; *m* 1614, in Eng., Mary (bap. 1590-1652), dau. of Robert White, of Eng., *m* 1585, Bridget Allgar.

LORD, Thomas (1585/86-1667; son of Richard, of Towcester, Co. Northampton, Eng. *m* Joan–), from Eng. in the "Elizabeth and Ann," to Cambridge, Mass., 1635; joined Rev. Thomas Hooker's party in founding of Hartford, Conn., 1636; an original propr. of Hartford; *m* 1610/11, Dorothy (*b* 1589-*d* Eng.), dau. of Rev. Edwd. Bulkeley, and sis. of Rev. Peter (qv); *m* 2d, 1616, Dorothy (1589-1670), dau. of Robert Bird.

LORILLARD, Peter (1746-76), Huguenot, from Holland; settled at Hackensack, N.J.; killed during Am. Rev.; *m* Catherine Moore.

LORING, Thomas (*d* 1661), from Eng. to Dorchester, Mass., 1634, with his wife and sons, Thomas and John; removed to Hingham, where he was one of the first deacons of the church established there, 1634; freeman, 1636; settled at Hull 1646; *m* in Eng., Jane Newton.

LOTHROP, see Lathrop.

LOVEJOY, John (ca. 1622-1690; son of Rowland), from Eng. in the "Mary and John," 1633/34; settled at Andover, Mass.; served in King Philip's War; *m* 1651, Mary (*d* 1675), dau. Christopher Osgood (qv); *m* 2d, 1676, Hannah–, widow of William Pritchard.

LOVEWELL (Lowell), John, said to have served in Cromwell's army; at Boston, 1657; granted land at Rehoboth, Mass., 1669; to Lynn, ca.1680, to Dunstable, 1648; he and his sons,

John and Joseph, were among the early settlers of the town; selectman, 1689; at Sudbury, 1700; m 1658. Elizabeth, dau. Richard Sylvester (qv).

LOW (Louw), Peter Cornelissen, from Holstein, 1659, settled at Esopus, N.Y.; m 1668 Elizabeth, dau. of Mattheus Blanchan, m Maddelen Jorisse, from Artois, France, 1660.

LOWELL (Lowle), Percival (1571-1665; son of Richard), merchant, from Eng. with his wife and sons, John and Richard, and daughter, Joan, in the "Jonathan," to Newbury, Mass., 1639; m Rebecca –.

LOWNDES, Christopher (1713-85), from Eng. ca. 1738; settled in Prince George's Co., Md., where he was justice and judge; m 1747, Elizabeth (d 1789), dau. Benjamin Tasker, pres. Council and dep. gov. of Md.

LOWTHER, William (d 1750), a Quaker, came from Ireland with his wife, Martha, to Abingdon, Pa., ca. 1727, settled finally in Bucks Co., Pa.

LUCE, Henry (ca.1640-ante 1689), appears as juror as Scituate, Mass., 1666; propr. at Rehoboth, 1668; settled at Tisbury, Martha's Vineyard ante 1671; surveyor of highways, 1675, juror, 1677, selectman, 1687; m 1666, Remember (1644-living 108), dau. Lawrence Litchfield (qv).

LUDLOW, Roger (1590-1665), from Eng. to Dorchester, Mass., 1630; removed to Windsor, Conn., 1635, to Fairfield, 1639; to Va., 1654; gov.'s asst., 1630; dep. gov., Colony of Mass. Bay, 1634, of Conn., 1639; served in Pequot War.

LUDLOW (Ludlam, Ludlum), William (1600-65), from Eng. to Boston; known as "The Miller"; to Southampton, L.I., where he received 40 acres at the head of Mecox Bay, from the Court, 1659; m Clemence– (Coe or Fordham?).

LUDWELL, Philip, came to Va., ca. 1660; mem. Council; dep. sec. of Va.; gov. of North and South Carolina, 1693; returned to Eng. where he d post 1704, was buried at Bow Ch., nr. Stratford in Middlesex; m 1667, as her 3d husband, Lucy, dau. Capt. Robert Higginson.

LUKENS (Lucken, Luckens), Jan (1666-1744), with his wife, Mary, together with twelve other families came from Crefeld, Germany, sailed from Rotterdam, Holland, to Eng., thence to America in the "Concord," July 17, 1683, arrived at Phila., Oct. 8, 1683; an original settler of Germantown, Pa.; was constable, burgess, sheriff and bailiff; m 1683, Mary–(1660-1742).

LUNT, Henry (d 1662), from Eng. in the "Mary and John," 1633; settled at Ipswich, Mass., later at Newbury; m Anne –.

LUSK, John (1702-88), from Scotland with his father, Stephen, to Wethersfield, Conn.; m Janet – (d 1742); m 2d, Jane Trumbell (d 1788).

LYFORD, Francis (1645-1723), London to Boston, 1667; mariner; Exeter, 1683; juryman, 1683; selectman, 1689-90; served in King William's War, 1696; comd. sloop "Elizabeth." Exeter, impressed by Capt. John Perkins to bring distressed inhabitants from Saco and Portsmouth "when Indians were burning and destroying all about them"; m 1st, ca. 1670, Elizabeth, dau. Thomas Smith, builder of Boston (m Elizabeth–); m 2d, Rebecca, dau. Rev. Samuel Dudley (son of Gov. Thomas Dudley, qv).

LYGON, Lt. Col. Thomas, see Ligon.

LYMAN, Richard (1580-1640), from Eng. in the "Lion," with his wife and children, to Boston, 1631; freeman, 1633; an original propr. of Hartford, Conn., 1636; m in Eng., Sarah, dau. Roger Osborne.

LYNDE, Simon (bap. 1624-d 1687; 3d son of Enoch, m Elizabeth Digby); came to Boston, Mass., 1650; clk. and sgt. A. and H. A. Co.; gov.'s asst., 1668-1679; served in King Philip's War; m 1652, Hannah (1635-84), dau. of John Newgate, emigrant.

LYNDE, Thomas (1593/94-1671), from Eng., settled at Charlestown, Mass., 1634; dep. Gen. Ct., 1636-37. 1645-52.

LYON, Henry (ca. 1625-1703), from Scotland to New Milford, Conn., 1648; one of the first settlers at Newark, N.J., 1666, where was dep., mem. Council and first treas.; removed to Elizabeth Town, N.J., but returned to Newark; m 1652, Elizabeth Bateman.

LYON, William (1620-92; son of William, of Heston, Co. Middlesex, Eng.); from Eng. in the "Hopewell," Sept. 11, 1635, aet. 14; settled at Roxbury, Mass. (home still standing on Belle-

view Av., nr. Atwood St., Roxbury); mem. A. and H. A. Co., 1645; m 1646, Sarah (bap. 1629-d 1688), dau. John Ruggles, of Nazing, Co. Essex, Eng., m Mary Curtis.

McCOOK, George (Scotch descent), from Ireland, 1780, settled at Canonsburg, Pa.; founder of Jefferson Coll.; m Mary McCormick (parents of "The Fighting McCooks," 2 sons and 14 g. sons in army or navy in Civil War).

McCORMICK, Thomas (1702-1762), from Ireland, settled in Lancaster Co., Pa., ca. 1734; moved to E. Pennsboro Tp., Cumberland Co., Pa., ca. 1745; m 1728, Elizabeth (1705-66), dau. Adam Carruth.

McCULLOCH, Roderick (d 1745; of the Clan McCulloch, Ardwall, Galloway, Scotland), came to Va., with Gov. Gooch and Commissary Blair, 1727; rector Washington Parish, Westmoreland Co., Va.; m Elizabeth Weedon.

McDONALD, Angus (1727-78), from Scotland to Falmouth, Va., 1746, to Winchester ca. 1760; served in French and Indian War, 1754-63; maj. militia, 1765; vestryman old Frederick Parish (Episcopal), 1768; one of the founders of Hiram Lodge No. 12, A. F. & A. M., at Winchester; agent for Lord Fairfax; built first fort at Wheeling, 1774; lt. col. of Va. militia, 1774; sheriff, 1775; justice and dep. sheriff, 1776; m Anna Thompson.

McDOWELL, Ephraim (1672-1774), soldier in siege of Londonderry and battle of Boyne; Scotch descent; came from Ireland, with two sons John and James to Pa., 1729-35; settled in Burden's Grant (now Rockbridge Co.), Va., 1737; m Margaret, dau. of James Irvine, m Mary Wylie.

McINTOSH, John Mohr (1700-61), from Scotland with Gov. Oglethorpe, to Darien, Ga., 1734; capt., Highland Light Inf., under Spaniards, 1740; wounded and captured at Ft. Moosa, Fla.; m Jean Gordon.

MACK, John (1652/53-1721), from Scotland to Salisbury, Conn., 1680; later at Lyme; m 1681, Sarah (b 1663), dau. of Orlando Bagley, m Mary Colby.

MACKALL, James (1630-d ca. 1693), from Scotland before 1666, settled at "The Clifts," Calvert Co., Md.; m Mary Grahame (1649-1717).

McKIM, Thomas (1710-1784-86; son Sir John, knighted by King William III), from Ireland, 1734; settled at Phila., Pa., later at Brandywine, Del.; was justice of quarter sessions and judge Ct. Common Pleas; lt. of militia, 1756.

McKINLEY, David (ca. 1705-1761), was called "David the Weaver"; from Dervock House, Co. Antrim, Ire., to York Co., Pa., 1743; m in Ire., Esther–; their son, John, was "The Martyred President of Delaware."

McLANE (MacLean), Allan (1719-76), from Scotland to Phila., Pa., 1740; m Jane, dau. Samuel Erwin, of Falls of Schuylkill.

McLEAN, Allan (1715-86), received grant of land from King for services as lt. in British Army during French and Indian War; came from Scotland to Boston, 1760; moved to Hartford, Conn., finally settled at North Bolton (now Vernon), Conn.; m 2d, 1744, Mary Loomis.

MacNUTT, Alexander (1656-1746; of the family MacNaught, of Scotland), from Scotland to Palmer, Mass., ca. 1720 (others of the family settled in Augusta Co., Va., and in Nova Scotia, 1760); m Sarah – (d 1744, aet. 84).

MACY, Thomas (1608-82), from Eng. to Newbury, Mass., bet. 1635-39; a founder of Salisbury, Mass., 1639; dep. from Salisbury to Gen. Ct. of Elections, Boston, 1654; was one of ten men to purchase island of Nantucket, 1659; chief magistrate of Nantucket, 1675, and first recorder of deeds; m 1639, Sarah Hopcott (or Hopcut, or Hopeat; 1612-1706).

MAGRUDER, Alexander (b Perthshire, Scot., 1610-d "Anchovie Hills," 1677; son of Alexander [b 1569], m 1605, Lady Margaret [Campbell] Drummond, dau. of Campbell, 1st Laird of Keithock), officer in army of Charles II, and sent as prisoner of war to Va., 1651; to Md., 1652; large landowner in Calvert (now Prince Georges) Co., Md.; m Margaret, dau. of William Braithwaite, mem. 1st Gen. Assembly and actg. gov. of Md.; m 2d, ante 1658, Sarah–(d 1671); m 3d, 1672, Elizabeth– (Hawkins or Greene?).

MAINDORT, Doodes, see Minor.

MAKEPEACE, Thomas (ca. 1592-1666/67), from Eng. to Boston, 1635; served in Narragansett War; mem. A. and H. A. Co.; *m* 2d, Mrs. Elizabeth (Hawkredd) Coney Mellowes.

MANCHESTER, John (*d* 1708), from Holland, 1636; settled at Tiverton, R.I.; *m* prob. Elizabeth Grinell (*d* 1708).

MANCHESTER, Thomas (*b* 1620), Eng. to New Haven, Conn., 1638; settled at Newport, R.I.; one of 3 jurymen chosen at meeting of free inhabitants of Portsmouth, 1643; *m* Margaret Wood.

MANIERRE, Louis (1757-94), Huguenot, from France; soldier Am. Rev.; settled at New London, Conn., 1785; *m* Rebecca Miner.

MANIGAULT, Pierre, or Peter (*d* 1729), from France to S.C., ca. 1691; *m* ca. 1699, Judith (Gitton) Royer, a widow, who left France, 1685.

MANN, Richard (*d* 1655), from Eng. to Scituate, Mass., ca. 1640; took oath of fidelity, 1644; juror, 1655; lived on Mann's Hill; *m* Rebecca–.

MANN, William (1607-62), came to Cambridge, Mass., 1634; *m* 1643, Mary Jerauld (or Gerald); *m* 2d, 1657, Alice Teel.

MANNING, William (*d* 1665/66), from Eng. as early as 1634, to Mass. Bay Colony; removed from Roxbury to Cambridge, 1638; propr., 1638; freeman, 1640; to Boston post 1650; *m* 1st, ante 1614, — (*d* on voyage to America); *m* 2d, Susanna–(*d* 1650); *m* 3d, Elizabeth–.

MANSFIELD, Richard (*d* 1655), from Eng., 1643, settled at New Haven, Conn.; propr.; mem. New Haven watch; *m* 1636, Gillian Drake (*d* 1669).

MAPES, Thomas (1628-86), from Eng. to Southold, L.I., before 1640; ensign, Suffolk Co. militia, 1686; *m* Sarah, dau. Capt. William Purrier, of Southold.

MARCH, Hugh (1620-93), from Eng. in the "Confidence," 1638; settled at Newbury, Mass.; *m* Judith – (*d* 1675); *m* 2d, 1676, Dorcas Blackleach; *m* 3d, 1685, Sarah Healy.

MARIS, George (1630-1705), from Eng., 1683, to Darby, Chester Co., Pa.; Provincial Councillor and colonial justice of Pa.; settled at "The Home House," Springfield Tp., Chester Co.; *m* Alice – (1623-99).

MARSH, John (*d* ca.1674; son of John [*d* 1627], clothier of Branktry, Co. Essex, Eng.,*m* Grace–, *d* 1657), came in the "Mary and John," 1633/34; propr., Salem; cordwainer; *m* ca.1635, Susanna, dau. Rev. Samuel Skelton.

MARSH, John (prob. 1618-1688), from Eng. ca.1635; at Hartford, Conn., 1639; at Hadley, Mass., 1660; to Northampton, thence to Hartford; *m* ca.1642, Anne (*d* 1662), dau. Gov. John Webster (qv).

MARSH, Samuel (*d* 1683/84), from Essex, Eng., 1641, resided at New Haven, Conn.; one of Elizabethtown associates, 1665; later at Mananday, N.J.; *m* ca.1647, Comfort Mann (*d* post 1684/85).

MARSHALL, John (1596-1660; 9th in descent from Gilbert, *d* 1150); capt. of cav. in army of Charles I, came from Eng. to Jamestown, Va., ca. 1650; settled in Westmoreland Co., served in Indian wars in Va.

MARSTON, John (1615-81), from Ormsby, Norfolk, Eng., in the "Rosa," 1637, settled at Salem; freeman, 1641; *m* 1640, Alice Eden (*b* 1619), also came in the "Rosa," 1637.

MARTIAN (Martiau), Nicholas (1591-1657), a Frenchman who was naturalized in England and came to America in the "Francis Bonaventure," 1620; resided in the Colony of Va.; justice of York for Kiskyache, 1622-57; burgess, 1623, 31, 33; owned the site of Yorktown; *m* 1627, Jane –, widow of Edward Berkeley; *m* 3d, Isabella Beach.

MARTIN, Abraham (*b* 1645; a younger son of an English family which owned large estates nr. Galway, Ire.), came to Albemarle Co., Va., 1680; Colonial officer.

MARTIN, Lt. Samuel (*d* 1683), from England to Wethersfield, Conn., ca. 1640 or 45; soldier in King Philip's War; was in Great Swamp Fight; *m* 1646, Phebe (Bisby) Bracey, dau. of William Bisby.

MARVIN, Matthew (bap. 1600-1679/80), was sr. warden St. Mary's, Great Bentley, Essex, Eng.; came in the "Increase," 1635, with wife Elizabeth and five children; his name is on monument in honor of the first settlers of Hartford, Conn.; surveyor of highways, 1639, 47; to Norwalk, Conn., 1650; deputy, 1654; *m* ca. 1622, Elizabeth – (ca. 1604-1640); *m* 2d, ca. 1647, Alice – (ca. 1610-1680/81), widow of John Bouton.

MARVIN, Reynold (or Reinold), (ante 1594-1662), from Eng., was at Hartford, Conn., 1638; later at Farmington, thence to Saybrook; *d* Lyme, Conn.; *m* Marie –.

MASON, Lt. Francis (1595-1648), from Eng., 1613; burgess; justice of Lower Norfolk Co., Va.; *m* 1624, Alice –.

MASON, George (1629-86), from Eng. to Norfolk, Va., ca. 1651; county lt., Stafford Co., 1675; mem. Bacon's Assembly, 1676; in Indian wars, 1675-84; *m* Mary French; *m* 2d, Frances Norgrave.

MASON, Hugh (1605/06-1678), from Eng. in the "Frances," 1634; settled at Watertown, Mass.; tanner; freeman, 1635; lt., 1645; capt., 1652-78; dep. Gen. Ct., 1635, et seq.; mem. Council of War, 1676; cdr. of volunteers against Manhattoes, 1664; cdr. company in King Philip's War; *m* 1632/33, Hester, dau. of Thomas Wells.

MASON, John (ca. 1600-1672), from Eng. to Dorchester, Mass., 1630 or 1632; freeman, 1635; settled at Windsor, Conn.; a leader in mil. and civil affairs; in chief command of forces at close of Pequot War, 1637; at Saybrook, 1647, Norwich, 1659; rep. Gen. Ct., 1637-41; asst., 1641-59; commr. United Colonies, 1647-61; dep. gov., 1659-69; dep. gov. under charter of Charles II, 1662; maj. and cdr.-in-chief of Conn. militia; organized the first troop of horse in the colony, 1657-58; *m* 2d, 1640, Anna, dau. Rev. Robert Peck, from Eng., 1637.

MASON, Sampson (*d* 1676), from Eng. to Dorchester, Mass., 1651; at Rehoboth, 1657; Swansea, 1667; shoemaker; *m* Mary Butterworth (*d* 1714).

MATHER, Richard (1596-1669; son of Thomas), non-conformist; from Eng. in the "James," to Boston, 1635; settled as teacher over the church at Dorchester, 1636; regarded as one of the most useful men in the colony; eminent theologian and author; *m* 1st, 1624, Catharine, dau. Edmund Holt (or Hoult); *m* 2d, 1656, Sarah Story, widow of John Cotton.

MATLACK, William (1648-1728), from Cropwell Bishop, Nottinghamshire, Eng., in the "Kent," 1677; settled at Burlington, N.J.; *m* 1682, Mary Hancock (1664-1728), who came from Eng., in the "Paradise," 1681.

MATTHEWS (Mathews), James (*d* 1686), from Eng. to Charlestown, Mass., ca. 1634; was at Yarmouth, 1639; mem. Yarmouth mil. company, 1643; dep. Gen. Ct. of Plymouth Colony, 1644. from Yarmouth, 1664.

MATTOON, Hubartus, settled at Kittery, Me., ante 1654.

MAULE, Dr. Patrick (*d* Apr. 1736, Bath Beaufort Precinct, Bath Co., N.C.), from Scotland, to N.C., 1714; trustee, Bath Pub. Library; vestryman St. Thomas's Parish, 1715; dep. surveyor; dep. surveyor gen.; mem. grand jury, 1721; mem. Gen. Assembly; justice of peace; dep. admiralty judge, 1733; *m* Elizabeth –.

MAULE (Mauld), Thomas (ca. 1643-1701; nephew of Sir Patrick Maule, Earl of Panmure, Baron Maule of Brechin and Navarre), from Eng. to the Barbados ca. 1655, at age of 12, thence to Salem, Mass.; joined the Quakers; twice whipped for "ill words"; shopkeeper; *m* 2d, 1670, Naomi –; *m* 3d, Mary –.

MAUPIN, Gabriel (*b* in bas Pyrennes, France, 1651 or 75?-will proved in 1720; son of Amos), Huguenot; officer army of Navarre; fled from France to Eng., ca. 1699; arrived at Yorktown, Va., in the "Nassau," Mar. 1700, with about 191 refugee Huguenots; comdt. royal arsenal at Williamsburg; a founder of Manakin Town, Va.; *m* Marie, dau. of Earl Spencer, of Eng.

MAURY, Matthew (*d* 1752), fled from France to Eng. after the revocation of the Edict of Nantes, 1685; came to Va., 1717; *m* 1716, at Dublin, Ireland, Mary Anne (1690-1755), dau. Rev. James de la Fontaine.

MAVERICK, Rev. John (bap. Awliscombe, Co. Devon, Dec. 28, 1578-*d* Dorchester, Mass., Feb. 3, 1635/36; son of Peter, *m* Dorothy Tucke), B.A., Exeter Coll., Oxford, 1599, M.A., 1603; ordained deacon, Exeter, Co. Devon, 1597; vicar of Beaworthy, Co. Devon, 1615-1629/30; teacher of Puritan Ch., Plymouth, Eng., 1629-30; came in the "Mary and John," 1630; founder of Dorchester, Mass.; freeman, 1631; minister, 1631-1635/36; *m* Ilsington, Co. Devon, Oct. 28, 1600, Mary Gye (living Oct. 9, 1666).

MAY (Maies, Mayes, Mays), John (1590-1670), from Eng. to Roxbury, Mass., ca. 1640; freeman. 1641; in Roxbury mil. company, 1647; *m* Sarah –.

MAYHEW, Thomas (1592-1681), from Eng. to Mass. with his son Thomas, 1631; settled at Edgartown, 1642; Indian teacher; dep. Gen. Ct. from Watertown, Mass., 1636-37; gov. and cdr. of Martha's Vineyard, Province of N.Y., 1647-81, under commissions from Governors Lovelace and Nichols; *m* Abigail Parkus, or Martha Parkhurst; *m* 2d, Jane (Gallion) Paine, widow of Thomas Paine.

MAYNARD, John (1620-78), from Eng. with Winthrop; settled at Cambridge, 1634; original propr. of Sudbury, Mass., 1638; freeman, 1644; selectman, 1646; a petitioner for grant at Marlboro, 1656; *m* in Eng.; *m* 2d, 1646, Mary Axdell.

MAYO, John (1629-88; son of Thomas), came with his mother Elizabeth (*m* 2d, Robert Gamlin, Jr.), in the "William and Francis," 1632; settled at Roxbury, Mass.; deacon; *m* 1654, Hannah (1636-99), dau. of John Graves.

MAYO, Rev. John (*d* 1676), from Eng., 1636; teacher at Barnstable, Mass., to 1644; minister at Eastham, 1646-55, at Boston, 1655-73; later settled at Yarmouth, Cape Cod; *m* Tamsen– (*d* 1682).

MAYO, William (1684-1744; son of Joseph [1656-91], of Co. Wilts., Eng., *m* Elizabeth Hooper; g.son of William [*d* 1707], *m* Jane—; g.g.son of William [*d* 1640], *m* Margaret—); went from Eng. to the Barbados, which island he surveyed; came to Va. ca. 1723; was at Richmond, 1729; col.Goochland Co. troop, provincial forces of Va., 1740; *m* Frances, dau. Enoch Gold, of Barbados; *m* 2d, ca. 1732, Ann (*d* 1773), dau. John Perratt, of St. Philip's, Barbados, *m* Ann-.

MEACHAM, Jeremiah (*b* Somersetshire, Eng., 1613-*d* 1695), from Eng. to Boston, Mass., 1636, with wife Margaret and a bro. John (who never *m*); weaver at Southold, 1650, and Easthampton, L.I., 1653, where he was known as "Goodman Meacham"; clothier at Salem in his later years and operated a fulling mill; made his will at Salem, where he had lived thru the witchcraft delusion; *m* Margaret-(*d* post 1679); *m* 2d, post 1684, Alice (*d* 1704), dau. of Osmund Dutch and widow of both John Newman and John Dane.

MEAD, Gabriel (1588-1666), from Eng. to Dorchester, Mass.; admitted freeman, 1638; *m* 2d, Joanna –.

MEAD (Meade, Meades, Mede), William (1600-63), from Eng. in the "Elizabeth," to Mass., 1635; removed to Hempstead, L.I., later to Wethersfield, Conn., and to Stamford, 1641.

MEADE, Andrew (*d* 1745), from Ireland to Eng., thence to N.Y., ca. 1685; settled in Nansemond Co., Va.; burgess, co. judge, col. militia; *m* Mary, dau. of Daniel Latham, of Flushing, L.I.

MEANS, Robert (1742-1823; son of Thomas), from Ireland, 1766; settled at Merrimac, N. H., later at Amherst, N. H., where he was a weaver; later a merchant; rep. Gen. Ct. of N.H. several sessions; state senator 2 yrs.; treas. Hillsborough Co., N.H., long period; *m* 1774, Mary, dau. Rev. David McGregor, of Londonderry, N. H.

MEEKER (Mecar, Meaker), Robert, from Eng. to Quinnipiack (New Haven), Conn., before 1651; removed to Fairfield before 1670; *m* 1651, Susan Tuberfeeld.

MEEKES, Thomas, see Mix.

MEIGS (Meggs), Vincent (ca. 1583-1658), from Eng. with his sons John and Mark, to Weymouth, Mass., ca. 1639; to Rehoboth, 1642; to New Haven, Conn., 1644, later at Milford, Guilford and what is now Killingworth; *m* 1606, –Churchill.

MELYN (Meleyn), Cornelis (1600-ca. 1662), from Holland to New Netherlands, 1638; went to Holland, 1640, for his wife and children, and returned to New Amsterdam, 1641, with an order granting him nearly the whole of Staten Island; planted a colony, 1641, dispersed by Indian War, 1643; pres. "Council of Eight," under Dir. Gen. Kieft, 1643-47; removed to New Amsterdam, returned again to Holland when banished by Peter Stuyvesant for espousing popular side in politics; returned to Staten Island, 1649; after Indian massacre of 1655, removed to New Haven, Conn.; *m* at Amsterdam, 1627, Jannetje Adriaens (1604-81).

MERCER, Gen. Hugh (1720-77; son of William, *m* Anne, dau. of Sir Robert Munro, of Scotland); came from Scotland to Pa., 1747; re-

moved to Fredericksburg, Va.; brig. gen. Cont. Army; physician; capt. in army at Braddock's defeat, 1755; capt. Military Assn. of Western Pa., 1756; capt. in command of a garrison, Shippensburg, 1757; maj. in command of forces in Pa., 1757; maj. in command of expdn. of Gen. Forbes against Ft. Duquesne, Jan. 12, 1777; brig. gen. U.S.A., wounded at battle of Princeton and died of these wounds; *m* Isabella, dau. of John Gordon.

MERIWETHER, Nicholas (*b* in Wales, 1631-*d* James City Co., Va., Dec. 15, 1678), came to Va., and had grant of 600 acres in Northumberland Co., and 300 acres in Lancaster Co., 1653; received 4,350 in Westmoreland Co., 1654; clk. Surry Co., 1655; received additional grants 1656; apptd. clk. of Council, 1656; *m* Elizabeth-, prob. dau. of Hy. or Thos. Woodhouse (they had: Nicholas [1677-1744]; vestryman of St. Peter's Ch., 1685-98; burgess of Va. from New Kent Co., 1702-14, from Hanover, 1723; *m* 1688/89, Elizabeth, dau. of David Crawford, of Assasquin, New Kent Co., Va.]; Wm.; David; Francis).

MERRIAM, Joseph (*d* 1640/41; son of William, of Tudeley, Co. Kent, Eng., *m* Sara–), from Eng. in the "Castle," 1638; freeman, Mass. Bay Colony, 1638/39; settled at "Merriam's Corner," Concord, Mass.; *m* ca. 1623, Sarah, dau. of John Goldstone, *m* Frances Jefferie.

MERRIAM, William (*d* 1635), from Eng., 1638; settled at Concord, Mass.; farmer, weaver and clothier.

MERRICK, Thomas (1620-1703), from Wales aet. 10, with 2 bros., to Roxbury, 1630; removed to Springfield, Mass., ca. 1636; constable; *m* 1639, Sarah Stebbins; *m* 2d, 1653, Elizabeth Tilley.

MERRICK (Mirick, Myrick), William (1603-89), from Wales with three younger brothers in the "James," 1636; an original propr. of Duxbury; lt. under Capt. Standish 6 yrs.; original propr. of Bridgewater; sold his Duxbury property and removed to Eastham, 1652; *m* 1642, Rebecca (Tracy?).

MERRILL (Merrell), Nathaniel (1610-55): desc. de Merle family, French Huguenots, name changed to Merrill in Eng.), from Eng. to Ipswich, Mass., 1633; settled at Newbury, 1635; *m* Susanah Wilterton, or Walterton (she *m* 2d Stephen Jordan).

MERRITT, Thomas (ca. 1634-ca. 1725), from Eng. to Wethersfield, Conn., 1662; dep. Conn. Gen. Assembly, 1699; settled at Rye, N. Y., 1673; vestryman, trustee, etc; *m* 1656, Jane (1636-85), dau. of Thomas Sherwood; *m* 2d, ante 1688, Abigail (1660-ca. 1721), dau. Robert Francis, of Wethersfield, Conn.; *m* 3d, Mary, dau. Jeffrey Ferris, and widow of Jonathan Lockwood.

MERWIN, Miles (1623-97), from Eng., settled at Windsor, later at Milford, Conn.; tanner and shipping mcht.; *m* Elizabeth Baldwin (*d* 1664); *m* 2d, Sarah Platt Beach (*d* 1670).

METCALF (Metcalfe), Michael (*b* Tatterford, Norfolk Co., Eng., June 17, 1587-*d* 1664; son of Rev. Leonard, rector of Tatterford); to Boston, 1637; settled at Dedham; freeman, 1640 or 1642; *m* Oct. 13, 1616, Sarah (June 17, 1593-1644), dau. of Thomas Elwyn; *m* 2d, 1645, Martha –, widow of Thomas Piggs, or Pidge.

METHENY (Mathena, Matheny), Daniel (ca. 1638-1689), of "Wentworth-Woodhouse," plantation, Charles Co., Md., 1664; soldier, Capt. Brent's (Charles Co.) rangers, 1680; political exile from Md. as leader of "Protestant Revolution," in 1681; removed to "Hope plantation," Stafford Co., Va., 1681; *m* 1665, Sarah (1648-1700), dau. Thomas Wentworth, of "Wentworth's Delight," Charles Co., Md.

MICOU, Dr. Paul (1658-1736), Huguenot, from France after the revocation of the Edict of Nantes, 1685; settled in Essex Co., Va., ante 1695; justice 1700-20; physician; lawyer; *m* Margaret LeRoy.

MIDDLETON, Edward (*d* 1685), from Eng. to the Barbados, thence to S.C., 1678, where he received large tracts of land; was lord proprietor's dep. and asst. justice; mem. Grand Council, 1678-84, Province of S.C.; *m* 2d, 1680, Sarah - (widow of Richard Fowell, of the Barbados).

MILES (Myles), John (1603-93), from Eng. to Concord, Mass., ante 1637; freeman, 1638; large landowner; *m* 2d, 1679, Susannah (1647-post 1698), dau. of Thomas Goodnow.

MILLARD, John, was one of three brothers who came from Eng., 1643, and settled at Rehoboth; *m* Elizabeth – (*d* 1680).

MILLER, John (1609-64), from Eng., 1635, settled at Wethersfield, Conn.; at Stamford, 1641; *m* 1638, Mary Angel? (*d* post 1657).

MILLER, Joseph (1617-97; 13th child, 9th son of "Maister" Thomas Miller, M.A., of Bishop's Stortford, Co. Herts., Eng., *d* 1627, *m* Agnes –; and g.son of John Myllar [*d* 1584], *m* Joan Thorowgood, also of Stortford); came in the "Hopewell," 1635, settled at Cambridge, Mass.; *m* Mary, dau. of Walter Pope, of Charlestown.

MIMS, Thomas, according to tradition was *b* in Wales, came to Va. with father; received grant of 800 acres, Flower-de-Hundred, Va., 1662; *m* Ann–.

MINER (Minor), Thomas (1608-90), from Eng. in the "Arbella," 1630; settled at Salem and later at Charlestown, Mass., 1632; a founder of the church at Charlestown; founder of Pequot (New London), Conn., 1645, and of Stonington, Conn., 1653-54; lt. and capt. King Philip's War; dep. Gen. Ct. for New London, 1650-51, for Stonington, bet. 1665-89; chief mil. officer at Mystic, 1665; *m* 1634, Grace, dau. of Walter Palmer (qv).

MINOR (Maindort), Doodes (*d* 1687), from Holland to Middlesex Co., Va., 1640; *m* Mary Johnson.

MINOT, George (1594-1671; son of Thomas); from Eng. to Dorchester, Mass., 1630; freeman, 1634; rep. Gen. Ct., 1635; ruling elder 30 yrs.; *m* Martha – (1597-1657).

MITCHELL, John (1763-1840), from Eng. to Pendleton Co., Va., later in Harrison Co.; pioneer minister and a founder of Meth. Church; pensioner Am. Rev.; *m* Margaret Teter.

MITCHELL, Matthew (1590-1645), from Eng. with Rev. Richard Mather in the "James," to Mass., 1635; was at Concord, later at Springfield, and signed compact there, 1636; removed to Saybrook, Conn.; one of his sons was roasted alive by the Indians; dep. Gen. Ct., 1637, which voted war against the Pequot Indians, and served in garrison at Saybrook Fort; *m* 1616, Susan Butterfield.

MIX (Meekes), Thomas, from Eng. to New Haven, Conn., 1643; one of the first grantees there; *m* 1649, Rebecca, dau. of Capt. Nathaniel Turner.

MONCURE, John (1709-64) from Eng. to Stafford Co., Va., 1733; *m* Frances (*b* 1713), dau. Dr. Gustavus Brown (*m* Frances, dau. Col. Gerrard Fowke, Jr.).

MONROE, Andrew (*d* 1668; son of David, *m* Agnes Munro, cousins, of Scotland), maj. in the Battle of Preston, in Scotland, Aug. 17, 1648; he was under his distinguished kinsman, Sir George Munro, and was taken prisoner, and banished to America; received land grant in Northumberland Co., Va., June 8, 1650; moved to Westmoreland Co., Va., where he died; mem. Westmoreland Assembly, 1659; *m* Elizabeth –, who *m* 2d, George Horner.

MONTAGUE (Jean de la Montagne), Dr. Johannes (1595-1670), studied at U. of Leyden, 1616; from Holland, 1624; settled at Harlem, N.Y.; physician; returned to Leyden, but came back to N.Y., 1647-55; school master of first pub. sch., 1652; mem. gov.'s council; vice-dir. gen. Fort Orange, 1656-64; *m* 1626, Rachel de Forest (*d* 1643).

MONTAGUE, Peter (1603-59; 2d son of Peter. *m* Eleanor Allen; desc. Droge de Monteacute, from Normandy to Eng. with William the Conqueror); came in the "Charles" to Jamestown, Va., 1621; was burgess from Nansemond, 1652, from Lancaster Co., 1651, 58; *m* Cicely, dau. Gov. Mathews, of Va. Colony.

MONTAGUE (Montague), Richard (ca. 1614-81; 3d son of Peter *m* Eleanor Allen); came in the "Speedwell," 1634; resided at Wells, Me., 1646; removed to Boston, Mass.; to Wethersfield, Conn., 1651-59, selectman 1671, 77; to Hadley, Mass., 1680; freeman, 1680; clk. of writs, 1681; *m* ca. 1637, Abigail (*d* 1694), dau. of Rev. Dr. Downing, of Norwich, Eng.

MOODY, John (1593-1655), from Eng., admitted freeman at Roxbury, Mass., 1633; *m* Sarah Fox (1598-1671).

MOORE, John (*b* ca. 1620-*d* Oct. 13, 1657), to Lynn, Mass., 1641; an original settler of Southampton, L.I., 1641; freeman, 1649; minister at Hempstead, L.I., ca. 1650; an original purchaser

and minister at Newtown, L.I., 1657; dep. and commr.; *m* Margaret (bap. 1622), dau. of Edward Howell (qv), she *m* 2d, Francis Doughty.

MOORE, John (*d* 1677), from Eng. in the "Mary and John," to Dorchester, Mass.; freeman, 1631; went to Windsor, 1635 or 1636, rep. Gen. Ct.

MOORE, John (1658-1732), from Eng. to Charleston, S.C., 1680; sec. of the Province, 1682; receiver gen., 1683; mem. Gov.'s Council, 1684; moved to Phila., bet. 1687-90, where he was crown advocate and dep. judge, 1695; atty. gen. of the Province, 1698-1700; registrar gen. of Pa., 1693-1703; registrar of wills, 1701-04; founder and vestryman of Christ's Church, Phila.; *m* Katherine–; *m* 2d, 1685, Lady Rebecca, dau. Landgrave Daniel Axtell (son of Lt. Col. Daniel Axtell, dau. of Kilkenny, Ireland).

MOORMAN, Zachariah (*b* 1620), capt. in Cromwell's army in the invasion of Ire.; later returned to Isle of Wight, Eng.; to the Barbados, 1669; to S.C., 1671, among first settlers at Charleston; *m* a dau. of Lt. William Candler, of Cromwell's army, who was awarded estates in Ire.

MORE, Richard (bap. Shipton, Shropshire, Eng., 1613/14-*d* ante Apr. 20, 1696; son of Samuel, *m* Katherine–), came with William Brewster in the "Mayflower," 1620, and resided with his family; at Duxbury, Mass., 1637; fisherman and master mariner, called capt.; had wharf and warehouse at Salem, Mass., 1643; received grants at Swansea and Taunton; inn-keeper at Salem, 1674; his gravestone still stands at Salem; *m* 1636, Christian Hunt (*d* Mar. 18, 1676, aet. 60); *m* 2d, Jane (*d* 1686, aet. 55), dau. of Richard Hollingsworth.

MOREHEAD, Charles (1609-1705; son of David, of London); came from Scotland to look after his father's interest which was partial ownership of the Isle of Kent project with William Claiborne, 1630; settled in the Northern Neck of Va.; *m* twice.

MOREY, Roger, from Eng. in the "Lion," 1630, to Boston; freeman, 1631; later at Salem, thence to Providence, R.I., 1643; freeman, 1655; commr., 1658, juryman, 1661; *m* Mary (*d* 1679), dau. John Johnson, *m* Margery–.

MORGAN, David, Quaker; from Wales, settled in America, ca. 1700; probably came by way of Jamaica.

MORGAN, Francis, from Eng.; burgess, 1647, 52, 53; settled in York Co., Va.

MORGAN, James (1607-85; son of William); from Wales in the "Mary," to Sandy Bay, nr. Gloucester, Mass., 1636; freeman at Roxbury, 1643; settled at New London, Conn., ca. 1650; mem. 1st Colonial Assembly of Conn.; soldier Pequot War; *m* Aug. 6, 1640, Margery Hill, of Roxbury.

MORGAN, Capt. Miles (1616-99; son of William); from Eng., 1636; a founder of Springfield, Mass., ca. 1640; built a block house which he defended against the Indians in the sacking of Springfield, 1675; *m* Prudence Gilbert (*d* 1660); *m* 2d, 1669, Elizabeth Bliss (*d* 1683).

MORRILL (Morrell), Abraham (1586-1662), from Eng. in the "Lion," to Cambridge, Mass., 1632; settled at Salisbury, 1634; he and Henry Sawood built a corn mill on the Powow, 1642; commoner, and taxed in 1650; signed petition of 1658; *m* June 10, 1645, Sarah Clement (she *m* 2d, 1665, Thomas Mudgett).

MORRIS, Anthony, 2d (1654-1721), Quaker, from Eng. to Burlington, N.J., 1682; removed to Phila., Pa., 1685; was presiding justice Ct. of Common Pleas of Phila.; justice Supreme Ct. of Pa., 1693-98; mayor of Phila., 1703-04; provincial councillor, 1696; rep. Assembly of Province, 1698-1704; *m* 1676, Mary Jones (*d* 1688); *m* 2d, 1689, Agnes – (*d* 1692), widow of Cornelius Barr; *m* 3d, Mary – (*d* 1699), widow of Thomas Coddington; *m* 4th, 1700, Elizabeth, dau. Luke Watson.

MORRIS, Lt. Edward (1630-90; son of Thomas, *m* Grace Hewson), from Eng.; granted land at Roxbury, Mass., 1652; chmn. com. to survey the common land; constable, 1664; selectman, 1674; juror, 1675; dep. Gen. Ct., 1678-86; a founder of Woodstock, Conn.; selectman, 1689, 90; *m* 1655, Grace Bett (*d* 1689).

MORRIS, Richard (*d* ca. 1673), capt. English army, from Eng. to the Barbados, 1654, thence to New York; obtained a land grant, 1668, with manorial privileges, 3000 acres nr. Harlem, which became known as Morrisania; bro. of Col. Lewis Morris; *m* Sarah Pole (*d* ca. 1672).

MORRIS, Thomas (d 1673), from Eng. in the "Hector," to Boston, 1637; at Quinnipiack (New Haven), 1638; signer of the Plantation Covenant, 1639; m Elizabeth –.

MORSE, Anthony (1606-86), from Eng. in the "James," to Newbury, Mass., 1635; freeman, 1636; lt. of militia; shoemaker; treas. Colony of Mass.; m Mary—; m 2d, Ann-.

MORSE, Joseph (1587-1646), from Co. Suffolk, Eng., 1634, settled at Ipswich, Mass.; m Dorothy–.

MORSE, Joseph (1619-91; son of Joseph, qv), from Eng. in the "Elizabeth," 1634, freeman, 1635, an early propr. of Watertown, Mass.; m Hester, dau. of John Pierce (qv).

MORSE, Samuel (1587-1654), from Eng. in the "Increase," to Watertown, Mass., 1635; a founder and first treas. of Dedham, 1637; freeman, 1640; settled at Medfield, 1649; m Elizabeth Jasper (b ca. 1587).

MORSE, William (1614-83), from Eng. in the "James," 1635, settled at Newbury, Mass.; cordwainer, from Marlboro; m Elizabeth–(accused of witchcraft, called "Witch of Newbury").

MORTON (Mourt), George (1585-1624), financial agent at London of the Mayflower Pilgrims; came in the "Ann" to Plymouth, Mass., 1623, with his wife and five children; settled at Middleboro, Mass.; m at Leyden, 1612, Juliana (1584-1665), dau. Alexander Carpenter.

MOSBY, Edward (ca. 1660-1742), Henrico Co., Va.; m 1st, 1688/89, Sarah (b ca. 1668), dau. Robert Woodson, of Varina Parish, Henrico Co., m ca. 1656, Elizabeth, dau. Richard Ferris.

MOSELEY (Maudesley), John (d Aug. 29, 1661), settled at Dorchester, Mass., buried at Dorchester, a few feet north of Rev. Richard Mather (qv); signature is on document establishing the first free school; m Cecily, or Cecilia – (d Dec. 1661).

MOTT, Adam (1620-86), b Eng.; came to New Amsterdam ca. 1640; purchased, 1660, a tract of land at Great Neck, L.I., part of which is still occupied by some of his descendants; lt. provincial forces; commr. to settle dispute between Dutch and English residents of L.I., 1666; m 1643, Jane Hulet; m 2d, 1667, Elizabeth Redman, step-dau. of John Richbell, first patentee of Mamaroneck.

MOTT, James (d 1707), from Eng. before 1670, settled at Mamaroneck, Westchester Co., N.Y.; capt. of a company of foot; justice; vestryman; m 1670, Mary (d ca. 1685), dau. John Richbell; m 2d, 1690, Elizabeth Bloomer.

MOULTON, Robert (b Norfolk Co., Eng. - d Feb. 20, 1655), from Eng. to Salem, Mass., 1629; ship builder and owner; mem. Colonial Legislature; rep. Gen. Ct., 1634; built house at Moulton's Pt. (present site of Charlestown Navy Yard), 1630, where British landed before battle of Bunker Hill; m Deborah – (d 1656).

MOULTON, William (1617-64), from Eng. to Newburyport, Mass., 1637; one of the first settlers of Hampton, N.H., ca. 1639; m Margaret, dau. of Robert Page.

MUDGE (Mugge), Thomas (b ca. 1624), from Eng., 1654 or earlier; settled at Malden, Mass.; in garrison at Wading River, 1675; m Mary –.

MULLINS, William (d 1621), 10th signer of the Mayflower Compact; m Alice – (d 1621).

MUMFORD, Thomas (1625-92), from Eng. to Portsmouth, R.I., ca. 1650; purchased land and settled at S. Kingston, nr. Point Judith, R.I., 1655; m Sarah, dau. Philip Sherman, 1st sec. of Providence Plantations.

MUNGER, Nicholas (d 1668), from Eng., 1639, settled at Guilford, Conn., with the Whitfield colony; m 1659, Sarah (d 1689), dau. William Hall, m Esther–.

MUNROE (Monroe), William (1625-1717), of Inverness, Scot., sent over by Cromwell as political prisoner after Battle of Worcester; early settler at Cambridge Farms (later Lexington), Mass.; m ante 1666, Martha George; m 2d, Mary Ball (d 1692); m 3d, Elizabeth (Johnson) Wyer (d 1715).

MUNSON, Thomas (1612-85), from Eng. to Hartford, Conn., 1637; received a grant of land in recognition of his services in the Pequot War; granted land at New Haven; rep. Colonial Assembly 27 sessions; capt. New Haven Co. forces King Philip's War; m Joanna–(ca. 1610-1678).

MURDOCK, Robert (1665-1754), from Scot. to Roxbury, Mass., ca. 1690; settled at Newton, 1703; owned 120 acres; m 1692, Hannah (1667-1727), dau. of Nathaniel Stedman.

MYGATT, Joseph (1596-1680), from Eng. in the "Griffin," to Charlestown, Mass., 1633; freeman, 1635; a founder and original propr., Hartford, Conn., 1635; townsman 4 terms; dep., 1658; deacon 1st church; m Ann–(ca. 1602-1686), (their dau. Sarah, m John Webster, the father of Daniel, also ancestor of Noah Webster).

NAPIER, Dr. Patrick (1610-69; son of Robert, of Edinburgh, Scotland, and desc. of Sir John Napier, of Merchistown, who m Lady Elizabeth Monteith); came to Va., 1655; m Elizabeth (1645-1672), dau. of Robert Booth (1619-64), from Eng. to York Co., Va., clerk, 1639, justice, 1652, burgess, 1653-64.

NASH, Thomas (1587-May 12, 1658), from Eng. with wife and five children; was at Guilford, Conn., 1639; signed Guilford Covenant; at New Haven, 1643, or earlier; signed Fundamental Agreement of New Haven; m Margery (d bet. Feb. 11, 1655-Aug. 1657), dau. of Nicholas Baker (son of John, m Margery Madistard), of Hertsfordshire, Eng., m Mary Hodgetts.

NEEDHAM, Anthony (1628-1705; son of Anthony); from Eng., 1653; settled at Salem, Mass.; corpl. Salem Old Troop, 1665; lt. in King Philip's War, 1675; lt., Troop of Horse, 1678; m 1655, Ann (d 1695), dau. of Humphrey Potter, of Coventry, Eng., killed in Irish massacre at Dublin, 1641; g.dau. of Thomas Potter, mayor of Coventry, 1622.

NELSON, Thomas, "Scotch Tom" (1677-1745), from Scotland to Va., ca. 1690; founded and laid out the town of York, 1705; built the first custom house in the colonies; founded "Nelson House," which was rebuilt by his son Gov. William, 1740; m Margaret, dau. of Robert Reade (son of Col. George Reade, qv); m 2d, Mrs. Tucker.

NEVIUS, Johannes (1627-72), from Holland, 1651; schepen of New Amsterdam, 1654-55; sec., 1657-65; m Arientje Blyck.

NEWBERRY, Thomas (1594-1636), from Eng. to Dorchester, Mass., ca. 1630; freeman, 1634; rep. Gen. Ct., 1635; by his will left large property; m in Eng., 1619, Joan Dabinott; m 2d, Jane (probably Jane Dabinott, a cousin of his first wife), she m 2d, Rev. John Warham.

NEWCOMB (Newcombe), Andrew (1618-86) master mariner, from Eng. to Va., where he married; thence to Mass., ca. 1640, where he died m Grace –, widow of William Rix.

NEWCOMB, Francis (ca. 1605-1692), from Eng to Boston, 1635; settled at Braintree ca. 1639 m Rachel –.

NEWELL, Abraham (1581-1672), from Eng., 1634, settled at Roxbury, Mass.; m Frances - (b 1594).

NEWELL, Thomas (d 1689), from Hertfordshire, Eng., to Farmington, Conn., 1653; m Rebecca Olmstead (d 1698), to Boston, 1632.

NEWHALL, Thomas (d 1674), from Eng. to Salem, Mass., 1630; settled at Lynn; mem. Train Band at Lynn, released, 1649; m Mary – (d 1665).

NEWLIN, Nicholas (1620-99), from Ire. to Concord, Chester Co., Pa., 1683; justice County Ct.; mem. Provincial Council; m Elizabeth Paggott.

NEWTON, Richard (b ca. 1601-1609-d 1701), was a founder of Sudbury, Mass.; freeman, 1645; m Ann, sister of Henrie Loker, d Bures St. Mary, Essex, Eng., 1630.

NEWTON, Roger (d 1687), from Eng., settled in Mass. before 1645, later moved to Conn.; m 1645, Mary (b 1616), dau. Rev. Thomas Hooker (qv).

NEWTON, Thomas (d ante May 1683), original settler at Fairfield, Conn.; one of five farmers at Greens Farms (Westport), 1648; dep., 1645; settled at Newtown, L.I.; capt. under Peter Stuyvesant; m 2d, 1648, Joan (d 1664), dau. Richard Smith.

NICHOLS (Nicholl), Francis (1600-50), from Eng. to Stratford, Conn., 1639; training sgt. for Stratford, 1639; m 2d, Anna Wines.

NICHOLS, Thomas (d 1710), from Eng. to Amesbury, Mass., before 1665; owned lands on Merrimac River.

NICOLL, Matthias (1626-87), from Eng. to New York, 1664; sec. Province of N.Y., 1664-80; mem. King's Council, 1667-80; speaker Provincial Assembly, 1683; judge Ct. of Admiralty, 1686; mayor of New York, 1672; *m* Abigail Johns.

NIGHTINGALE, William (1637-1714), settled at Braintree, Mass., before 1690; *m* Bethia (*b* 1649), dau. Samuel Deering.

NILES, John (1602/03-1693/94), from Wales, said to have been a passenger in the "Speedwell"; settled in Mass.; at Squantun, 1632, Dorchester, 1634, Braintree, 1636; *m* 1635, Jane (*d* 1654), dau. William Reed, *m* Lucy Hennage.

NOBLE, Thomas (*b* ca. 1632-Jan. 20, 1704), admitted inhabitant of Boston, Jan. 5, 1653; an early settler at Springfield, Mass., 1653; removed to Westfield, Mass., Jan. 16, 1669; constable; took oath of allegiance to King, Jan. 23, 1678; freeman, Oct. 12, 1682; co. surveyor, Mar. 2, 1696; *m* Nov. 1, 1660, Hannah (Aug. 17, 1643-ante May 12, 1721), dau. of William Warriner (qv).

NORRIS (Norrice), Isaac (1671-1735); son of Thomas, who settled in Jamaica, B.W.I., 1678), came to Phila., Pa., 1693; established "Fairhill"; was mem. Gov.'s Council over 30 yrs.; speaker Assembly; presiding judge Ct. Common Pleas; mayor of Phila., 1724; trustee under William Penn's will and atty. for Hannah Penn; *m* 1694, Mary, dau. Thomas Lloyd, 1st dep. gov. and pres. Council of Pa.

NORRIS, Nicholas (ca. 1640-ca. 1725), resided at Hampton and Exeter, N.H.; soldier King Philip's War; *m* 1664, Sarah, dau. Moses Coxe, of Hampton, N.H.

NORTH, John (1615-91), from Eng. in the "Susan and Ellen," 1635; an original landowner of Farmington, Conn., and an early settler of Hartford; *m* Hannah Bird.

NORTHRUP, Joseph (*d* 1669), from Eng. to Boston, Mass., 1637; a first settler at Milford, Conn.; *m* 1648, Mary (*d* 1683), dau. of Francis Norton.

NORTON, Nicholas (1610-90), from Eng., 1635, to Weymouth, later settled at Edgartown, Marthas Vineyard, 1659; tanner; served in Pequot War; *m* Elizabeth–(*d* 1690).

NORTON, Thomas (1582-1648), from Eng. with Whitfield, 1639; of Guilford, Conn.; signed Plantation Covenant; *m* 1631, Grace (Wells?).

NORTON, William (*d* 1694), from Eng. in the "Hopewell," to Ipswich, Mass., 1635; freeman, 1636; *m* Lucy, dau. Emmanuel Downing.

NOYES, James (1608-56; son of Rev. William), ed. Brasenose Coll., Oxford U.; from Eng. in the "Mary and John," to Mass., 1634; preached at Medford; freeman, 1634; settled at Newbury, 1635, where he was teacher of the church for more than 20 yrs.; *m* in Eng., 1634, Sarah, eld. dau. Joseph Brown, of Southampton.

NOYES, Nicholas (1614-1701; brother of Rev. James; son of Rev. William, *m* Ann Stephens); came in the "Mary and John," to Mass., 1634; freeman, 1637; rep. Gen. Ct., 1660 and later; deacon; *m* 1640, Mary (*d* 1689), dau. Capt. John Cutting.

NUTTING, John (1620-25-1676), from Eng. to Woburn, Mass.; at Chelmsford, Mass., 1656; settled finally at Groton, Mass., 1663; helped lay out a highway to Chelmsford, 1663; selectman, 1663, 67, 69; constable, 1668; one of a com. to see that the minister's maintenance was paid, 1669; fence viewer, 1673; surveyor of highways, 1675; *m* 1650, Sarah Eggleston.

NYE, Benjamin (1620-1704), from Eng. in the "Abigail," to Lynn, Mass., 1635; to Sandwich, 1640; *m* 1640, Katharine, dau. of Rev. Thomas Tupper, of Sandwich, Mass.

NYSSEN, Theunis, see Denise.

OAKES, Edward (*b* Eng. 1604-*d* Concord, Mass., Oct. 13, 1689), came to Cambridge, Mass., 1640; q.m. Middlesex Co. troop, 1656; dep. Gen. Ct., 1659-61 and 1668-81; to Concord, 1683; *m* Jane – (*d* post 1691).

ODIORNE, John (ca. 1627-1707), granted 42 acres on Great Island (now Newcastle); later received grant now known as "Odiorne's Point," nr. Portsmouth, N.H.; mem. grand jury, 1686; resided at Sandy Beach (now Rye, then a part of Portsmouth); *m* Mary, dau. James Johnson, *m* Mary–.

OFFLEY, David, of Boston; mem. A. and H. A. Co., 1638; removed to Plymouth, 1643, but on account of complaints of Indians against him it is declared he returned to Boston.

OGDEN, David (1655-1705), from Eng. in the "Welcome," with William Penn; settled at Phila., Pa., 1682; *m* 1686, Martha, dau. of John Houlston.

OGDEN, John (1610-81/82), from Eng. ca. 1641, settled at Stamford, Conn., where he was a magistrate; removed to Hempstead and Southampton, L.I.; was a founder of Elizabethtown, N.J.; magistrate, 1656; mem. Upper House of Gen. Ct., 1660-61; mem. King's Council, 1665; schout and actg. gov. of English Colony in East Jersey, 1673; a patentee in the Royal Charter for Conn., 1662; *m* 1637, Jane, dau. Jonathan Bond.

OLDHAM, John, from Eng. in the "Elizabeth and Ann," 1635; settled in Westmoreland Co., Va.

OLDS (Ould), Robert (1645-1727/28; son of John of Sherborne, Co. Dorset, Eng.); at Windsor Conn., 1667; removed to Suffield, Conn., 1673; called Dr.; granted land at Suffield; one of 1st proprs.' agts. for town to Gen. Ct., 1694; *m* 1669, Susannah Hanford (*d* 1688); *m* 2d, 1689, Dorothy (*d* 1728), dau. Launcelot Granger (qv).

OLIVER, Thomas (1567-1658; son of John, g son of Thomas); physician and surgeon of Bristol, Eng.; came in the "William and Francis," 1632; settled at Boston; ruling elder 1st ch.; *m* 1st, – (*d* 1635); *m* 2d, Ann – (*d* 1662).

OLMSTED, James (1580-1640), from Great Leighs, Essex, Eng., in the "Lyon," 1632, settled 1st at Mt. Wollaston (now Quincy), Mass., later at Newton (Cambridge), one of the 12 men, apptd. by Rev. Thomas Hooker (qv), who selected the site of Hartford, Conn., and lead the migration thither, 1635; *m* 1605, Joyce Cornish (*d* Fairsted, Essex, Eng., 1621).

OLMSTED (Olmstead), Richard (1612-86), from Eng. in the "Lyon," to Cambridge, Mass., 1632; an original settler at Hartford, Conn.; a founder of Norwalk; rep. Gen. Ct. many yrs.; commr. for Norwalk, 1668; was sgt., lt., muster master, and capt.; *m* twice.

OLNEY, Thomas (1600-82), from Eng. in the "Planter," 1635; freeman, Salem, 1637; one of 12 persons to whom Roger Williams deeded land, 1638; treas. R.I., 1638; commr., 1647; asst., 1648-63; judge Justices Ct., 1655; commr., 1657-63; named in R.I. charter given by Charles II, 1663; dep., 1665-71; mem. town councils, 1665-81; mem. Gen. Assembly; *m* Mary Ashton (1605-79).

ORCUTT, William (*d* 1693), from Eng.; resided at Weymouth, Scituate and Bridgewater, Mass.; *m* at Hingham, Mass., 1664, Mary (*b* 1646), dau. Andrew Lane; *m* 2d, Martha–.

ORTON, Thomas (1613-88), from Eng. to Mass., 1636; of record at Windsor, Conn., 1641, at Farmington, 1655; dep. Gen. Ct.; *m* 1641, Margaret Pratt.

ORVIS, George (*d* 1664), referred to as "the emigrant"; from Eng., 1629; one of the first settlers and original proprs. of Farmington, Conn. ante 1639; *m* 1652, Elizabeth – (*d* 1694), widow of David Carpenter.

OSBORN, John (1604-86), from Eng. in the "Hector," 1638; settled at East Windsor, Conn. 1644; *m* 1645, Ann, dau. of Richard Oldage.

OSBORN, Matthew (1650?-1738), from Eng., 1675?; settled in Sussex Co., Del.; *m* Mary–.

OSBORN (Osborne), Richard (1612-86), from Eng.; at Hingham, Mass., 1635; served in Pequot War, 1637; at New Haven, 1639, Fairfield, 1652; settled finally at Westchester. N.Y.; *m* —(by whom children); *m* 2d, post 1677, Mary–, widow of Mordecai Bedient, and Roger Townsend.

OSBORNE, Capt. Thomas, from Eng. ante 1620, settled at "Coxendale," on the James River; justice, 1631; burgess.

OSGOOD, Christopher (*d* 1650), from Eng. in the "Mary and John," to Ipswich, Mass., 1634; *m* 1632, Mary Everett (*d* 1633); *m* 2d, 1633, Margery (bap. 1615), dau. of Philip Fowler, who also came in the "Mary and John," *m* Mary Windey or Window.

OSGOOD, John (1595-1651), from Eng. to Ipswich, Mass., 1638; settled finally at Andover, 1645; dep. Gen. Ct., 1651; *m* ca. 1627, Sarah Booth.

OTEY, John (desc. Chief High Chamberlain, of James II), from Eng. settled in St. Peter's Parish, New Kent Co., Va.; mem. of com. to check on tobacco planters, 1724, 25, 28, 29.

OTIS (Ottis), John (ca. 1581-1657), from Eng. to Hingham, Mass., 1635; freeman, 1636; selectman; removed to Weymouth after 1653; *m* in

Eng., Margaret – (*d* 1653/54); *m* 2d, Elizabeth Streame, widow.

OUTWATER (Van Oudewater, Oudwater), Frans Jacobsen (*b* ca. 1632), from Holland; at Albany (Ft. Orange), N.Y., 1657.

OVERTON, William (*b* Dec. 3, 1638; son of Col. Robert [*b* ca. 1609], who was a distinguished soldier of the Parliamentary wars, *m* 1630, Anne Gardiner); came to Va., 1669; received grant of 4,600 acres for bringing over 92 persons, grant dated Apr. 23, 1681, the land on the south side of the Pamunkey River in New Kent (now Hanover) Co.; granted land in St. Peter's Parish, New Kent Co., 1690; *m* Nov. 24, 1670, Mary Elizabeth Waters, of St. Sepulchre's Parish, London.

OWEN, Thomas (ca. 1660-1744), with bros. John and William, to Va. ante 1700; settled in Henrico Co.; *m* 1690, Elizabeth, dau. Thomas Brooks, *m* Joana–.

PABODIE, see Peabody.

PACKARD, Samuel (*d* 1684), from Eng. in the "Diligent," 1638; settled at West Bridgewater, Mass.; *m* Elizabeth –.

PADDOCK, Robert (*d* 1650), from Eng. to Duxbury, Mass., 1634; mem. military co., Plymouth, 1643; *m* Mary – (*d* 1650).

PAGE, John (1586-1676), from Eng. with Gov. Winthrop, to Boston, Mass., 1630; at Dedham, 1636; freeman, 1640; *m* Phebe –; *m* 2d, Mary Paine.

PAGE, John (1627-Jan. 23, 1691), from Eng. to Va. ca. 1650; civil and military officer for York Co., Va.; justice before 1655; burgess, 1655-56; mem. Colonial Council of Va., 1681-91; gave the ground and aided in the erection of Bruton Parish Church, at Williamsburg, Va.; maj. 1676; col. and county lt., 1680-85; *m* ca. 1656, Alice (ca. 1635-ca. 1698), dau. of Sir Edward Lukens, of Essex, Eng.

PAGE, Robert (1604-79; son of Robert, Co. Norfolk, Eng.), from Eng. to Hampton, N.H., 1637; *m* Lucy–(*d* 1665).

PAIGE, Nathaniel (*d* 1692), from Eng. with his wife and three children ca. 1685, and settled at Roxbury, Mass.; marshal of Suffolk Co., 1686; purchased land and lived at Billerica for a brief time; one of the eight purchasers of Hardwick, 1686: *m* Joanna –

PAINE, Moses (1581-1643; son of Nicholas), from Eng. to Cambridge, Mass., 1638; *m* 1st, Mary Benison; *m* 2d, ca. 1618, Elizabeth – (*d* in Eng., 1632); *m* 3d, Judith – (*d* 1654), widow of Edmund Quincy.

PAINE, Stephen (*d* 1679) from Eng. in the "Diligent," with his wife, three children and four servants, to Hingham, Mass., 1638; freeman, 1639; a founder and early propr. of Rehoboth, 1643; rep. Gen. Ct. of Mass., until his death: *m* Rose (also called Neele) – (*d* 1660); *m* 2d, 1662, Alice – (*d* 1682), widow of William Parker, of Taunton.

PAINE (Payne), Thomas (1586-1650), from Eng., with his son Thomas, to Plymouth, Mass., 1621; settled at Yarmouth; freeman, 1639; 1st dep. Gen. Ct.; *m* Margaret, dau. Sir Thomas Pultney.

PAINE (Payne), Thomas (*b* Dec. 11, 1588-*d* 1640: son of Thomas Payne [ca. 1540-1631], of Cooklie, Co. Suffolk, Eng., *m* Katherine Harssant), weaver, from Wrentown, Co. Suffolk, Eng., in his own ship, the "Mary Ann," 1637; settled at Salem, Mass.; *m* Nov. 22, 1610, Elizabeth–.

PAINE, William (1598-1660; son of William, of Nowton, Co. Suffolk, Eng.); came to Ipswich and Boston, Mass.; *m* Hannah–.

PALFREY (Palfery, Palfry, Palfray), Peter (*d* 1663), from Eng., was at Salem, Mass., 1626; freeman, 1630; rep. Gen. Ct., 1635; removed to Reading; *m* Edith –; *m* 2d, Elizabeth –, widow of John Fairchild; *m* 3d, Alice –.

PALGRAVE, Dr. Richard (*d* 1651), Eng. to Charlestown, Mass.; distinguished physician and writer; *m* Anna Harris.

PALMER, Walter (1585-1661/62), from Eng. to Salem, Mass., 1628; at Charlestown, 1629-43; freeman, 1634; constable, 1633; removed to Rehoboth; 1st rep. Gen. Ct. from that town, 1646, 47; a founder of Stonington, Conn., 1653; *m* Ann (Elizabeth)–; *m* 2d, 1633, Rebecca Short; *m* 3d, Esther–.

PALMER, William, from Eng., was at Watertown, Mass., 1636-37; at Newbury, 1637, and one of the original settlers and patentees of the town of Hampton, N.H., 1638; *m* 2d, Ann –.

PALMER, William (ca. 1585-1638), from Eng. in the "Fortune," to Plymouth, Mass., 1621; later at Duxbury; *m* Frances –, who came in the "Anne," 1623.

PANCOAST, John (*d* 1694), from Northamptonshire, Eng., 1675; brought his children in the "Paradice," Oct. 1680; a framer of the first constitution of lower N.J., the "Concessions and Agreements of the Proprietors, Freeholders and Inhabitants of West N.J. in America," signed in Eng., Mar. 3, 1676 (William Penn also a signer); regulator of weights and measures, Burlington Co., 1681; constable of Yorkshire Tenth, 1682; mem. Assembly of West Jersey at Burlington, 1685; signer of the memorial address to the Quakers, in the Keithian controversy, 1692; *m* in Eng., Elizabeth – (*d* in Eng.).

PARDEE, George (bap. Feb. 19, 1624-Apr. 1700; son of Rev. Anthony); from Pitminster and Taunton, Somerset, Eng., to New Haven, Conn., 1644; rector Hopkins Grammar Sch.; *m* Oct. 20, 1650, Martha, dau. of Richard Miles (*d* Jan. 7, 1667), from Eng., to New Haven; *m* 2d, 1662, Katherine Lane.

PARK, Arthur (*d* Jan. 1739), of Scotch-Irish descent; from Ireland with his wife and son, Joseph, to Westchester Co., Pa.; settled in Union Co., S.C.; *m* Mary – (*d* ca. 1760).

PARK (Parke), Richard (ca. 1602-1665), from Eng. in the "Defense," 1635, settled at Cambridge, Mass.; propr., 1636; *m* Margery –; *m* 2d, Sarah, dau. William Collier, and widow of Love Brewster.

PARKE (Park), Sir Robert (1580-1665), came from Eng. in the "Arbella," 1630, as sec. to John Winthrop; removed to Wethersfield, Conn., 1639; to Pequot (now New London), 1649; later to Mystic (now Stonington); was dep. Gen. Ct. and selectman; served in Colonial Wars; *m* 1st, 1602, Martha Chaplin (1584-ante 1644); *m* 2d, Alice, widow of John Thompson, of Preston, Eng.

PARKER, Elisha (*d* after July 24, 1701), from Eng. to Barnstable, Mass.; *m* 1657, Elizabeth Hinckley (*b* 1635; sister of Gov. Thomas).

PARKER, Richard (*d* 1680), from Eng., settled on the Nansemond River, Va., 1650; high sheriff, Nansemond Co., 1654-73; had land grants for 2,500 acres, 1654-65; *m* Elizabeth, dau. Capt. Richard Bailey, of London.

PARKER, Thomas (1609-83), from Eng. in the "Susan and Ellen," 1635; freeman at Lynn, Mass., 1637; one of the first settlers at Reading ca. 1638; selectman, 1661; deacon, 1645-83; *m* ca. 1635, Amy–(*d* 1690).

PARKER, William (1660-1736), from Eng. to Portsmouth, N.H., 1703; *m* 1703, Zerviah Stanley (1665-1718; dau. Earl of Derby).

PARKHURST, George (1618-1698/99; son of George), from Eng., 1635; propr. of 12 acres, Watertown, Mass., 1642; freeman, 1643; to Boston, 1645; *m* 1st, Phebe––; *m* 2d, Widow Susanna Simpson.

PARKMAN, Elias (son of Thomas), from Sidmouth, Co. Devon, Eng., to Dorchester, Mass., 1632; freeman, 1635; *m* Bridget–.

PARMELEE (Palmerley, Permerly, Permerlee, Parmele), John (*d* New Haven, Conn., Nov. 1659; will probated Jan. 3, 1659/60); from Eng. in the "Elizabeth and Ann," 1635, and settled at Guilford, Conn.; signer of the Plantation Covenant, 1639; *m* 1st, in Eng., Hannah –; *m* 2d, 1653, Elizabeth Bradley (*d* 1683; she *m* 4th, 1663, John Evarts).

PARMENTER (de Parmentier), Dea. John (1588-1671; son of William, of Co. Essex, Eng., *m* Margery–; g.son of George), Huguenot, from Little Yeldham, Eng., to Sudbury, Mass., 1635, with his wife and son John; deacon and commr.; removed to Roxbury, 1660; *m* 1609, Bridget–(*d* 1660); *m* 2d, 1660, Mrs. Annis Chandler-Dane (*d* 1682/83).

PARRISH, Edward (1640-80), to Md., 1655; settled in Anne Arundel Co., Md.; *m* 1664, Clara– (*d* ante 1720).

PARROTT, Richard (*d* 1686), from Barbados, an early settler in Lancaster Co., Va., 1649; sr. justice, 1673-86; commr., 1650; high sheriff, 1657; *m* Margaret – (*d* 1687).

PARSHALL (Pershall), Jonas (1600-60), came from Eng. 1620, to Va., thence to N.Y.

PARSONS, Joseph (1618-83), from Eng. to Springfield, Mass., 1635; mem. A. and H. A. Co.; grantee in Indian deed to Springfield, 1636; a founder of Northampton; freeman, 1669; cornet of the horse; again settled at Springfield, 1679, and was one of the richest men there; *m* 1646, Mary (1620-1712), dau. Thomas Bliss; she was charged with witchcraft, sent to Boston, tried and acquitted.

PARTRIDGE (Partrigg), William (*d* 1668), from Eng. to Hartford, Conn., 1640; removed to Hadley, Mass., 1659; cooper; *m* Mary Smith (1625-1680), of Hartford.

PASCHALL, Thomas (1634-1717/18; son of William. g.son of Thomas), from Eng. to Phila.; freeman, 1661; mem. Pa. Provincial Assembly, 1686-89; mem. Pa. Common Council, 1701, 04; *m* ante 1665, Joanna Sloper (1634-1707).

PATTEN, William (*d* 1668), from Eng. to Cambridge, Mass., ca. 1635; served in Pequot War; original propr. of Billerica; mem. A. and H. A. Co.; *m* in Eng. Mary – (*d* 1673).

PATTERSON, James (1633-1701), arrived at Charlestown, in the "John and Sarah," 1652; an adherent of Charles II, taken captive by Cromwell's army and transported to America, 1652; soldier in King Philip's War and Canadian expdn.; settled at Billerica; *m* 1662, Rebecca, dau. of Andrew Stevenson, of Cambridge, Mass.

PATTON, Robert (1755-1814), from Ireland to Phila., Pa., 1762; maj. Pa. Line; a founder of Soc. Cincinnati; was the first postmaster of Phila., under the new constitution, nearly 20 yrs.; *m* Cornelia Bridges.

PAUL, Joseph (1657-1717), from Eng., 1685, mem. Provincial Assembly of Pa., 1687; *m* 1680, Margaret Roberts.

PAUL, William (*d* 1704), Scotsman; from Eng. to Bermuda, thence to Mass., 1635; weaver; large landowner, Taunton, 1637; one of purchasers of Taunton South Purchase (now Dighton), Mass.; *m* ca. 1657, Mary (1639-1715), dau. John Richmond (*b* Ashton, Keynes, Wiltshire, Eng., 1594, soldier and trader).

PAULDING, Joost (Joseph), from Cassant, Holland, 1664; settled at Eastchester, Westchester Co., N.Y.; thence to Philipse Manor, where he was dea. and treas., Old Dutch Ch.; to New York City, 1710; *m* 1688, Catharine Jans (*b* 1664), dau. Hans Duyts, of Harlem, N.Y.; *m* 2d, 1709, Sophia–, widow of Teunis Krankheit.

PAYNE, Sir John, came to America; he and his brother, Sir William Payne, were both knighted by King James II; they received from the King a grant of land 12 miles square nr. Alexandria, Va., called "Payne Manor"; Sir John settled in the manorial estate in (then) Fairfax Co.

PAYSON, Edward (1613-91), from Eng. to Roxbury, Mass., ca. 1633; freeman 1640; removed to Dorchester; *m* 1640, Ann Park (*d* 1641); *m* 2d, 1642, Mary Elliot (bap. in Eng., Oct. 1613).

PEABODY, Francis (1614-97; son of John, qv); from Eng. in the "Planter," to Ipswich, Mass., 1635; an original settler at Hampton, N.H., 1639; freeman, 1642; removed to Topsfield before 1657; selectman at Hampton and Topsfield; town clk.; lt. local mil. company; *m* Lydia –; *m* 2d, Mary (Foster) Wood (1618-1705), dau. of Reginald Foster (qv).

PEABODY (Pabody, Paybodie, Pabodie, Peabodie), John (ca. 1590-ca. 1667), from Eng. to Plymouth, Mass., 1640; an original propr. of Bridgewater, Mass., 1645; *m* Isabel –.

PEARCE, see Pierce.

PEARSON, John (1615-79), from Eng., settled at Lynn, Mass., 1637; *m* Maudlin –.

PEASE, Robert (1607-44; son of Robert, *m* Margaret –), from Eng. in the "Francis," to Boston, ca. 1634; later at Salem; *m* Marie –, a Huguenot.

PECK, Henry (*b* bet. 1615-20-*d* 1651), said to have come from Eng. in the "Hector," 1637, with Rev. John Davenport; appeared at New Haven, 1638; signed the New Haven Compact, 1639; *m* Joan – (*d* post 1663); she *m* 2d, Andrew Low.

PECK, Joseph (ca. 1587-1663/64), from Eng. in the "Diligent," to Hingham, Mass., 1638; freeman, 1639; rep. Gen. Ct., 1639-42; removed to Rehoboth, 1645; commr. for Hingham, 1639; served in Indian wars; *m* 1617, Rebecca Clark.

PECKHAM, John (1595-1681), from Eng., settled at Aquidneck (Newport), R.I.; *m* Mary (1607-48), dau. of Thomas Clarke, of Bedfordshire, Eng.; *m* 2d, Eleanor –.

PEET (Peat), John (1597-1684), from Seven Oaks, Derbyshire, Eng., in the "Hopewell,"

1635; settled at Stratford, Conn., 1638; first sexton Congl. ch., Stratford.

PEGRAM, Edward, from Eng. with Col. Daniel Baker, 1699; was Queen's surveyor in the colonies; *m* Mary Scott, dau. of Col. Daniel Baker.

PEIRCE, see also Pierce.

PEIRCE, Daniel (1611-77), blacksmith; came from Ipswich, Co. Suffolk, Eng., in the "Elizabeth," 1634; settled at Watertown, Mass.; propr., 1636-37; freeman, 1638; removed to Newbury, 1638; *m* in Eng., Sarah–(*d* 1654); *m* 2d, 1654, Mrs. Ann Milward (*d* 1690).

PEIRCE, George (1659-1734), from Eng. with his wife and three children, 1684, settled in what is now Thornbury Tp., Chester Co., Pa.; mem. Provincial Assembly, 1706; removed to Sadsbury Tp. in (now) Lancaster Co., Pa., 1715; Quaker; *m* 1679, Ann, dau. William Gayner, or Gainer (ca. 1617-post 1681), *m* 1641, Ann Jones (*d* 1684).

PELL, John (1643-drowned 1702; son of Rev. John, 1609/10-1685, distinguished clergyman and mathematician, whose brother Thomas, 1608-69, surgeon in Pequot War, dep., etc., established "Pelham Manor," Westchester Co., N.Y., and willed all his property to his nephew, John), came from Eng. to Boston, 1670, as the 2d lord of Pelham Manor, N.Y.; capt. of horse, 1684, maj., 1692; first judge Ct. of Common Pleas, Westchester Co., 1688; mem. Provincial Assembly, 1691-95; mem. Com. for Defense of the Frontier and chmn. of the Grand Com.; *m* Rachel, dau. Philip Pinckney.

PENDLETON, Brian (1599-1681), from Eng., admitted freeman, Watertown, Mass., 1634; settled at Sudbury, 1638, later at Ipswich, Mass., Portsmouth, N.H., and Saco, Me.; capt. of Portsmouth mil. company, 1664; maj. at Saco, 1668; dep. Mass. Gen. Ct. from Watertown, 1635, from Sudbury and from Portsmouth; dep. gov. Province of Me.; joined A. and H. A. Co., 1646; *m* 1619, Eleanor Price.

PENDLETON, Philip (1654-1721), from Eng. to Caroline Co., Va., 1674; *m* 1682, Isabella Hurt.

PENNEBACKER (Pennebecker), Hendrick (1674-1754; son of Johannes, of Crefelt, Germany, and g.g.g.son of Herr J. Pfannebecker, of Holland). from Crefelt, Germany, to Germantown, Pa., ante 1699; of fine education, he became surveyor for the Penns; purchased Bebber's Tp., Phila. Co., and became one of the three Dutch patroons of Pa.; *m* 1699, Eve (*b* 1676), dau. of Hans Peter Umstadt, and g. dau. of Nicholas Umstadt.

PENNIMAN, James (ca. 1600-will proved 1664/65), from Eng. in the "Lyon," 1631, with John Winthrop, Jr.; admitted to the church, Boston, 1631; removed to Braintree, 1639; freeman; mem. A. and H. A. Co.; *m* Lydia Eliot (*b* 1616), she was a sister of Apostle John Eliot (she *m* 2d, Thomas Wight, of Dedham).

PENROSE, Bartholomew (bap. 1674-*d* 1711), from Eng. to Phila., Pa., ca. 1700; shipbuilder; *m* 1703, Esther, dau. Tobias Leech.

PEPPER, Robert (*d* 1684), from Eng., settled at Roxbury, Mass.; freeman, 1643; *m* 1643, Elizabeth Johnson (*d* 1684).

PEPPERRELL, William (1647-1733), *b* in Wales, apprenticed to the captain of a fishing schooner on the coast of N.E.; settled at Isle of Shoals, later at Kittery, Me.; capt. provincial militia, 1714; cdr. of fort at Kittery Point, 1714 later lt. col. of militia of York Co.; justice Ct Common Pleas, 1715-30; dep. Gen. Ct. of Mass. 1696, et seq.; *m* Margery (*d* 1741), dau. of John Bray, of Kittery, Me.

PERKINS, Abraham (1613-83), from Eng. t Hampton, N.H., 1639; *m* Mary Wise (1618-1706)

PERKINS, Edmund (*d* 1693), from Eng. witl his widowed mother, to Salem, Mass., ca. 1650; *m* Susannah, dau. of Francis Hudson, and widow of John Howlett.

PERKINS, John (1583-1654), from Eng. in the "Lion," with Roger Williams, to Mass., 1631; freeman, 1631; went to Ipswich with John Winthrop, the younger, 1633; rep. Gen. Court, 1636; sgt. in war with the Tarratines, 1631; *m* 1608, Judith, dau. Michael Gater.

PERRINE (Perrin), Daniel (ca. 1640-1719; son of Pierre Perrin, of the Isle of Jersey); came from the Isle of Jersey in the "Philip," 1665; settled at Elizabethtown Plantations, N.J.; later on Staten Island; *m* 1666, Maria Thorel (*b*

Rouen, France, ca. 1640-*d* post 1687); *m* 2d, post 1687, Elizabeth – (*d* post 1719).

PERRY (Pury), Edward (*b* ca. 1630-*d* 1695; son of Edmund, *m* Sarah—), from Eng. with his mother and bro. Ezra, first to Plymouth, then to Saugus, Mass.; settled at Sandwich, Mass., 1637; grand juror, 1653; surveyor of highways, 1657, 68, 74; recorder of deeds, 1674; *m* 1653, Mary, dau. of Edmund Freeman, acting gov. of Plymouth.

PERRY, John (1604-74), from Eng. to Watertown, Mass., 1666; *m* Johannah Holland.

PERRY, Richard, from Eng. to New Haven Colony, 1640; at Fairfield, Conn., 1649, when he received a grant of land there; *m* Grace—, widow of John Nichols.

PERS, see Pierce.

PERSHING (Pfershing), Frederick (1724-94), from Alsace, in the "Jacob," to Phila., 1749, lived in York Co., Pa., where he was naturalized, 1765; removed to Westmoreland (then Cumberland) Co., nr. Youngstown, 1769, *m* 1751, Maria Elizabeth Weygandt (1738-1824).

PETERS, Andrew (1634/35-1713), from Eng. to Boston, 1659; removed to Ipswich, 1665, thence to Andover; distiller; two sons killed by Indians, 1689; soldier in Narragansett campaign, King Philip's War; *m* Mercy, dau. William Beamsley.

PETERS, William (1702-89), from England to Phila., Pa., ca. 1735, where he erected Belmont Mansion (still standing in Fairmount Park, Phila.); was register of the admiralty; judge common pleas, quarter sessions and orphans cts., Phila.; mem. Assembly and sec. of the Land Office; *m* 1741, Mary, dau. John Brientnall.

PETTINGELL, Richard (ca. 1620-ca. 1695), was settled at Salem, Mass., before 1641, when he was admitted freeman; removed to Wenham, 1649, to Newbury, 1651, where he bought land; *m* ca. 1643, Joanna (ca. 1625-1692/93), dau. Richard Ingersoll.

PETTIT, Thomas (ca.1610-1690; son of Henry, of Saffron Waldon. Essex, Eng.), from Eng. to Boston, Mass., 1630; granted house plot on Boston Commons, 1637, on which the State House at Boston stands; banished from Boston because of the Ann Hutchinson religious controversy, 1638; with 35 others founded Exeter Combination, July 4, 1639; cdr. of mil. co.; selectman, 1652; to English colony on L.I., 1657; marshal of Newtown, 1657; freeholder, 1666; assessor, 1687-90; with bro. John signed Donegan Charter of New York; *m* Christena (*b* ca. 1621), dau. Oliver Mellowes, from Eng., 1634, *m* 1620, Marie James); g. dau. Abraham Mellowes, *m* Martha Bulkley.

PETTUS, Thomas (1610-60; son of Sir John), from Eng. to Va., 1638; of "Littleton," James City Co., Va.; mem. Council, 1640-60; col.; *m* Elizabeth Mourning, widow of Richard Durant.

PHELPS, George (1605 or 06-1687), from Tewksbury, Eng., in the "Mary and John," to Dorchester, Mass., May 30, 1630; founded Windsor, Conn., 1635; finally settled at Westfield, Mass., 1670; mem. Council of Ten; *m* 1637, Phillury Randall; *m* 2d, 1648, Frances Dewey.

PHELPS, William (1599-1672; son of William, bailiff of Tewksbury, Eng.), from Eng. in the "Mary and John," to Dorchester, Mass., 1630; freeman, 1631; rep. 1st Gen. Court of Mass., 1634; selectman, 1634, 35; removed to Windsor, Conn., 1636; one of 8 commissioners apptd. by Colony of Mass. Bay to govern Colony of Conn., in 1636; gov.'s asst., 1636-42, 1658-62; rep. Gen. Court, 1645-57; mem. Council, 1637; magistrate; *m* Elizabeth – (*d* 1635); *m* 2d, ante 1639, Mary Dover.

PHILBRICK, Thomas (*d* 1667), from Eng. with Gov. Winthrop, Sir Richard Saltonstall and others, arrived in Mass. Bay, 1630; settled at Watertown, Mass.; removed to Hampton, N.H., 1645; *m* Elizabeth – (*d* 1663).

PHILLIPS, George (1593-1644), A.B., Cambridge, 1613; from Eng. in the "Arbella," to Salem, Mass., 1630; a founder of Watertown, where he founded the first Congl. Ch. in America; *m* 1st. 1631, Elizabeth, dau. of Richard Sergeant; *m* 2d, Mrs. Elizabeth Welden.

PHILLIPS, Maj. William (*d* 1683), of Cambridge, Mass.; removed to Boston, 1646, to Saco, Me., 1660; commr., justice, maj. and cdr. mil. forces, 1665; returned to Boston, 1675; *m* Mary– (*d* 1646).

PHIPS, James (father of Sir William); gunsmith; founded Phippsburg, Me., nr. mouth of Kennebec River before 1649.

PICKERING, John (1615-ca. 1657), from Eng. to Ipswich, Mass., 1634; removed to Salem, 1637; carpenter; *m* 1636, Elizabeth–(*d* 1662).

PICKETT (Pigot, Picquette), Capt. William (*d* 1640), mem. Va. Company, but did not come to America; *m* Sarah Stonor (*d* 1663).

PIERCE, Abraham (1605-73; g.son of John Pierce, M.P., granted a charter for the Mayflower Pilgrims, and owned and outfitted the "Fortune"), came in the "Fortune," 1622, bringing the charter to the Pilgrims; served in Capt. Myles Standish's mil. co., 1633; an original purchaser and founder of Bridgewater, Mass., 1645; *m* 1650, Rebecca–.

PIERCE (Pers), John (ca. 1588-1661), from Norwich, Co. Norfolk, Eng.; weaver with his wife, Elizabeth and four children, John, Barbare, Elizabeth and Judeth, came in the "John and Dorothy" or the "Rose," to Watertown, Mass., 1637; some of his children must have preceded him; *m* Elizabeth–(*b* ca. 1601-*d* Mar. 12, 1666/67).

PIERCE, Capt. Michael (ca. 1615-1676), from Eng., settled at Hingham, Mass., 1646; at Scituate, 1647; commd. capt., 1669; with the 49 Englishmen in his command killed in battle with Narragansett Indians; *m* 1st, —Ames (*d* ca. 1662); *m* 2d, ca. 1663, Mrs. Anna James, of Marshfield.

PIERCE (Pearce), Robert (*d* Jan. 6, 1665), from Eng. to Dorchester, Mass., 1630; built home on land which is still in possession of his descendants; *m* Ann (1591-1695, aet. 104), dau. of John Greenway, from Eng. in the "Mary and John."

PIERCE (Pers), Thomas (1583/84-1666). from Eng., 1633/34, settled at Charlestown; freeman, 1635; one of 21 commrs. apptd. by Gen. Ct. "to see that Saltpetre heapes were made by all the farmers of the Colony," 1642; *m* Elizabeth – (*b* 1595/96).

PIERPONT (Pierrepont), James (*d* ante 1664), from Eng., settled at Ipswich, Mass.; *m* Margaret – (*d* 1664).

PIERSON, Rev. Abraham (*b* Yorkshire, Eng., 1613-*d* Aug. 9, 1678), grad. Trinity Coll., Cambridge, 1632, and ordained; came to Boston, 1639. but soon removed to Lynn, Mass.; established a settlement at Southampton, L.I., 1640-1641; removed to Branford, Conn., with many of his congregation; Indian interpreter and translated the catechism into the Indian dialect; later at Newark, N.J., where he died; *m* Abigail, dau. of Rev. John Wheelwright, of Lincolnshire. Eng. (his son, Abraham Pierson [1641-1707], was first pres. of Yale Coll., 1701-07).

PIERSON (Pearson, Parsune, Person), Henry (1618-ca. 1680), from Eng. to Boston, 1639; to Southampton, L.I., 1640; clerk of Suffolk Co. Ct., 1669; founder of the public school system; *m* Mary, dau. of John Cooper, of Lynn, Mass., from Eng. in the "Hopewell," to Southampton, 1685.

PILLSBURY, William (1615-86). from Eng. to Dorchester, Mass., 1641; removed to Newbury, 1651; freeman, 1668; *m* Dorothy Crosby.

PINGRY (Pingree), Dea. Moses (*d* 1695/96), at Ipswich. Mass., 1641; established salt works, 1652; selectman; dep., 1665; *m* Lydia (*d* 1676/77), dau. Robert Clement, of Haverhill.

PITKIN, William (1635-94), from Eng., 1659; settled at Hartford, Conn.; prosecutor for Conn. Colony; atty. gen. for the King; rep. Hartford, 1675-90; treas. Com. to United Colonies; *m* 1661, Hannah (1637-1724), dau. of Ozias Goodwin, an original settler of Hartford.

PITNEY, James (1583/84-1663), from Eng. to New Brunswick, N.J., ante 1622; settled at Basking Ridge; *m* Sarah Smythe (1612/13-1658).

PLATER, George (*d* 1707), from Eng., resided in Md., 1685-1707; atty. for the king, 1691; collector of customs, Patuxent Dist., 1692; *m* Ann–.

PLATT, Richard (ca. 1603-1684), from Eng. with his wife and four children, to New Haven Colony, 1638; a founder of Milford, Conn., 1639; deacon; *m* Mary –.

PLEASANTS, John (1644-98), from Eng. to Va., 1665; settled at Curles Neck, Henrico Co.; *m* 1670, Jane Larcome (*d* 1708), widow of Samuel Tucker.

PLIMPTON (Plympton), John (ca. 1620-1677), from Eng. ca. 1630; was at Dedham, Mass., before he settled at Deerfield, ca. 1673; sgt. mil.

company; captured and burned at the stake by Indians, 1677; *m* 1644, Jane Dammant.

PLUMB, John (July 28, 1594-July 1648), came from Spaynes Hall, Great Yeldham, Essex Co., Eng., in his own ship, 1635; an early settler and propr. of Wethersfield, Conn.; shipowner; traded with Indians; mem. Wethersfield Ct.; probably with Capt. Mason in Pequot War, 1637; removed to Branford, 1644; town clk., 1645; *m* ca. 1616, Dorothy – (*d* post 1669).

PLUMMER (Plumer), Francis (ca. 1595-1672/1673), from Wales in the "Elizabeth Dorcas," to Newbury, Mass., 1633; admitted freeman, Ipswich, 1634; Newbury, Mass., 1634; linen weaver; kept the first tavern; *m* Ruth–; *m* 2d, 1648, Widow Ann Palmer (*d* 1665); *m* 3d, 1665, Beatrice–, widow of William Cantlebury.

POLK, Capt. Robert (*d* bet. May 6, 1699, date of his will, and June 5, 1704, when it was proved), from Ireland to Somerset Co., Md., bet. 1672-80; received from the Lords Baltimore grants of land in the Eastern Shore, "Polk's Lott," May 7, 1687, and "Polk's Folly," 1700; *m* in Ireland, Magdalen (Tasker) Porter (*d* "White Hall," Eastern Shore, 1726), dau. of Colonel Tasker, of Broomfield Castle, nr. Londonderry, a chancellor of Ireland, and widow of Colonel Porter in whose regt., a part of the Parliamentary forces under Cromwell, Robert Polk served as captain.

POMEROY (Pomroy, Pummery, Pumry), Eltweed (1585-1673; son of Richard), from Beaminster, Co. Dorset, Eng., in the "Mary and John," 1630; settled at Dorchester; freeman, 1632; selectman, 1633; to Windsor, where he received a grant of 1,000 acres, 1636; to Northampton, 1672; *m* 1617, Johannah Keech (*d* 1620); *m* 2d, 1629, Margery (christened Mary, but called Margery) Rockett (1605-55); *m* 3d, 1661, Lydia Brown, widow of Thomas Parsons.

POND, Daniel (1627-98), came from Eng. with Winthrop's fleet, 1630; settled at Dedham, Mass.; selectman, 1660; settled; lt. of Dedham, Mass., troops, 1672; *m* 1652, Abigail Shepard.

POND, Samuel (*d* 1654), from Eng. with Winthrop's fleet, 1630; *m* 1642, Sarah Ware.

POOLE (Poal, Pole), Edward (1609-64), from Eng. to Boston, Mass., 1635; settled at Weymouth, the same year; capt. militia; propr. of a sawmill, and a large amount of land; *m* bet. 1641-45, Sarah, dau. John Pynney.

POOR (Poore), John (1615-84), from Wiltshire, Eng., to Newbury, Mass., 1635; juror many times; took oath of fidelity, 1678; *m* Sarah–(*d* 1702).

POPE, Col. Nathaniel (ca. 1610-Apr. 1660), from Eng. to Va., 1634; resided in Md., 1637-50; mem. Md. Assembly, 1637, 1641-42; removed to Va., 1650; settled at "The Cliffs," Pope's Creek Westmoreland Co., Va., upon a grant from Charles I; lt. col. Westmoreland Co., 1655; *m* Lucy –.

POPE, Thomas (1608-83), from Eng. in the "Mary and John," settled at Dorchester, Mass., 1630, at Dartmouth, ca. 1674; *m* 1637, Ann, dau. Gabriel Fallowell; *m* 2d, 1646, Sarah, dau. John Jenney.

PORTER, John (1590-1648); desc. in the 16th generation from William de la Grande, a Norman Knight of Kenilworth in Warwickshire, 1066), from Co. Essex, Eng.; settled at Windsor, Conn., 1638; received large grant; constable, 1639-40; juror, 1641; grand juror, 1643; dep., 1646, 47; *m* in Eng., Oct. 18, 1620, Anna (bap. 1600), dau. Robert White, *m* Bridget Allgar.

POSEY, Francis (ca. 1610-1657), mem. Lower House of Burgesses, from St. Mary's Co., Md., 1640-50; one of first settlers in St. Mary's Co.

POST, Richard (1617-ca. 1689), from Eng., at Southampton, L.I., 1640; one of first settlers of New London, Conn., 1646 or 47; blacksmith; *m* ca. 1640. Dorothy Johnson (1625-ca. 1689).

POST, Stephen (*d* 1659), from Eng., ca.1630; was at Cambridge, Mass., 1634; freeman, 1634; a founder of Hartford, Conn., 1636; to Saybrook, 1645; *m* Eleanor–(*d* 1670).

POTTER, Nathaniel (*d* ante 1644), from Eng.; admitted inhabitant at Aquidneck Island, 1639; *m* Dorothy–(1617-96).

POTTER, Nicholas (ca.1600-1677), from Eng.; granted land at Lynn, Mass., 1638; freeman, 1638; interested in iron works; to Salem, 1660; *m* ante 1630, Emma–(*d* ante 1658); *m* 2d, Alice–,

widow of Thomas Weeks, of Salem.

POTTER, Robert (1610-55), from Eng. to Lynn, Mass., 1630; freeman, 1634; removed to Newport, R.I., 1638; a founder of Warwick, 1641; taken prisoner to Boston on account of preaching a "monstrous doctrine," was banished and went to Eng. and secured restoration of his estate; kept an inn at Warwick and *d* there; *m* Isabel –; *m* 2d, Sarah–.

POVALL, Robert (1650-1728), from Eng. to Henrico Co., Va., 1681; made voyage to Eng., 1682; upon return to America came into possession of estate called "Malvern Hills," Henrico Co., Va.; *m* 1683, Elizabeth, dau. Lord Hooker.

POWELL, Walter (ca.1645-1695), Accomac Co., Va., to Somerset Co., Md., 1668; *m* ca.1667, Margaret Berry (*d* 1679).

POWELL, Capt. William, from Wales to Va., 1607, with Capt. John Smith; subscriber to London Co.; rep. from James City in first House of Burgesses, 1619; killed by Indians on Chickahominy River, 1623; *m* Elizabeth, dau. of Joseph Welles.

POWERS, Walter (1639-1708), from Eng. to Concord Village, Mass., 1660; bought town of Nashoba from Indians; *m* 1661, Trial, dau. of Ralph Shepherd (qv);

POYTHRESS, Capt. Francis, from Eng. to Va., 1633; burgess for Charles City 1645, 47; commanded against the Indians, 1645; burgess for Northumberland, 1649.

PRATT, John (*d* 1655), from Eng. 1632; a founder of Hartford, Conn., 1636; dep. Gen. Ct., 1639, et seq.; *m* Elizabeth –.

PRATT, Joshua (*d* 1656), from Eng. in the "Anne," 1623, settled at Plymouth, Mass.; constable; *m* ca. 1630, Bathsheba Fay.

PRATT, Matthew (1600-72), from Eng., settled at Weymouth, Mass.; freeman, 1640; removed to Rehoboth; *m* Elizabeth Bate.

PRATT, Richard (1615-91), from Eng. to Charlestown, Mass., ca. 1640; removed to Malden, Mass.; *m* 1643, Mary – (*d* ca. 1691).

PRATT, William (1622-78; son of Rev. William Pratt), from Eng. with Rev. Thomas Hooker; an original settler at Hartford, Conn., 1636; dep. Gen. Ct., 1666, et seq.; mem. Council of War, 1642; removed to Saybrook, 1645; lt. of Saybrook forces in Pequot War; *m* Elizabeth, dau. John Clark, one of the 19 patentees named in the Royal Charter from Charles II.

PREBLE, Abraham (1603-63), from Eng. to Scituate, Mass., 1637, removed to York, Me., 1642, magistrate 1650; freeman, 1652; treas. of Me. Company, 1659; commr. for York, 1655-57, 1659-60; held first mil. appointment with rank of major; *m* Judith, dau. Nathaniel Tilden.

PRENCE (Prince), Thomas (1601-Mar. 29, 1673), from Eng. to Plymouth, Mass., 1621; asst. Plymouth Colony, 1635; gov., 1634, 38, 1657-73; mem. Council of War, and served in Pequot War; commr. United Colonies, 1645; removed to Duxbury, 1635, to Eastham, Mass., 1645; *m* 1624, Patience, dau. Elder William Brewster (qv).

PRENTICE (Prentis), Capt. Thomas (1621-1710), from Eng. to Cambridge, Mass., ante 1652; freeman, 1652; lt. horse troop, 1656; laid out Worcester, 1667; rep. Gen. Ct., 1672-74; capt. Indian war, 1675, in Pequot and Narragansett wars; commr. to rebuild Lancaster, Mass., 1689; overseer of Indians, 1691; *m* ca. 1643, Grace –.

PRENTISS (Prentice), Valentine (*d* 1633), from Eng. in the "Lyon," 1631; settled at Roxbury, Mass.; *m* Alice–.

PRESCOTT, James (1642-1728; g.g.son James, lord of the manor of Driby, Lincolnshire, *m* Alice, dau. Sir Richard Mollyneux, of Sefton); from Eng. to Hampton, N.H., 1655; took oath of allegiance, 1678; *m* Mary, dau. Nathaniel Boulter.

PRESCOTT, John (ca. 1604-1683), from Eng. to the Barbados, 1638, thence to Watertown, Mass., 1640; with others bought from Indians a large tract of land and became a founder of Lancaster, Mass., 1645 or 46; took oath of allegiance, 1652; admitted freeman, 1669; blacksmith and miller; *m* in Eng., 1629, Mary Platts (*d* 1674).

PRESTON, John (1699-1747), from Ireland to Augusta Co., Va., 1740; grantee with Breckenridge and Patton of 12,000 acres; *m* 1725, Elizabeth Patton (1700-76).

PRESTON, Roger (1614-1666), from Eng. in the "Elizabeth," 1635; settled at Ipswich, Mass., 1639, at Salem, 1659-60; *m* 1642, Martha—(*b* 1622).

PRICE, John (1584-1628), came from Eng. first time in the "Starr," to Jamestown, Va., 1610; lived on "Ye Neck of Land," Charles City, on 150 acres granted him Feb. 20, 1619. by Sir George Yeardley; mem. Provincial Council; *m* Mary –; *m* 2d, Ann – (*b* 1599), who came in the "Francis Bonaventure," 1620.

PRICE, Thomas (*d* 1701), from Eng. in the "Ark" and "Dove" expdn. to St. Mary's Co., Md., 1638; mem. Council; *m* Elizabeth, dau. Robert Phillips, of Calvert Co., Md.

PRICHARD, Roger (*d* 1670/71), from Eng., 1640, settled at Wethersfield, Conn.; at Springfield, 1643, Milford, 1653; *m* 1653, Elizabeth (Pruden) Slough, dau. of James Pruden.

PRIEST, Degory (ca. 1579-1621), 29th signer of the Mayflower Compact; *m* at Leyden, Holland, 1611, Sarah (Allerton) Vincent, widow of John Vincent.

PRIME, Mark (*d* 1683), from Eng., settled at Rowley, Mass.; propr. ante 1650; judge of Delinquents, 1663-64; voted on minister's stipend, 1674; *m* 1647, Anne–(*d* 1672).

PRINCE, John (1610-76), from Eng. to Mass., 1633, freeman at Watertown, 1635; removed to Hull; ruling elder; *m* Alice Honour (*d* 1668); *m* 2d, 1670, Anna Hubbard, widow of William Barstow (qv).

PROVOOST, David (1608-85; 3d from Guillaume Prevost [*b* 1545], of Paris, *m* Margaretta Ten Waert); came to N.Y., 1624; cdr., Ft. Good Hope for Dutch West India Co.; head of the "Nine Men," New Amsterdam schepen 1645, of Breucklen, Midwout and Amersfoort until death; mem. Gov.'s Council.

PRUDDEN, Rev. Peter (1600-56), from Hertfordshire, Eng., settled at New Haven and Milford; pastor of the first ch. at Milford, Conn., 1640-56; *m* Joanna Boyse, from Eng.

PRUYN, Franz Janse (*d* 1712), from Holland to Albany, N.Y., ca. 1661; *m* Aeltje –.

PUGH, Francis, I (son of a Welsh squire of Glendower Hall, Carnavon, Wales); came to America, 1665, with his brothers, Thomas and Daniel, and settled in Upper Nansemond, Surry Co., Va., where they built a manor house of English brick upon an estate called "Jericho."

PULLIAM, (Pullum) Edward (*b* 1600), from Eng. to Henrico Co., Va., 1636; paid his passage.

PUREFOY, Capt. Thomas (ca. 1578-ca. 1652-55; son of Humphrie, g.son of Sir Nicholas Purefoy, of royal descent); came to America in "The George," 1621; settled in Elizabeth City Co., Va.; commr.; justice and principal cdr. Elizabeth City Co., 1628; mem. Council, 1631; burgess; settled on "Drayton," a tract of 1,000 acres; *m* 1620, Lucy Ransom (1598-1657-60).

PUTNAM, John (bap. 1579-1662), from Eng., to Salem, Mass., 1634; received a land grant of 100 acres in Salem Village (now Danvers), Mass.; became principal landowner there; *m* 1611/12, Priscilla Deacon (or Gould).

PYNCHON (Pincheon), William (1590-1662), from Eng. with Winthrop's fleet to Roxbury, Mass., 1630, a founder of Springfield, Mass. 1636; governing magistrate of Conn., 1637-38; governor's asst., treas., 1632-34; gov. of Springfield, 1641-50; returned to Eng., 1652, and devoted himself to theological writing; *m* Anna, dau. William Andrew; *m* 2d, Frances Sanford.

QUINCY, Edmund (1602-35), from Eng. to Mass., 1628; returned to Eng., but came again with John Cotton, 1633, to Quincy, Mass.; freeman, 1634; rep. Gen. Ct., 1634; a founder of Braintree, 1635; *m* Judith Pares.

RAGLAND, John, from Wales to Eng., thence to Va. ca. 1720, with his wife and 10 children; settled in Henrico Co.; was granted 15,000 acres in Hanover Co.; his home "Ripping Hall," on the Chickahominy was burned in 1825; *m* Ann Beaufort, his kinswoman.

RAMBO, Peter Gunnarsson (*b* in Sweden, 1605-*d* in Pa., 1698), from Rambo, in northeastern Sweden, 1638, settled at New Sweden (later called Upper Merion, now Phila.); a founder of the Swedish colony in America; deputy under Gov. Rising, 1665; councilman under Dutch regime; magistrate, 1658; commr. under Duke of York, 1664; *m* ca. 1648, Bretta – (*d* 1684).

RANDALL, Thomas (1688 or 90-1759). from Eng. to King George Co., Va., 1717-20; provincial judge; was of "Tuckahoe," and Henrico and Goochland cos., Va.; burgess, 1720-22; col.

and county lt. of Goochland, 1727; *m* 1728, Jane Davis.

RANDOLPH (Fitz Randolph), Edward (bap. 1607-*d* ante 1685; of royal and surety baron descent), from Nottinghamshire, Eng., to Barnstable, Mass., 1630; juryman, 1641; settled at Piscataway, N.J., ca.1668; *m* 1637, Elizabeth (*b* Holland, 1620-*d* 1713), dau. of Dea. Thomas Blossom (qv).

RANDOLPH, William (*b* Parish of Moreton, Mobrell, Eng., 1650-*d* Turkey Island, Henrico Co., Va., Apr. 11, 1711); from Eng. to Jamestown, Va., 1672; settled on Turkey Island. James River, Henrico Co., Va., 1674; was clk. of Henrico Co., burgess, atty. gen. and mem. Royal Council; capt., lt. col.; a founder of William and Mary College; *m* Mary, dau. Henry Isham (qv).

RANNEY, Thomas (1616-1713), from Scotland to Middletown, Conn., ca. 1657; *m* 1659, Mary (1641/42-1721), dau. George Hubbard.

RAPELJE (de Rapalie), Joris Jansen (ca. 1600-ca. 1663; desc. noble family of Brittany), Huguenot, fled from France to Holland, thence in the "Unity" to New Amsterdam, 1623; at Albany, 1623-37; resided at Wallabout; magistrate; one of the "Twelve Men," Brooklyn; *m* Catalyntie (1605-89), dau. of Joris Trico, of Paris.

RATHBUN (Rathbone), Richard (*b* ca.1574), from Eng. to Mass., 1628; *m* ca.1596, Marion (ante 1583-post 1610), dau. Matthew Whipple.

RAVENEL (de Ravenal), Rene (*b* 1656; sieur de la Haute, Massais), Huguenot, from France, 1682, before the revocation of the Edict of Nantes, to Charleston, S.C.; mem. Assembly; *m* 1687, Charlotte, dau. Pierre de St. Julien (sieur de Malacare, Brittany).

RAWSON, Edward (1615-93), came from Eng., 1636-37; settled at Newbury, 1637; town clk., 1638-47; at Boston, 1650; selectman; commr.; dep. Gen. Ct.; officer to enforce English naval laws, 1663; *m* in Eng., Rachel, dau. of Richard Perne, Gent., of Dorset, *m* Rachel—.

RAYMOND, Capt. Richard (ca. 1602-1692), was at Salem, Mass., ante 1634; founder of Norwalk, Conn., 1662; called "Honored fore-father of Saybrook"; *m* Judith -.

RAYMOND, Capt. William (1637-1709), came from Eng. in boyhood with his bro., John, to Beverly, Mass., 1651; in Narragansett Fight, 1675; mem. Gen. Ct., 1683; lt. and cdr. Expdn. to Can., 1690; *m* Hannah (1646-1738), dau. Edward Bishop.

READE, Col. George (*d* 1671), from Eng. to Va., 1637; sec. Colony of Va., 1637; acting gov., 1638; burgess, 1649, 56; mem. King's Council, 1657-71; *m* Elizabeth (1627-87), dau. of Nicholas Martian (qv).

READING, Col. John (*d* 1717), from Eng. to Gloucester Co., N.J., 1684; mem. Assembly, 1685; co. clk., 1688-1702; removed to Burlington (later Amwell Tp., Hunterdon) Co., 1709; capt. N.J., Militia, 1713; lt. col., 1715; *m* Elizabeth –.

REDMAN, see Rodman.

REED (Read), John (1598-1685; son of William, *m* Lucy Henage, of Co. Kent, Eng.); desc. of Sir William Read, *m* Ann Menis), from Eng. with the "Great Fleet," 1630; at Weymouth, Mass., 1637, at Dorchester, 1638, Rehoboth, 1643; constable; *m* Sarah, dau. William Lessie.

REED, William (1587-1656), from Eng. in the "Defence," 1635; settled at Boston, Mass.; constable, Scituate, Mass., 1644; to Woburn, 1648; returned to Eng. with his wife, and *d* at Newcastle-on-Tyne, ca.1656; *m* ca. 1628, Mabel (ca. 1605-1690), dau. John Kendall (she *m* 2d, Henry Summers).

REED, William (1605-63), from Eng. in the "Assurance," to Boston, 1635; rep. Gen. Ct., 1636, 38; townsman, 1651; *m* Avis (Deacon or Chapman).

REMINGTON (Rimmington), John (1617-67), from Eng. to Rowley, Mass., 1637; removed to Newbury; freeman, 1639; later at Greenwich, R.I.; lt. mil. company; soldier Pequot War; *m* Elizabeth – (*d* 1657), *m* 2d, Rhoda –, widow of John Gore.

REMSEN (Rem Jensen Vanderbeeck), Rem (*d* 1681), probably from Westphalia, to New Netherland, 1642; resided at Albany, later at Wallabout, L.I.; *m* Jannette de Rapalje.

REVERE (Rivoire), Apollos (1702-54), from France to Island of Guernsey, thence to Boston, 1715; goldsmith; *m* 1729, Deborah Hichborne (1704-77).

REYNOLDS, James (ca. 1620-1700), settled at Potowomut Neck, nr. E. Greenwich, North Kingston, R.I., ca. 1665; *m* ca. 1648, Deborah – (ca. 1620-ante 1692).

REYNOLDS, John (*b* ca. 1612), first recorded mention is in Watertown, Mass., where he was made a freeman, 1635; *m* Sarah – (*b* ca. 1614).

REYNOLDS, Robert (*d* Apr. 27, 1659), from Eng. with Winthrop's fleet, 1630; admitted to first church at Boston, 1634; freeman, 1634; *m* ca. 1610, Mary –.

RHETT (Lwirete-Rhett, from Lwirte), George, from Eng. to Carolina, 1671, later to Charlestown, Mass.; *m* Sarah Boyleston.

RHINELANDER, Philip Jacob (*d* 1737), a Huguenot, from France after the revocation of the Edict of Nantes, settled at New Rochelle, N.Y., 1686.

RHOADES, Henry (1608-1703; son of George and g.son of James of Lancashire, Eng.), from Eng., 1640; rep. Gen. Ct., 1657; ironmonger, farmer and miller at Lynn, Mass.; in King Philip's War; *m* Elizabeth White, or Paul (*d* 1700).

RHODES, Zachariah (1603-65), a first settler of Pawtuxet, R.I.; joined Roger Williams in Bapt. belief; *m* 1646, Joanna (1617-92), dau. William Arnold (qv).

RICE, Edmund (1594-1663), from Eng., 1638; a founder of Sudbury, Mass.; freeman, 1640; rep. Gen. Ct.; magistrate; an early settler of Marlborough; selectman; *m* Tamazine– (1600-54); *m* 2d, 1655, Mercy, widow of Thomas Brigham.

RICHARDS, Edward (ca. 1610-84), from Eng. in the "Lion" with Roger Williams, 1631; at Dedham, Mass., 1632; freeman, 1641; *m* 1638, Susanna Hunting.

RICHARDSON, Amos (ante 1618-1683), Eng. to Boston, ante 1639; tailor and trader bet. the Colonies; owned vessels which traded with W.I.; large landowner; atty. at Boston; mem. Narragansett Co.; agt. for Stephen Winthrop and later of his bro., Gov. John Winthrop; propr. Groton, Conn.; to Stonington, Conn., 1663; freeman, 1665; dep. to Conn. Gen. Ct., 1676-81; *m* ca.1642, Mary (1617-prob. 1683), dau. John Smith, who came in the "Planter," 1635, at Sudbury, Mass., 1643

RICHARDSON (Richeson), Ezekiel (1602-47), from Eng. in the "Arbella," with Gov. Winthrop, to Charlestown, Mass., 1630; freeman, 1631; constable, 1633; rep. Gen. Ct., 1635; selectman; a founder of Woburn; *m* in Eng., Susanna –.

RICHARDSON, Samuel (ca. 1610-1658), from Eng. with two brothers, Ezekiel and Thomas, in the "Arbella," with Gov. Winthrop, 1630, settled at Charlestown, Mass., 1636; founder and largest landowner of Woburn, Mass.; *m* Joanna –.

RICHARDSON, Thomas (*d* 1651), from Eng. in the "Arbella," with Gov. Winthrop, 1630, to Charlestown, Mass.; freeman, 1638; a founder of Woburn, 1642; *m* Mary –.

RICHMOND, John (1594-1664; son of Edmund), from Eng. to Mass., ca. 1635; one of the first purchasers of land at Taunton, 1637; in R.I., 1655, but returned to Taunton, 1656; mem. R.I. Ct. of Commissioners, 1656; *m* Elizabeth Nicholas.

RICKARD, Giles (1597-1684), from Wales, settled at Plymouth, Mass., 1635; freeman, 1640; surveyor and constable; *m* 1st, 1622, Judith – (*d* 1661); *m* 2d, 1662, Joan Tilson.

RIDGELY, Henry (1625-1710), from Devonshire, Eng., settled on the Patuxent River, Prince Georges Co., Md., 1659; justice for Anne Arundel Co., 1656-92; mem. Gov.'s Council and Assembly; col. militia; *m* Elizabeth Howard; *m* 2d, Sarah Warner; *m* 3d, Mary (Stanton) DuVall.

RIDGELY, Robert (*d* 1682), from Eng. in the "Assurance," to St. Mary's Co., Md., 1634/35; one of the principal attorneys for the province and clk. House of Assembly many yrs.; principal sec., 1671; examiner High Ct. of Chancery; probate judge; keeper of lesser seals; *m* Martha –.

RIGGS, Edward (1590-1672), from Eng. to Boston, 1633; settled at Roxbury, Mass.; freeman, 1634; served in Pequot War; *m* Elizabeth– (*d* 1635).

RIPLEY, William (1600-56), from Eng. in the "Diligent," ca. 1638, settled at Hingham, Mass.; admitted freeman, 1642; *m* 2d, 1654, Elizabeth –

(*d* 1660), widow of Thomas Thaxter, of Hingham; she *m* 3d, 1657/58, John Dwight, of Dedham.

RISLEY, Richard (*b* ante 1615), from Eng. in "Griffin," to Boston, 1633; original propr. Hartford, Conn; served Pequot War; participated in adoption of the "Fundamental Order," 1st written constn. known in history; *m* ca.1640, Mary Arnold (*d* ante 1669), she *m* 2d, Will Hills.

RITTENHOUSE (Rettinghausen), B i s h o p Wilhelm (*b* nr. Mulheim-Ruhr, Ger., 1644-*d* Feb. 18, 1708; desc. of medieval baronial family von Rodinghausen of Westphalia); learned paper-making art and later practiced it at Arnhem, Gelderland, Netherlands; to Germantown, Phila. Co., 1688; established first paper factory in America, 1690; an organizer and first preacher, Germantown Mennonite Ch. (the earliest 1690), and first bishop (1707) of that denomination in America; *m* 1665, —.

ROBBINS, John (*d* 1660), from Eng., 1638, settled at Wethersfield, Conn.; selectman, 1652, 53, 56, 57; rep. Gen. Ct., 1657-59; *m* Mary Welles (1616-59), dau. of Robert Welles and sister of Gov. Thomas Welles.

ROBBINS, Richard (*d* after 1683), from Eng. to Charlestown, Mass., 1639; removed to Boston, thence to Cambridge; *m* Rebecca –.

ROBERT, Rev. Pierre (1656-1715; son of Daniel, of St. Imier, Basle, Switzerland), from France, 1686; settled at Charleston, S.C.; 1st Huguenot pastor in S.C.; *m* 1674, Jeanne (1660-1717), dau. Jehu Braye, *m* Susanne–.

ROBERTS, Hugh (*d* 1702), from Wales with his widowed mother (*d* 1699), to Pa., 1683; settled in Merion Tp.; Quaker; mem. Provincial Council of Pa.; *m* Jane, dau. Owen ap Evan; *m* 2d, Elizabeth John.

ROBERTS, John, from Wales to Montgomery Co., Pa., 1683; *m* Gainor Hugh.

ROBERTS, Thomas (1600-1673/74; son of Thomas, of Co. Worcester, Eng.), from Eng., 1624; acquired a tract of land at Dover, N.H., 1628 (which remained in continuous possession of the family for 300 yrs.); pres. of the ct., 1638; elected 4th and last gov. of Dover Colony, 1640, and served until the colony was taken over by Mass. Bay Colony, 1642; *m* 1627, Rebecca Hilton.

ROBERTSON, William, from Scotland to Charles City, Va., was receiver of York River and sec. of Council of State, 1719, under Gov. Spottswood; *m* Christian Ferguson.

ROBESON, Andrew (1654-1719/20), from Scotland to Gloucester Co., N.J., ca. 1676; moved to Philadelphia Co., Pa., 1702; purchased, 1690, "Shoomac Park," now known as Fairmount Park; chief justice of Pa., 1693-98; *m* 1685, Mary Spencer (1666-1716), of Stuart descent.

ROBINS, John (*d* 1623), from Eng. in the "Margaret and John," 1622; returned to Eng., and died on voyage to Va.

ROBINSON, Alexander (1750-1845), from Ireland to Baltimore, Md.; *m* Priscilla (Lyles) Booth (1760-90), widow of Robert Booth; *m* 2d, a dau. of Charles Wilson Peale.

ROBINSON, Isaac (1610-1704; son of Rev. John), from Eng. in the "Lion," 1631; was at Duxbury, Mass., 1635; at Scituate, 1636, at Barnstable, 1639; mem. Grand Inquest for the colony, 1639, 48; dep. Gen. Ct. from Barnstable, 1645, 51; receiver of excise; recorder at Tisbury; *m* 1636, Margaret Hanford.

ROBINSON, John (ca. 1576-1625), M.A., Cambridge, 1599; from Eng. to Holland, and settled at Leyden, 1609; pastor at Leyden of the Pilgrims; regarded as "the most learned, polished and modest spirit that ever separated from the Church of England"; active in promoting emigration to America; *m* Bridget White.

ROBINSON, William (1616-68), from Eng., 1637; at Dorchester, Mass., name first appears as member of the church there, 1639; freeman, 1642; mem. A. and H. A. Co., 1643; *m* 1st, 1637, Margaret Beach.

ROCKEFELLER, Johan Peter (1681-1766), from Germany, settled in Somerset Co., N.J., later at Amwell, Hunterdon Co., N.J.; *m* Anna Maria Remagen (1684-1719); *m* 2d, 1720, Elizabeth Christina Runkel.

ROCKWELL, John (*d* 1676), from Eng., settled at Stamford, Conn., 1641; removed to Rye, Westchester Co., N.Y.; *m* Elizabeth, dau. Jonas Weed (qv).

ROCKWELL, William (bap. 1591-1640), from Eng. to Dorchester, Mass., 1630; freeman, 1631; removed to Windsor, Conn., ca. 1636; *m* 1624, Susan Capen (1602-66); she *m* 2d, 1645, Matthew Grant.

RODMAN (Redman), John (1653-1731; son of John, who settled in the Barbados), from Eng. to Barbados, thence to Newport, R.I., ca. 1682; freeman, 1684; removed to Block Island, ca. 1688, to Flushing, L.I., 1691; freeman, New York City, 1698; physician; Quaker; *m* Mary Scammon (1663-1748).

RODMAN, Dr. Thomas (1640-1728; son of John [*d* 1686], from Eng. to Ireland, 1654, planter in the Barbados, *m* ca. 1638, Elizabeth –); a Quaker; came to Newport, R.I., 1675; eminent physician and surgeon; large landowner in N.J. and Pa.; *m* 2d, 1682, Patience Easton (1655-90), dau. of Peter Easton, *m* Ann, dau. of John Coggeshall (qv).

ROE, Hugh (*d* 1689), from Eng.; at Weymouth, Mass., 1642; to Marthas Vineyard, 1658, thence to Hartford, Conn.; freeman, 1669; sealer of leather, 1663; at Suffield, 1674; constable, 1684, 85, 88; *m* 2d, 1656, Abigail–(*d* 1689).

ROE, John (1628-will probated 1714), from Ire. to Boston, 1641; later at Setauket, L.I., 1655; signed treaty with Indians for land in Suffolk Co., L.I.; *m* ca.1655, Hannah (Furrier?).

ROGERS, Giles (*b* Edinburgh, 1653-*d* King and Queen Co., Va., 1730), ed. at Edinburgh, after maturity moved to Worcestershire, Eng., from there he emigrated to Va., where he patented land, Apr. 18, 1670; *m* 1672, Rachael Eastham (Esam), in Eng.; he returned to Va., 1680, arriving in his own ship and settled on his land grant, on Dragon Swamp, Stratton Major Parish, King and Queen Co., Va.

ROGERS, James (1615-87), from Eng. in the "Increase," 1635; at Stratford, Milford and New London, Conn.; freeman, 1660/61; baker; rep. Gen. Ct. 6 times; in Pequot War, 1637; a founder of "Rogerenes"; brought to America the Bible of the martyr, John Rogers; *m* Elizabeth (1621-1709), dau. Samuel Rowland.

ROGERS, Nathaniel (1598-1655), A.B., Cambridge, 1617; from Eng. to Boston, Mass., 1636; pastor at Ipswich, 1638-55; *m* 2d, Margaret, dau. Robert Crane.

ROGERS, Thomas (*b* 1586/87-*d* 1621), 18th signer of the Mayflower Compact; came in the "Mayflower" with his eldest son; *m* ca. 1606, Grace –.

ROGERS, William, from Eng. to Conn., 1635; with two others bought from the Indians what was called the Eastern land purchase, on which the town of Huntington, L.I., was founded.

ROLFE, John (*b* Beacham Hall, May 6, 1585-*d* 1622; son of John, of Beacham Hall, Co. Suffolk. Eng., *m* Dorothea Mason); capt. English army; came to Va., 1607; was mem. Council and the first sec. and recorder general of Colony of Va.; *m* 1613, Pocahontas (Rebecca Matoaka), (1595-1617), dau. of Powhatan, Indian chieftain of Va.

ROLLINS (Rawlins), James (will proved July 25, 1691), from Eng., 1632, settled at Ipswich, Mass.; at Newbury, 1634; Dover, N.H., 1644; *m* Hannah –.

ROOSA, Albert (Aldert) Hymanse (1621-79), from Herwynen, Gelderland, Holland, in the "Spotted Cow," to New Netherlands, 1660; settled at Hurley, Ulster Co., N.Y.; one of the 1st schepens; overseer, 1669; sgt. mil. co., 1670; capt., 1673; *m* Wyntie Ariense, as widow received a grant of 320 acres in recognition of husband's public service.

ROOSEVELT (Van Rosenvelt), Claes Martensen (*d* ca. 1658), from Holland, seems to have first appeared in New Netherland, 1638; *m* Jannetie Samuels, or Hamel, or Thomas (*d* 1660).

ROOT (Roote), John (1608-84, son of John, of Badby, Eng., *m* Ann Russell), from Eng., 1640, settled at Farmington, Conn.; freeman, 1657; *m* Mary (1619-97), dau. Thomas Kilborne (qv).

ROOT (Roote), Thomas (1605-94; son of John, of Badby, Eng., *m* Ann Russell), came to Conn., 1637; an early settler at Hartford, Conn.; soldier in Pequot War; to Northampton, Mass., 1654; weaver.

ROSE, Robert (1594-1664), from Eng. in the "Francis," to Mass., 1634; thence to Wethersfield, Conn.; constable, 1640; rep. Gen. Ct. 3 terms; removed to Stratford before 1648; served in Pequot War; *m* Margery– (*b* 1594).

ROSSITER, Edward (*d* 1630), from Eng. in the "Mary and John," to Dorchester, Mass., 1630, with son Brian; was gov.'s asst., Mass. Bay Colony.

ROWELL, Thomas (*d* 1662), from Windsor, Eng., 1638; resided at Salisbury, Ipswich and Andover, Mass.

ROYAL, William (*d* Dorchester, Mass., 1676), from Eng., 1629, settled at Salem, Mass.; at Casco Bay, Me., 1635; received land grant, 1639; purchased 250 acres at N. Yarmouth, Me., 1643; ct. asst., 1636, 48; councillor at York, 1640; clk. of the writs, 1667; *m* Phoebe Green, step-dau. of Samuel Cole.

ROYALL, Joseph (1600-58), from Eng. in the "Charitie" to Jamestown, Va., 1622; settled on James River above Shirley Hundred; large landowner, fought in the Indian wars; *m* ante 1637, Thomassia–; *m* 2d, Ann–; *m* 3d, ca. 1645, Katherine Banks of Canterbury, Eng., who *m* 2d, Henry Isham (qv).

RUGGLES, Thomas (1584-1644), from Eng., 1637; settled at Roxbury, Mass.; *m* 1620, Mary (1586-1674), dau. Thomas Curtis, *m* Mary Camp.

RUMSEY (Rumsie), Robert, from Wales to Fairfield, Conn., ca. 1664; *m* Rachel –.

RUNK (Runck), Jacob (ca. 1716-ca. 1771), from the Palatinate in the "Winter Galley," to Phila., Pa., 1738; purchased farm and settled in Amwell Tp., Hunterdon Co., N.J.; *m* Ann (bap. 1724-ca. 1771), dau. Johann Peter Rockefeller.

RUNYAN (Rongnion), Vincent, Huguenot, from Poitiers, Province of Ancienne Poitou, France to Elizabethtown, N.J., ca.1665; later to Piscataway, N.J.; carpenter; juror; *m* 1668, Ann Boutcher.

RUSH, John (1620-99), from Eng., 1683, settled at Byberry, Pa.; cdr. of horse in Cromwell's Army, also his personal friend; *m* 1648, Susanna Lucas, of Hornton.

RUSSELL, John (1597-1680), from Wales ca. 1632; freeman at Cambridge, Mass., 1636; removed to Wethersfield, Conn., 1649, to Hadley, Mass., 1659; *m* Elizabeth –.

RUSSELL, John (1608-95), an original propr. and settler at Dartmouth, Mass.; freeman, 1676; took oath of fidelity, 1684; rep. Gen. Ct., 1665-83, except two yrs.; in expedn. against Narragansett Indians, 1645; *m* Dorothy – (*d* 1687).

RUSSELL, Richard (1611 in Eng.-1676; son of Paul), to Charlestown, Mass., 1640; mem. A. and H. A. Co.; dep. Gen. Ct., 7 times; speaker; treas. of colony; gov.'s asst.; *m* in Eng., 1640, Maud (*d* 1642), dau. of William Pitt.

RUSSELL, William (*d* 1661/62), from Eng., 1636-45; resided first at Menotomy (now Arlington), Mass., later at Cambridge; carpenter; *m* Martha—(*d* 1694), she *m* 2d, 1665, Humphrey Bradshaw, and 3d, 1683, Thomas Hall.

RUTHERFOORD, Thomas (*b* 1766), from Scotland, settled at Richmond, Va., 1784; *m* 1790, Sallie Winston.

RYERSON (Reyerszen), Marten (*d* ca. 1687), from Holland to Wallabout, L.I. (present site of Brooklyn Navy Yard), ca. 1647; *m* 1663, Annetje Joris, dau. Joris Jansen de Rapelje, from France in the first ship sent out by West India Co.

SABIN, William (ca. 1620-1687), mem. of Huguenot family which sought refuge in Eng.; came from Co. Hampshire, Eng., ca.1640, settled at Rehoboth, Mass., later to Plymouth, Mass.; advanced money for King Philip's War, 1675; *m* 1st, ca.1640,—(*d* 1660); *m* 2d, 1663, Martha (*b* 1641), dau. of James Allen (qv).

SAFFORD, Thomas (*d* 1666/67), came to Mass., 1630; at Ipswich, 1641; freeman, 1630 and 1648; propr.; *m* Elizabeth–(*d* 1670/71).

SAGE, David (1639-Mar. 31, 1703), from Wales, 1650; one of first settlers at Middletown, Conn., 1652; freeman, 1667; *m* Elizabeth (1646-72), dau. John Kirby; *m* 2d, 1672-74, Mary, or Marcy–(*d* Dec. 7, 1711).

ST. JOHN (Sention, Sension), Matthias (1603-99; son of Sir Oliver, of London, Eng., *m* Sarah Buckley, *b* Cayshoe, Bedfordshire, Eng.); to Dorchester, Mass., 1631/32, settled at Norwalk, 1634, Windsor, Conn., 1640, Hartford, 1650; freeman, 1699; *m* Elizabeth –.

SALISBURY, William (*d* 1675), from Eng., settled at Dorchester, Mass., ca.1648; shipbuilder and lived nr. mouth of Gulliver's Creek; at Milton, Mass., 1652; mem. militia;

killed by Indians in King Philip's War; *m*
Susanna–(*d* post 1677).

SALTAR, Richard (*d* ca. 1724), settled in Monmouth Co., N.J., ca. 1687; mem. House of Deps.
to Gen. Assembly 1695, 1704; mem. Gen. Assembly, 1706, 11; justice of the peace, 1704,
05, 08; captain; supported claims for supremacy of the Nicolls Patent, 1700-01; judge
Monmouth Co., N.J. until 1724; *m* 1693, Sarah (*b*
1669), dau. of John Bowne (qv).

SALTONSTALL, Sir Richard (bap. 1586-ca.
1660), from Eng. in the "Arbella" with Gov.
Winthrop, to Watertown, Mass., 1630; gov.'s
asst.; returned to Eng., 1631; active friend of
the colonists; *m* in Eng., Grace, dau. Robert
Kaye; *m* 2d, Elizabeth West (sister of Sir
Thomas West, 3d Lord De la Warr); *m* 3d,
Martha Wilfred.

SAMSON (Sampson), Abraham, from Eng.,
settled at Plymouth, Mass., ca. 1629-30; his
name appears on the list of persons in Plymouth "able to bear arms," 1643; one of the
original 54 grantees of Bridgewater, 1645; surveyor of highways, 1648; constable, 1653; admitted freeman, 1654; *m* the dau. of Lt. Samuel Nash, of the Duxbury Co.

SAMSON (Sampson), Henry (*d* 1685), Mayflower Pilgrim, 1620; freeman, Duxbury, Mass.,
1635; *m* at Plymouth, Mass., 1636, Ann Plummer
(*d* bet. 1669-85).

SANBORN (Samborne), John (1620-92), from
Eng. with his grandfather, Rev. Stephen Bachiler, to Boston, 1632; settled at Hampton, N.H.,
1638; ensign and lt., Hampton mil. company;
rep. Gen. Ct.; served in King William's War; *m*
Mary (*d* 1668), dau. Robert Tuck; *m* 2d, Margaret,
dau. Robert Page, and widow of William Moulton.

SANBORN (Samborne), William (1622-92),
from Eng. with his grandfather, Rev. Stephen
Bachiler, to Boston, 1632; at Hampton, Mass.
(now N.H.), 1638; served in King Philip's War,
selectman 4 yrs., etc.; *m* Mary Moulton.

SANDERSON, Edward, of Watertown, Mass.;
m 1645, Mary Eggleston, of Dorchester.

SANDS (Sandes, Sandys), James (1622-95),
from Eng. to Boston, 1635; settled at Portsmouth, R.I., 1640; later at Block Island; dep.
Gen. Ct. for New Shoreham Co., 1665; asst. warden, 1676; cdr. militia co. in King Philip's War;
m Sarah (*d* 1709), dau. John Walker.

SANFORD, Thomas (1607/08-1681), from Eng
in the "Arbella," with Gov. John Winthrop
1630; settled at Milford, Conn., 1637; *m* 1636/37,
Sarah – (*d* 1681).

SANGER, Richard (*d* 1661), from Eng. in the
"Confidence," to Hingham, Mass., 1638; settled
at Watertown, 1646; at Watertown, 1649; blacksmith.

SARGENT, James (*d* 1795), from Eng. to Frederick Co., Md., before 1735; *m* Eleanor Taylor.

SARGENT, William (1602-75), from Eng. to
Ipswich, Mass., 1633; later at Newbury, Hampton, Salisbury, and an original settler at Amesbury; *m* 1633, Elizabeth (*b* 1611), dau. John Perkins; *m* 2d, 1670, Joanna (Pindor) Rowell.

SARGENT, William (bap. 1602-82; son of
Roger), from Eng. to Charlestown, Mass., 1638;
mem. of the ch., 1639; freeman the same year;
resident of Malden, where he was a lay preacher, 1648-50; removed to Barnstable, 1656; freeman Plymouth Colony, 1658; *m* Hannah – (*d*
1632); *m* 2d, Marie – (*d* 1637); *m* 3d, Sarah – (*d*
1688/89), widow of William Minshall.

SATTERLEE, Benedict (desc. Sir Edmund
de Sotterley, 1223; and son of Rev. William, vicar
of St. Ide, Devonshire, Eng.); settled at New
London. Conn., ca. 1688; *m* Rebecca, dau. of
James Bemis.

SAVAGE, Capt. Anthony (will dated 1695),
from Eng.; in Va., ca.1607; justice Gloucester
Co., 1660; high sheriff; justice, Richmond Co.;
capt. militia; *m* Alice, dau. Humphrey Stafford.

SAVAGE, John (*d* 1684/85; desc. Thomas
Savage, to Eng. in army of William the Conqueror and survived the Battle of Hastings,
1066, was bishop of Rochester, London and
York), to America, 1652; freeman, 1654; 7th on
list of organizing members First Congl. Ch. of
Middletown, Conn., 1668; sgt.; *m* 1652, Elizabeth
Dubbin, or D'Aubin (*d* ca.1696).

SAVAGE, Thomas (1592 or 94-1627), from Eng.
to Jamestown, Va., 1607; at 13, was exchanged
as hostage for "Namontock," an Indian from
Powhatan's tribe; ens. in Indian war, 1624;

given 9,000 acres, known as Savage's Neck, by
Indians; *m* 1621, Hannah –.

SAVAGE, Thomas (1607-82; son of William,
of Taunton, Eng.); to Boston, 1635; went to
Providence, 1638, but returned to Boston the
following yr.; later at Hingham and Andover,
Mass.; tailor; lt. and capt. A. and H. A. Co.;
capt. Suffolk regt. before 1655; maj. comdg. Mass.
forces in Mt. Hope campaign, King Philip's
War, 1675; dep. Gen. Ct., 1654, et seq.; and speaker, 1659, et seq.; gov.'s asst., 1680-81; *m* 1637, Faith,
dau. William Hutchinson.

SAWYER, Thomas (1616-1706; son of John);
from Eng. to Rowley, Mass., 1636; an original
settler at Lancaster, 1647; *m* 1648, Mary, dau.
of John Prescott (qv).

SAYLES, John (1633-81), from Eng. 1645; was
at Providence, R.I., 1654; was commr., assistant,
treas., warden, mem. Gen. Council, and dep.
Gen. Ct.; *m* ca. 1650, Mary (1633-81), eldest dau.
of Roger Williams (qv).

SAYRE (Sayer, Sayres), Thomas (1597-1670;
son of Francis), from Leighton Buzzard, Co.
Bedford, Eng., 1630; farmer and tanner; first
recorded at Lynn, Mass., 1638; a founder of
Southampton, L.I., 1640; where he built a house
still standing; served as a scout against the
Indians at Southampton.

SCARBOROUGH (Scarburgh), Capt. Edmund (1584-1635/36; son of Henry [1565-1619], *m*
Mary, dau. of John Humberstone); from Eng.,
1620, settled in Accomac Co., Va.; burgess, Va.,
1629-35; first cdr. Plantation of Accomac, 1631; *m*
Hannah, dau. of Robert Butler.

SCATTERGOOD, Thomas (*d* 1697), from Eng.
to Burlington, N.J., ca. 1676; *m* 1667, Elizabeth
Jarvis.

SCHENCK (Shenk), Johannes (1656-1747/48),
from Holland to New Netherland, was first at
New Amsterdam, 1684-85; at Esopus, 1685-89, at
Flatbush, L.I., 1691-ca. 1712; town clk., 1691-94;
schoolmaster, 1700-12; supervisor at Bushwick,
1719.

SCHENCK, Roelof Martense (1619-1704), from
Holland to New Amsterdam, 1650; removed to
Flatlands, L.I.; capt. of horse, Kings Co., 1690;
m 1660, Neeltje (1641-72), dau. of Garret W.
Van Couwenhoven.

**SCHERMERHORN (van Schermerhooren),
Jacob Janse** (1622-88; son of Jan, of Waterland,
Holland), from Holland in the "Arms of Rensselaerwyck," 1636, to Beverwych (Albany);
commissary to the Gen. Privileged West Indies
Company; one of 3 magistrates at Beverwyck
and Ft. Orange, 1652, 54, 56, 57, 64, 66, 74, 75; Indian
trader; owner of large estates; moved to
Schenectady 1686; *m* ca.1650, Jannetie Egmont
(1633-1700), dau. of Cornelius Segerse Egmont
Van Voorhout, *m* Bregje Jacobsen, from Holland to Beverwyck, 1642.

SCHIEFFELIN, Jacob (*d* 1769), from Germany to Phila., Pa., ca. 1734; *m* 1756, Regina Margarette Ritschausin.

SCHLEY, John Thomas (1712-89), from the
Palatinate to Phila., Pa., 1737; settled in the
Catochin Valley, Frederick Co., Md., 1745, at the
head of about 100 families, and founded Frederick City, Md.; educator; *m* 1735, Margaret
Winz von Winz.

SCHOFF, Jacob (bet. 1725-30-after 1806), from
Germany to Braintree, Mass., 1752; at Ashburnham, 1757, later at Maidstone, Vt.; *m* Mary –.

SCHOOLEY (Scholey), Thomas (ca.1647-1723;
son of John, of Co. York, Eng., *m* Alice–), mem.
of Farnsworth Soc. of Friends in Yorkshire,
Eng.; came from Hull, Eng., in the "Martha,"
to Chesterfield, Burlington Co., N.J.; 1677;
Schooley's Mtn., N.J., named for him, 1714; *m*
1686, Sarah Parker.

SCHOONMAKER, Lt. Hendrick Jochense (*d*
1681), from Hamburg, Germany; lt. in mil. service of Holland, settled at Ft. Orange (Albany),
ante 1654; later at Esopus, N.Y.; leader against
the Indians; *m* Elsie Janse Van Breestede.

SCHUYLER, Philip Pieterse, van (ca. 1628-83),
from Holland to Rensselaerwyck, N.Y., 1650;
settled at Beverwyck (Albany); general merchant and trader and a dealer in land; commissionary at Ft. Orange, 1655, a magistrate
there for many terms; commr. of Albany, 1678;
del. to Mohawk Indians, 1655; vice-dir. or dep.
under Govs. Stuyvesant and Nicolls; he had the
first commn. of captain at Albany, 1667, at
Schenectady, 1669; in 1662 he, with others, laid

out "New Village," at Esopus (Kingston); *m* 1650, Margarita (1628-1711), dau. Brant Arentse Van Slichtenhorst, first resident director of Rensselaerwyck, 1646.

SCOTT, Richard (1607-post 1680), from Eng.; one of the 13 signers of the first written compact of Providence Plantations, 1637; of Ipswich, Mass., and Providence, R.I.; *m* Catherine Marbury (1617-87).

SCOTT, Robert (1607-80), came in the "Griffin," 1634, settled in R.I.; *m* Catherine, dau. Francis Marbury.

SCRANTON, John (1609-71), from Eng. to Boston, 1637; an original settler at Guilford, Conn., and at New haven, 1638; dep. Gen. Ct.; *m* 1666, Adaline Hill.

SCRIBNER (Scrivener), Benjamin (*d* 1704), from Eng., was at Norwalk, Conn., before 1680; *m* 1679, Hannah (*b* 1662), dau. of John Crampton.

SCUDDER, Thomas (*d* 1658), from Eng. to Salem, Mass., ca. 1635; awarded grant of land, 1648; *m* Elizabeth Somers (*d* 1666).

SEABURY, John, from Eng. to Barbados, 1638, thence to Boston, Mass., 1639.

SEARS (Sares), Richard (*d* 1676), from Eng. ca. 1630; first appears on tax list at Plymouth, Mass., 1633; awarded grant of land at Salem, 1638; a founder of Yarmouth, 1639; dep. Plymouth Colony, 1662; *m* Dorothy Jones? (*d* 1678/79).

SEAVER, Robert (*d* 1683, aet.75), from Eng. in the "Jane," 1635; selectman, Roxbury, Mass., 1665; *m* 1634, Elizabeth Ballard.

SEDGWICK, Robert (1611-56), from Eng. in the "Truelove," to Mass., 1635; settled at Charlestown, 1636; freeman, 1637; rep. Gen. Ct. 17 terms; cdr. at the Castle, 1641; a founder and capt. A. and H. A. Co.; sgt. maj. Middlesex regt., 1643-44; cdr.-in-chief, 1652; with Capt. Leverett organized an expdn. against the Dutch in Manhattan, 1654; cdr. fleet of four vessels against Acadia, 1654; cdr. regt. to occupy Jamaica, 1655, and apptd. commr. to govern the island; maj. gen., 1656; *m* Joanna Blake.

SEELEY (Cilley), Robert (1601-67), and wife Mary landed at Salem, Mass., with Governor Winthrop, 1630; lt. in Pequot War, 1637; a founder of Watertown, Mass., 1630, Wethersfield, 1635, New Haven, 1638, Fairfield and Stamford, Conn.; of Huntington, L.I., and Elizabethtown, N.J.; marshal of New Haven Colony and cdr. of its militia; *m* at St. Stephens Ch., London, Eng., Dec. 15, 1626, Mary Mason.

SELDEN, Thomas (*b* Ticehurst, Co. Sussex, Eng., bap. Mar. 17, 1616/17-*d* 1655; son of John, *m* Mary Baldock; desc. ancient yeoman family located in Sussex Co., 1210); an original settler at Hartford, Conn., 1636; constable, 1650; *m* Hester (bap. 1617), dau. of Francis Wakeman, of Bewdley, Eng.

SELLÆCK, David (ca.1614-1654), from Eng., settled at Dorchester, Mass., 1633; to Boston, 1641; soap maker, ship owner and coast trader; *m* ca.1637, Susannah (*d* 1657), dau. Henry Kibby, mem. A. and H.A. Co.; *m* Rachel–.

SELLERS, Samuel (1655-1732), from Eng. with William Penn, to Chester Co., Pa., 1682; *m* Anna Gibbons.

SERGEANT, Jonathan (*d* 1667), came from Eng. to Branford, Conn., ca. 1644; founder of Newark, N.J., 1667.

SETTLE, John (son Josias [will dated 1667], Co. Bedford, Eng.), came to Va. ante 1660; *m* Elizabeth Slaughter.

SEVERANCE (Severns, Severans), John (*d* 1682), from Eng. to Ipswich, Mass., 1634; an original propr. of Salisbury; freeman, 1637, before the town was settled; mem. A. and H. A. Co.; *m* 2d, 1653, Abigail Kimball (*d* 1658); *m* 3d, Susanna–, widow of Henry Ambrose.

SEWALL, Henry (bap. 1576-1657), from Eng. and settled at Newbury, Mass., 1635; removed to Rowley; *m* Ellen–.

SEWALL (Sewell, Seawell), Henry (1614-1700), from Eng., in the "Elizabeth and Dorcas," to Newbury, Mass., 1634; wintered at Ipswich and helped begin that plantation, furnishing English with meat, cattle and provisions; dep. Gen. Ct., 1661; *m* 1646, Jane Dummer.

SEWARD, William (1627-89), from Eng., settled at Taunton, Mass.; moved to Guilford, Conn., ca. 1654; lt. in colonial wars; *m* 1651, Grace Norton.

SEYMOUR (Seimor, Seamor, Seamer), Richard (*b* 1596, bap. 1604/05-*d* 1655; son of Robert Seymer, *m* Elizabeth, dau. John Waller of Eng., g.son of John Semare), from Hertford, Sawbridgeworth, Co. Herts, Eng., to Hartford, Conn., 1639; a first settler of Norwalk, Conn., ca.1651; selectman, 1655; *m* Apr. 18, 1631, in Eng., Mary or Mercy (*b* 1610), dau. Roger Ruscoe (she *m* 2d, IIon. John Steele, qv).

SHACKFORD, William, of Newington, N.H.; appears in records, 1662; marker has been erected at Breakfast Hill, Rye, N.H., where Capt. Shackford surprised and killed the band of Indians who had massacred inhabitants of Portsmouth Plains; *m* ca.1671, Deborah (*b* ca. 1646), dau. Thomas Trickey, *m* Elizabeth–.

SHAPLEIGH (Shapley, Sharpley), Alexander (1585-ca. 1650), from Eng., ca. 1635, in his own ship "Benediction," to Kittery, Me., where he built the first house; he returned to England and died there; *m* Mary–.

SHARPLESS (Sharples), John (1624-85), from Wybunbury, Cheshire, Eng., with William Penn, to nr. Chester, Pa., 1682; *m* 1662, Jane Moore (1638-1722).

SHATTUCK (Shathock), William (1614-72), from Eng. ca. 1630; was at Watertown, Mass., 1630, where he received land grant, 1642; *m* 1642, Susanna– (*d* 1686).

SHAW, Abraham (1585-1638), from Eng., settled at Dedham and Watertown, Mass., 1636-1638; *m* 1616. Elizabeth (Bridget) Best (*b* 1592).

SHAW, Roger (bap. 1594-*d* 1660), from Eng. to Cambridge, Mass., 1636; mem. Mass. Gen. Ct., 1636; selectman, 1641-42, 1644-45; town clk., 1642; removed to Hampton, N.H., 1648; rep. from N.H. to Mass. Gen. Ct., 1651-52; *m* Ann–(*d* 1661).

SHEARMAN, see Sherman.

SHEDD (Shed), Daniel (1620-1708), from Eng., and was an original settler at Braintree, Mass.; at Shed's Neck, Germantown, 1639/40; land owner at Billerica, 1659; assigned to garrison house, Billerica, 1667; corpl. in King Philip's War, 1675; *m* 1st, Mary – (1628-1658/59).

SHEFFIELD, Edward (1615-1705), from Eng.; *m* Mary Woods.

SHELBY, Evan (ca. 1694-1750/51), came from Wales to Pa., 1735; purchased and patented land; removed to Prince George's Co., Md., 1739; became a large landowner; *m* Catherine Davies.

SHELDON, Isaac (1629-1708; son of Ralph, of Ashton, Co. Derby, Eng., *m* Barbara Stone), from Eng. to Mass.; at Windsor, Conn., 1640; settled at Northampton, Mass., 1654; selectman, 1656-57; freeman, 1663; tithingman, 1678, 79; mem. highway com., 1681; overseer of poor, 1698; *m* 1653, Mary (*d* 1684), dau. of Thomas Woodford, (qv); *m* 2d, ca.1685, Mehitable, dau. Thomas Gunn, and the divorced wife of David Ensign.

SHELDON, John (1630-1708; nephew of Gilbert Sheldon, bishop of London, archbishop of Canterbury, primate of all England), came to America and joined Roger Williams' Colony at Providence, R.I.; *m* 1660, Joan Vincent.

SHEPARD (Shepherd), Edward (*d* 1679/80), from Eng. to Cambridge, Mass., 1639; freeman, 1643; *m* Violet Stanley (*d* 1649); *m* 2d, Mary –, widow of Robert Pond, of Dorchester.

SHEPARD, John (1599-1650), from Eng. in the "Defense," 1635, with his wife (age 35), and his son Thomas; settled at Braintree, Mass.; admitted freeman, 1643; one of the 30 petitioners for the R.I. grant before Roger Williams secured it; *m* Margaret –.

SHEPARD (Shepherd, Shepheard), Ralph (1603-93), from Eng. in the "Abigail," to Charlestown, Mass., 1635; lived at Dedham, Rehoboth, Weymouth, Concord and Malden, Mass.; *m* Thanks Lord (1612-93).

SHEPARD, Thomas (1632-1719), from Eng. to Malden, Mass., 1658; *m* Hannah Ensign (*d* 1698), of Scituate, Mass.

SHEPLEY (Sheple, Shipley), John (ca.1587-1678), from Eng., 1637; had a grant of land at Salem, Mass., 1637; moved to Chelmsford; *m* Ann–(*d* 1685).

SHERBURNE (Sherbourne), John (1615-93; son Joseph Sherburne [*d* 1621], of Odiham, Hampshire, Eng.; desc. of Henry Sherburne, of Beam Hall, Oxford, Eng., and Sir Richard Sherburne, of Stonyhurst), came from Eng. in the "James," 1632, settled at Portsmouth, N.H.; assessor, selectman, commr., large landowner, held many offices; sgt. militia, 1675; *m* 1645/46, Elizabeth, dau. Robert Tucke, one of the historic founders of N.H.

SHERMAN, Edmund (1595-1641), from Eng. in the "Elizabeth," to Boston, Mass.; 1634; an original propr. of Wethersfield, Conn., 1636; freeman at New Haven, Conn., 1640; *m* Joan Makin.

SHERMAN (Shearman), John (ca. 1613-ca. 1691), from Eng. to Watertown, Mass., 1634; freeman, 1637; selectman many yrs.; town clk.; rep. Gen. Ct., 1651, 53. 63; ensign, 1654; capt., 1680; *m* Martha, dau. of William Palmer.

SHERMAN (Shearman) Philip (1610-87), from Eng. to Roxbury, Mass., 1633; freeman, 1634; banished, 1637, on account of religious differences; settled in R.I.; first sec. or recorder; mem. Ct. of Commrs., 1656; dep. Gen. Ct., 1665-1667; mem. Council, King Philip's War; *m* Sarah Odding.

SHERMAN, Samuel (1618-1700), from Eng. to Mass., ca. 1634; at Wethersfield and Stratford, Conn., and among the first residents of Stamford; dep. Gen. Ct. of Conn., 1637, which declared war against the Pequots; asst., 1663-1668; active in settlement of Woodbury, 1672; *m* Sarah, dau. Matthew Mitchell (qv).

SHERWIN, John (1644-1726), from Eng., settled at Ipswich, Mass.; *m* 1667, Frances Lomas, or Loomis.

SHERWOOD, Thomas (1586-1655), from Eng. in the "Francis," to Boston, 1634; land records of Conn. show his name in many transactions; moved from Wethersfield to Fairfield, 1644; built 1st grist mill on Mill Plain; original will with signature still at Fairfield, Conn., Town Hall; *m* ca. 1610, Alice — (*b* 1587); *m* 2d, 1641, Mary (*d* 1693/94), dau. of Thomas Fitch (she *m* 2d, John Banks, qv).

SHIPLEY, Adam (*b* ca.1650; son of Hugh, "Gentleman," a grantee of 2d charter of The Virginia Co., 1609), came to America ante 1668; had 200 acres surveyed, 1681, on the south side of the Severn River, known as "Shipley's Choice"; owned land in Baltimore, Carroll and Howard cos., Md.; *m* Lois–.

SHIPMAN, Edward (*d* 1697), from Eng., 1639; to Saybrook, Conn., ca. 1650; freeman, 1667; given 3,000 acres of land "within sight of Hartford," in will of Indian Sachem Uncas, 1676; *m* 1st, 1651, Elizabeth (*d* 1659), dau. William Comstock (qv); *m* 2d, 1663, Mary Anderson.

SHIPPEN, Edward (1639-1712; son of William [ca. 1600-1681], of Methley, Yorkshire, Eng., *m* 1626, Mary [1592-1672], dau. of John Nunes, *b* 1584, Effam Crosfeld); from Eng. to Boston, 1668, where he was mem. A. and H. A. Co., 1669; removed to Phila., Pa., 1693/94; speaker Pa. Assembly, 1695; mem. Provincial Council, 1696-1712, and pres., 1702-04; dep. gov., 1703; first mayor of Phila., 1701; presiding justice Common Pleas and Quarter Sessions courts; treas. of Phila., 1705; *m* 1671, Elizabeth Lybrand (*d* 1688); *m* 2d, 1689, Rebecca (Howard) Richardson (*d* 1692), dau. John Howard and widow of Francis Richardson; *m* 3d, 1704, Esther (Wilcox) James (1673-1724), dau. Barnabas Wilcox, and widow of Philip James, of Bristol, Eng.

SHOE (Shuey, Shewey), Daniel (*d* 1777), Huguenot; from France to the Palatinate, thence in the "Johnson," to Phila., 1732; settled in Lancaster Co., Pa.; *m* 1719, Mary Martha–.

SHOEMAKER (Schumacher), Thomas, arrived at New York, 1710; settled at Little Falls, later at Mohawk, N.Y.; lt. colonial forces; *m* Anna Dorothea, dau. of Rudolph Curring.

SHRIVER (Schreiber), Andreas (ca. 1673-ca. 1723), from Germany to Phila., Pa., 1721; settled on the Schuylkill; *m* 1706, Anna Margaretta (Hess) Jung, dau. Hans Theobold Hess, and widow of John Jung.

SHUMWAY, Peter (1635-will dated 1693), to America bet. 1660-75; resided at Topsfield, Mass.; later at Boxford; served in King Philip's War; *m* Frances– (*d* 1714).

SIBLEY (Sebley, Sybley), John (*d* 1661), from St. Albans, Eng., in Winthrop's Fleet, 1630; later at Salem; freeman, 1634; selectman, 1636; at Manchester, 1637; dep. Gen. Ct.; *m* 2d, Rachel, dau. John Pickworth.

SILLIMAN, Daniel (*d* 1690), from Holland, ca. 1630, settled at Fairfield, Conn. where he received a land grant and established "Holland Hill"; *m* Peaceable –, widow of John Eggleton.

SILSBEE (Sillsbey), Henry (*b* before 1618), from Eng. to Naumkeag (Salem) Mass., 1639; removed to Ipswich, and to Lynn, 1651; shoemaker; *m* Dorothy – (*d* 1676); *m* 2d, 1680, Grace –, widow of Jonas Eaton, of Reading, Mass.

SIMMONS, Moses (*d* 1697), from Eng. in the "Fortune," to Plymouth, Mass., 1621; settled at Duxbury, 1637; *m* Sarah –.

SINGLETARY (Singeltary), Richard (*d* 1687), from Eng. to Salem, Mass., 1637; freeman, Newbury, 1638; at Haverhill, 1652; *m* Susanne Cook (*d* 1682).

SINGLETON, Col. Matthew (*b* Isle of Wight, 1730-*d* 1787), came to Va., thence to S.C., 1752; received land grant from George II, 1756, which has since remained in the family; mem. Gen. Assembly, 1772, 76; vestryman St. Mark's Parish, 1770; capt., later col. troop of horse during Am. Rev. under Gen. Francis Marion; *m* 1750, Mary, dau. of Sherwood James, *m* Ann –.

SISSON, Richard (1608-84), from Wales; freeman, Portsmouth, R.I., 1653; mem. grand jury, Dartmouth; large landowner; surveyor; *m* Mary – (*d* 1692).

SKIFF, James (*d* 1688), from Eng., settled at Sandwich, Mass., 1637; *m* Mary Reeves (*d* 1673).

SKINNER, John (*d* 1650), from Eng.; an original propr. of Hartford, Conn.; *m* 1638, Mary (ca. 1620-1680), dau. Joseph Loomis (qv).

SKINNER, Sgt. Thomas (1617-1703/04), from Eng. bet. 1649-51; settled at Malden, Mass.; freeman, 1653; constable; *m* in Eng., Mary (*d* 1671), dau. of Richard Pratt; *m* 2d, Lydia (*d* 1723), dau. of Daniel Shepardson, *m* Joanna–.

SKIPWITH, Sir Grey (*d* 1680), from Eng. to Va., established "Prestwould"; *m* Elizabeth –.

SLAUGHTER, Capt. John, from Eng., 1619; settled in Rappahannock Co., Va.; received numerous land grants.

SLECHT, Cornelis Barentse (*d* 1671), from Holland, was at Esopus, N.Y., 1655; sgt. of mil. company which built the stockade at Esopus; mem. first Bd. of Schepens, 1661; mem. Ct. of Sessions; *m* Tryntje Tysse Bos.

SMALLEY, John, from Eng. in the "William and Francis." to Plymouth, 1632; with first settlers at Eastham; constable, 1646; surveyor of highways, 1649; grand inquest, 1654; *m* 1638, Ann Waldon.

SMEDLEY, Baptiste (*d* 1675), probably from Parish Odell, Bedfordshire, to Concord, Mass., ante 1639; *m* 1645, Katherine Shorthouse (*d* 1679).

SMITH, George, from Eng. in the "James," 1635; settled at Dover, N.H.; tailor; town clk.; 1646; at the head of the tax list, 1648; lt. of mil. company, 1645; asso. justice of the county.

SMITH, Sir Henry (son of Sir Hugh Smith, of Ashton, Somerset, Eng.); with his wife, Elizabeth Gorges, came to N.E., 1630, as chaplain in charge of fleet with Gov. Winthrop.

SMITH, John (ca. 1698-1776), officer British army, from Ireland to Augusta Co., Va., ca. 1730; capt. Va., militia, 1742-60, served in Col. George Washington's regt. in French and Indian War; cdr. Ft. Vause, which was captured by French. 1756. and sent to France as a prisoner of war, 1756-58; *m* in Ireland, 1719, Margaret –.

SMITH, Joseph (*b* Eng.-*d* ante Feb. 20. 1689/90), bro. of Christopher, of Northampton, Mass.; at Hartford, Conn., 1655; freeman, 1667; *m* 1656, Lydia (*d* 1710). dau. of Rev. Ephraim Huit, *m* Isabel–.

SMITH, Maj. Lawrence (*d* 1700), settled in Gloucester Co., Va., ante 1660; lawyer, burgess; maj. 1675-76; served as col. of Va. militia, against Bacon, 1676; c.-i.-c. of Gloucester Co. forces; *m* Mary–

SMITH, Rev. Nehemiah (1605-86), from Eng.; at Plymouth, 1637/38; removed to Conn.; an original propr. Norwich; *m* 1639/40, Sarah Anne (ca. 1615-post 1684), dau. of Thomas Bourne (qv).

SMITH, Richard (ca. 1620-1692/93), from Eng. ca. 1643; prominent settler at Southampton, L.I.; patentee of 35,000 acres, called Smithtown, 1664; freeman, 1647; constable, 1648; became a patroon or lord of the manor by patent from Gov. Andros and James, Duke of York, 1677; *m* ca. 1645, Sarah Folger (ca. 1625-1708).

SMITH, Samuel (1602-80), from Eng. in the "Elizabeth," with his wife and four children, to Watertown, Mass.; 1634; freeman, 1634; a founder of Wethersfield. Conn., where he was "antient serjeant" and "fellmonger"; dep. Gen.

Ct., 1637-56; founder of Hadley, 1659; dep. Mass. Bay Colony, 1661-73; lt. Hadley troop, 1663-78; commr. to the Mohawks, 1667, magistrate; *m* Elizabeth Chileab (1602-1685).

SMITH, Thomas (1648-94), from Eng. to Carolina, 1684; settled at Charles Town, S.C.; landgrave and gov. of S.C.; granted 48,000 acres (4 baronies); *m* 1st, his stepsister, Barbara Atkins (*d* 1687); *m* 2d, 1687, Sabina de Vignon, widow (*d* 1689).

SMOOT, William (*b* prob. Holland, 1596), from Eng. ante 1642; taxed for 400 acres in York Co., Va., 1642; took part in expdn. against Indians; moved to Charles Co., Md., 1646, where he was a planter, and engaged extensively in commercial pursuits and shipbuilding; juror, 1650; signed the famous Protestant Declaration proclaiming complete religious freedom in Md., 1650; *m* ca. 1634, Grace Wood (*d* 1666), a widow.

SNOW, Nicholas (*d* 1676), from Eng. in the "Ann," to Plymouth, Mass., 1623; a founder of Eastham, 1645; first town clerk 17 yrs. and selectman 7 yrs.; dep. Gen. Ct.; *m* 1623/24, Constance, dau. Stephen Hopkins (qv).

SNOWDEN, Richard (*d* 1711), from Wales to South River, Md., ca. 1652; large landowner; capt. provincial forces of Md., 1700-03.

SOHIER, Edward, III (*b* 1724), from Eng. to Boston, ca. 1750; *m* Susanne Brimmer.

SOMERVELL (Somerville), James (1694-1754), from Eng. to Md., 1719; physician; justice and high sheriff for Calvert Co.; *m* 1722, Sarah, dau. Thomas Howe, of Calvert Co., Md.

SOULE, George (*d* 1680), 35th signer of the Mayflower Compact; dep. Gen. Ct., from Duxbury, 1645-54; volunteer in Pequot War, 1637; *m* at Plymouth, Mass., before 1627, Mary Becket, or Bucket (*d* 1676), came in the "Anne," 1621.

SOUTHGATE, Richard (bap. 1670/71-1758), from Eng. to Boston, 1715; settled at Leicester, Mass., where he was the first town treas.; *m* 1700, Elizabeth, dau. William Steward.

SOUTHWICK, Lawrence (*d* 1660), came on 2d voyage of "Mayflower," returned to Eng. but brought family, 1630, and settled at Salem, Mass., 1636; with his wife was fined, whipped and banished for being Quakers; on L.I., 1659; *m* Cassandra – (*d* 1660).

SOUTHWORTH (Southard), Constant (1615-1679; son of Edward, whose widow, Alice [Carpenter] Southworth, came in the "William and Mary," to Plymouth, Mass., 1623, and *m* 2d, Gov. William Bradford), came from Eng. at 13 (1628); freeman at Plymouth 1637; soldier Pequot War; dep. 22 yrs.; dep. treas. Plymouth Colony; mem. Council of War, 1658, commr. for United Colonies, 1668; commissary gen. King Philip's War; *m* Elizabeth, dau. William Collier.

SPARHAWK, Nathaniel (bap. Dedham, Co. Essex, Eng., Feb. 16, 1598-*d* June 28, 1647), from Eng. to Cambridge, Mass., 1636; rep. Gen. Ct., 1642-47; deacon; *m* Mary Angier (*d* 1644); *m* 2d, Katherine Haddon (*d* 1647); *m* 3d?, Ann Sherman.

SPARROW, Richard (1580-1660/61), from Eng. to Plymouth, Mass., 1632; freeman, 1633; surveyor of highways 7 terms; juror many times; constable, 1640, 41; settled at Eastham, Mass., ca. 1653; dep. Gen. Ct.; *m* Pandora–.

SPAULDING (Spalding), Edward (*d* 1670), who came to Jamestown, Va., with Sir George Yeardley, 1619, later removed to Braintree, Mass., 1630; freeman, 1640; removed to Wenham, 1645; was an original incorporator of Chelmsford, Mass., 1653, where he died; mem. 1st Bd. of Selectmen; *m* Margaret – (*d* 1640); *m* 2d, Rachel –.

SPENCER, Gerard (bap. St. Mary's Stotfold, Co. Bedford, Eng., Apr. 25, 1614-will probated Sept. 3, 1685; son of Gerrard Spencer), with older bros., William, Thomas, and Michael, came to N.E., ca. 1632; received grant at Cambridge, Mass., 1634; freeman, 1636/37; at Lynn, Mass., 1637; ens. mil. co., 1656; to Hartford, Conn., thence to Haddam, Conn.; ens. Train Band, 1675; served in King Philip's War; rep. Gen. Ct., 1674-83; *m* Hannah–(*d* 1683).

SPENCER, Thomas (1607-87), from Eng. to Cambridge, Mass., 1633; settled at Hartford, Conn., ca. 1637; received land grants; soldier in Pequot War; constable, 1657; surveyor, 1672; chimney viewer, 1649; *m* Sarah, dau. Nathaniel Bearding.

SPENCER, Hon. William (1601-40), came to America, 1633; a founder A. and H. A. Co. of Boston; rep. Mass. Bay Gen. Ct., 1634, 1639-40; *m* Agnes Heane.

SPICER, Peter (*d* ca. 1694), prob. of English descent; to Va., 1656; landholder, New London, Conn., 1666; granted 20 acres, 1692; received 140 acres at Voluntown for services in King Philip's War; *m* 1670, Mary, dau. Peter Busecot, of Warwick, R.I., *m* Mary–.

SPOONER, William (*d* 1684), to Plymouth, Mass., 1637; freeman, 1654; surveyor, grand juror; to Dartmouth, Mass., ante 1670; *m* 2d, 1652, Hannah, dau. Joshua Pratt (qv).

SPOTTSWOOD (Spottiswoode, Spotswode), Alexander (1676-1740), officer in British Army; apptd. gov. of Va., 1710, and brought from the king the right of habeas corpus, hitherto denied to Virginians; gov., 1710-22; dep. postmaster gen. of the colonies, 1730-39, and postmaster of Pa.; maj. gen., 1740; formed the "Knights of the Golden Horseshoe," for exploration; *m* Anne Butler, dau. Edward Brayne.

SPRAGUE, Ralph (1603-50; brother of William), came from Eng. to Salem, Mass., ca. 1626; removed to Charlestown, 1629; constable, 1631; dep. Gen. Ct., 1635, et seq.; ensign for Charlestown, 1646; lt., 1637-41, 1647-49; mem. A. and H. A. Co., 1637; *m* 1623, Joan, dau. Richard Warren of Fordington, Co. Dorset, Eng.

SPRAGUE, William (1609-75; brother of Ralph), came from Eng. to Charlestown, Mass., 1629; removed to Hingham, Mass., 1636; *m* 1635, Millicent, dau. of Anthony Eames (qv).

SPRIGG, Thomas (1630-1704), from Eng. to Va., and resided in Northampton Co.; removed to Md.; served against Nanticoke Indians before 1678; commr. for Calvert Co., 1661; justice, 1667-1674; presiding justice, 1674; high sheriff, 1663-64; *m* Katherine –; *m* 2d, before 1668, Eleanor, dau. John Nuthall.

SPRING, John (*b* Eng., 1589), came in the "Elizabeth," 1634, with his wife Elinor, age 46, and children Mary, 11, Henry 6, John 4, and William, 9 mos.; settled at Watertown, 1636; took oath of fidelity, 1652; *m* 2d, Grace–, widow of Thomas Hatch, at Scituate.

STACKPOLE, James (1652-1736), from Ire. ca. 1680, settled at Dover, N.H.; mem. militia; *m* ante 1680, Margaret, dau. James Warren, Berwick, Me.

STACY, Mahlon (1638-1704), from Eng. in the "Shield," with his family, to Burlington, West Jersey, 1678; settled under a proprietary land grant of several thousand acres, at the Falls of the Delaware, 1679 (now Trenton, N.J.); signer of the Constitution of West New Jersey, 1676; mem. Assembly, 1681, et seq.; House of Reps., 1697-1701; Gov.'s Council, 1682-83; Council of Proprietors, 1688; *m* 1668, Rebecca (*d* 1711), dau. Richard Ely.

STAFFORD, Thomas (1605-77), from Eng. to Plymouth, Mass., ca. 1626, and is said to have built there the first grist mill operated by water power in America; removed to Newport, R.I.; later to Warwick; dep. Gen. Assembly; *m* Elizabeth – (*d* 1677).

STANDISH, Myles (*d* 1656), 6th signer of the Mayflower Compact; captain and military leader of Plymouth Colony, 1621; asst. 1631-50; six years treas.; general-in-chief of all the companies in the colony, 1649; *m* 1st, Rose – (*d* 1621); *m* 2d, at Plymouth, Mass., 1623/24, Barbara Allen (*d* 1659).

STANLEY, John (*d* 1698), from Eng. to Md., 1683; surveyor gen.; mem. Lower House of Assembly, 1689; capt. of troop, Talbot Co., Md., 1689; maj., 1692.

STANLEY, Capt. John (1624-1706; son of John, who *d* enroute to America), from Eng. to Hartford, Conn., 1634/35, settled finally at Farmington, Conn.; dep. Gen. Ct., 1659-95; capt. King Philip's War; *m* 1645, Sarah (*d* 1661), dau. Thomas Scott, *m* Anna–.

STANLEY, Thomas (1597-1663; son of John, *m* 1590, Susan Lancock [*d* 1619], of Ashford, Co. Kent, Eng.), from Co. Kent, Eng., 1634; freeman, 1634/35; dep. to Gen. Ct. from Lynn, Mass., 1635; one of the founders of Hartford, Conn., 1636; constable, 1644, 1648 and 1653; removed to Hadley, Mass., 1659; *m* in Eng., 1630, Bennet Tritton (1609-64), dau. of Daniel Tritton, *m* Alice, dau. Robert Goldhatch.

STANTON, Robert (1599-1672), from Eng.; signed compact, Portsmouth, R.I., 1638; freeman, 1641; sgt., 1644; dep., 1670; d Newport, R.I.; m Avis –.

STANTON, Thomas (1616-Dec. 2, 1677), from Eng., 1635; at Boston, 1636; served in Pequot War; at Hartford, Conn., 1639; settled at New London, 1651, at Stonington, 1658; Indian interpreter to the Gen. Ct. of Conn. in all controversies; apptd. magistrate, 1664; co. judge, 1666-77; mem. Gen. Ct., 1666-74; m 1637, Anna (1621-88), dau. of Thomas Lord (qv).

STARBUCK, Edward (ca. 1604-1690), from Eng., to Dover, N.H., ca. 1635; leading elder in the ch., among "associates chosen by the first proprs."; one of commrs. chosen by Dover and Kittery to lay out the boundary bet. the towns; rep. from Dover, 1643-46; at Nantucket, Mass., 1659; chief magistrate at Nantucket; m 1636, Katharine Reynolds.

STARK, Aaron (1608-85), settled at Stonington, Conn., ca. 1653; of New London, Conn.; served as soldier under Capt. Mason in the Pequot War, 1637, and in the Narragansett War; settled on Mystic River, 1669; freeman, 1666; soldier in King Philip's War; m ca. 1653.

STARR, Comfort (bap. Cranbrooke, Co. Kent, Eng., July 6, 1589-d Jan. 2, 1659; son of Thomas), physician and surgeon at Ashford, Co. Kent, 1631-32; came to Boston in the "Hercules," 1635; later at Cambridge, Duxbury and Dedham, Mass.; dep. Gen. Ct., 1642; charter fellow of Harvard Coll., 1650; m Elizabeth- (1595-1658).

STATHAM, Hugh (b ca. 1638-d 1700; of the 27th generation from Richard I, Sire de Saint Sauveur, of Cotentin, Normandy, vide ca. 890-930, and thru Nigel III, of the 6th generation who came into Eng. with the Conqueror in 1066; first of the name found in Va., 1667, as tutor and guardian in family of John Percy, or Pearcy.

STEARNES (Stearns), Charles (bet. 1620-30-bet. 1680-1700), settled at Watertown, Mass.; m 1654, Rebecca, dau. John Gibson, m Rebecca–.

STEARNS (Stearne, Sterne), Isaac (d 1671), from Stoke Nayland, Co. Suffolk, Eng., in the "Arbella," to Salem, 1630; freeman, 1631; selectman; m Mary (d 1677), dau. of John Barker, m Margaret–.

STEBBINS (Stebings), Rowland (bap. 1592-d 1671; son of Thomas Stebings, of Bocking, Co. Essex, Eng.), came in the "Frances," 1634, with 4 children and a relative, Mary Winche, aet. 15; settled at Roxbury, Mass.; at Springfield, 1639; townsman, 1664; to Northampton, 1664; m 1618, at St. Mary's Ch., Bocking, Sarah Whiting (1591-1649).

STEDMAN, Isaac (1605-78), from Eng. in the "Elizabeth," to Scituate, Mass., 1635, where he built the old stone mill, still standing; removed to Boston, 1650; an organizer of Brookline; m in Eng., Elizabeth –.

STEELE, George (d 1663), from Eng. to Cambridge, 1631/32; to Hartford, 1635; commr. United Colonies; rep., 1637-60; in Pequot War; m Rachel – (d 1653).

STEELE, John (prob. 1591-1661), from Eng. to Newton, Mass., 1631; freeman, 1634; rep. Gen. Ct., 1634; to Hartford, 1635, one of eight commrs. to govern Colony of Conn., 1636-37; sec. of the colony, 1636-1639; dep. Com. Gen. Assembly, 1637, 39, 1640-43, 1645-48; town clk; removed to Farmington, Conn., 1645; m Rachel (d 1653), dau. John Talcott; m 2d, 1655, Mary, or Mercy (Ruscoe) Seymour, widow of Richard Seymour (qv).

STETSON, Robert (1613-1703), from Eng. to Scituate, Mass., 1634; dep. Gen. Ct., 1655, et seq.; mem. Council of War, 1661, 71, 81; cornet, first body of Plymouth Horse; press master, 1675; commr. for settling boundary with colonies of Mass. and Plymouth; m 1st, Honor –; m 2d, Mary Hiland, widow of John Bryant.

STEVENS, Henry (ca. 1653-1726), from Eng. ca. 1660; was at Narragansett, later at Stonington, Conn.; selectman, 1696-99, 1702-04, '07; rep. Gen. Ct., 1699-1707; received land grant at Voluntown, Conn., for services in King Philip's War; m Elizabeth, dau. Capt. John Gallup.

STEVENS, John (1605-62), from Caversham, Oxford Co., Eng., in the "Confidence," 1638; a founder of Andover, Mass., 1640; freeman, 1642; m Elizabeth Parker (d 1684, aet. 80).

STEVENS, William (1617-53), from Eng. in the "Confidence"; became landowner and propr.,

Newbury, Mass.; m 1645, Elizabeth Bitfield (d 1652/53).

STICKNEY, William (bap. 1592-d 1664/65; son of William, of Frampton, Lincs., Eng., m 1585, Margaret Peirson); from Eng. with wife and 3 children ca. 1638; among first settlers of Rowley, Mass.; freeman, 1640; selectman, 1652, 57, 60, 62; m Elizabeth –.

STILES, John (1595-1662), from Eng. to Windsor, Conn., 1635; m Rachel – (d 1674).

STILLMAN, George (1654-1728), from Eng. to Hadley, Mass., 1683; later at Wethersfield, Conn.; merchant in West Indies trade; juror, selectman; large landowner; m Jane Pickering (1659-84); m 2d, Rebecca (b 1668), dau. of Philip Smith.

STILLWELL, Nicholas (d 1671), from Surrey, Eng., ca. 1635, to York Co., Va.; apptd. tobacco viewer, Va., 1639; commd. lt., war against Indians, 1644; removed to New Amsterdam, N.Y., 1646, to Gravesend, L.I., 1649; magistrate there, 1649-63; lt. under the Dutch, Esopus War, 1663; m ante 1647, Anne – (d 1686).

STIMSON (Stimpson), George (b 1641), settled at Ipswich, 1668; soldier King Philip's War; m 1676, Alice Philips.

STIMSON, John (b 1605), from Eng. in the "Truelove," 1635, settled at Watertown Mass.; m Susanna–.

STIRLING, James (1752-1820), from Scotland to Baltimore, Md., ca. 1774; soldier Am. Rev.; m Elizabeth, dau. Judge Andrew Gibson, of Pa.

STITES, Dr. John (1595-1717, aet. 122), surgeon in Col. John Hampden's Regt. in revolution of 1640, and was said to have been one of the physicians designated to certify to the death of Charles I; was excepted from the amnesty proclamation of Charles II, and had to flee for his life to Holland; came to Plymouth, Mass., 1633; to Hempstead, L.I., 1657; surgeon and physician to the colonists.

STITH, Maj. John (d post 1692), from Eng. to Va., ante 1656; with Samuel Earle, had grant of 550 acres on north side of James River, in Charles City Co., Va., 1663; also had grants in 1664 and 1675; purchased other tracts and on his death left a large landed estate; lt. Charles City Co. militia, 1656, capt., 1676, maj., 1680; magistrate and lawyer; burgess, 1685-86, 92; sheriff, 1691; m 1656, Jane–, widow of both John Gregory and Joseph Parsons.

STOCKBRIDGE, John (1608-57), from Eng. in the "Blessing," to Scituate, Mass., 1635; wheelwright; removed to Boston, where he died; m Ann –; m 2d, 1643, Elizabeth Sloane.

STOCKLEY, John, Gent. (ca.1621-1673), from Eng.; settled in Accomac Co., Va.; burgess, 1672; m Elizabeth–(d bet. 1697-1707), she m 2d, John Stratton (d ca. 1697).

STOCKTON, Richard (ca. 1630-1707; son of John, Lord of Stockton Manor, Malpas Parish, Cheshire, Eng.); from Eng. ante 1656; settled at Flushing, L.I.; lt. of Flushing Troop of Horse, 1665; converted to Quaker faith; moved to Burlington, N.J.; 1660; m 1652, Abigail –.

STOCKWELL, William (ca.1650-ante Dec. 30, 1731), from Eng. or Scot.; settled at Ipswich, Mass., later at Salem and Sutton; m 1684/85, Sarah Lambert (1661-post 1744), prob. dau. William Lambert of Ipswich.

STODDARD (Stodder), Anthony (d 1687), from Eng. to Boston, Mass., 1639; freeman, 1640; constable; rep. Gen. Ct. 23 yrs.; clk., 1642, et seq. and 3d sgt., 1650, A. and H. A. Co.; linen draper; m Mary Downing (d 1647; sister of Sir George Downing, celebrated English politician), dau. of Emand Downing, m Lucy Winthrop, sister of Gov. Winthrop; m 2d, 1647, Barbara Clapp (d 1655), widow of Capt. Joseph Weld (qv); m 3d, Christian –; m 4th, Mary, dau. Rev. Zachariah Symmes, and widow of Maj. Thomas Savage.

STODDARD (Stodder), John (b 1612-d ca. 1676), from Eng. in the "Diligent" to Hingham, Mass., 1638; later a founder of New London, Conn.; m Catherine-(she m 2d, John Sampson).

STODDARD, John (ca.1620-1664), from Eng. ante 1642, settled at Wethersfield, Conn.; juror, 1642; m 1642?, Mary (ca. 1623-post 1685), dau. Nathaniel Foote (qv).

STOKES, Christopher (d 1646), from Eng., ca.1624, settled in southeastern Va.; burgess for Warwick River, 1629, for Denby in Warwick Co., 1629-30.

STONE, Gregory (1590-1672; son of Rev. Timothy, of Great Bromley, Essex, Eng.), bro. of John and Simon (qv); from Eng. ca. 1635; admitted freeman at Watertown, Mass., 1636; settled at Cambridge, 1638, where he was extensive landowner; deacon; dep. Gen. Ct.; *m* Margaret Garrard; *m* 2d, Mrs. Lydia Cooper.

STONE, John, bro. of Gregory (qv); from Eng. in the "Increase," to Watertown, Mass., 1635; with his brother, Rev. Simon, was one of the early settlers of Guilford, Conn., 1639; *m* Sarah—.

STONE, Simon (1585-1665), bro. of Gregory (qv); from Eng. in the "Increase," to Watertown, Mass., 1635; freeman, 1636; *m* Joan (*b* ca. 1597), dau. William Clarke; *m* 2d, 1654, Sarah—, widow of Richard Lumpkin, of Ipswich.

STONE, William (1603-95), from Eng., 1633, settled in Accomac Co., Va., later to Md.; gov. of Md., 1649-54; *m* Verlinda (*d* 1675), dau. Andrew Cotton, *m* Joan—.

STORM, Dirck, from Holland with his wife and three children, to New Amsterdam, 1662; was sec. at Brooklyn, 1670, and town clk. of Flatbush, L.I.; lived in Orange Co., and later in Westchester Co., N.Y.; *m* Maria Pieters.

STORRS, Samuel (1640-1719; son of Thomas, *m* Mary-), from Eng. to Barnstable, Mass., 1663; removed to Mansfield, Conn., 1698; *m* 1666, Mary (1646-83), dau. Thomas Huckins (1617-79); *m* Mary Wells (*d* 1648); *m* 2d, 1685, Widow Esther Egard (1641-1730).

STOUGHTON, Thomas (ca. 1600-1661; son of Thomas, rector of Coggshall Ch., Co. Essex); from Eng. with his bro. Israel in the "Mary and John," to Dorchester, Mass., 1630; freeman, 1631; constable; an early settler of Windsor, Conn., 1640; made lt., 1640; *m* 1st, in Eng. —Montpeson; *m* 2d, 1635, Margaret Barrett, widow of Simon Huntington (qv).

STOUT, Richard (1604-1703), ran away from home and enlisted or was pressed in British navy; probably deserted at New Amsterdam; owned a plantation at Gravesend, 1643; bought land at Monmouth, N.J., 1644; *m* 1644, Penelope von Princis (or von Princin), a widow who came from Holland with her first husband, 1640, when the vessel was wrecked at Sandy Hook.

STOVALL, Bartholomew (*d* 1721), from Eng., 1683, settled in the tidewater section of Va.; *d* in Henrico Co.; *m* 1693, Ann Burton.

STOWE, John (1581-1653; son of John, of Biddenden, Co. Kent, Eng.), came from Eng. in Winthrop's Fleet, 1634; settled at Roxbury, Mass., later at Concord; rep., 1639; mem. A. and H. A. Co., 1638; one of first teachers at Roxbury grammar sch.; transcribed the Roxbury public school records for which he was granted 80 acres; *m* 1608, Elizabeth (*d* 1638), dau. of John Bigge, *m* Rachel Martin.

STOWELL, Samuel (*d* 1683), came from Eng. ca. 1635, settled at Hingham, Mass., blacksmith; granted land at Cohasset, 1670 and 77; *m* 1649, Mary (1633-1708), dau. of John Farrow, Eng. to Hingham, 1635. *m* Frances-.

STRATTON, Samuel (ca.1592-1672); from Eng. to Watertown, Mass., 1633 or 1647; freeman, 1653; *m* in Eng., Alice-(*d* ante 1657).

STREET, Nicholas (1603-74), B.A., Oxford, 1624/25; minister at Taunton, Mass., 1637-59, and New Haven, Conn., 1659-74; *m* Ann (Pole) Waldron, sister of Elizabeth Pole, foundress of Taunton, 1637, and dau. of Sir William Pole (1561-1635), of Colyton Devon. *m* Marie, dau. of Sir William Periam, lord chief baron of the exchequer, 1597-1604; *m* 2d, Mary-, widow of Gov. Francis Newman.

STREETER, Stephen (*d* 1652) shoemaker; resident of Gloucester, 1642; later removed to Charlestown, Mass.; he and his wife doubtless arrived with the settlers as early as 1635 or before; will probated July 24, 1652; *m* Ursula Adams (1600-73; said to have been dau. of Henry Adams, of Braintree).

STRONG, Elder John (*b* ca. 1610-*d* 1699; son of John, of Chard; g.son of George), came from Chard, Co. Somerset, Eng., in the "Mary and John," to Nantasket, Mass., 1630; said to have been at Dorchester, 1630; 1st found at Hingham, 1635-36, Taunton, 1638; constable, 1638; at Windsor, Conn., 1646, Northampton, Mass., 1659/60; first ruling elder of Northampton ch.; *m* in Eng., Margery (*d* ca. 1634-35), dau. of

William Deane; *m* 2d, 1635/36, Abigail (bap. 1619-*d* 1688), dau. of Thomas Ford (qv).

STROTHER, William (ca. 1630-1702), from Eng. to Va., ca. 1650; settled nr. present site of Port Conway; *m* ca. 1651, Dorothy (living 1716), dau. of Capt. Anthony Savage, sheriff, Gloucester Co., Va.

STRYCKER, Jan (1615-97), from Holland to New Amsterdam, 1652; chief magistrate and rep. in great landtag; schepen; *m* Lambertje Seubering.

STURGIS, Edward (1613-95; son of Philip, of Hannington, Eng.); from Eng. to Charlestown, Mass., ca. 1634; at Sandwich; removed to Yarmouth, 1639; dep. Gen. Ct.; *m* Elizabeth Hinckley.

STURTEVANT, Samuel (1622-69), from Eng., to Plymouth, Mass., ca. 1643; mem. Plymouth mil. company; soldier colonial wars; *m* 1643, Ann -.

STUYVESANT, Peter (1591-1671), entered mil. service of Holland at an early age; fought in the West Indies and became gov. of Island of Curacoa; lost a leg in expdn. against the Island of St. Martin; apptd., 1646, by the West India Co., dir.-gen. of the New Netherlands, in which office he remained until 1664, when New Amsterdam passed into the hands of the English; *m* Judith, dau. of Samuel Bayard.

SULLIVAN, John (Owen O'Sullivan, "Master John, of Berwick," 1690-1795, aet. 105), came from Ireland, settled at York, Mass. (now Me.), ca. 1720; *m* ca. 1735, Margery Brown (1714-1801).

SUMNER, William (1604/05-1691; son of Roger, *m* 1601, Joane Franklin), from Eng. to Dorchester, Mass., 1636; admitted freeman, 1637; dep. Gen. Ct., 1658, et seq.; clk. of the Train Band, 1663; *m* 1625, Mary West (*d* 1676).

SUTPHEN (van Zutphen), Dirck Jansen (1645-1706), from Holland to New Amsterdam, N.Y., 1676; settled at New Utrecht, later Flatbush, L.I.; *m* 1680, Lysbett, dau. Aucke van Nuys.

SUTTON, George (ca.1610-1669), Quaker; prob. from Tenterden, Co. Kent, Eng., to Boston, in the "Hercules," 1634; at Scituate, Mass., thence to Perquimans Co., N.C., 1668; *m* 1636, Sarah (1613-77), dau. Elder Nathaniel Tilden (qv).

SUTTON, William (1642/43-1718), a Quaker; from Eng., settled at Hingham and Eastham, Mass.; yeoman, town clk., constable; at Piscataway, N.J., 1672; *m* 1666, Damaris (1646-82), dau. of Richard Bishop, of Plymouth, *m* Alice (Martin) Clark, dau. Christopher Martin, Mayf. Pil.

SUYDAM (van Zuyt Dam), Hendrick Rycken (*d* 1701), from Holland to New Amsterdam, 1663 a patentee of Flatbush, L.I., ca. 1679; *m* 1666, Ida Jacobs.

SWAN, Richard (1600-78), from Eng. to Boston, Mass., ca. 1634; removed to Rowley, 1639; freeman, 1635; rep. Gen. Ct., 1666-77; in King Philip's War and in expdn. to Canada; *m* Ann—(*d* Apr. 1, 1658), widow of Nathaniel Hopkinson; *m* 2d, Ann Trumble, widow of John Trumbull (qv).

SWEARINGEN, Garret (Gerett), van (1636-1698), from Holland to New Amstel (New Castle), Del., 1655; councillor at Amstel on the Delaware, 1659; schout, 1660; commr. to Holland, 1661-62; removed to Md., 1664; commr. to Holland, 1661-62; sheriff of St. Marys Co., 1686-87; mem. Council, 1694; commissary gen.; *m* 1st, 1659, Barbara de Barrette (*d* 1670), Huguenot.

SWEET, John, from Wales to Salem, Mass., ca. 1630; later at Warwick or Kingston, R.I.; *m* at Newport, R.I., Mary-(*d* 1681), or Elizabeth-(*d* 1688).

SWETLAND, William, reported as a seafaring man, and to have sailed, 1675, as capt. of the "James," from Barbados to N.Y.; at Salem, Mass., 1676, Salem, Conn., 1703; *m* Agnes-.

SWETT, John (1580-1651), admitted freeman, Mass. Bay Colony, 1642; grantee of Newbury, Mass., 1642; *m* Sarah-(*d* 1650).

SWIFT (Swyft), William (*d* 1644), from Eng. ca. 1630; a propr. of Watertown, Mass., 1636; removed to Sudbury, and to Sandwich ca. 1637; served in Lt. John Blackmer's company, 1643; *m* Joan—(*d* 1643).

SYLVESTER, Richard (*d* 1663), from Eng., settled at Weymouth, Mass.; freeman, 1633; removed to Scituate, 1663; *m* ca. 1632, Naomi Torrey.

TABB, Humphrey (1609-58), from Eng., 1637, settled in Elizabeth City Co., Va.; burgess, 1652; *m* 1646, Joanna –.

TABOR (Taber), Philip (1605-69), from Eng. to Watertown, Mass., 1634; freeman, 1634; one of first settlers of Yarmouth; mem. earliest Assembly of Plymouth Colony, 1639, 40; was at Vineyard, New London, Conn., 1651, Portsmouth, Providence and Tiverton; rep. Gen. Court, from Providence, 1661; *m* Lydia Masters.

TAFT (Taffe), Robert (ca. 1640-1725), from Eng., was at Braintree, Mass., and an original settler at Mendon, when it was set off from Braintree, 1667; mem. first Bd. of Selectmen, 1680; *m* Sarah – (*d* 1725).

TAINTER (Tayntor, Taintor), Joseph (1613-90), from Eng. in the "Confidence," to Watertown, Mass., 1638; served in King Philip's War, as did three of his sons; *m* Mary, dau. Nicholas Guy.

TAINTOR, Charles (*d* 1654), from Wales, ca. 1640, settled at Wethersfield, Conn., 1643; later at Branford and Fairfield; dep. Gen. Ct., 1643-1646; dep. from Fairfield, Conn., 1647-48.

TALBOT, Peter (1652-1704), from Lancashire, Eng., supposed to have been victim of a press-gang that carried him to an American-bound ship from which he escaped and swam ashore to coast of R.I.; settled at Dorchester, Mass., 1675; at Milton, and Chelmsford, 1684; *m* 1st, Dec. 29, 1687, Hannah (Clark) Frizell (*b* Feb. 13, 1646), dau. of William Clark (1595-Mar. 15, 1682), *m* Margaret – (1599-Nov. 11, 1694).

TALBOTT (Talbot), Richard (*d* 1666), was in Md., 1652; purchased "Poplar Knowle" plantation, on West River, Anne Arundel Co., Md., 1656; *m* 1656, Elizabeth, dau. Maj. Richard Ewen, speaker of Maryland Assembly.

TALCOTT (Tailecoat, Taylcoat), John, "The Worshipful" (ante 1604-1660), from Eng. in the "Lion," with Rev. Thomas Hooker's company, to Boston, 1632; freeman, 1632; removed with Hooker to Hartford, 1636; rep. first Gen. Ct., 1637-54; gov.'s asst., 1654-60; treas. of colony, 1652-60; commr., 1656-58; *m* Dorothy (*d* 1670), dau. of Mark Mott, Esq., *m* Frances Gutter, of Braintree, Essex Co., Eng.

TALIAFERRO, Robert (ca.1626-1687/88), first of name in Va.; witnessed will in York Co., 1647; patented lands in Gloucester Co., 1655; jointly with Maj. Lawrence Smith, patented 6,300 acres on Rappahannock River, 1662; *m* Sarah, dau. Rev. Charles Grymes (qv).

TALLMADGE (Talmadge, Talmage), Thomas (*d* 1653; bro. of John Talmadge, of Newton Stacy, Hants., Eng.), came from Eng. to Charlestown, Mass., in the "Plough," 1631; removed to Boston, thence to Lynn, Mass.; freeman, 1634; granted 200 acres, 1638, and his son Thomas (qv), received 20 acres; removed to Southampton, L.I., N.Y., 1640, where he was granted home lot (in first ward), 1642; freeman, 1649; fined for absence from Easthampton town meeting, 1651.

TALLMADGE, Thomas (*d* 1691; son of Thomas, qv), of record at Lynn, Mass., 1638, when he received 20 acres of land; removed to Southampton, L.I., where he was granted a town lot in 2d ward, 1642; lt., 1665; dep. Gen. Ct.; recorder, Easthampton, L.I., 1650.

TAPPAN (Toppan), Abraham (bap. Apr. 10, 1606—*d* Nov. 5, 1672; son of William, *m* Cecelia—); from Eng. in the "Mary Ann," 1637, settled at Newbury, Mass.; *m* 1607, Susanna Taylor (1607-89).

TARBELL, Thomas (*d* ca. 1678 or 81), from Eng., was at Watertown, Mass., ca. 1644; removed to Groton, 1663, thence to Charlestown; soldier King Philip's War; *m* Mary – (1620-74); *m* 2d, 1676, Susanna –, widow of John Lawrence.

TATNALL, Edward (1704-90), from Eng. with his mother and 4 brothers, to Pa., 1725; was at Wilmington, Del., ca. 1735; *m* Elizabeth Pennock.

TAYLOR, Edward (1642-1729), from Eng. to Westfield, Mass., ca. 1669; A.B., Harvard, 1671, A.M., 1720; clergyman; *m* 1674, Elizabeth (*d* 1689), dau. James Fitch; *m* 2d, Ruth, dau. Samuel Wyllys, mem. Colonial Congress (and g.dau. of Gov. John Haynes).

TAYLOR, James (*b* ca. 1615-*d* Sept. 22, 1698), from Eng. ca. 1635; established "Hare Forest," in Va.; *m* 1st, Frances Walker (*d* 1680); *m* 2d,

1682, Mary (1665-1747), dau. of John Gregory, of Va.

TAYLOR, John (*d* 1647), from Eng. in the "Arbella," to Mass. with Gov. Winthrop, 1630; settled at Windsor, Conn., 1639; sailed for Eng. in the "Phantom Ship," 1647, and was lost at sea; *m* 1640, Rhoda –, a widow.

TAYLOR, Richard (*d* 1624, aet. 50), from Co. Kent, Eng., in the "Mary Margaret" to Jamestown, Va., 1608; listed in the 1624 muster as inhabitant of Colledge Land; *m* Dorothy–(*b* 1603), came in the "London Merchant," 1620.

TAYLOR, Richard (ca. 1619-1673), "the tailor"; from Eng. in the "Truelove," 1635; settled at Yarmouth, Mass.; *m* 1646, Ruth (*d* 1673), dau. Gabriel Whelden.

TAYLOR, Samuel (*d* 1723), a Quaker, came from Eng. to Chesterfield, Burlington Co., N.J., 1677; a propr. of West Jersey; his house and farm are still in possession of the family; *m* Susanna Horsman.

TAYLOR (Taylour, Tailer), William (*b* 1609), from Eng. to Barbados, 1635; came to Wethersfield, Conn., 1640; *m* Mary –.

TEN BROECK, Dirck Wesselse (1638-1717; son of Wessel, who was supposed to have come from Holland with Peter Minuit, 1626), appeared at Albany as early as 1662; was magistrate, commissary, alderman and recorder, and mayor of Albany, 1696-98; mem. 1st to 5th Provincial Assemblies; commr. of Indian affairs many yrs.; political agent to Canada four times; *m* 1663, Christyna Van Buren (1644-1729).

TEN BROECK, Wessel W. (1635-1704; eldest son of Wessel, who was supposed to have come from Holland with Peter Minuit in 1626); came from Munster, Westphalia, in the "Faith," 1659; removed to Kingston (then Esopus), N.Y., 1670; received grant of land there, 1676; erected a stone house now known as the "Senate House of the State of N.Y." in which 1st constn. of the State was adopted, 1777; *m* Dec. 17, 1670, Maria (*d* 1694), dau. of Conraedt Ten Eyck; *m* 2d, Laurentia Kellenaer, widow of both Dominie Van Gaasbeek and Maj. Thomas Chambers, lord of the Manor of Foshall, Kingston, N.Y.

TENNEY (Tenny), Thomas (1614-1699/1700), from Eng. to Salem, Mass., 1638; at Rowley, 1640; later at Bradford, Mass.; sgt. and ensign of Rowley foot company, 1677; *m* Ann Parratt (*d* 1657).

TERHUNE (Terheun), Albert Albertse (*d* in 1685), Huguenot, went from France to Holland and thence to New Utrecht, L.I., 1641; settled at Gravesend, L.I., 1642; *m* Geertje De Nyce.

TERRELL (Tyrrell, Terrill), William (son of Robert, *m* Jane Baldwin), from Eng. ante 1667, settled in New Kent Co., Va.; *m* Susannah Waters.

TERRY, Sgt. Samuel (1633-1730), from Eng. to Boston, 1650; granted land at Agawam, 1650; an original settler at Enfield, Conn.; *m* 1660, Anna Lobdell (*d* 1684, aet. ca. 50), of Springfield.

TERRY, Thomas (1607-72), from Eng. in the "James," 1635; resided at Braintree, Mass., and New Haven, Conn.; a founder of Southold, L.I.; freeman of Conn., 1662; *m* Marie – (*d* 1659).

TEWKSBURY, Henry (ca. 1635-living 1697), from Eng., settled at Newbury, Mass., 1661; took Oath of Allegiance, 1677; mem. Amesbury Train Band, 1680; freeman, 1690; tithingman, 1693; *m* 1658, Martha (Copp) Harvey (ca. 1633-1729?), dau. William Copp (qv).

THACHER (Thatcher), Thomas (1620-78; son of Rev. Peter, rector Parish of St. Edmunds, Salisbury, Eng.), from Eng. in the "James," to Boston, 1635; prepared for the ministry under Rev. Charles Chauncey, of Scituate; ordained at Weymouth, 1644/45; was first minister of Old South Ch. at Boston, 1670-78; *m* 1642, Elizabeth (*d* 1664), dau. Rev. Ralph Partridge, of Duxbury; *m* 2d, Margaret, dau. of Rev. Henry Webb, of Boston, and widow of Jacob Sheaffe.

THATCHER (Thacher), Anthony (1588/89-1667), from Eng. to Mass., 1635; was taxpayer at Marblehead, Mass., 1637; removed to Yarmouth; clergyman; rep. Gen. Ct., 1643, et seq.; mem. militia and of Council of War, 1642; *m* 1635, Elizabeth Jones.

THAYER, Richard (bap. 1601-*d* 1668), Eng. to Mass., with his brother, Thomas, 1630; admitted freeman at Braintree, 1630; later settled at Boston; *m* Dorothy (*d* 1640), dau. of William Mortimer.

THAYER, Richard (1621-1705; son of Richard, qv), from Eng., admitted freeman at Braintree, Mass., 1640; was at Boston, 1641; *m* 1654, Dorothy Pray.

THEBALD (Theobald), Clement (*d* 1675), from Eng., was in Lower Norfolk Co., Va., 1641, in Md., 1654; *m* 2d, Mary –.

THOMAS, David (*d* 1689), came in the "Elampoon," 1640; original propr. at Middleboro, Mass.; *m* Joanna–.

THOMAS, Evan, from Llanykeavne, Pembrokeshire, Wales, to Pa.; purchased 250 acres, 1682; *m* Mary–.

THOMAS, James, from Wales to Kent Co., Md., 1702; *m* 2d, Elizabeth Hackett.

THOMAS, John (1629-71), from Eng. in the "Hopewell," to Marshfield, Mass., 1635; *m* 1648, Sarah, dau. James Pitney, of Marshfield.

THOMAS, Peter (*d* 1722), from Wales, ca. 1682-85; settled in Chester Co., Pa.; *m* 1686, Sarah Stedman, from Eng.

THOMAS, Philip (1600-1674/75), from Eng., 1651, settled in West River, Md.; lt. provincial forces before 1655; high commr. governing Md., 1656-58, and one of those effecting the surrender of the province to Lord Baltimore, 1658; *m* Sarah Harrison (*d* 1687).

THOMAS, Thomas (will proved 1671), from Eng. with his wife, son James and servants, to St. Marys Co., Md., ca. 1639; received land warrant on Patuxent River, near Buzzard Island; high commr. of Provincial Ct.; *m* Elizabeth, dau. William Barton.

THOMAS, William (1573-1651), from Eng. to Plymouth, Mass., in the "Mary and Ann," 1630; settled at Greens Harbor (Marshfield), Mass., ca. 1640; freeman, 1642; governor's asst., 1642, 43, 44, 47, 51; mem. Council of War; dep. Gen. Ct., 1640, 44.

THOMPSON (Tomson, Thomson, Tompson), Anthony (1612-47), from Eng. in the "Hector," 1637; a founder of Quinnipiack (New Haven), 1638, and a signer of the Compact; soldier in Indian troubles, 1642; *m* 2d, Katherine –.

THOMPSON, James (1593-1682), from Eng. in Winthrop's fleet, to Charlestown, Mass., 1630; freeman, 1634; original settler at Woburn, 1640; *m* in Eng., Elizabeth – (*d* 1643); *m* 2d, 1644, Susanna –, widow of Thomas Blodget, of Cambridge.

THOMPSON, John (1616-96), dep. Gen. Ct. from Barnstable, Mass., 1671-72, from Middleboro, 1674, et seq.; sgt. mil. company, 1673; lt., 1675; cdr. garrison in King Philip's War, 1675; *m* 1645, Mary (1626-1714), dau. of Francis Cooke (qv).

THOMPSON, John (1730-78), from Scotland to Hunterdon Co., N.J., moved to Shamokin on West Susquehanna, 1776; soldier Cont. Army; killed by Tories and Indians, nr. Cherry Valley; *m* Judith Bodine (1735-96; g.dau. Jean Bodin, *d* 1695, a Huguenot, naturalized at London, 1681).

THOMPSON, John Lewis (1640-1726), from Wales with a brother, to Va., ca. 1650; *m* Elizabeth McGrath.

THOMSON, Alexander (1722-1800), from Scotland to Chambersburg, Cumberland Valley, Pa., 1772; soldier Am. Rev.; *m* 1748, Elizabeth Edmundstone.

THOMSON, David (1592-1628; son of Richard Tomson, *m* at Clerkenwell, Eng., 1579, Florence Cromlan), gentleman, scholar, apothecary, chartist, sea capt. and atty. for Sir Gorges; from Eng. in the "Jonathan," as apptd. leader to "found a plantation on the Piscataqua River"; had grant of 6,000 acres and an island "any place in N.E."; settled off Odiorne's Pt. (Portsmouth), N.H.; to Thomson's Island (Boston Harbor), 1626; *m* 1613, Amyas (1st white woman to N.H.), dau. William Colle, *m* 1594, Agnes Bryante, or Briant.

THORN (Thorne), William, supposed to have landed at Boston, 1629; admitted freeman at Lynn, Mass., 1638; later one of the patentees of Flushing, L.I., 1645; a propr. of Jamaica, L.I., 1657; *m* Sarah –.

THORNDIKE, John (ca. 1603-1668-70), from Eng. to Boston, Mass., 1632; a founder of Ipswich, 1633; returned to Eng., 1668, leaving his son Paul at Beverly; *m* Elizabeth Stratton; *m* 2d, Alice Coleman.

THORNTON, William, Gent. of the "Hills," Yorkshire, Eng. (son of William [*d* 1600], of noble ancestry); came to Va., ante 1641; settled in Petsworth Parish, now Gloucester Co.; moved to Stafford Co.

THOROGOOD (Thoroughgood, Thorowgood), Capt. Adam (1602-40; son of William of Norfolk Co., Eng.); came to Va. in the "Charles," 1621; later settled at Lynnhaven, Princess Anne Co., Va.; commr. and burgess for Elizabeth City; mem. Council; presiding justice Co. Ct. of Lower Norfolk, 1637; *m* 1627; Sarah (1609-57), dau. of Robert Offley, *m* Anne, dau. of Sir Edward Osborne, Kt., lord mayor of London, 1583.

THRALL, William (1606-79), from Eng. in the "Mary and John," 1630; settled at Windsor, Conn., 1633; served in Pequot War; *m* Miss Goode (*d* 1676).

THROCKMORTON, John (*d* 1687), from Eng. in the "Lion," to Boston, 1631; moved to Providence, R.I., 1638; one of the 13 original proprs. with Roger Williams of R.I.; lands conveyed to him by Roger Williams, 1637; obtained a grant of land for himself and 35 associates, from Governor Kieft, in New York, July 6, 1640, which was called Throgg's Neck, an abbreviation of Throckmorton; dep. to R.I. Gen. Assembly, 1664-68, 1670-75; treas., 1667; mem. Gen. Assembly at Newport, R.I., 1664-65; moved to Monmouth Co., N.J., 1673; *m* Mary –.

THROCKMORTON, Robert, lord of the Manor of Ellington, Huntingdonshire, Eng. (bap. Aug. 15, 1609-*d* Sept. 1657); received a grant of 300 acres in Charles River (now Gloucester) Co., Aug. 24, 1637, for transporting five persons into the Colony of Va., and a grant of 650 acres in Upper Norfolk Co., Sept. 16, 1644; subsequently returned to Eng. where he died.

THRUSTON, Edward (1638/39-1717), from Eng., settled first in Lower Norfolk Co., Va., 1663; returned to Eng., 1670, but again came to Va., 1717, to join son; *m* 2d, Susannah Perry.

THURBER, John (*d* 1706), from Eng., 1671, settled at New Meadow Neck, Rehoboth, Mass. (now a part of Barrington, R.I.); with 53 others made application for admittance to the town of Swansea, Mass., 1669; *m* in Eng., Priscilla–.

THURSTON, John (1601-85), from Eng. with wife and two sons in the "Mary Anne," 1637; freeman, 1643; settled at Medfield, Mass.; *m* Margaret–(ca. 1605-1662).

THWING, Benjamin (1619-72), from Eng. in the "Susan and Ellen," to Boston, 1635; townsman, 1642; propr. Watertown and Concord; *m* 1641, Deborah Savage.

TICKNOR (Tickner, Tickenor), William, from Eng. to Scituate, Mass., ca. 1646; soldier King Philip's War; *m* Hannah (*d* 1665), dau. John Stockbridge; *m* 2d, 1666, Deborah, dau. Thomas Hyland.

TIFFANY, Humphrey (*d* 1685), from Eng. to Mass., ca. 1660; settled at Rehoboth, Mass., 1663; later at Swansea; killed by lightning; *m* Elizabeth –.

TILDEN, Nathaniel (1583-1641), from Tenderden, Co. Kent, Eng., in the "Hercules," 1635, with his wife, Lydia, and seven children and seven servants; settled at Scituate, Mass., where he was ruling elder; *m* Lydia, dau. of Stephen Huckster, of Tenderden, Eng.

TILESTON, Thomas (1611-94), was at Dorchester, Mass., 1636; *m* Elizabeth–.

TILGHMAN, Richard (1626-76), English surgeon, came in the "Elizabeth and Mary," 1661, settled at "The Hermitage," Talbot Co., Md.; high sheriff, 1669-71; *m* Mary Foxley.

TILLEY, John (1586-1621), 16th signer of the Mayflower Compact.

TILLINGHAST, Pardon (1622-1718), from Eng. to Providence, R.I., ca. 1643, where built at own expense, 1st Bapt. church in America, and gave it to the society; pastor 40 years; dep. Gen. Ct., 1672, 80, 94, 97, 1700; *m* 2d, 1664, Lydia (1640-1720), dau. Philip Tabor (qv).

TILLMAN, Roger, from Eng. to Va., ante 1689; landgrant, south side of Appomatox River, Charles City Co., nr. Bristol; *m* 1680, Mrs. Susanna Parham (Parram) (1647-*d* Prince George Co., 1717).

TILSON (Tillson), Edmund (*d* 1660), from Eng. to Plymouth, Mass., 1635; *m* Joanna–.

TILTON, John (*d* 1688), from Eng. bet. 1630-1640; settled at Saugus (Lynn) Mass.; a founder of Gravesend, L.I., 1643, where he was town clk. 20 yrs.; an original purchaser of land from the Carnasie Indians, and purchased Barren Island, L.I., from the Indians, 1664; an explorer and interpreter in the purchase of lands in Monmouth Co., N.J., from the Indians, 1664/65, on behalf of himself and eleven associates known as "John Tilton and Co."; *m* Mary – (*d* 1683).

TILTON, William (ante 1618-ca. 1653), from Eng. to Lynn, Mass., 1640; freeman; *m* Susanna –.

TINGLEY, Palmer (*b* 1614), from Kingston-on-Thames, Eng., in the "Planter," 1635; at Ipswich, Mass., 1639, where he received land for services in Pequot War; *m* bet. 1635-40, Anna (1615-81), dau. Stephen Fosdick (she *m* 2d, James Barrett).

TINKER, John (*d* 1662; son of Henry, of Eng., and nr. kinsman Thomas of the Mayflower); came to Boston, 1635; a founder of Lancaster, Mass.; asst. gov. of Conn.; *m* 2d, 1651, Alice (1629-1714), dau. of John Smith.

TISDALE, John (1618-killed in King Philip's War, 1675), first known at Duxbury, Mass., where he is recorded, 1636, as owner of land; removed to Taunton, ca. 1650, where he owned land in what is now Berkley; shareholder in the "Ancient Iron Works," Taunton, 1653, 54; one of proprs. of Taunton North Purchase, and of Assonet; dep. Gen. Ct.; constable; selectman, 1650-58; *m* Sarah Walker (*d* 1676, aet. 58), from Eng. in the "Elizabeth," with her bro., James, 1635.

TITUS, Robert (*b* 1600), from Eng. in the "Hopewell" to Boston, 1635; settled at Weymouth, Mass.

TODD, Christopher (1617-86; son of William, of York, Eng., *m* Katherine Ward); came in the "Hector," to Boston, 1637; a founder of New Haven Colony, 1638, and a signer of the covenant; owned the present site of Yale U.; *m* Grace, dau. of Michael Middlebrook.

TODD, John (*b* 1621), from Eng. to Charlestown, Mass., 1637; an early settler of Rowley, 1648; rep. Gen. Ct., 1664, 86; *m* Susanna –.

TODD, Thomas (1619-76), from Eng. to Gloucester Co., Va., 1640; built original "Toddsbury," for which two other homes were named, 1654; built second home nr. Baltimore, Md., 1664; mem. Assembly, 1675; *m* 1657, Anne (1638-95), dau. of Rev. John Gorsuch, of Eng., *m* Anne, dau. of Sir William Lovelace.

TOLMAN, Thomas (1608-90), from Eng. in the "Mary and John," 1630, settled at Dorchester, Mass.; freeman, 1640; constable, 1661; *m* Sarah–; *m* 2d, Kathrine–.

TOMPKINS, John, from Eng., 1636; settled at Concord, Mass., 1640-44; *m* Ruth Taylor.

TOMPKINS, Nathaniel (1650-1724), from Eng. to Newport, R.I., 1671; temporarily resided at Boston; later at Little Compton, R.I.; merchant; *m* 1671, Elizabeth (1651-1714), dau. John Allen.

TORREY, William (1608-abt. 1690), from Eng. to Weymouth, Mass., ca. 1640; freeman, 1642; rep. Gen. Ct., 1642, et seq.; lt. and capt.; clk. Ho. of Deputies, 1648, et seq.; *m* Agnes Combe (*d* ante Feb. 14, 1630); *m* 2d, Jane (*d* Apr. 17, 1639), dau. of Robert Haviland, *m* Elizabeth Guise; *m* 3d, Elizabeth, dau. of George Frye.

TOUSLEY (Towsley), Michael (*d* Nov. 3, 1712), of Salisbury, Mass.; settled at Suffield, Conn.; served in Indian wars; *m* 1678, Mary Husse, or Hussey (*d* 1729).

TOWER (Towers), John (1609-1702; son of Robert, *m* Dorithe Damon); from Eng. to Hingham, Mass., 1637; freeman, 1638; removed to Lancaster, 1654; served in garrison house in King Philip's War; *m* 1639, Margaret (1617-1700), dau. of Richard Ibrook.

TOWN (Towne), William (1600-72), from Eng., 1635, settled at Salem, Mass.; at Topsfield, 1651; *m* 1620, Joanna Blessing (*d* 1682), among their daus., was Rebecca (Towne) Nourse, who was executed for witchcraft; the monument to her memory at Danvers, Mass., is inscribed with the inscription by Whittier: "A Christian martyr who for truth could die, When all about there owned the hideous lie. The world redeemed from superstition's sway, Is breathing freer for thy sake to-day."

TOWNLEY, Col. Richard (ca. 1654-1711; son of Nicholas, of Eastbourne; g.son of Nicholas, of Littleton Place [*d* 1687, aet. 75], and desc. of Richard de Towneley [*b* 1387, of Spartlingus, 1st Dean of Whalley on record), came from Littleton Place, Middlesex, Eng., to Va.; settled at Elizabethtown, N.J.; col. Train Band; mem. Gov.'s Council; justice Co. Ct. of Common Rights; capt. of foot; commr.; assemblyman and presiding judge of the Quarter Session; founded St. John's P.E. Ch.; *m* 1684, Elizabeth (Smith) Lawrence Cartaret (*d* 1712), dau. Richard Smith (qv).

TOWNSEND, John (1578[?]-1668/69), from Eng. with brothers Henry and Richard, to Lynn, Mass., 1643; removed to Providence, R.I., 1644, and to Oyster Bay, L.I., 1645; *m* Elizabeth Montgomery.

TOWNSEND, Martin (1596-1675; son of Walter, of Hinton, Eng., *m* Katherine, dau. Martin Brown), came from Eng. to Watertown, Mass., 1634; *m* Martha–.

TOWNSEND, Thomas (bap. 1594-*d* 1677), from Eng. to Lynn, Mass., 1637; freeman, 1639; *m* Mary (*d* 1692), dau. of Philippe Newgate, *m* Jane Hoo.

TRACEY (Tracy), Stephen (1596-1655; son of Stephen, *m* Agnes Erdley); from Eng. in the "Ann," to Plymouth, 1623; settled at Duxbury, Mass., 1633; returned to Eng., 1654, and *d* there; *m* 1621, Tryphosa Lee.

TRACY, Thomas (1610-85), from Eng. to Watertown, Mass., 1636; to Salem, Mass., 1637; removed soon to Saybrook, Conn., to Wethersfield and finally settled at Norwich, of which he was an original propr., 1659; rep. Gen. Ct., 1662 and for many yrs.; ensign and lt.; commissary and q.m. in King Philip's War; *m* 1641, Mary—; *m* 2d, 1679, Martha, dau. Thomas Bourne, and widow of John Bradford.

TRAIN (Traine), John (ca. 1610-1681), from Eng. in the "Susan and Ellen," to Watertown, Mass., 1635; mem. Watertown Train Band, 1652; *m* Margaret Dix (*d* 1660); *m* 2d, 1675, Abigail Bent (*d* 1691).

TREADWAY, Nathaniel (1605-89), from Eng.; propr. at Sudbury, 1639; later removed to Watertown, Mass.; *m* 1638, Sufferance (*d* 1682), dau. Elder Edward Howe, *m* Margaret–.

TREAT, Richard (1584-1669), from Eng. to Watertown, Mass., 1635; at Wethersfield, Conn., 1637; dep. Gen. Ct., 1637-44; gov.'s asst., 1657-65; patentee of Conn. under royal charter of Charles II, 1662; mem. Gov. John Winthrop's Council, 1663-65; *m* Alice Gaylord.

TREDWELL (Treadwell), Edward (*d* ca. 1660-1661), from Eng. to Ipswich, Mass., 1637; settled at Hempstead, L.I., 1660; *m* Sarah –.

TREMAINE (Treman, Truman), Joseph (*d* 1697), from Nottinghamshire, Eng., 1666; settled with his wife at New London, Conn.; dealt in real estate; operated tanneries, and a flour mill.

TRIGG, Daniel (ca. 1650-1716), to Middlesex Co., Va., ante 1684; *m* Susan Johns (*d* 1687).

TRIPP, Hon. John (1610/11-1678), from Eng.; first record of him in America, when he became an original founder and propr. of Portsmouth, R.I., 1638; in 1660 he deposed in court and stated his age as about 49; dep. R.I. Gen. Assembly, 1648, 1654-58, 1661-64, 1666-69, 72; commr. Ct. of Commissioners, 1655; asst. or mem. Gov.'s Council, 1670, 1673-75; *m* 1639, Mary (*d* 1687), dau. of Anthony Paine, *m* Rose Potter.

TRIPPE, Henry (1632-1697/98); from Eng. to Dorchester Co., Md., 1663, where he took up land; mem. Lower House of Assembly, 1671-81; maj. of horse, 1689; lt. col. of field officers, 1694; *m* 1665, Frances –, widow of Michael Brooke, of Calvert Co., Md.; *m* 2d, Elizabeth –.

TROWBRIDGE, Thomas (*d* 1672/73), from Eng. to Dorchester, Mass., 1634; settled at New Haven, Conn., 1639; returned to England leaving his sons; of their direct male descendants 56 fought in Am. Rev.; 41 in War of 1812; 152 in Civil War; *m* 1627, Elizabeth (1602/03-1641/42), dau. of John Marshall.

TRUAX (du Trieux), Philip (ca. 1586-*d* bet. 1649-53), a Walloon; worsted dyer, from Holland to New Amsterdam, in the "New Netherlands," ante 1624; marshal of New Netherland; court messenger, 1638—; *m* Jacqueline (or Jacquemine) Noiret (*d* 1620-21); *m* 2d, 1621, Susanna de Chesne (living 1654).

TRUE, Henry (*d* ante 1659), from Eng. to Salem, Mass., ca. 1644; a founder of Salisbury, Mass.; *m* 1644, Israel (*d* 1699), dau. John Pike, Eng. to Newbury, 1635; and sister of "the worshipful Maj. Robert Pike," distinguished in early colon'al history.

TRUESDELL, Samuel (bap. St. Botoloph's, Boston, Lincolnshire, Eng., Mar. 13, 1647-d Newton, Mass., Mar. 2, 1694/95; son of Thomas, of Boston, Eng.), *m* ca. 1671, Mary, dau. Dea. John Jackson.

TRUMAN, Joseph, see Tremaine.

TRUMBULL, John (*d* 1657), from Eng. to Roxbury, Mass., 1639; freeman, 1640; later at Rowley, Mass.; town clk., 1655, et seq.; *m* Ellen–(*d* 1648/49); *m* 2d, 1650, Ann–, widow of Michael Hopkinson (she *m* 3d, Richard Swan).

TRYON (Triall, Tryan), William (1646-1711), from Eng. to Wethersfield. Conn.; *m* Saint (1656-1711), dau. Thomas Robinson (*d* 1689), of Hartford, Conn.

TUCK (Tucke, Tewk), Robert (*d* 1664), from Eng. to Watertown, Mass., 1636; removed to Hampton, N.H., 1638; obtained license for first inn at Hampton; *m* Joanna –.

TUCKEE, Robert (1604-82), from Eng. to Weymouth, Mass., 1635; removed to Dorchester, later to Milton, Mass.; rep. Gen. Ct., 1669, 80, 81; *m* Elizabeth Allen.

TUCKER, St. George, LL.D. (1752-1827), from the Bermudas to Williamsburg, Va., 1771; lt. col. Am. Rev.; mem. Council of State, 1781; county lt. and del. to the Annapolis conv., 1786, for amendment of the Articles of Confederation; judge Gen. Ct. of Va., 1788-1804; prof. law, Coll. of William and Mary, 1790-1804; judge Ct. of Appeals of Va., 1804-13; U.S. dist. judge, 1813-25; eminent legal author; *m* 1778, Frances (Bland) Randolph (mother of John Randolph, of Roanoke), dau. of Theodoric Bland, and widow of John Randolph, of "Matoax"; *m* 2d, 1791, Lelia (Skipwith) Carter, dau. of Sir Peyton Skipwith, of "Prestwould," and widow of George Carter, of "Corotoman."

TUCKERMAN, John (1624-98), from Eng. to Boston, Mass., 1649; *m* Sarah –.

TUFTS, Peter (*b* 1617), from Eng., founder of Malden, Mass., 1638; *m* 1640, Mary Pierce (*d* 1701).

TUPPER, Capt. Thomas (1578-1676), from Eng. in the "Abigail," 1635; at Lynn, Mass., until 1637; a founder of Sandwich, Mass., 1637; dep. Gen. Ct., 1646-65; capt., 1663; mem. Council of War, 1675; selectman, 1667-72; commd. justice; *m* Anne– (1586-1676).

TURNER (de Tourneur), Daniel (1626-73), fled from France to Leyden, Holland, ca. 1648, thence, with his wife and son Daniel, to New Netherland, 1652; corp. mil. company at Midwout for defense against English, 1654, against Indians, 1660; magistrate, 1660-63; patentee of Harlem; *m* 1650, Jacqueline de Parisis (*d* 1700).

TURNER, Humphrey (ca. 1593-1673), from Eng. to Plymouth. Mass., 1628; removed to Scituate, 1633; a founder of the ch. there, 1635, constable; rep. Gen. Ct., 1640, 52, 53; pvt. in mil. company; *m* Lydia Gamer.

TURNER, John, 22d signer of the Mayflower Compact (*d* at Plymouth, Mass., bet. Jan. 11 and April 10, 1621).

TURNER, Capt. Nathaniel (*d* 1646), from Eng., with Gov. Winthrop, 1630; constable at Lynn, Mass.; rep. in 1st Gen. Ct., Boston; served with Capt. Endicott against the Pequots, 1637; removed to New Haven, Conn.; magistrate; assisted in organizing Congl. Ch.; *m* ante 1630, Margaret (Leachland?).

TURNER, Robert (1611-51), from Eng. in the "Blessing," 1635; settled at Boston; shoemaker; mem. A. and H. A. Co., 1643; *m* Elizabeth (*b* in Eng.), dau. Richard Freestone.

TUTHILL, Henry (1612-1648-50), from Eng. in the "Planter," 1635; settled at Hingham, Mass.; freeman, 1638; constable, 1640; removed to Southold, L.I., with Rev. Young's company, 1644; *m* Bridget –.

TUTTLE, Richard (ca. 1593-1640), husbandman from Ringstead, Northants, Eng., in the "Planter," 1635; settled at Boston; *m* Anne–(*b* 1594).

TUTTLE, William (1609-73; son of Henry Tuthill, of Tharston, Co. Norfolk, Eng.; bro. of Henry Tuthill, qv), from Ringstead, Northants, Eng., in the "Planter," to Boston, 1635; had a mill on Tower Hill, 1635; a propr. of Charlestown, 1636; removed to New Haven, Conn., 1638; fence-viewer, 1644; served in the night watch at New Haven, 1646; part owner

of the ketch "Zebulon"; road commr., 1646; propr. of New Haven, 1659; constable, 1666; *m* ca. 1630, Elizabeth–(1612-84).

TWOMBLY, Ralph (*d* 1656), from Eng. ca. 1656, settled at Dover, N.H.; *m* Elizabeth –.

TYLER, Henry (1604-72), from Eng. to Middle Plantation (now Williamsburg), Va., ca. 1645; justice for York Co.; *m* 2d, Ann–, widow of John Orchard.

TYLER, Job (ca. 1619-1700), from Eng., was at Portsmouth or Newport, R.I., 1638; removed to Andover, Mass., 1640; to Roxbury, 1665, to Mendon, 1669; later to Rowley; *m* Mary –.

TYLER, Robert (1637/38-1674), from Eng., 1663; settled in Anne Arundel Co., Md., where he had several grants of land; also a grant of about 750 acres called "Brough," on west side of north fork of Patuxent River, Calvert Co., which remained in the Tyler family until 1866; *m* at Deptford, Kent, Eng., June 29, 1663, Joanna Ravens.

TYLER, Roger (*d* 1673/74), at Lynn, Mass., 1640; to New Haven, Conn., 1650; later at Branford; *m* Ann–.

TYLER, Thomas (*d* 1703), from Eng. to Boston, Mass., ca. 1680; *m* Miriam Simpkins (1663-1730).

TYSON, Rhiner, or Reynier (1659-1745), from Germany, with his brother Derrick, in the "Concord," to Phila., Pa., 1683; an original incorporator of Germantown, Pa.; burgess, 1692, 93, 94, 06; purchased land and settled at Abington, Pa.; *m* Margaret, prob. Striepers.

UNDERHILL, John (1597-1672), from Eng. with Winthrop, as capt. of mil. forces; freeman, 1630; officer A. and H. A. Co.; dep. Gen. Ct. several times; selectman; officer in Pequot War; driven out of the colony for "heresy" and went to New Hampshire; gov. of Exeter and Dover, N.H.; soon left for New Amsterdam and settled on L.I.; led the Dutch troops against the Simaroy Indians, 1644; mem. Council of New Netherland; *m* Helena Kruger (*d* 1658); *m* 2d, 1658/59, Elizabeth (1633-1674/75), dau. Lt. Robert Feake.

UPDEGRAFF (Op-den-Graeff), Abraham (ca. 1660-1731; son of Isaac, g.son of Herman), from Crefeld, Germany, via Eng., with William Penn, in the "Concord," 1683; moved from Germantown, Pa., to Perkiomen, nr. Phila.; mem. Pa. Assembly, 1689-90, 92; *m* 2d, ante 1704, Trintje–.

UPHAM, John (1598-1682), from Eng., with the Hull colony to Mass.; settled at Weymouth, 1635; freeman, 1638; removed to Malden, 1648; rep. Gen. Ct., 1636-42; mem. Provincial Assembly; *m* in Eng., Elizabeth Slade (or Webb; *d* 1671); *m* 2d, 1671, Catharine –, widow of Angel Hollard, of Boston.

USHER, Robert (*d* 1669), from Eng. to Newtown, Mass., ca. 1637; settled at New Haven, Conn.; admitted freeman, 1644; removed to Stamford, 1647; constable, 1665, 1667; selectman, 1668; rep. Gen. Ct., 1665-67; *m* 1659, Elizabeth –, widow of Jeremy Jagger.

UTLEY, Samuel (1622-62), from Eng. ca. 1643, settled at Scituate Mass.; freeman; *m* 1658, Hannah (*b* ca. 1638), dau. Thomas Hatch, of Scituate (qv).

VAIL (Vale), Jeremiah (1618-87), settled at Salem, Mass., 1639; to Easthampton, L.I., 1655; to Southold, 1659; blacksmith; *m* Catherine–; *m* 2d?, 1660, Mary–, widow of Peter Paine.

VAIL (Vayle), Thomas (*d* 1687), from Eng. with his wife, Sarah, to Salem, Mass., 1640; moved to Southampton, L.I., 1649; with Thomas Pell and others bought a tract of land from the Indians (for which they received a grant from Conn. Colony, 1654), on which they founded Westchester, now in the boundaries of N.Y. City, where he was magistrate.

VAN BOERUM (Booraem), Hendrick Willemse (*b* 1642), at Newtown, L.I., 1666; *m* Maria Arlaense, or Adrians.

VAN BOERUM (Booraem), Willem Jacobse (1617-98; son of Jacobse, *b* 1570); came from Gröningen, via Amsterdam, 1649; at Flatbush, L.I.; magistrate, 1657, 62, 63; on assessment roll, 1675; took oath of allegiance, 1687; rep. Dutch Convention, 1664; *m* Geertje Hendrickse.

VAN BUSKIRK, Laurens Andriessen (*d* 1694), from Holland, first appeared in records in America, 1654, on the occasion of the baptism of a child; removed to west shore of Hudson

River, 1662; mem. Gov. Carteret's council; first coroner of Bergen Co.; justice; pres. English Ct. of Bergen; magistrate; mem. Ct. of Common Rights; *m* 1658, Jannetje Jans (*d* 1694).

VANCE (Vans), Andrew (*b* Co. Cavon, Ire.; son of John, of Coagh; g.son Dr. Launcelot, surgeon, Londonderry Regt.; g.g.son Rev. John, rector of Kilmacrenan; desc. of Robert Bruce, King of Scotland), came to America ca. 1700; settled at Opecquon Creek, Winchester, Va., 1735; *m* Elizabeth Colvin.

VAN CLEAVE (Van Cleef), Jan (*b* 1628), from Holland, 1653; at Gravesend, L.I., 1656; to New Utrecht, L.I., 1659; patentee; rep. Buskwick Colony in Representative Conv. of 1664; constable, 1678; took oath of allegiance, 1687; *m* ante 1661, Angelica, dau. Peter Lawrence; *m* 2d, ante Mar. 10, 1681, Engeltie Louwerens, dau. of Louwerens Pieterse.

VAN CORTLANDT, Oloff Stevenson (1610-84; son of Oliver, of Courland, South Holland, *m* Catherine-), from Holland to New Amsterdam, in the "Haring," 1637; one of the eight men to adopt measures against the Indians, 1645; col. Burgher Corps, 1649, 1655-64; burgomaster, 1655, 56, 58, 60, 62, 63; schepen, 1654; commr. to settle boundaries bet. New Netherland and New England; commr. to surrender New Netherland to the English, 1664; *m* 1642, Annetje Loockermans, sister of Gouvert Loockermans (*d* 1684).

VAN COUWENHOVEN, Wolfert Gerretse, see Couwenhoven.

VANDERBEEK, Paulus (1623-80), came from Bremen, Ger.; the earliest mention of him in America is his marriage, Oct. 9, 1644; resided at New Amsterdam until about 1656; is said to have been at Brooklyn, N.Y., 1655; mem. of conv., 1653; farmer of the revenue, 1656-61; surgeon in service of Dutch West India Co., and served in Curacoa and on board the company's ships; ferry master bet. Manhattan and Brooklyn, 1662; a great burgher, 1657; *m* 1644, as her 3d husband, Mary Thomas Baddie, dau. Aeltje Brackhoengie (widow of Jacob Verdon and William Adrianese Bennet).

VANDERBILT, Jan Aertsen (*d* 1705), from Bilt or der Bilt, nr. Zeyst, Friesland, Holland, to New Amsterdam, ca. 1650; settled at Flatbush, L.I.; to Bergen, N.J., ante 1694; *m* 1650, Anneken Hendricks (*b* Bergen, Norway); *m* 2d, Dierber Cornelis; *m* 3d, 1681, Magdalena Hanse, widow of Hendrick Jansen Spier.

VAN DEURSEN (Van Deusen), Abraham Pietersen (*b* 1607), Holland to New Amsterdam, 1630; took possession of Quetenesse Island, 1638; one of the 12 men to serve as advisers to Gov. Gen. Keift, 1641-42, which constituted the first group of popular reps. in New Amsterdam; apptd. on bd. of 8 men, 1642-47; official miller of the Dutch West India Co.; took oath of allegiance Sept. 5, 1664, after Dir. Gen. Peter Stuyvesant had surrendered New Amsterdam to the English; *m* Dec. 9, 1629, in the Groote Kerk at Haarlem, Holland, Tryntje (Catherine) Melchiors (*b* Groningen, Holland-living at New Amsterdam, 1678).

VAN DE WATER, Jacobus (1626-1712), from Holland to New Amsterdam, 1660; town mayor, 1674; settled at Bedford, L.I., 1677; county clerk of Kings Co., L.I.: *m* Engeltje Juriaans.

VAN DYKE (Van Dyk, Van Dyck), Jan Thomasse (1605-73), came with his father, Thomasse Janse (qv) settled at New Utrecht, L.I., 1657; was 1st magistrate there; sgt., 1657; *m* Tryntje Haegen (living 1678).

VAN DYKE, Thomasse Janse (ca. 1580-ca. 1665), from Holland to New Amsterdam, 1652; *m* Sytie Dirks.

VAN HARDENBERGH, Jan, see Hardenbergh.

VAN HOESEN, Jan Franse (*d* 1667; son of Francis); came from Huisen on the Zuyder Zee, Netherlands, 1645; settled at Beverwyck (Albany), N.Y., 1646; *m* Volkie Jurianse (*d* 1703), dau. of Wilhelm Jurrian.

VAN HORN, Christian Barentsen (*d* 1658), from Holland, settled in New Amsterdam ante 1653; prominent officer of New Amsterdam; *m* Jannetje (*d* 1694), dau. of Tyman Jansen Jans, *m* Martije Webber.

VAN HORN (Van Hoorn), Jan Cornelisen (*d* ante 1669), at New Amsterdam as early as 1640; took oath of allegiance, 1664; 3d teacher

of pub. sch. of Dutch Ch., 1648-50; *m* Hillegonda Joris.

VAN METER, Jan Joosten (*d* 1706), from Holland in the "Fox," 1662, settled at Kingston (Wyltwick), N.Y.; *m* ca. 1646, Macyken Hendricksen.

VAN PETTEN, Claas Frederickse (1641-1728; son of Frederick), from Holland to Schenectady, N.Y., 1664; moved to Papsne, nr. Albany, 1683; mem. Dutch Reformed Ch.; justice of peace, 1690; *m* Aifie, dau. of Arentse Bradt, from Holland to Albany, then to Schenectady where he was an original propr., killed in massacre of 1690, *m* Catalina, dau. of Andrew de Vos, Huguenot, dep. dir. of Rensselaerwyck.

VAN RENSSELAER, Jeremias (1632-74; son of Kiliaen), from Holland to Rensselaerwyck, 1658, of which he was 3d patroon; col. of militia; mem. Colonial Assembly and speaker, 1664; capt. Troop of Horse, 1670; *m* 1662, Maria, (1645-89), dau. of Oloff Stevensen Van Cortlandt (qv).

VAN RENSSELAER, Kiliaen (1585-1643), was one of the lords directors of the Dutch West India Co., purchased from the Indians a very large tract of land now including part of Albany and Rensselaer counties, New Netherland, which he named Rensselaerwyck; title of "patroon" conferred on him, 1624; the grant was divided into two manors, 1704, and title changed to "lord of the manor"; the patroonship vested in Rensselaerwyck; never came to America; *m* 2d, Anna van Wely (*d* 1670).

VANSANT, Garret Stoeffel (Christopher), (1630-1706), from Holland to New Utrecht, L.I., 1651; *m* Lysbeth, dau. Cornelius Gerritz.

VAN SANTVOORD, Cornelius (1686-1752), grad. U. of Leyden; from Holland to Staten Island, N.Y., ca. 1717, where he was preacher; removed to Schenectady, N.Y., 1742, and was pastor Old Dutch Church there; scholar and writer; *m* Anna Staats.

VAN SCHAICK, Gozen (Goosen) Gerritse (*d* 1676), from Westerbroeck, Holland, 1637; tapster and tanner; mem. ct., 1648-51; removed to Albany, 1650; magistrate, Ft. Orange, 1664; lt. of militia, 1670, capt., 1676; *m* Geertie Brantse Peelen van Nieuwkerk (*d* ca. 1656); *m* 2d, 1657, Annetje Lievens.

VAN SCHOONHOVEN, Guert Hendrikse (*d* 1702), from Holland to Albany Co., N.Y., before 1681; *m* Maritie Cornelie.

VAN VOAST (Van Vorst), Gerrit Janszen (1618-42), from Holland ante 1639, settled at Corlear's Hook, New Amsterdam, New Netherlands; *m* Geertruyd-.

VAN WIE (Ver Wey, Verweyen), Hendrick Gerritse (*d* 1692; son of Gerrit), from Holland in the "De Endracht," 1664; settled at Fort Orange; bought land at Van Wie's Point, Albany Co., N.Y., 1679; wounded at Frary, Can., while on expdn. to Can.; *m* Aytje Ariaanze (Ariese).

VAN WINKLE, Jacob Wallingen (1599-1657), from Holland ante 1633; settled at Rensselaerwyck, 1636; returned to Manhattan and secured a grant at Pavonia (now Jersey City), N.J.; became one of "The Twelve Men" of the Province of N.J.; *m* ante 1647, Tryntje Jacobs (*d* 1677).

VAN WYCK, Cornelius Barentse (desc. of Chevalier Hendrick Van Wyck, of Wyck, nr. Teck, Holland, living in 1400), came to New Amsterdam, 1660; *m* Anna, dau. Theodorus Polhemus, 1st Dutch Reformed minister on L.I.

VAN ZANDT, Gerret Stoffelse (son of Christoffle, of the Netherlands, among the early settlers in Kings Co.); came from Holland, ca. 1651; settled at New Utrecht; patentee, 1668; supervisor Richmond Co. records; magistrate, 1681; rep., 1712, 14, 19; *m* Lisbeth (*d* ante 1706), dau. of Cornelus Gerrets, of New Utrecht, L.I.

VAUGHN, John, from Wales to Salem, Mass., 1636; settled at Newport, R.I., ca.1638; freeman, 1655.

VEDDER, Harmen Albertse (*d* 1715?), from Holland, 1630; first mentioned in Albany records, 1657; one of the three commissioners of Schenectady.

VEEDER, Simon Volkertse (1624-96), sailed between Amsterdam and New Amsterdam, 1644-1652; settled at New Amsterdam, 1652; removed to Beaverwyck, 1654, to Schenectady, 1662; soldier French and Indian War; *m* Engeltie –.

VENABLE, Abraham, from Eng. in the "Friend's Adventure," to New Kent Co., Va., ca. 1685; *m* Sara – (*d* 1687), *m* 2d, Elizabeth (Lewis) Hicks, dau. of Capt. Hugh ap Lewis.

VERMILYA (Vermeille, Vermelje, Vermilyea), Isaac (1601-76; son of Joanne [*b* 1580], *m* Marie Roubley, Walloon refugees to London), came in the "Purmarland Church," 1662; settled at Harlem; joined New Amsterdam Ch., 1663; overseer Harlem Ct.; *m* 1627, Jacomina Jacobs.

VER PLANCK, Abraham Isaacsen (*d* ca. 1680), from Holland to New Amsterdam, 1636; one of the "Twelve Men," 1641; *m* 1630, Maria (Vinge) Roos, dau. Geyeyn Vinge.

VILAS, Peter (1704-56), believed to have come from Eng., ca. 1720, settled at or nr. Dedham, Mass.; *m* Mercy, dau. John Gay.

VOORHEES (Van Voor Hees), Hon. Steven Coerte (ca. 1610-Feb. 16, 1684), from Hees, prov. Drente, Netherlands, in the "Bonte Koe" with his family to New Amsterdam, Apr. 1660; settled at Flatlands, L.I.; magistrate; *m* 2d, Willemjie (1619-90), dau. of Roelof Seubering.

WADE, (Armigall) Armiger (*d* 1676; desc. of Armigall, of Bellsize, nr. Hampstead, Eng.); to Va. ante 1655; burgess for York Co., Va., 1655-56.

WADE, Nicholas (1616-83), from Eng. in the "Falcon," 1635; settled at Scituate, Mass.; served in colonial wars; *m* 1638, Elizabeth (*d* 1708), dau. of Thomas Ensign.

WADHAMS (Wadham), John, from Eng. to Wethersfield, Conn., ca. 1645.

WADLEIGH, John (ca. 1600-1671), from Eng. with Richard Vines' Company, 1630; settled at Biddeford, Saco, Wells and Kittery, Me.; *m* Mary –.

WADSWORTH, Christopher (*d* 1677 or 78), Eng. to Boston, 1632; dep., selectman, rep., constable, surveyor; *m* Grace Cole (*d* 1688).

WADSWORTH, William (1595-1675), from Long Buckby, Northamptonshire, Eng.; resident at Braintree, Co. Essex, Eng.; came in the "Lyon," to Cambridge, Mass., 1632; freeman, 1632; selectman, 1634-35; at Hartford, Conn., with Rev. Thomas Hooker, 1636; rep. Gen. Ct. many times, bet. 1656-75; *m* 2d, 1644, Elizabeth Stone (*d* 1682), sister of Rev. Samuel Stone.

WAIT (Wayte), Capt. John (ca.1618-1693), from Eng. probably in the "Susan and Ellen," 1638; early settler at Malden, Mass.; in Mar. 1647-48 the colony allowed him ₤4 18s., "for his writing one booke of the lawes, and for finding paper for both bookes" (this was the ms. of the celebrated Mass. Laws of 1648, compiled and perfected by Joseph Hills, his father-in-law, the first civil and religious affairs of Malden); succeeded Joseph Hills in Ho. of Deps., 1666, representing the town 18 yrs.; comd. a co. in active service during King Philip's War; with others was chosen to prepare papers for the agents in Eng., 1681-82; received nomination for the magistracy, 1683; *m* Mary (*d* 1674), dau. Joseph Hills, *m* Rose Clarke.

WAIT, Richard (ca. 1596-1680, aet. 84), of Boston; tailor; admitted to church, 1634; freeman, 1637; sgt., 1647; commissary in Pequot War; spl. commissary to the Narragansetts, 1664; *m* Elizabeth – (*d* ca 1651); *m* 2d, Rebecca Hepbourne.

WAIT (Waite, Waight), Richard (1608-1668/69), from Eng. to Watertown, Mass., 1637, where he had land grants; *m* 1656-78).

WAIT (Waite, Wayte), Thomas (1601-77), from Eng.; went to Portsmouth, R.I., 1638, with Ann Hutchinson and her associates; freeman, Boston, 1640; freeman, Newport, 1641.

WAKEFIELD, John (ca. 1614-1667), from Eng., landing either in Va. or Md., was at Martha's Vineyard, Mass., before 1647; at Boston, ca. 1650; *m* Ann–.

WAKEMAN, Capt. John (1598/99-1661), from Eng. to New Haven Colony, 1638; a signer of the New Haven Compact, 1639; dep. Gen. Ct., 1641-44, 1646-48, 56, 61; treas. of the Colony, 1655-1660; capt. of colonial forces; *m* 1628, Elizabeth Hopkins (bap. 1610-*d* 1658).

WALCOTT, Capt. William (living 1648), from Devon, Eng.; settled at Salem, Mass.; freeman, 1636; granted 30 acres, 1636; *m* ante 1643, Alice, dau. Richard Ingersoll (qv).

WALDO, Cornelius (*b* 1624-*d* Jan. 3, 1700/01), came from Eng., resided at Ipswich, Mass., until ca. 1665; deacon at Chelmsford, ca. 1668;

selectman, 1698; served in King Philip's War; tavern keeper, 1690; *m* 1651, Hannah (1624-1704), dau. of John Cogswell (qv).

WALDRON, Resolved (1610-90), from Holland, 1654, settled at New Amsterdam; dep. sheriff; one of five patentees named in Nicolls' patent; constable, 1665; overseer, 1668; assessor, 1683; elder of the church; *m* 1st, 1645, Rebecca Hendricks; *m* 2d, Tennecke, dau. of Barent Nagel, of Groningen, Holland.

WALDRON (Walderne), Maj. Richard (1614-89), from Eng. to Dover, Mass., 1635; at Dover Neck until 1655; capt. of a militia co., 1652, maj., 1674; cdr.-in-chief (colonel) of Eastern military forces in King Philip's War; dep. for Dover in Mass. Gen. Ct., 1652-79; speaker of the House several sessions; royal councillor and dep. gov. of the Province of N.H., when it was organized, 1680; chief justice Superior Ct. of the Province, 1683; his garrison was captured and burned by the Indians, June 28, 1689, and he was killed; *m* in Eng., 1637, – (ca. 1617-1680).

WALES, Nathaniel (bap. 1586-*d* 1661), shipwright; from Eng. in the "James," to Mass., 1635; freeman, 1637; *m* Susanna Greenway.

WALKER, James (1619-91), from Eng. to Taunton, Mass., ca. 1633; freeman, 1650; dep. Gen. Ct. 16 yrs.; mem. and chmn. Council of War, 1667, 75, 78; mem. Plymouth Council of War, 1658, 61, 71, 81; constable, selectman; *m* Elizabeth (1620-78), dau. of William Phillips, *m* Elizabeth Parker.

WALKER, Capt. Richard (*d* 1687, aet. 95), from Eng., 1630, settled at Lynn, Mass.; freeman, 1634; ens., 1637, lt., 1646, capt. 1652; dep. Mass. Gen. Ct. for Reading, 1640-42, 1648-50, 1660; *m* Jane, dau. Joe Talmadge, of Eng.

WALKER, Robert (*b* 1607), from Eng., settled at Boston; freeman, 1632.

WALLER, John (1617-88; of royal ancestry), from Newport Paganel, Buckinghamshire, England, to Va., 1635; settled in Gloucester Co., Va., later at "Enfield," King William Co., Va.; *m* Mary Key, or Kay; their son Col. John (1673-1754), settled in King and Queen Co.; sheriff, 1702; rep. King William Co., 1719-21; first clk., St. George's Parish; founder and organizer of Spotsylvania Co.; with his wife, is buried at "Newport," Spotsylvania Co.; *m* Dorothy King (1675-1759).

WALN, Nicholas (ca. 1650-1721), from Eng. in the "Welcome," with William Penn, 1682; purchased 1000 acres; settled in Middletown Tp., Pa., on the Neshaminy River, 1682/83-96; removed to Phila. Co., 1696; mem. first Assembly many yrs.; sheriff of Bucks Co., 1685; director of public schools, etc.; *m* 1673, Jane Turner.

WALTON, Rev. William (ca. 1598-1668), Puritan; M.A., Emanuel Coll., Cambridge, 1625; D.D., 1625; came to Mass., 1635; settled at Marblehead where he was pastor over 30 yrs.; *m* Elizabeth –.

WARD, Andrew (ca. 1600-1659), from Eng. to Mass., 1630; freeman at Watertown, Mass., 1634; removed to Wethersfield, Conn., 1635, to Stamford, 1641, later to Fairfield, where he died; one of commrs. apptd. by Colony of Mass. Bay to govern Colony of Conn., 1635-36; magistrate, 1636, 37; dep. Gen. Ct., 1638, 39, 1653-56, 1658; mem. com. to press men for the expdn. against the Dutch, 1653, and against the Narragansets, 1654; *m* Hester Sherman.

WARD, Capt. John (*b* 1598), came to Va., 1619; burgess; rep. "Ward's Plantation," or "Ward's Hundred"; grantee of a patent for 350 acres in Henrico Co., 1643.

WARD, William (1603-87), from Eng. to Sudbury, Mass., 1639; freeman, 1643; selectman; rep. Gen. Ct., 1644; a founder of Marlborough, 1660; again rep., 1666; in garrison at Marlborough in King Philip's War; *m* 2d, Elizabeth – (1613-1700)

WARE (Weares), Robert (*d* 1699), from Eng. to Dedham, Mass., 1642; freeman, 1647; mem. co. arty., 1644; *m* 1644/45, Margaret Huntinge (*d* 1670), dau. of John Huntinge; *m* 2d, 1676, Hannah Jones (1636-1721), dau. of Thomas Jones, of Dorchester.

WARFIELD, Richard (*d* 1703/04), from Eng., settled nr. Annapolis, Anne Arundel Co., Md.; mil. officer of the county, 1696; large landowner; vestryman; *m* 1670, Elinor, dau. Capt John Browne.

WARHAM, John (ca. 1595-1670), minister at Exeter, Devon, Eng.; came from Plymouth,

Eng., in the "Mary and John," 1630, and settled at Dorchester, Mass.; at Hartford, 1637; minister at Windsor, Conn., until death; *m* 1st, —(*d* 1634); *m* 2d, Abigail—, widow of John Branker; *m* 3d, Jane (Dabinott) Newbury (*d* 1655), widow of Thomas Newbury (qv).

WARING, Benjamin (*d* 1713), from Lea, nr. Wolverhampton, Staffordshire, Eng., in the "Loyal Jamaica," settled at Pine Hill, S.C.; mem. House of Commons, 1685; mem. Assembly from Berkeley Co., 1693; maj. of militia in Indian wars; commr. of taxes, 1703-11; *m* Elizabeth Beamer.

WARING, Sampson (1618-68), from Eng. to Lower Norfolk Co., Va., ca. 1643; removed to "The Clifts," Calvert Co., Md., ca. 1646; lawyer. mem. Council, 1655-59; capt. of militia; mem. Assembly; *m* 1648, Sarah, dau. of Francis Leigh.

WARNER, Andrew (ca. 1595-1684), from Eng to Cambridge, Mass., 1632; freeman, 1634; a founder of Hartford, Conn., and of Hadley, Mass., 1659; deacon; *m* 1st, Mary Pureas; *m* 2d, Esther, or Hester Wakeman, widow of Thomas Selden (qv).

WARNER, Augustine (1610-74), from Eng. to York Co., Va., 1628; burgess, 1652, 1658, 59; councillor, 1669; *m* Mary – (1614-62).

WARNER, John (1615-79), from Eng. to Hartford, Conn., 1635, to Farmington, 1644; soldier Pequot War, and received land grant for his services; *m* 1649, Ann, dau. of Thomas Norton.

WARNER, Capt. William (1627-1706), from Eng. to Salem, N.J., 1675; settled at "Blockley," Phila., 1677; mem. first Council of Province of Pa.; *m* Anne Dide (or Dyde).

WARREN, John (1585-1667), from Eng. in the "Arbella," to Salem, Mass., 1630; settled at Watertown; freeman, 1631; selectman, 1636-40; *m* Margaret – (*d* 1662).

WARREN, Richard (*d* 1628), 12th signer of the Mayflower Compact; in the "First Encounter," 1620; *m* Elizabeth-, came with five children, 1623.

WARREN (Waren, Warin, Waring), Richard (*b* 1616), from Eng. in the "Endeavor," to Boston, 1664; removed to Oyster Bay, L.I., ca. 1670.

WARREN, William (*d* 1746), from Eng. with his wife and son William, in the "Expectation," to Boston, 1715; purchased land and settled at Leicester, 1727; *m* Dorothea—.

WARRINER, William (*d* 1676), Westfield, Mass.; *m* 1639, Joanna Scant (*d* 1661).

WARTHEN, Thomas, from Eng. in the "Susan Constance," 1635, settled at Port Tobacco, Md.; came in Lord Baltimore's Colony.

WASHBURN (Washburne), John (bap. 1597-*d* 1670; son of John), sec. in Eng. of the Governor and Company of Mass. Bay in N.E.; from Eng., was at Duxbury, Mass., 1631 where he was made freeman; purchased land from Massasoit, the Indian, and founded Bridgewater, to which place he removed, 1645; served in expdn. against the Narragansets, 1645; *m* in Eng., 1618, Margery (*b* 1586), dau. Robert Moore.

WASHINGTON, John, of Surry Co. (son of Sir John, Knight, of Thrapston, Northamptonshire, Eng., and bro. to Lawrence, rector of Purleigh, Essex, Eng.), to Barbados ca.1650, to Va., 1658, settled in Surry Co.; *m* 1658, Mary Flood (widow of both Richard Blount and Charles Ford).

WASHINGTON, Col. John, of Westmoreland Co. (1632-77; son of Lawrence, rector of Purleigh, Co. Essex, Eng.), from Eng., 1656; settled in Washington Parish, Westmoreland Co., Va.; j.p., 1662; burgess, 1666, 75, 77; pres. of the Westmoreland Co. Ct., 1672; col. of Va. troops in Indian war, 1675; *m* 1658, Ann (*b* St. Mary's Parish, Md.-*d* ca. 1668), dau. of Col. Nathaniel Pope (qv); *m* 2d, 1669, Anne (Gerrard?), widow successively of Col. Walter Broadhurst and of Henry Brett; *m* 3d, May 1676, Frances, dau. of Thomas Gerrard, mem. Md. Council, and widow successively of Col. Thomas Speke (*d* 1660), Col. Valentine Peyton (*d* 1665), and Capt. John Appleton (*d* 1675); after Col. John Washington's death she *m* 5th, Col. Samuel Hayward.

WASHINGTON, Lawrence (1635-1677), bro. of Col. John, of Westmoreland Co. (qv); was in Va., 1659; and again in 1661; settled there permanently, 1666; of "Westphalia," Rappahannock (now Essex) Co., Va.; *m* 1660, Mary, dau. of Edmund Jones; *m* 2d, 1670, Joyce (Haw-

kins?), widow of Capt. Alexander Fleming (she *m* 3d, James Yeats of Rappahannock Co.).

WATERMAN, Richard (1590-1673), from Eng., 1629, settled at Salem, Mass.; at Providence, R.I., 1638; one of twelve to whom Roger Williams deeded land at Providence; an original mem. 1st Bapt. ch. in America, 1639; freeman, 1665; commr.; juryman; warden; col. militia; *m* Bethia–(*d* 1680).

WATERMAN, Robert (*d* 1652; son of Thomas, of Norwich, Eng.), from Eng., was at Salem, Mass., 1636; at Plymouth, 1638; settled finally at Marshfield; rep. Gen. Ct., 1644-49; *m* 1638, Elizabeth, dau. of Thomas Bourne (qv).

WATERS, Lt. Edward, Gent. (1568-1630), mem. London Co. organized for the purpose of colonizing Va.; from Eng. in the "Sea Venture," returned to Eng., ship-wrecked on the Bermudas, returned to Va. ca. 1618 and settled on south bank of the James River; commr.; mem. Co. Ct.; burgess; lt., capt. Va. militia; *m* 1618, Grace O'Neil (*b* 1603).

WATHEN, John (ca.1625-ca.1698), from Eng. ante 1647, as trader and shipper; settled in St. Mary's Co., Md.; later returned to Eng. and *d* there; *m* ca. 1650, Mary Mullett (ca. 1630-post 1698).

WATKINS, Henry (1638-1715/16), Wales to Va., 1687; of Malvern Hall, Henrico Co.; *m* Rachel– (were g.g.g. parents of Henry Clay).

WATSON, Josiah (1748-1828), from Pa. to Alexandria, Va., ca. 1771, landowner in Tenn., Ky., and Va.; *m* Jane Taylor (1752-1830).

WEARE, Peter (1618-1691/92), from Eng., 1635, settled at Kittery, Me., later at York; dep. from Kittery to Mass. Gen. Ct., 1660, from York, 1665-69; killed by Indians; *m* 2d, 1666, Mary Puddington (1633/34-1718/19).

WEAVER, Clement (*d* 1683; son of Clement, *m* Rebecca Holbrook); from Eng. to Newport, R.I., ca. 1630; admitted freeman, 1655; mem. Colonial Assembly, 1678; *m* Mary (*b* 1627), dau. of William Freeborn, of R.I.

WEBB, Christopher (*b* 1590), from Eng. prob. 1628, settled at Braintree, Mass.; town clk.; removed to Billerica ca.1655; *m* Humility–.

WEBB, Richard (*d* 1665), from Eng. to Cambridge, Mass., 1632; freeman, 1632; a founder of Hartford, Conn., 1636; mem. grand jury, 1643; one of first settlers of Norwalk, Conn.; was at Stamford, 1655; *m* Elizabeth (*d* 1680), dau. John Gregory.

WEBSTER, John (*b* Cossington, Co. Leicester, Eng., ca.1585-*d* May 5, 1661; son of Matthew, *m* Elizabeth–), from Eng. to Mass.; one of original proprs. of Hartford, Conn., 1636; dep. Gen. Ct., 1637; gov.'s asst., 1639-55; magistrate, 1639-55; commr. for United Colonies, 1654; dep. gov., 1654; a founder of Hadley, Mass., 1659; freeman in Mass., 1660; magistrate at Hadley, 1660; *m* in Eng., 1609, Agnes Smith (*d* 1667).

WEBSTER, Thomas (1631-1715), from Eng. to Watertown, Mass., with his mother, Margary –, and his stepfather, William Godfrey; removed to Hampton, N.H.; *m* 1657, Sarah, dau. of Thomas Brewer, of Roxbury, Mass.; *m* 2d (?), Susannah Batchelder.

WEED, Jonas (*d* 1676), came in the "Arbella," 1630; settled at Watertown, Mass.; freeman, 1631; first settler at Wethersfield, Conn., 1635; a founder of Stamford, Conn., 1641; *m* Mary–(*d* 1690).

WEEKS (Weekes), Francis (1616-89; prob. son of Francis, who *d* at James City, Va., 1627), from Eng. to Va., thence according to tradition, to Dorchester, Mass., 1635; at Providence, 1636, New Amsterdam, 1641, Gravesend, 1648, Hempstead, 1657, Oyster Bay, 1660; banished from Mass. with Roger Williams; signer of Covenant of R.I., 1637; constable and overseer, Oyster Bay, 1667-68; surveyor, 1668-72; arbitrator, 1670; *m* ante 1640, Elizabeth–.

WEEKS (Weekes), George (1605-50), from Devonshire, Eng., in the same ship with Richard Mather, to Dorchester, Mass., 1635; freeman, 1640; *m* in Eng., Jane, sister of Roger Clap.

WELD, Joseph (ca. 1595-1646), from Eng. to Roxbury, Mass., ca. 1635; mem. A. and H. A. Co.; dep. Gen. Ct., 1637; freeman, 1639; capt. and first comdg. officer in service of colony; *m* Elizabeth—; *m* 2d, Barbara Clapp.

WELD, Rev. Thomas (1590-1661), ed. Trinity Coll., Cambridge; excommunicated from Ch. of Eng. by the Archbishop of London; came in the

"William and Francis," to Boston, 1632, with his wife, Margaret, and three children; was pastor of the first church at Roxbury.

WELLES (Wells), Thomas (1598-1660), from Eng. in the "Susan and Ellen," 1635; to Saybrook, Conn., 1636, to Hartford, 1637; magistrate, 1637-60; treas., 1639-51; sec., 1640-48; gov. pro tem., 1651; dep. gov., 1654, et seq.; gov. Colony of Conn., 1655-58; commr. for United Colonies, 1649; *m* 1st, Alice (*d* 1646), dau. of John Tomes; *m* 2d, Elizabeth Deming, widow of Nathaniel Foote (qv).

WELLS (Welles), Hugh (ca. 1590-1645; bro. of Thomas Welles, qv), from Colchester, Co. Essex, Eng., to Mass., 1635; a founder of Hartford, Conn.; ensign; later resided at Wethersfield, Conn., and Hadley, Mass.; *m* 1619, Frances Belcher (*d* 1678).

WELLS, Nathaniel (*b* 1600), wealthy shipbuilder of London; came to Boston. ca. 1629; a founder of Salem; removed to Wellstown, R.I.

WELLS (Welles), Thomas (1605-66), from Eng. in the "Susan and Ellen," to Boston, 1635; freeman, 1637; an original settler of Ipswich, Mass.; mem. A. and H. A. Co.; ensign "Mil. Co. of the Massachusetts"; *m* Abigail Warner.

WELSH, Maj. John (*d* 1683), settled in Anne Arundel Co., Md., ante 1668; justice, 1666; *m* Anne-, widow of Henry Grosse.

WENDELL, Evert Jansen (*b* Emblen, E. Friesland, 1615-*d* 1709), from Holland, 1640; settled at New Amsterdam, for 5 yrs.; Indian trader at Ft. Orange, 1645; magistrate, 1660-61; ruling elder, 1656; *m* 1644, Susanna du Trieux (*d* 1660), dau. of Philip (du Trieux) Truax (qv); *m* 2d, 1663, Maritje Abrahamse (Vosburgh) Mingael, dau. of Abraham Pieterse Vosburgh, and widow of Thomas Jansen Mingael; *m* 3d, Ariaantje-.

WENTWORTH, William (1615/16-1696/97), from Eng. to Boston, 1636; a founder of Exeter, N.H., 1639; removed to Wells, Me., 1642, to Dover, N.H., 1649; *m* Elizabeth Kenney.

WEST, Francis (*d* 1692, aet. 86), came from Salisbury, Eng., to N.E.; carpenter; settled at Duxbury, Mass.; mem. grand jury, 1640, 42; freeman, Plymouth Colony, 1656; surveyor of highways, 1658; constable, 1661; mem. grand inquest 6 yrs.; *m* Feb. 27, 1639, Margery Reeves.

WEST, John (1590-1659; son of Sir Thomas West, 2d Lord Delaware [new creation], *m* Anne, dau. of Sir Francis Knollys, K.G.), B.A., Magdalen Coll., Cambridge U., 1613; came to Va.; mem. Council of Va. 29 yrs.; gov. and capt.-gen., 1635-37; settled on West Point estate, 1650; *m* Anne—.

WEST, Mathew (*d* post 1677), was at Lynn, Mass., 1636; removed to Newport, R.I., ca. 1646; mem. Ct. of Commrs., for Providence, R.I.

WEST, Sir Thomas (1577-1618; son of Sir Thomas West [1555-1603], *m* Anne, dau. of Sir Francis Knollys, K.G. and treas. of household of Queen Elizabeth), 3d Lord De la Warr, and bro. of John (qv); M.A., Oxford U.; knighted 1599; apptd. gov. and capt. gen. of Va. 1609; arrived at Jamestown in his own ship, 1610; returned to Eng., 1611, where he worked to preserve the colony; *d* while on return voyage to Va.; *m* 1602, Cecelie, dau. of Sir Thomas Sherley, Kt. of Wiston, Eng.

WESTCOTT (Wescott, Westcoatt), Stukeley (1592-1677), from Eng., settled at Salem, Mass., 1636; a founder of Providence Plantations; removed to Warwick, R.I., 1648; dep. Gen. Ct., 1650; commr., 1651, et seq.; gov.'s asst., 1656, et seq.; freeman, 1636; *m* 1619, Julian Marchante.

WESTON, John (ca. 1630-1723), from Eng., 1644, settled at Salem, Mass.; to Reading, ca. 1652; large land propr.; *m* 1653, Sarah, dau. Dea. Zachariah Fitch; *m* Mary—.

WETMORE (Whitmore), Thomas (*b* 1615-*d* Dec. 11, 1681), from Eng. to Conn., 1635; landowner, Wethersfield, 1639/40; to Hartford, thence to Middletown, 1654/55; propr. and freeholder, 1670; freeman; rep. Middletown in Gen. Ct., 1654-55; *m* 1645, Sarah (*d* 1664), dau. John Hall, *m* Ann Willcocke; *m* 2d, 1667, Mary (Platt) Atkinson (*d* 1669), dau. of Richard Platt, and widow of Luke Atkinson; *m* 3d, 1673, Katherine (Leet) Robards (*d* 1693).

WHARTON, Thomas (1664-1718; son of Richard, of Kellorth, Westmorelandshire, Eng.), settled at Phila., Pa., ca. 1683; mem. Phila Council; *m* Rachel Thomas.

WHEATON, Robert (1605-96), from Wales to Salem, Mass., 1636; removed to Rehoboth, Mass., 1645; one of founders, 1st Bapt. Ch. in Mass.; *m* Alice Bowen (*d* 1696).

WHEELER, John (*d* 1670, aet. 52), from Salisbury, Wiltshire, Eng., in the "Mary and John," 1633/34, to Hampton, N.H.; an original propr. and received land at Salisbury, Mass., 1641; removed to, Newbury, Mass., ante 1650; *m* Anne-(*d* 1662).

WHEELER, Moses (1598-ca. 1690), from Eng. to New Haven, Conn., 1638; removed to Stratford, 1648; charter from Conn. Gen. Court for ferry on Housatonic River; freeman, 1669; shipwright; *m* Miriam Hawley.

WHEELER, Thomas (1602-86), from Eng. to Lynn, Mass., 1635; constable; freeman, 1642; removed to Stonington, Conn., 1667; mem. Gen. Ct., 1673; *m* 1645, Mary-.

WHEELER, Sgt. Thomas (ca. 1625-1704), a freeman at Concord, Mass., 1642; sgt. Concord mil. company; *m* Sarah (ca. 1627-1676), dau. Joseph Meriam, who *m* Sarah Goldstone.

WHEELOCK, Ralph (1600-83), A.B., A.M., Cambridge U.; from Eng. with his wife and daughter to Watertown, Mass., 1637; removed to Dedham, 1638; founded town of Medfield, 1650; dep. Gen. Ct. from Dedham and Medfield several yrs.; *m* Rebecca – (*d* before 1651); *m* 2d, Hannah – (*d* 1682).

WHIPPLE, Dea. John (1605-69), from Eng., settled at Ipswich, Mass., 1638; freeman, 1640; dep. Gen. Ct., 1640-42, 46, 50, 54; deacon, ruling elder, 1658; agent for "The Worshipful Mr. Saltonstall" in his business affairs; selectman; the "Whipple House" is now the home of the Ipswich Hist. Soc.; *m* Sarah Hawkins; *m* 2d, Jennett–.

WHITAKER, Jabez (*b* 1596; posthumous son of Rev. William [1548-95], noted Puritan preacher in the Ch. of Eng. and distinguished scholar, master of St. John's Coll., Cambridge, 1586-95); came to Va.; commended by name in the records of the Va. Co., 1620, and at other times for his service to the colony; mem. House of Burgesses which met, 1623/24, from "Elizabeth City beyond Hampton River"; councillor, 1626, 28; referred to as capt., 1622, and later; *m* Mary, dau. of Sir John Bourchier, of the Parish of Lambert, Surrey Co., Eng.

WHITCOMB, John (1588-1663), from Taunton, Co. Somerset, Eng., 1633/34; at Dorchester, Mass.; freeman; propr., 1636; a founder of Lancaster, Mass.; *m* 1623, Frances Coggan (1604-71).

WHITE, John (ca. 1595-ca. 1683; son of Robert, yeoman, of Shelford, Co. Essex, Eng., *m* 1585, Bridget, dau. William Algar); came in the "Lyon," to Boston, Mass., 1632; settled at Newtown (Cambridge); freeman, 1633; an original propr. of Hartford, 1636, and mem. of the Hooker colony; removed to Hadley, 1659; rep. Gen. Ct., 1664, 69; returned to Hartford, ca. 1670; elder South Ch. until his death; *m* in Eng., 1622, Mary Levit (*d* post 1666).

WHITE, Nicholas (*d* 1697), from Eng., freeman at Dorchester, Mass., 1643; moved to Taunton bet. 1652-55; *m* ca. 1643, Susanna, dau. of Jonas Humphrey, *m* Frances –.

WHITE, Peregrine (*b* in the Mayflower, Cape Cod Harbor, bet. Dec. 7 and 10, 1620-*d* 1704; son of William), capt. Mass troops; mem. Council of War, 1675; *m* 1649, Sarah (1630-1711), dau. William Bassett.

WHITE, Capt. Thomas (1599-1679), from Eng., a founder of Weymouth, Mass., ante 1635; freeman, 1635; lawyer; capt. of a military company; selectman; rep. Gen. Ct.; rep. Colonial Legislature, 1636-37.

WHITE, Thomas (*d* 1664), was at Cambridge, Mass., 1635-36; at Watertown, Mass., 1637; later at Sudbury and Charlestown; *m* Margaret-(*d* 1649).

WHITE, William (*d* 1621; son of Bishop John White), 11th signer of the Mayflower Compact; *m* at Leyden, Holland, 1612, Susanna Fuller, who *m* 2d, Edward Winslow.

WHITE, William (1610-90), from Eng. in the "Mary and John," to Ipswich, Mass., 1634; freeman at Newbury, 1642; one of the first settlers at Haverhill, where he died; capt. of first mil. company at Haverhill; *m* 1st, Mary – (*d* 1681, aet. 75).

WHITELEY, Arthur (1652-1732), from Eng. to Dorchester Co., Md., 1676; *m* 1705, Elizabeth –, widow of William Rich, of Md.; *m* 2d, 1719, Joan –.

WHITFIELD, William (1688-ca. 1770), from Eng. in his own ship, "The Providence," in early part of the 18th Century, and settled at Nansemond, Va., finally in Lenoir Co., N.C.; *m* 1713, Elizabeth Goodman (ca. 1697-1773), of Gates Co., N.C.

WHITING, Nathaniel (ca. 1609-1682), from Eng. to Dedham, Mass., ca. 1635; granted land at Lynn; *m* 1643, Hannah (1625-1714), dau. of John Dwight.

WHITING, Samuel (1597-1679), son of John, mayor of Boston, Lincolnshire, Eng.), from Eng. to Boston, Mass., 1636, settled at Lynn, where he was freeman, 1636; clergyman; *m* 2d, Elizabeth St. John.

WHITING, William (*d* 1647), from Eng. to Cambridge, Mass., 1633; an original settler at Hartford, 1636; dep. Gen. Ct., 1637; 2d colonial treas. of Conn., 1641-47; maj. in colonial forces; magistrate, 1642-47; *m* Susanna–.

WHITMAN (Whiteman), John (ca. 1603-1692), from Eng. to Dorchester, Mass., 1635; freeman, 1639; removed to Weymouth, ca. 1641; ensign, mil. company, 1645; apptd. by Gen. Ct. "to end small causes"; *m* Ruth—(*d* 1662).

WHITMORE (Wightman), John (1599-ca. 1663; son of Rev. Edward Wightman, a Separatist, and the last of the religious martyrs in Eng. to be burned at the stake, 1612), came from Eng., 1654, to Wickford, R.I.

WHITMORE, John (*d* 1648), from Eng. in the 1630's with his wife and 5 children; appeared at Wethersfield, Conn., 1638; a founder of Stamford, 1641; freeman, 1642; dep. Gen. Ct., 1643; rep., 1647; his murder by the Indians, 1648, was the direct cause of the Colonial govt. resolving to declare war upon them; *m* 2d, Widow Jessup.

WHITMORE, Thomas, see Wetmore.

WHITNEY, John (ca. 1589-1673; son of Thomas and g.son of Sir Robert, knighted by Queen Mary, 1553), from Eng., in the "Elizabeth and Ann," to Watertown, Mass., 1635; freeman, 1636; constable, 1641; selectman and town clk.; garrison duty during King Philip's War; *m* Elinor – (1599-ca. 1670); *m* 2d, Judah Clement.

WHITON (ca. 1599-1664; son of William, of Nethercott, Oxfordshire?, *m* Catherine Ardene), from Hook Norton, Oxfordshire, Eng., in the "Elizabeth and Ann," 1635; settled at Plymouth, Mass., 1637, and granted 7 acres; propr., 1638; *m* Audrey–(*b* ca. 1590); *m* 2d, 1639, Winifred Harding (*d* 1660).

WHITRIDGE (Whitred, Whitteredd, Whittredge, Whittridge, Whitrig), William (1599-1668), from Eng. in the "Elizabeth," with his wife and son Thomas, 1635; settled at Ipswich, Mass., 1637; *m* Elizabeth –; *m* 2d, Susanna –, widow of Anthony Colby.

WHITSETT, William (1709-98), came from Ireland to Pa., 1740; with his two brothers, John and Joseph; *m* in Ireland, Elizabeth Dawson, and had two sons also born in Ireland, Henry (*b* 1730), and William (*b* 1731).

WHITTELSEY, John (1623-1704), from Eng., and settled at Saybrook, Conn.; *m* 1664, Ruth (1645-1714), dau. William Dudley, *m* Jane Lutman.

WHITTEMORE, Thomas (1593/94-1660/61; a desc. of Sir John, knighted on the battlefield for valorous conduct, 1230, and received a tract of land called "Whytemere" or White Meadow, whence came his title, Lord John de Whytemere), came from Hitchen, Eng., with his wife and 5 children, 1642; settled at Charlestown, Mass.; *m* Hannah–.

WHITTINGHAM, John (*d* 1649; son of Baruch, of Southerton, Eng.), from Eng. to Ipswich, Mass.; *m* Martha, dau. of William Hubbard (qv).

WICK, John (1617-67), from Eng., 1637, to Plymouth, Mass.; removed to Aquidneck, L.I., N.Y., 1639.

WICKES, John (1609-75), from Eng., 1634; a signer of the Aquidneck Compact; dep. Gen. Ct.; gov.'s asst., 1650-55; killed by Indians in King Philip's War; *m* Mary –.

WICKHAM, Thomas (1624-1688/89), from Eng., was at Wethersfield, Conn., 1648; freeman, 1658; *m* Sarah Churchill (1630-1700).

WICKLIFFE, David (*b* Yorkshire, Eng.-*d* 1643), came in the "Evelyn" expedition to Md., 1635; mem. Md. Assembly from St. George's Hundred, 1636-43; *m* Jane–.

WIGHT, Thomas (ca. 1600-1674), from Isle of Wight, 1635; settled at Watertown, Mass., 1637, later at Dedham; was one of members from Dedham who voted to tax himself for first free sch. in Mass.; to Medfield and later to Middlesex, Mass.; selectman; *m* ca. 1622, Alice– (ca. 1605-1665); *m* 2d, 1665, Lydia, dau. Bennett Eliot, and sister of Rev. John Eliot (qv).

WILBUR (Wilboare, Wilber, Wilbor, Willbore, Wildbore), Samuel (*d* 1656), from Eng. to Boston, 1633; admitted to the church at Boston, 1633; banished on account of religious differences and was an original propr. of Aquidneck, R.I., 1638; returned to Boston after a number of yrs.; *m* in Eng., Ann (*d* Sept. 24, 1656), dau. Thomas Bradford; *m* 2d, Elizabeth Letchford.

WILCOX (Willcocks), John, of Hartford (*b* ca. 1595-will dated 1651; a desc. of Capt. John Wilcox who commanded 1,000 lancers against William the Conqueror), came from Lancashire, Eng., ca. 1635; a propr. of Hartford; surveyor of highways, 1642-44; juror, 1645; called senior, 1648; selectman, 1649; his name appears as a founder, on the monument erected by the City of Hartford, Conn.; *m* Mary–(ca. 1597-1669).

WILCOXSON (Wilcooks, Wilcox, Wilcockson), William (1601-1652/53), from Eng. in the "Planter," to Concord, Mass., 1635; freeman at Cambridge, 1636; removed to Stratford, Conn., 1639, later to Hartford and Windsor; rep. Gen. Ct., 1647; *m* Margaret Birdseye (*b* 1611), she *m* 2d, ca. 1663, William Hayden.

WILDER, Thomas (ca. 1618-1667), from Eng., was at Charlestown, Mass., 1638; freeman, 1641; settled at Lancaster, 1659; selectman; *m* 1641, Anna Eames (*d* 1692).

WILKINSON, Lawrence (*d* 1692), cavalier, officer in army of Charles I; came to Providence, R.I., 1645; dep. R.I. Assembly; *m* ca. 1649, Susannah (*d* 1692), dau. of Christopher Smith, of R.I.

WILKINSON, Rev. William (1612-63), from Eng. to Va., 1635; settled in Md., 1650; was 1st Ch. of Eng. minister with an established church in Md.; *m* Naomi–.

WILLARD, Simon (1605-76), from Eng. to Cambridge, Mass., 1634; removed to Concord, 1635, thence to Lancaster, 1657; dep. Gen. Ct., 1636-54; gov.'s asst., 1654-76; lt., 1637; capt., 1646; maj., 1655; cdr.-in-chief of expdn. against Minigret, 1655; mayor of Middlesex, 1655-76; cdr. Middlesex regt. in King Philip's War; was given 1,000 acres of land by the govt.; *m* in Eng., Mary (bap. 1614-ca. 1650), dau. Henry Sharpe; *m* 2d, Elizabeth Dunster; *m* 3d, Mary Dunster.

WILLET (Willett), Thomas (1610/11-1674), from Eng. to Plymouth, Mass., 1632; settled at Swansea, Mass.; capt. Plymouth colonial militia, 1648; mem. Council of War, 1653; Gen. Council, 1672; served in expdn. which captured New Amsterdam from the Dutch, 1664, and became the first English mayor of New York; returned to Swansea, where he died; *m* 1636, Mary (*d* 1669), dau. of John Brown of Swansea.

WILLETT, Thomas (1621-1646/47), from Bristol, Eng., to L.I.; *m* 1643, in New Amsterdam, Sara, dau. of Thomas Cornell (qv).

WILLIAMS, Gov. Francis (1602-48), from Eng. or Wales, settled at Laconia, now N.H., 1631; first colonial gov. of N.H.; *m* Mary –.

WILLIAMS, George, from Wales to Phila., Pa., ca. 1690; shortly after removed to Prince Georges Co., Md.

WILLIAMS, James (*d* 1735), from England to Fredericksburg, Va., ca. 1726; *m* Ann Johnson.

WILLIAMS, John (ca. 1600-1674), came probably from Newbury, Eng., 1633; settled at Newbury, Mass., on the Merrimac River; one of the founders of Haverhill; freeman, 1642; original propr., 1667; *m* 2d, Jane–(*d* 1680).

WILLIAMS, Richard (*b* 1599), *b* in Wales; came to Salem, Mass., 1633; a founder of Taunton, Mass., 1637; rep. Gen. Ct., 1646-48, 50.

WILLIAMS, Richard (1606-93), from Eng. 1636; settled at Dorchester; founder of Taunton, Mass., called "Father of Taunton"; freeman, 1639; mem. Gen. Ct., 1640-60; one of original purchasers of "North Purchase"; *m* 1632, Frances (1611-1706), dau. John Dighton, *m* Jane Bassett.

WILLIAMS, Robert (1607-93; son of Stephen of Great Yarmouth); was freeman and alderman of Norwich, Eng.; came to Roxbury, Mass., June, 1637; freeman, 1638; selectman; trustee Roxbury school; mem. A. and H. A. Co.; *m* in England, Elisabeth (1597-1674), dau. of John Stalham, jurat, *m* Alice Gibson; *m* 2d, 1675, Margaret (*d* 1690), widow of John Fearing (qv).

WILLIAMS, Roger (1599-1683), grad. Pembroke Coll., Cambridge U., 1627; ordained minister Ch. of Eng.; came from Eng. in "Lyon," to Boston, Mass., 1631; teacher of the church at Salem, 1631-33; again at Salem, 1633-35; banished from the colony and founded R.I. and Providence Plantations, 1636; secured a charter for the colony in Eng., 1644; gov. of the Plantations, 1654-56, later gov.'s asst. and dep.; *m* Mary Barnard.

WILLIS, Henry (1628-1714; son of Henry, of Wiltshire, Eng.), from Spittlefield, London, Eng., ca. 1674, to Oyster Bay, L.I., N.Y.; a founder of Westbury, L.I.; *m* Mary Peace (1632-1714).

WILLISTON, Joseph (1667-1747); was at Westfield, and Springfield, Mass.; *m* Mary (*d* 1711), dau. of Joseph Parsons and widow of Joseph Ashley; *m* 2d, 1714, Sarah –, widow of Thomas Stebbins.

WILTSIE (Wiltsee), Philippe Maton (ca. 1598-1632), soldier under Prince Maurice in War bet. Holland and Spain; sent from Holland in the "New Netherland," by the Dutch West India Co., 1623; aided in erection of Fort Orange, 1624; settled at Waal-Bogt, nr. Hellgate, L.I.; killed by Indians while on a visit to Swaanendael, Del.; *m* ca. 1616, Sophia Ter Bosch (*b* 1598), of Overyssel, Holland, said to have returned to Holland in 1632.

WINCHESTER, John (1616-94), from Eng. in the "Elizabeth," to Boston, Mass., 1635; removed to Hingham, 1636; freeman, 1637; removed to Boston after 1650; mem. A. and H. A. Co.; *m* 1638, Hannah, dau. Dea. Richard Sealis, of Scituate.

WINDER, Lt. Col. John (ca. 1635-1698), of Cumberland, Eng.; came to Del., 1682; served with Colonial forces, 1697; planter and mariner; settled at Princess Anne, Somerset Co., Md.; commd. officer of Colonial army; apptd. j.p., 1665; lt. col., 1697; *m* Bridget–(*d* 1697).

WING, Daniel (*b* ca. 1616-will dated May 3, 1659, *d* 1664; son of Rev. John, qv); from Eng. with his mother, in the "William and Francis," 1632; *d* at Sandwich, Mass.; *m* 1641, Hannah (ca. 1620-1664), dau. of William or John Swift.

WING, Rev. John (1584-1630; son of Mathew, of Banbury, Oxford); entered Oxford Coll., 1599; grad. Queen's Coll., 1604; preached at Flushing and Middlebury, Holland; *d* at London; *m* 1609/10, Deborah Batchellor (*b* ca. 1592; dau. of Rev. Stephen Batchelder, qv), who with four sons came in the "William and Francis," to Lynn. Mass., 1632, settled at Sandwich, 1637.

WINN, Capt. John (ca. 1627-ca. 1694), was of Westmoreland Co., Va.; *m* ca. 1650, Elizabeth–, said to have been dau. of John Minor, Westmoreland Co.

WINSHIP (Winshope, Windship), Edward (1612/13-1688), from Eng. in the "Defense," to Newtown, Mass., 1634; freeman, 1635; selectman many yrs.; rep. Gen. Ct., 1663, et seq.; mem. A. and H. A. Co.; *m* Jane –; *m* 2d, Elizabeth –.

WINSLOW, Edward (1595-1655; son of Edward [*b* 1560], of Droitwich, Eng., *m* 2d, 1594, Magdalene Ollyver); 3d signer of the Mayflower Compact; 3d gov. of the Colony, 1633, 36, 44; commr. United Colonies, 1643; *m* 1st, at Leyden, Holland, 1618, Elizabeth Barker (*d* in 1621); *m* 2d, at Plymouth, Mass., 1621, Susanna (Fuller) White, widow of William White (qv).

WINSLOW, John (1597-1674; brother of Gov. Edward, qv); from Eng. to Plymouth, Mass., 1623; mem. Council of War, 1646; rep. Gen. Court, 1653-55; removed to Boston, 1657, and was a mcht. there; freeman, 1672; *m* 1627, Mary (Mayflower Pilgrim), dau. James Chilton.

WINSLOW, Kenelm (bap. 1599-1672; brother of Gov. Edward, qv), from England to Plymouth, Mass., 1629; admitted freeman, 1632; surveyor, town of Plymouth; original propr. of Assonet (Freetown), 1659; rep. Gen. Ct., 1642, et seq.; engaged in settlement of Yarmouth and other towns; mem. Marshfield mil. company; *m* 1634, Ellen (Newton) Adams (1598-1681), widow of John Adams (qv).

WINSOR (Windsor), Joshua, from Eng., was at Providence, R.I., 1638; an original purchaser of that town, with Roger Williams.

WINSTON, William (*d* 1702), from Eng., settled in New Kent Co., Va.; later in Hanover Co.; patented land, 1687.

WINTHROP, John (1588-1649), elected gov. of the Mass. Company, 1629; leader of a fleet which arrived at Salem, Mass., 1630; served as gov. 1630-34, 1637-40, 1642, 1646-49, first pres. United Colonies of N.E., 1643; *m* at 17, in Eng., Mary (*d* June 26, 1615), dau. of John Forth; *m* 2d, Dec. 6. 1615, Thomasine (*d* Dec. 8, 1616), dau. of William Clopton; *m* 3d, Apr. 29, 1618, Margaret (*d* June 14, 1647), dau. of Sir John Tyndal; *m* 4th, Dec. 4, 1647, Martha, dau. of Capt. William Rainsborough, of Royal Navy, and widow of Thomas Coytmore.

WISNER, Johannes (1676-1744), from Eng., 1714, settled on the Wawayanda Patent, Orange Co., N.Y.; *m* 1697, Elizabeth Dumbaugh.

WITHERSPOON, John (*b* 1670; son of David, *m* Lucy, dau. Rev. John Welch), from Scot. in the "Good Intent," to Williamsburg, S.C., 1734; granted land, Columbia, S.C., 1734; aided in building 1st ch. at Kingstree, S.C.; 1st person buried there; *m* 1693, his cousin, Janet Witherspoon (*b* 1670-*d* at sea, 1734).

WITHINGTON, Henry (1589/90-1666/67), from Eng., probably in the "James," to Dorchester, Mass., ca. 1636; one of the 6 founders of the ch. there; selectman, 1636; never a freeman; *m* 1st, Anne Leech (*d* 1621); *m* in Eng., Elizabeth Smith (*d* 1661); *m* 2d, 1662, Margaret—, widow of Richard Paul.

WITTER, William (ca. 1584-1659), from Eng., 1629, settled at Lynn, Mass.; later purchased for two pestle stones, from Poquonnum, the Indian Sagamore, all the land now occupied by Swampscott, Sagamore Hill and Nahant, Mass.; active religious worker; *m* Annis –.

WODELL, William (1604-93; son of Matthew), one of first settlers of Shawmut, R.I., 1642; a founder of the historic charter colony of Warwick, R.I., 1642; freeman, 1655; commr., 1656-63; dep. Gen. Ct., 1664, et seq.; served in Colonial wars; mem. spl. council, Colony of R.I., King Philip's War, 1675; apptd. asst., 1684; *m* Mary– (*d* 1676).

WOLCOTT, Henry (bap. Lidiard, Eng., Dec. 6, 1578-*d* May 30, 1655), came to Dorchester, Mass., ca. 1628; came in first co., May 30, 1630, with family landed at Nantasket; an original settler of Dorchester; on first list of freemen, Oct. 19, 1630; selectman; to Windsor, Conn., 1636/37; mem. first Gen. Assembly of Conn., 1637, House of Magistrates of Conn., 1643; *m* Jan. 19, 1606, at Tolland, Eng., Elizabeth (*d* 1655), dau. Thomas Saunders.

WOOD, see also Atwood and Woods.

WOOD, Henry (1594-1670), from Eng. to Plymouth, Mass.; was with Pilgrims in Leyden, Holland; at Falmouth and Middleboro, Mass.; *m* 1644, Abigail (1619 in Leyden, Holland-1690), dau. of John Jenney (*d* 1644), gov.'s asst., 1637, 1640, dep., 1641-43; *m* Sarah Carey (*d* 1655).

WOODBRIDGE, John (1613-95; son of Rev. John, of Stanton, Wiltshire, Eng., *m* a dau. of Rev. Robert Parker), from Eng. in the "Mary and John," 1634; settled at Newbury, Mass.; first town clk., 1638; dep. Gen. Ct., 1637, 40, 41; commr. to hear small causes, 1638, 41; a founder of Andover; ordained minister, 1645; returned to Eng., 1647, but came again in 1663; settled at Boston; gov.'s asst., 1683, 84; mem. A. and H. A. Co.; *m* 1639, Mercy (*d* 1691), dau. of Gov. Thomas Dudley (qv).

WOODBURY, William (ca. 1589-1677), bro. of "Father John"; came from Somersetshire, Eng., to Beverly, Mass., ca. 1630; rep. Gen. Ct., 1635, 38; *m* 1616, Elizabeth Patch.

WOODFORD, Thomas (*d* 1667), from Eng. in the "Francis and Mary," to Cambridge and Roxbury, Mass., 1632; freeman, 1635; settled at Hartford, Conn., 1636; town crier; at Northampton, Mass., 1655; selectman, 1658; juryman, 1659; *m* ca.1632, Mary, dau. of Robert Blott.

WOODMAN, Edward (1612-ante 1694), from Eng. in the "James," to Newbury, Mass., 1635; dep. Gen. Ct., 1636-37, 1639-43; lt. mil. co., 1637; *m* Elizabeth–(*d* 1677).

WOODRUFF, John (1607-70; son of John, of Fordwich, Eng., *m* Elizabeth Cartwright; g.son of Robert; g.g.son of William; g.g.g.son of Thomas Woodrove); came to Lynn, Mass., with his mother and stepfather, John Gosmer; thence to Southampton, L.I., 1640-41, where he was church warden; *m* Anne, dau. of John Hyde, *m* Elizabeth Gosmer.

WOODRUFF (Woodrove, Woodroffe), Matthew (*b* ca. 1612-*d* 1682), from England, ca. 1640: settled at Hartford, Conn.; at Farmington, Conn., 1640/41; freeman, 1657; *m* Hannah –.

WOODS, Michael (*b* Ulster, Ireland, 1684-*d* 1762), migrated to Pa., 1725, then to Va., 1732, settled in Albemarle Co., 1734; founded the estate in after years known as "Blair Park"; *m* Mary Campbell (*d* 1762).

WOODS (Wood), Samuel (ca. 1636-ca. 1717/18), mem. Train Band, Watertown, 1653; later lived at Cambridge; moved to Groton, Mass., 1662, where he was an original propr., own'ng an 11 acre right; returned to Watertown, 1675-76; again at Groton, 1678; *m* 1659, Alice Rushton (ca. 1636-1712).

WOODS (Wood), Samuel (1686-1763), from Eng. to Chelmsford, Mass., ca. 1700; *m* 1717, Mary Parker.

WOODSON, Dr. John (1586-1644), grad. St. John's Coll., Oxford, 1604; came in the "George," 1619, as surgeon to a co. of soldiers, and settled at Fleur de Hundred, on the James River; killed in Indian massacre; *m* Sarah Winston.

WOODWARD, Dr. Henry (1646-1684-90), from Eng., 1666, settled among the Indians at Pt. Royal, S.C.; *m* Mary (Godfrey) Browne, dau. of Col. John Godfrey.

WOODWARD, Nathaniel (*d* after 1673), from Eng. to Boston, 1630; mathematician and surveyor; ran the line between Plymouth colony and Mass., 1638, also between Mass. and Conn.; also on Merrimac survey; *m* Margaret Jackson.

WOODWARD, Richard (1590-1665), from Eng. in the "Elizabeth," to Watertown, Mass., 1634; freeman, 1635; miller; *m* in Eng., Rose–(*d* 1662); *m* 2d, 1663, Ann (Hill) Gates, widow of Stephen Gates (qv).

WOODWORTH, Walter (*d* 1685/86), from Eng. to Plymouth, Mass., 1630; settled at Scituate, Mass., 1633; freeman, 1640/41; surveyor of highways, 1645, 46, 56; juror; mem. First Ch.

WOOLSEY, Joris, or George (1610-98), from Eng. to New Amsterdam, 1623; later at Plymouth, Mass.; at Flushing, L.I., 1647; cadet Burgher Corps; *m* Rebecca, dau. of Thomas Cornell.

WORCESTER, William (*d* 1662), Eng. to Salisbury, Mass., ca.1639; served in ministry in Eng.; the first minister at Salisbury; freeman, 1640; *m* in Eng., Sarah–(*d* 1650); *m* 2d, 1650, Rebecca Cornell, widow of John Hall (she had also been widow of Henry Byley).

WORTHINGTON, Capt. John (1650-1701; son of John, of Jesus Coll., Cambridge, Eng.); came to America with his brother, Samuel; was in Md., 1670; capt. Anne Arundel Co. militia; burgess; judge Provincial Ct.; mem. Quorum; *m* Sarah, dau. of Matthew Howard.

WORTHINGTON, Nicholas (*d* 1683), said to have owned considerable property nr. Liverpool, Co. Lancaster, Eng., which was confiscated, because he fought in Cromwellian wars; came to N.E. and settled at Saybrook, Conn., 1649-50; removed to Hartford, thence to Hatfield, Mass., where he took oath of allegiance, 1678; *m* ca. 1668, Sarah (Bunce) White (*d* 1676), dau. Thomas Bunce (qv).

WRIGHT, Peter (*b* ca. 1600-*d* post Dec. 13, 1660), from Co. Norfolk, Eng., with bros. Anthony and Nicholas, to Saugus (Lynn), Mass., 1635; to Sandwich, 1637; surveyor of highways; sgt. mil. co.; a founder of Oyster Bay, L.I., 1653; *m* ca. 1636, Alice—(*d* 1685).

WRIGHT, Samuel (1614-65; g.son of Sir John Wright, of Wrightsbridge, Eng., granted peerage 1690), from London, Eng., ca.1638, settled at Springfield, Mass.; dea., 1639; juror, early settler at Northampton; *m* 1632, Margaret–(*d* 1681).

WURTS (Wirtz), Johannes Conrad (1706-63), from Switzerland, 1735; clergyman in several of the colonies, settled at York, Pa., 1762; *m* Anna Goetchius.

WYATT, Rev. Hawte (1596-1638; son of Sir George Wyatt [1550-1625], who was restored to his rights by act of Parliament during the reign of Queen Elizabeth, *m* Jane, dau. Sir Thomas Finch); came from Eng., 1621, settled at Jamestown, Va.; minister, 1621-25; returned to Eng. and became vicar of Boxley, Kent Co.; *m* Barbara (Eliz.) Mitford (*d* 1626); *m* 2d, Ann – (*d* 1632).

WYCHE, Henry (1648-1714; son Rev. Henry, *m* Ellen, dau. of Ralph Bennett), settled in Surry Co., Va., 1679.

WYCKOFF, Pieter Claessen (1615-95; son of Claes Cornelissen, presumed to have come with his father, from the Netherlands, 1636; had a farm near Albany until about 1649; del. from Flatlands to conv. held at New Amsterdam, 1664; magistrate, Amesfoort, 1655, 1662-63; removed to New Amsterdam where he was magistrate and patentee in charters, 1667 and 1686; adopted the name Wyckoff (derived from Dutch words "refuge" and "city"); *m* 1649, Gretien, dau. of Cornelis Hendrickson van Nes (1600-81), from Holland, 1642, Indian commr., Ft. Orange 1665-66, capt., *m* 1625, Maykee Burghgraef.

WYLLYS, George (1589/90-1645), from Eng. 1638, settled at Hartford, Conn.; trooper in Pequot War; gov.'s asst., 1639; gov. Colony of Conn., 1641-42; *m* Bridget Young (*d* 1629); *m* 2d, Mary Smith.

WYMAN, Francis (bap. 1619-*d* 1699, aet. 82; son of Francis, of West Mill, Co. Herts., Eng., *m* Elizabeth Richardson), came to Charlestown, Mass., 1635; an original settler of Woburn, 1642; *m* 2d, 1650, Abigail, dau. of William Read, from Eng. in the "Defence," 1635, *m* Mabel–.

WYNNE, Dr. Thomas (ca. 1630-1692), physician to William Penn and came with him in the "Welcome," 1682; leader of the Welsh group which purchased the "Welsh Tract," nr. Phila., Pa.; was speaker of the Assembly; judge Provincial Supreme Ct.; author; *m* ca. 1655, Martha Buttall; *m* 2d, Elizabeth Rowden, widow.

YALE, Capt. Thomas (1616-83; son of Thomas Yale [*d* 1619], *m* Anne, dau. of George Lloyd, bishop of Chester, Eng.), came to Boston, Mass., 1637; settled at New Haven, Conn., 1638; *m* 1645, Mary (*d* 1704), dau. of Capt. Nathaniel Turner, of New Haven (their 3d son, Elihu, founded Yale Coll.).

YARDLEY, Thomas, from Eng. to Pa., 1704; mem. Pa. Assembly, 1715, 22; *m* 1706, Ann (*b* 1685), dau. William Biles.

YATES (Yate), George, from Eng. to Yorktown, Va., 1690; settled in Caroline Co., Va., and had large landed estate; *m* –Calvert.

YEAMANS, Sir John (ca. 1605-1674; son of Robert, high sheriff of Bristow and gov. of Isle of Wight); knighted by King Charles II, 1661; high sheriff of Bristow; gov. Isle of Wight; from Eng., to Barbados, 1655; apptd. gov. of Barbados; founded Clarendon Colony, Carolinas, 1665; apptd. landgrave and gov. of Carolinas, 1672; *m* Margaret Foster.

YEARDLEY, Sir George (1577-1627), dep. gov. of Va., 1616-17; gov. and captain general, 1618-26; *m* 1618, Temperance Flowerdew; she *m* 2d, Gov. Francis West.

YORK, James (1614-83), from Eng. in the "Philip," 1635, to Stonington, Conn.; *m* Joannah–(*d* 1685).

YOUNG (Yonges), Rev. John (1598-1671; son of Rev. Christopher Yonges, Vicar of Reydon and Southwold, Eng.); came to Salem, Mass., in the "Mary Anne," 1637; founder of Southold, L.I., 1640, and first pastor Presbyn. Ch.; *m* 1622, Joan Herrington (*d* 1630); *m* 2d, Joan Harris; *m* 3d, 1639, Mary Warren Gardner (*d* 1678).